I0137221

ISLAM EXPOSED
A Three-Volume Series

VOLUME II

The Koran:
Selected Sûrahs with
Commentary and
Bible Comparisons

J.P. Sloane, Ph.D.

AvingtonHouse
Publishing

Titles by Dr. J.P. Sloane
Available from AvingtonHouse Publishers:

☙❦❧

WHAT EVERY BIBLE BELIEVER NEEDS TO KNOW ABOUT ISLAM

•

ISLAM EXPOSED VOLUME I
A Simple Crash Course on Islam:
Are the Bible's God and Allah the Same?

•

ISLAM EXPOSED VOLUME II
The Koran:
Selected Sûrahs, Commentary and Bible Comparisons

•

ISLAM EXPOSED VOLUME III
Science—Bible—Archaeology and Myths.

•

WHAT EVERY BIBLE BELIEVER NEEDS TO KNOW ABOUT ISLAM

•

"ANTISEMITISM" THE HORRIBLE HISTORY OF
HATRED AND HOLOCAUSTS
Illustrated

•

DO OUR PETS GO TO HEAVEN?
A Biblically Based Book to
Prepare Children and Bring Them Comfort
When Losing a Pet

ISLAM EXPOSED
A Three-Volume Series

Volume II
THE KORAN: SELECTED SÛRAHS, COMMENTARY
AND BIBLE COMPARISONS

By J.P. Sloane, Ph.D.

© Copyright 2013 by J.P. Sloane, D. Min., Ph.D.
Printed in the United States of America

AvingtonHouse Publishers, Dallas

ISBN-13: 978-0692892862
SSBN-10: 0692892869

All Rights Reserved by the author. No part of this work may be reproduced, stored in a retrieval system, or transmitted in any form or by any means; for example, electronic, photocopy, or recording without the prior written permission of the publisher. The only exception is a brief quotation in printed reviews.

All Koran passages, unless otherwise designated, are taken from Marmaduke Pickthall's translation of the Koran, which is in the public domain in the United States because the author died in 1936. Works by this author are also in the public domain in countries and areas where the copyright term is the author's life plus 60 years or less. Works by this author may also be in the public domain in countries and areas with longer native copyright terms that apply the rule of the shorter term to foreign works.

All Scriptures, unless otherwise designated, have been taken from the King James Version of the Bible with "you," "ye," and "thou" converted to Modern English when applicable. The use of "you" and the Old English words, "thy" and "thine," have sometimes been translated into the contemporary word "your," as well as the expression "Lo!," which means "Look!," "See," "behold" or "Indeed." For further clarification, as necessary, words ending in the archaic plural suffixes "t," "est" and "eth" have been deleted and substituted with the modern ending. However, we sometimes leave the old English words alone for the sake of their poetic value. We may also add quotes to a verse for clarification. This is also applied to the archaic seventeenth century, English words used in the Koran.

Scriptures are taken from the New King James Version®. Copyright © 1982 by Thomas Nelson. Used by permission. All rights reserved.

Scripture quotations labeled "NIV" are from the HOLY BIBLE, NEW INTERNATIONAL VERSION® (Copyright © 1973, 1978, 1984, by International Bible Society). Used by permission from Zondervan Publishing House. All rights reserved.

We believe that Heaven and Hell are proper nouns that describe actual places; therefore, we have capitalized them in this work.

The same applies to the twentieth-century translations of the Koran we have referenced, which were also originally produced in the English of the seventeenth century including, but not limited to, Marmaduke Pickthall (published 1930), Abdullah Yusuf Ali (published 1934-38 revised 1939), Arthur John (A.J.) Arberry (published 1955) and Muhammad Habib Shakir (1866–1939) (published during 1981, but not without some controversy— see End Note #6 on page 345). The version we use in this book is Marmaduke Pickthall's public domain translation of the Koran. As for the three translations and any incidental translation we might use for cross-references, we do so under Section 107 of the Copyright Act of 1976, which reads in part: "Copyright Disclaimer Under Section 107 of the Copyright Act of 1976, allowance is made for 'fair use' for purposes such as criticism, comment, news reporting, teaching, scholarship, and research. Fair use is a use permitted by copyright statute that might otherwise be infringing." Please note that all bracketed clarifications in the koranic verses are those of this author.

Cover design has been taken from a NASA photo of the *Helix Nebula* (also known as the "Eye of God" (because of its remarkable appearance and similarity to the human eye), photographed using the Hubble Telescope.

CONTENTS

LIST OF ILLUSTRATIONS

CHARTS:

TABLES

FIGURES:

INTRODUCTION

The actual Koran (Arabic, *Qur'an*) has around 470 pages total. This book is slightly larger than that due to the commentary and Bible comparisons. If we were to do a complete commentary of the entire Koran, which has 114 sûrahs (i.e., chapters), this book would be between 1,500 and 2,000 pages and would be not only huge but also very expensive. Therefore, to make this book affordable and give you the most sûrahs in approximately 500 pages, we have selected sûrahs that might interest the average Bible believer—when comparing the Koran to the Bible. (NOTE: Unlike the Bible, there are no books in the Koran; rather, it has sûrahs and verses.)

Until recently, there was no standard method of numbering verses in the various translations of the Koran. In 1834, a man known by the name of G. Fluegel created his own numbering system when he first published his own translation of the Koran; however, Pickthall made use of the Indian numbering system (which accounts for verses being somewhat different from other translations). The majority of English translations use the Egyptian numbering system.[1]

The Koran is Islam's holiest book and is considered by Muslims not only to be on par with the Judeo-Christian Bible, but they also believe it supersedes it as the last and final word from god. The Koran is an interesting collection of revelations given to Muhammad over a 23-year time period. Because Muhammad could not read or write (Sûrah 7:157a), he memorized the information Allah gave to him through the angel, Gabriel. Muhammad's followers later wrote them down on various items, such as palm branches, the shoulder blades of camels, flat rocks, or anything else that was handy at that time. Those writings were kept until after Muhammad's death. His followers were shocked when he died because they believed they were living in the Last Days and that Muhammad was the last and greatest prophet; consequently,

9

they had not made any provisions for his successor. After Muhammad's death, his followers compiled all of his revelations into a book known as the Koran (i.e., "the recitation"). Many other close friends of the Prophet of Islam also wrote down various sayings, examples,

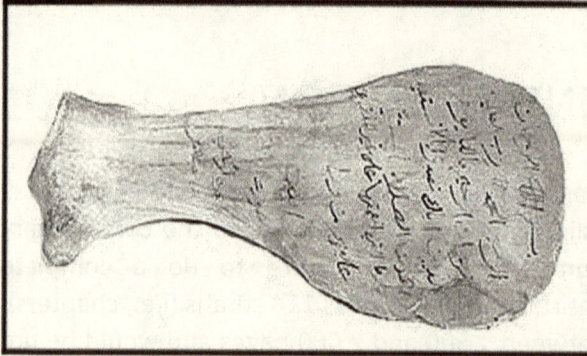

Fig. 1. A camel's shoulder blade with inscriptions

and historical events they had seen or heard him say. Those extra koranic observations were eventually written down for prosperity in the many volumes known as the Hadith {sayings).

One of the challenging features of the Koran is its somewhat disjointed accumulation of verses, stories, and events scattered throughout its text. Because the Koran is not put together in chronological order, many of the earlier revelations are contained toward the end of the second volume, while the later revelations are in the first volume.

Since some of the verses are also out of context, it makes it easier to be used by defenders of Islam to show an ignorant *Kafir* (i.e., a non-Muslim) how Islam is a "religion of peace." That was accomplished by presenting the Koran's peaceful conciliatory verses first, which instructs Muslims to use restraint. Defenders of Islam are quick to point out how the Koran teaches that people cannot be forced to convert to a religion. That is done whenever critics of Islam call attention to the "Verse of the Sword" (Sûrah 9:5) and the other jihadist passages which teach that Muslims must convert the Pagans, Christians, and Jews—or kill them. Never mind that these older conciliatory verses have been replaced by newer, more violent revelations from Allah.

From the beginning, when Muhammad first received his revelations in a cave near Mecca, he began transitioning through three stages of religious development:

☾ First Stage

The "courtship stage" was when Muhammad was proselytizing from military weakness in an attempt to convert Pagan polytheists to accept his new monotheistic religion.

☾ Second Stage

The "spurned lover" stage was when the Pagans—while tolerant of Muhammad's new religion—continued to reject his conversion courtship. The same was true with Christians and Jews who realized that many of the so-called biblical stories in the Koran were profoundly lacking in historical accuracy.

☾ Third (and Final) Stage

The "I'm over you, and I want revenge" stage came after Muhammad had gathered enough followers for his new religion of Islam and, therefore, was in a position to overthrow those he once courted but refused his advancements. This stage placed Muhammad in a position to force disbelievers to either accept him and his new religion—or pay a tax *(jizya)* for refusing—or be killed!

We will discuss these stages in greater detail in Volume III of our three-volume series, *Islam Exposed, Islam: Science—Bible—Archaeology and Myths* under the section titled, "The Romancing of Islam" in Chapter

The Koran contains 114 sûrahs, approximately the size of the New Testament. Like the Bible, it is comprised of two volumes; however, because of the extensive amount of sûrahs and verses in the two volumes of the Koran, we have selected 23 of the 114 sûrahs (more sûrahs than in Volume I of the Koran), which contain over 700 verses, that will be of interest to Christians and Jews. We have also included some of the first sûrahs revealed to Muhammad. For clarification, the koranic verses will be presented in **bold italics** with corresponding quotes and/or our commentary below each verse. Please note that the translators of the Koran sometimes insert clarifications, which are set off in parentheses; however, at times, it was necessary for us to add additional clarifications. Those are identified by the use of brackets.

Comparing the Koran with the Bible can be very confusing because of their many similarities. To shed biblical light and eliminate this problem, we created the icon on the right consisting of the Torah scroll and the Bible. Because both books can speak eloquently for themselves, you can now easily distinguish between those alleged Bible stories—which are presented as true in the Koran—and the *actual* Bible passages themselves.

As you will see, some verses in the Koran which claim to be biblical, are reasonably accurate, while others—on the other hand—are completely contrived. Some alleged Bible stories in the Koran are simply a retelling of myths as well as biblical stories, which mistakenly link together the wrong times, places, and people. Therefore, when you see this icon, you will know at a glance that a particular text is a legitimate biblical quote to aid you in comparing the accuracy of the Koran when it presents its version of factual stories from the Bible.

As we previously mentioned—contrary to the popular belief of many non-Muslims—the Koran was not given directly to Muhammad by Allah; rather it was given by a spiritual entity referring to himself as the angel, Gabriel, who spoke on Allah's behalf.[2] Keep in mind, the order of the sûrahs are not presented chronologically; they are generally arranged from the longest sûrahs with the most number of verses to the shortest sûrahs. Sûrah 108 is the shortest of all the sûrahs, while Sûrah 114 is the last and consists of one run-on sentence broken into six verses. The obvious exception to the rule of—the largest to the shortest—is the first sûrah, which is used as an introductory prayer to the Koran.

Another rule governing the interpretation of the Koran concerns the law of abrogation (Sûrah 2:106), also known as corrected revelations (retracted/repealed/nullified). When reading the Koran, many people might become confused by the many contradictions it contains. To begin with, there are two points of view in the Koran: (1) The revelations given to Muhammad at the beginning of his ministry in Mecca when he was militarily weak, and (2) the later, more militant revelations given to Muhammad when he became stronger and a warlord after his *Hijra* (migration) to Yathrib, later renamed "Medina" (also referred to as the "City of the Prophet") by Muhammad in his own honor.

Incidentally, Muhammad left Mecca in June of 622 A.D. to escape to Yathrib (Medina). To memorialize that year as the start of the Muslim era, the Muslims began their own lunar calendar identifying it as 622 A.H., the year of the *Hijri* (Latin, *Anno Hegirae*).[3] It has been reported that Medina was a town made up of Arabs, but it was actually a predominately Jewish town administrated by three Jewish tribes.[4]

Another interesting thing you will discover is that after Allah revealed something to Muhammad, sometimes things did not always go as planned, so the Prophet of Islam was forced to seek help from Allah, who then abrogated ("fixed" the problem). A new problem then arose regarding conflicting verses; which revelation were they supposed to follow? The solution was to use the last word on the subject as the deciding verse.

In an effort to further convince some of us in the naïve West to believe that Islam is a peaceful religion, Muslim apologists (i.e., defenders of their faith) offer us several conciliatory koranic proof-texts[5] from the koran to reinforce their claim. However, if we were to know the order in which the sûrahs were actually given—as any learned koranic student of Islam knows—(which is other passages revoke the conciliatory passages), they are left meaningless. Naturally, one would assume that Sûrah 2 would supersede or abrogate Sûrah 3, and Sûrah 3 would supersede Sûrah 4, etc. This could not be further from the truth, as the chart on the next few pages will show.

Many of the claims made in defense of Islam are based on conflicting verses found in the Koran. Some verses might be cited in the first sûrahs with the claim—because they are at the beginning of the Koran—that they are the last revelations given to Muhammad and, therefore, those peaceful proof-texts take precedence over the militant verses found in the higher numbered sûrahs.

The problem is that while verses in the last sûrahs (i.e., Sûrahs 1, 2, 3, 4, etc.) have replaced the smaller and (usually) older verses—that

13

scenario is not necessarily set in stone, but is more of a general rule of thumb. Not only are the sûrahs and verses constructed without any continuity, neither are they always placed in the Koran according to the time in which they were given to Muhammad. Confusing? As a result, the sûrahs are not placed in chronological order; rather they are placed in the Koran based on the number of verses a sûrah contains—from sûrahs with the most verses (which tend to be the later revelations) at the beginning of the Koran (except for the first or opening sûrah)—to sûrahs with the least amount of verses, which are usually the earlier revelations given to Muhammad. To make it even more confusing, the sûrahs are also arranged from the largest sûrahs first to the smallest sûrahs placed toward the end of the Koran. This means, in order to find out which verse might take precedence and reverse or replace an earlier verse, it is necessary for us to know when those verses and the sûrahs were written, thus the need to provide our comparison Table 1.

For your convenience, we have included a table you can easily reference to help you understand which sûrahs and verses came first. This is important because the last verse that was given is the deciding factor in replacing/abrogating any conflicting verses which came before it. The table provides us with the numerical order in which the sûrahs were placed in the Koran; they are located in the first column alongside the actual (chronological) order of sûrahs received by Muhammad, which you will see in the second column. This chart enables us to identify a contradiction in the Koran and understand which verse takes precedence. In other words:

(A) If you want to know whether or not the proof-text is legitimate or has been abrogated (replaced) by Allah with a more recent militant verse, (1) consult Table 1; (2) Then, refer to the sûrah containing the conciliatory verse in the order in which it is listed in the Koran (first column), and (3) then look at the column next to it on the right to see when the sûrah was *actually* revealed to Muhammad.

(B) Now do the same with the more militant verse, and you will be able to see, by the original order given, if the positive proof-text is valid or if it has been abrogated by the more militant verse. If the more recent of the two texts is negative, it will take precedence over the older, more positive, revoked text, which exposes their proof-text as a means of deception. Defenders of Islam use "proof-texts" in this manner to mislead the average non-Muslim reader through the use of a technique called *taqiyya*. *Taqiyya* is a permissible lie to further the cause of Islam.

Another example of Muslim deception is "*kitman*," which allows a believer to incorporate some truth in order to mislead a non-Muslim. One example of this technique is when Muslims take biblical verses out of context to make them seem supportive of their claims, while the verse in the Bible, in context, means something entirely different. (We discussed this in Chapter 9, Volume I of our three-volume series, *Islam Exposed, A Simple Crash Course on Islam,* where we focused on the Yale Covenant and the new movement to merge Christianity and Islam into a one-world religion, Chrislam.)

As we would expect, many defenders of Islam argue that they are not revisionists, but simply know the Koran better than those who cannot read Arabic or are reading various translations of the Koran. This creates an inability to discern the finer grammatical points contained in the Koran's original Arabic language. To reinforce that argument, many Muslim scholars quote Sûrah 19:97, which reads:

> *And We make (this Scripture) easy in your tongue [Arabic], (O Muhammad) only that you may bear good tidings therewith unto those who ward off (evil), and warn therewith the forward [contentious] folk (bracketed clarifications mine).*

There is controversy regarding who actually translated one of the versions of the Koran. It is believed that Muhammad Habib Shakir was not the actual translator of the English version (1866-1939, Cairo, Egypt) bearing his name because he believed that it was unlawful to translate the Koran into any language other than Arabic. The name M.H. Shakir is thought to be the pen name used by Mohammed Ali Habib, the son of Habib Esmail (1904-1959) of the House of Habib, who died in 1959. It was not until 1981, 22 years after his death, that his version of the Koran was published.

As we shared in Volume I of our three-volume series of *Islam Exposed: A Simple Crash Course on Islam*, the Koran has a recurring theme attacking the Divinity of Christ while embracing Him as one of their most important prophets. Consider that Allah claims he gave the Christians and Jews the Torah and Gospel (Sûrah 3:3) and that "... there is none that can alter the words (and decrees) of Allah ..." (Sûrah 6:34); and then the Koran contradicts itself by going against the gospel (Good News) message that God came to earth in the form of a man by denying, directly or indirectly. Jesus is the Son of God, which we will learn as we study the Quran and Hadith in this volume, one of our three-volume series titled, *Islam Exposed*. In the Koran alone, we are told 21 times that Allah has no son (Sûrahs, 2:116; 4:171; 6:101; 9:30; 10:68; 17:111; 18:4; 19:35; 19:88; 19:89; 19:90; 19:91; 19:92; 21:26; 23:91; 25;2; 37:152; 39:4; 43:81; 43;82; 72:3). In order to drive the message that Allah has no son, the Koran purposefully refers to Jesus as the son of Mary (not Allah) 23 times (Sûrahs 2:87; 2:253; 3:45; 4:157; 4:171; 5:17; 5:46; 5:72; 5:75; 5:78; 5:110; 5:112; 5:114; 5:116; 9:31; 19:34; 23:50; 33:7; 43:57; 57:27; 61:6; 61:14), it must also deny the Trinity (the Koran does so at least 65 times because that includes God the Son (Matthew 28:19), (Sûrahs, 3:64; 4:36; 4:48; 4:116; 5:72; 6:14; 6:81; 6:88; 6:106; 6:136; 6:137; 6:148; 6:151; 9:31; 10:28; 10:29; 12:108; 13:15; 13:33; 13:36; 16:51; 16:52; 16:53; 16:54; 16:55; 16:56; 16:57; 16:73; 16:86; 17:22; 17:39; 17:40; 17:56; 17:57; 18:12; 18:110; 22:31; 23:59; 23:117; 24:55; 25:68; 28:87; 28:88; 29:8; 30:31; 31:13; 35:13; 35:14; 39:64; 39:65; 40:41; 40:42; 40:43; 40:66; 41:6; 43:15; 43:45; 46:4 46:5; 46:6; 50:26; 51:51; 60:12; 72:2; 72:18).

The Contrast between the Order of the Sûrahs in the Koran and When They Were Actually Received[6]

Like the Bible, the Koran contains two volumes; Volume 1 has Sûrahs 1-20, and Volume 2 has Sûrahs 21-114. We can see below the order in which the sûrahs appear in the Koran, and the generally agreed on order when they were received. As we explained earlier, this allows us to know which verses were abrogated (replaced) earlier conflicting verses[7,]

Table 1: The Contrast Between the Order of Sûrahs and When They WereActually Received

Order They Appear in the Koran	Actual Order Originally Received	Sûrah Name	Number of Verses	City Where They Were Revealed
1	5	The Opening/al-Fatiha	7	Mecca
2	87	The Cow or Heifer/al-Baqara	286	Medina
3	89	The House (or Family) of 'Imran/al-i-Imran	200	Medina
4	92	Women/An-Nisa	176	Medina
5	112	The Repast (meal)/Al-Maeda	120	Medina
6	55	Cattle, Livestock/al-Anaam	165	Mecca
7	39	The Heights/al-Araf	206	Mecca
8	88	Spoils of War, Booty/ al-Anfal	75	Medina
9	113	Repentance/At-Taubah	129	Medina
10	51	Johna/Yunus	109	Mecca
11	52	Hud/Hud	123	Mecca
12	53	Joseph/Yusuf	111	Mecca
13	96	The Thunder/al-Rad	43	Medina
14	72	Abraham/Ibrahim	52	Mecca
15	54	Stone Land, Rock City /al-Hijr	99	Mecca
16	70	The Bee/An-Nahl	128	Mecca
17	50	The Night Journey The Children of Israel/al-Isra	111	Mecca
18	69	The Cave/al-Kahf	110	Mecca
19	44	Mary/Maryam	98	Mecca
20	45	Ta-ha/Taha	135	Mecca
21	73	The Prophets/al-Ambiya	112	Mecca
22	103	The Pilgrimage/al-Hajj	78	Medina
23	74	The Believers/al-Muminun	118	Mecca
24	102	Light/al-Nur	64	Medina

Order in Koran	Order Received	﷽ Sûrah Name	Number of Verses	City Revealed Continued. ..
25	42	The Criterion/al-Furgan	77	Mecca
26	47	The Poets/Ash-Shuara	227	Mecca
27	48	The Ants/An-Naml	93	Mecca
28	49	The Story, Stories/al-Qasas	88	Mecca
29	85	The Spider/al-Ankaboot	85	Mecca
30	84	The Romans/Ar-Rum	60	Mecca
31	57	Lugman/Lugman	34	Mecca
32	75	The Prostration/As-Sajda	30	Mecca
33	90	The Clans/al-Ahzab	73	Medina
34	58	Sheba/Saba	54	Mecca
35	43	The Angels, Originator/Fatir	45	Mecca
36	41	Ya-sin/Ya-Sin	83	Mecca
37	56	Those Who Set the Ranks/As-Saaffat	182	Mecca
38	38	The Letter Sad/Sad	88	Mecca
39	59	The Troops, Throngs/ Az-Zumar	75	Mecca
40	60	The Forgiver/al-Ghafir	85	Mecca
41	61	Signs Spelled Out/Fussilat	54	Mecca
42	62	Counsel/Ash-Shura	53	Mecca
43	63	Ornaments of Gold, Luxury/Az-Zukhruf	89	Mecca
44	64	Smoke/Ad-Dukhan	59	Mecca
45	65	Crouching/al-Jathiya	37	Mecca
46	66	The Dunes/al-Ahqaf	35	Mecca
47	95	Muhammad/Muhammad	38	Medina
48	111	Victory, Conquest/al-Fath	29	Medina
49	106	The Private Apartments/ al-Hujraat	18	Medina
50	34	The Letter Qaf/Qaf	45	Mecca
51	67	The Winnowing Winds/ Adh-Dhariyat	60	Mecca
52	76	The Mount/At-Tur	49	Mecca
53	23	The Star/An-Najm	62	Mecca
54	37	The Moon/al-Qamar	55	Mecca
55	97	The Beneficent (charitable)/ al-Rahman	78	Mecca
56	46	The Inevitable/al-Waqia	96	Mecca
57	94	Iron/al-Hadid	29	Nadina

Order in Koran	Order Received	Sûrah Name	Number of Verses	City Revealed Continued.
58	105	She that Disputes/ al-Mujadila	22	Medina
59	101	Exile, Banishment/al-Hashr	24	Medina
60	91	She that Is Examined/ al-Mumtahina	13	Medina
61	109	The Ranks/As-Saff	14	Medina
62	110	The Congregation/ al-Jumua	11	Medina
63	104	The Hypocrites/ al-Munafiqun	11	Medina
64	108	Mutual Disillution/ At-Taghabun	18	Medina
65	99	Divorce/At-Talag	12	Medina
66	107	Banning (Exclusion)/ At-Tahrim	12	Medina
67	77	The Sovereignty/al-Mulk	30	Mecca
68	2	The Pen/al-Qalam	52	Mecca
69	78	The Reality/al-Haaqqa	52	Mecca
70	79	The Ascending Stairway/ al-Maarij	44	Mecca
71	71	Noah/Nooh	28	Mecca
72	40	The Jinn (spirits, impish devils)/al-Jinn	28	Mecca
73	3	The Enshrouded or Bundled Up One/al-Muzzannil	20	Mecca
74	4	The Cloaked One/ al-Muddathir	56	Mecca
75	31	Resurrection/al-Qiyama	40	Mecca
76	98	Man/al-Insan	31	Medina
77	33	The Emissaries/al-Mursalat	50	Mecca
78	80	The Tidings/An-Naba	40	Mecca
79	81	Those Who Drag Forth/ An-Naziat	48	Mecca
80	24	He Frowned/Abasa	42	Mecca
81	7	The Overthrowing/ At-Takwir	29	Mecca
82	82	The Cleaving/al-Infitar	19	Mecca
83	86	Defrauding/al-Mutaffifin	36	Mecca
84	83	The Sundering (Dividing)	25	Mecca

Order in Koran	Order Received	Sûrah Name	Number of Verses	City Revealed
85	27	Constellations/al-Burooj	22	Mecca
86	36	The Morning Star/At-Tariq	17	Mecca
87	8	The Most High/al-Ala	19	Mecca
88	68	The Overwhelming/ al-Ghashiya	26	Medina
89	10	The Dawn /al-Fajr	30	Mecca
90	35	The City/al-Balad	20	Mecca
91	26	The Sun/Ash-Shams	15	Mecca
92	9	The Night/al-Lail	21	Mecca
93	11	The Morning Hours/ Ad-Dhuha	11	Mecca
94	12	Consolation/al-Inshirah	8	Mecca
95	28	The Fig/al-Tin	8	Mecca
96	1	The Clot/Alaq	19	Mecca
97	25	Power, Fate/al-Qadr	5	Mecca
98	100	The Clear Proof/Evidence al-Bayyina	8	Medina
99	93	The Earthquake/al-Zaizala	8	Mecca
100	14	The Coursers or Chargers/ al-Adiyat	11	Mecca
101		The Calamity/al-Qari'ah	11	Mecca
102	16	The Rivalry in Worldly Increases/al-Takathur	8	Mecca
103	13	The Declining Day/al-Asr	3	Mecca
104	32	The Gossipmonger or Traducer/al-Humaza	9	Mecca
105	19	The Elephant/al-Fil	5	Mecca
106	29	Winter or Quraysh/ Quraish	4	Mecca
107	17	Small Kindness/ al-Maun	7	Mecca
108	15	Abundance/al-Kauther	3	Mecca
109	18	The Disbelievers/ al-Kafiroon	6	Mecca
110	114	Succour or Divine Support/ al-Nasr	3	Medina
111	6	The Twisted Rope or Palm Fiber/al-Masad	5	Mecca
112	22	The Unity/Purity of Faith/	4	Mecca
113	20	The Daybreak, Dawn/al-lalaq	6	Mecca
114	21	Mankind/An-Nas	6	Mecca

In summary, we have learned that there are chronological inconsistencies in the Koran. One interesting and little-known fact we include is that a few sûrahs contain verses that were—for whatever reason—revealed at another time and place. Because they are rare occurrences, we have chosen not to include them in this book; however, keep in mind they are one of the contributing factors to the Koran's disjointed construction.[9] When reading a sûrah, the theme might radically change course and leave us wondering, "Where did that come from?!"

Now that you know some of the things to expect when reading the Koran, you are now ready to sit back and prepare to explore some of the sûrahs we specifically selected that should be of interest to you, especially Bible believers. We will also be using corresponding Bible verses with many of the Koran's own verses or versions in a "comparison" format when appropriate, similar to a parallel Bible where different versions of the Bible are placed side-by-side. We will also offer commentary from a biblical point of view for the difficult verses from various sûrahs contained in this volume. By studying the Koran in this manner, we are accepting the Koran's challenge, which states:

> *And We [Allah] caused Jesus, son of Mary, to follow in their [prophets] footsteps, confirming that which was (revealed) before him in the Torah, and We bestowed on him the Gospel wherein is guidance and a light, confirming that which was (revealed) before it in the Torah—a guidance and an admonition unto those who ward off (evil). Let the People of the Gospel judge by that which Allah hath revealed therein. Whoso judges not by that which Allah has revealed: such are evil-livers (Sûrah 5:46-47, bracketed clarification mine).*

> *Do they [Christians and Jews] not consider the Qur'an (with care)? Had it been from other than Allah, they would surely have found therein many discrepancies (Sûrah 4:82, Abdullah Yusuf Ali, bracketed clarification mine).*

21

The meaning of the word "discrepancies" in the last verse means discrepancies within the Koran itself in light of the Bible, which Allah declares he provided before the existence of the Koran (Sûrahs 3:48, 81, 184; 5:45; 32:23; 40:53, etc.).

NOTES:

1. *Encyclopaedia of Islam*, New Edition, Volume V (Ledin: E.J. Brill, 1986), 411. This encyclopaedia explains the various numbering systems of the various translations of the Koran (Qur'an), including the differences between the verse numbering of M. Pickthall and Y. Ali.

2. Fazlur Shaikh, Rehman, *Chronology of Prophetic Events* (West Norwood: Ta-Ha Publishers Ltd, 2001), p. 50. Islamic faithful believe that the Koran was sent down to Muhammad and verbally delivered to him by the angel, Jibril (Gabriel).

3. As with many Arabic words, there are several spellings of Hijra (Hegira, i.e., migration of Muhammad to Madina) Hijrah, Hegira, Hejira, or Hijrat.

4. Bernard Lewis, *The Arabs in History* (Oxford: Oxford Univ., 1993), 40. "The city of Medina, some 280 miles north of Mecca, had originally been settled by Jewish tribes from the north, especially the Banu Nadir and Banu Quraiza. The comparative richness of the town attracted an infiltration of pagan Arabs who came, at first, as clients of the Jews and ultimately succeeded in dominating them. Medina, or as it was known before Islam, Yathrib, had no form of a stable government at all. The town was torn by the feuds of the rival Arab tribes of Aus and Khazraj, with the Jews maintaining an uneasy balance of power. The latter, engaged mainly in agriculture and handicrafts, were economically and culturally superior to the Arabs and were consequently disliked.... As soon as the Arabs had attained unity through the agency of Muhammad, they attacked and ultimately eliminated the Jews."

5. A proof-text is a passage or verse from the Bible or Koran used in support of a particular theology argument or point.

6. Notice: The Koran's sûrahs are not arranged in the order in which they were received by Muhammad (as we saw in Table 1, column two), but arranged more or less according to their length. As

22

Muhammad became more confident, the sûrahs got longer. Some of the verses (i.e., passages) are taken from revelations received in Medina and inserted into the earlier sûrahs, which were first received in Mecca. To a lesser extent, some verses that were received in Medina have Meccan passages inserted as well. Not all revelations, however, were received in Mecca or Medina; a few were received during the prophet's Hijra. (The first time was when Muhammad relocated from Mecca to Medina and other times when he made the Hijra to Mecca.) Because it can become confusing and controversial as to which ones they actually are, and difficult to document, we will not include them in the chronological chart, which, as previously stated, is considered accurate overall by most Islamic scholars.

7. "Quran Verses in Chronological Order," *Qran.org.* اقرا قرآن في طريق آسون, n.d. Web. 30 March 2016.

8. "Chronological Order of the Qur'an," *WikiIslam.* N.p., n.d. Web. 30 March 2016.

9. "Tanzil Documents." *Http://Tanzil.net/*, ©2007-2017, tanzil.net/docs/revelation_order.

   (1) The History of the Quran by Abu Abd Allah al-Zanjani (pdf book, English translation).

   (2) Chronological Order of Quranic Surahs, rendered by Kevin P. Edgecomb.

   (3) Geschichte des Korans by Theodor Noldeke (pdf book, Arabic translation).

   One example of an insertion of a verse into a sûrah that was received at another place at another time can be found in Sûrah 2:281:

Table 2. Example of How Verse in Koran Misapplied

Koran Order	Name of Sûrah	City Received	Exception
2	The Cow	Medina	Verse 281 in this sûrah was not received in Medina but received in Mina (near Mecca) at the time of the Last Hajj.

NOTE: Sûrah 2, verse 281 is inserted between two verses dealing with money. Verses 280 and 282 deal with debt, while verse 281 deals with the afterlife (pages 226-227).

THE KORAN

VOLUME I

Volume I of the Koran consists of Sûrahs 1 through 20. In order to familiarize ourselves with the Koran, we will study Sûrahs (Chapters) 1, 2, 18, and 19, which are of particular interest to readers of the Bible.

SÛRAH 1

THE OPENING (Fātiḥ)
(Revealed at Mecca)

In the name of Allah, the Beneficent, the Merciful.

(1:1) Praise be to Allah, Lord of the Worlds,

(1:2) The Beneficent, the Merciful.

(1:3) Owner of the Day of Judgment,

(1:4) You (alone) we worship; You (alone) we ask for help.

(1:5) Show us the straight path,

(1:6) The path of those whom You have favoured;

(1:7) Not (the path) of those who earn Your anger nor of those who go astray.

An interesting and confusing problem with the Koran is their numbering system. As with the Bible, a numbering system was added to the Koran centuries later to make it easier to find a passage.

There are several methods of numbering the various translations of the Koran. One system is known as the "Indo-Pakistani" system; it usually acknowledges the stand-alone letters that begin some sûrahs as a verse. The other system is the Egyptian system; it also counts the letters at the beginning of sûrahs as a verse, but that is where the similarity ends. Therefore, most Korans use the Egyptian numbering system. In this case, Pickthall commingles the Arabic tradition from India with the Egyptian system; it does not number the letters as separate verses for the opening sûrah. Yet Pickthall is not the only one who has taken such liberties; Abdulla Yusuf Ali also prefers the Egyptian system, but he does not always follow it. That makes the readings of certain passages confusing, to say the least! For our purposes, we will use the Egyptian numbering system.

It can be confusing when associating a number with a verse only to look it up in a different Koran and find out that the number you have is not the verse you are looking for. Many verses in the Koran use the Hindi-Arabic numerical system, which uses a decimal point system (e.g., 1.11) instead of a colon system like the West uses when numbering their Bible verses (e.g., 1:11). Because most of us are familiar with the colon system, we will use the Western punctuation system for the Koran verses.

This short, opening sûrah was originally the fifth one given to Muhammad and was placed at the beginning of the Koran to be reflected on and used as a prayer to enable Muslims to be in a more reverent and receptive frame of mind before continuing to read the rest of the Koran. It is also invoked, at times, when a Muslim begins praying, not unlike the Lord's Prayer for Christians (Matthew 6:9-12).

Having said that, let's take a closer look at this from the Bible's point of view. At first glance, this short and simple prayer seems to be agreeable and inoffensive. After all, it is only six short stanzas, but on closer inspection, it contains an enormous number of troubling conflicts in light of the Bible. As we stated in Volume I of our three-volume series, *Islam Exposed: A Simple Crash Course on Islam,* you will see throughout the series—problems and conflicts between the Bible and the Koran, even though the Koran advises its readers to use the Bible to verify that the same person authored both books (Sûrahs 5:47; 4:82; 6:114). Let's begin the study of the Koran with Sûrah 1.

In the name of Allah, the Beneficent, the Merciful.

Marmaduke Pickthall presents the first verse in Sûrah 1 as a preamble, while Yusuf Ali, A.J. Arberry (who uses the Arabic numbering text from India), and Muhammad Habib Shakir number it as the first verse. As for the subject of this verse, Yusuf Ali and A.J. Arberry use the term "God" when referring to Allah, while Marmaduke Pickthall and Muhammad Habib Shakir use the proper name of Allah in place of God. However, Allah is the theophoric name (a name containing "God" like Godfrey) for the Muslim god in the Koran. Nevertheless, the name Allah is incorrectly (and deliberately) used interchangeably with the word "God" to make it appear that Allah is also the God of the Bible as he claims he is. We see this throughout the Koran and in everyday speech by Muslims and many Middle-Eastern Christians as well!

Allah has 99 names, some of which could arguably be referred to as attributes as opposed to proper names. Some translations substitute the word "God" for "Allah," which is either (1) out of ignorance, or (2) an attempt to be deceptive to further the propaganda that Allah is synonymous with our English word "God," proving, according to Muslims, that they worship the same deity as Christians and Jews, and they are only using different words to describe Him. Of course, this is deceptive and without fact.[1] (See *Volume 1* of our three-volume series of *Islam Exposed: A Simple Crash Course on Islam.*) In the Koran, not one of the names describing the Arab deity known as "Allah" is referring to "Elohim," a name mentioned in the Bible over 2,500 times. Not one is "I AM," which is the Hebrew Tetragrammaton, *YHWH* (Eng., "Jehovah") and is mentioned in the Bible over 9,000 times. Not one is the name "Jesus" *(*Hebrew, "Yeshua"*)* or in Arabic, "Isa," who is referred to in the Old Testament (Proverbs 30:4; Daniel 3:25; Isaiah 7:14, 9:6, 48:16, Chapter 53), as well as named "God" in the New Testament.

In the Bible, Moses directly asks God what His name is:

> And Moses said unto God, "Behold, when I come unto the children of Israel, and shall say unto them, 'The God of your fathers has sent me unto you;' and they shall say to me, 'What is His name? what shall I say unto them?'"

And God said unto Moses, "I AM THAT I AM:" and He said, "This shall you say unto the children of Israel, 'I AM hath sent me unto you' " (Exodus 3:13-14).

Jesus also uses the Tetragrammaton (four-letter name of God), a Hebrew theonym (the proper name of a deity), *YHWH (יהוה)*, meaning "I AM" to describe Himself:

> Jesus said to them, "Most assuredly, I say to you, before Abraham was, [two millennia before Christ came to earth] 'I Am!' " (John 8:58, NKJV, bracketed clarification mine.)

Regarding Jesus as God, consider the reason why Jesus was crucified. It was because He declared Himself to be the Son of God; thus Himself being God (John 5). We are also informed in the Bible that Jesus *(Isa)* is God (Titus 2):

> Therefore the Jews sought the more to kill Him because He not only had broken the Sabbath but said also that God was His Father, making Himself equal with God (John 5:18).

> Looking for that blessed hope, and the glorious appearing of the great God and our Savior Jesus Christ (Titus 2:13).

On the other hand, it is interesting to observe that while the Koran claims Allah is the author of the Bible, including the gospels, it denies the gospel message![2] Furthermore, the name "Allah" cannot be found in the Scriptures of the Bible even once.

(1:1) Praise be to Allah, Lord of the Worlds,

Notice that Allah created *"the worlds."* In Islamic cosmology, there are seven earths stacked above one another, and seven heavens nested like upside-down bowls (Sûrah 65:12). This is not found in the Bible, yet according to the Koran, since Allah says he gave us the Bible (Sûrahs 3:3; 5:49, 68; 6:114; 19:30), we wonder how he got something like this so wrong.

(1:2) The Beneficent [Charitable], the Merciful.

Here we see the preamble repeated again, proclaiming that Allah can bless and show mercy.

(1:3) Owner of the Day of Judgment

This opening theme presented in the preamble (sometimes quoted as verse 1 by other translators), along with verse 1.2, states, *"[Allah is] The Beneficent [Charitable], the Merciful"* (bracketed clarification mine). This statement seems to be a message of reassurance to Muslim believers; yet in addition to this claim of benevolence and love, Allah can choose to save some while rejecting others, and destroy others simply at his pleasure, as seen in the following sûrahs:

> *Those whom Allah (in His plan) wills to guide,—He opens their breast to Islam; those whom He wills to leave straying,—He makes their breast closed and constricted, as if they had to climb up to the skies: thus does Allah (heap) the penalty on those who refuse to believe (Sûrah 6:125, Abdullah Yusuf Ali).*

> *But Allah does call to the Home of Peace: He does guide whom He pleases to a way that is straight (Sûrah 10:25, Abdullah Yusuf Ali).*

This is a stark contrast to the God of the Bible who is desirous that none should perish (2 Peter 3:9).

(1:4) You (alone) we worship; You (alone) we ask for help.

This is the opening attack against the Divinity of Christ, which we will see repeated over and over again as an underlying theme throughout the Koran. Right at the start of the Koran, we see a conflict when it states, *"You (alone) we worship,"* meaning Allah has no son.

We would not be truthful if we did not point out that Yusuf Ali and Muhammad Habib Shakir did not add the clarification that it is Allah in the singular aspect (non-Trinitarian), as Marmaduke Pickthall and A.J. Arberry do:

> *You only we serve; to You alone we pray for succor [help]. (A.J. Arberry, bracketed clarification mine.)*

The Bible foresaw Muhammad and his false gospel when Paul, the apostle, said to the Gentiles:

But though we, or an angel from heaven, preach any other gospel unto you than that which we have preached unto you, let him be accursed.

As we said before, so say I now again, "if any man preach any other gospel unto you than that you have received, let him be accursed" (Galatians 1:8-9).

As we will see throughout the Koran, Muhammad preaches a different gospel!

At the very beginning of the Koran, we are presented with its recurring theme—attacks on the Divinity of Jesus (Arabic, *Isa*) and the Trinity. This is a fundamental error on two fronts: First, the biblical conflict with Islam denies the Trinity because it assumes each member of the Trinity has no common denominator (having the same essence as Allah) and second, it assumes Christians, who are assigned to Allah, Jesus, and Mary[3] are their associates who make up the other two members of the Trinity. The Koran repeats over and over, ad nauseam, that Allah does not have any associates or partners by adding (or associating) two separate human beings with him (incorrectly assuming that is what Christians believe).

Chart 1: The Koran's Conceptualized Formula of the Trinity Based on Sûrah 5:116

$$\frac{1 \ (Allah)}{1 \ (god/spirit)} + \frac{1 \ (Mary)}{1 \ (human)} + \frac{1 \ (Jesus)}{1 \ (human)} = \frac{3}{?} \ \frac{3 \ persons}{no \ common \ denominator}$$

We discuss, in greater detail, the biblical formula for the Trinity in Volume III of our three-volume series, *Islam Exposed, Islam: Science—Bible—Archaeology and Myths,* Chapter 1, under the section, "Is Allah Just Another Name for God?"

Contrary to this Koranic verse, the Bible tells us that there is another who is worshiped besides God in addition to the Holy Spirit. That person is Jesus, who has been worshipped from the very beginning of His life on

earth when the Wise Men followed the Star of Bethlehem to the place where He lay as a baby:

For unto us a child is born, unto us a Son is given: and the government shall be upon His shoulder: and His name shall be called Wonderful, Counselor, **The mighty God,** The everlasting Father, The Prince of Peace (Isaiah 9:6, bolded emphasis added).

And when they were come into the house, they saw the young child with Mary, His mother, and fell down, **and worshiped Him:** and when they had opened their treasures, they presented unto Him gifts; gold, and frankincense and myrrh (Matthew 2:11, bolded emphasis added).

(1:5) Show us the straight path,

The Bible teaches that Jesus *(Isa)* shows us the right way: Jesus said to him, "I am the way, the truth, and the life. No one comes to the Father except through Me" (John 14:6, NKJV).

(1:6) The path of those whom You have favoured;

"What path has God "favored?" The answer is in the Psalms, which Allah says he gave to "us" (Sûrah 3:184)[4] along with the gospel (Sûrah 3:3).[5] In the Psalms we read:

Thy word is a lamp unto my feet and a light unto my path (Psalm 119:105).

The Bible explains that the path we need to walk is revealed through God's light, but now we need to ask what that light is. The answer is in the Gospel of John:

Then spoke Jesus again unto them, saying, "I am the light of the world: he that follows me shall not walk in darkness, but shall have the light of life" (John 8:12).

(1:7) Not (the path) of those who earn Your anger nor of those who go astray.

This is a continuation of verse 6, which gives us more clarification when we read them together, **The path of those whom You have favoured; Not (the path) of those who earn Your anger nor of those who go astray.**

As for verses 6 and 7, in light of the Bible, we see how to recognize the right from wrong paths and who will lead us astray:

"Enter by the narrow gate; for wide *is* the gate and broad *is* the way that leads to destruction, and there are many who go in by it. Because narrow *is* the gate and difficult *is* the way which leads to life, and there are few who find it. Beware of false prophets, who come to you in sheep's clothing, but inwardly they are ravenous wolves" (Matthew 7:13-15, NKJV).

Also, regarding this last verse, which reads, *"Not the (path) of those who earn your anger nor of those who go astray."* A.J. Arberry translates it closer to the original wording in the Koran, which reads:

...not of those against whom You are wrathful, nor those who are astray.

Using the translation of Muhammad Habib Shakir of this verse, Mahmoud M. Ayoub, a Muslim scholar, and professor of religious and interfaith studies, explains who "those" are that are on the receiving end of Allah's anger:

"Those who have incurred Your wrath" is usually seen as referring to the Jews and the phrase "those who are the neglectful wanderers" (is more clearly translated as "those who have gone astray") is seen as referring to the Christians.[6]

To be fair, it must be pointed out that Ayoub admits that not all Muslim scholars believe this way—and the few who believe this part of the passage simply apply it to anyone who is not a Muslim.

NOTES:

1. "... Allah is the best of schemers [deceivers]" (Sûrah 3:54, bracketed clarification mine). "... Allah is the best of plotters" (Sûrah 8:31).

   "He [Allah] hath revealed unto you (Muhammad) the Scripture with truth, confirming that which was (revealed) before it, even as He [Allah] revealed the Torah and the gospel" (Sûrah 3:3, bracketed clarifications mine); yet as we explained in Chapter 1 of our three-volume series exposing Islam, *Volume I, A Simple Crash Course on Islam*, the Koran denies over and over again the very heart of the gospel (the Good News of Jesus Christ), which Allah claims he *gave* to Jesus. Curiously, the claim—Allah gave the *Good News [gospel] of Jesus Christ* to Jesus Christ—while at the same time, he denies the very essence of the gospel message. As we see here, the gospel could not be *given* to Jesus because the Good News *is about* Jesus. The books containing the gospel were created to tell the world about the life of Jesus, not during His time on earth, but afterward by Matthew, Mark, Luke, and John; therefore, it makes no sense Allah gave it to Jesus during His life on earth. (We revisit this topic again in Volume III of our three-volume series, *Islam Exposed, Islam: Science—Bible—Archaeology and Myths,* at the end of Chapter 1).

2. It is of great help to know that the Bible always interprets itself, and that includes what constitutes the gospel message, as we can see here:

   "Moreover, brethren, I declare to you the gospel which I preached to you...by which also you are saved, if you hold fast that word which I preached to you—unless you believed in vain. For I delivered to you first of all that which I also received: that Christ died for our sins according to the Scriptures, and that He was buried, and that He rose again the third day according to the Scriptures, and that He was seen by Cephas, then by the twelve. After that, He was seen by over five hundred brethren at once, of whom the greater part remain to the present, but some have fallen asleep. After that, He was seen by James, then by all the apostles. Then last of all He was seen by me also, as by one born out of due time" (1 Corinthians 15:2-8, NKJV).

3. "And when Allah saith: 'O Jesus, son of Mary! Didst you say unto mankind: 'Take me and my mother for two gods beside Allah?' " (Sûrah 5:116a.) This is a rhetorical question, which has to be answered in the negative, thus forcing the Jesus of the Koran to deny His Divinity.

4. The Koran says that Allah gave the Psalms. Also see Sûrahs 3:184; 4:163; 17:55; 21:105; 34:10; 35:25.

5. The Koran says that Allah gave the gospel. Also see Sûrahs 3:2; 3, 48, 65; 5:46, 47, 66, 68, 110; 7:157; 9:111; 48:29; 578:27.

6. Mahmoud M. Ayoub, *The Qur'an and Its Interpreters:* Vol. 1 (Albany: State University of New York Press, 1984), 49.

☾☆

SÛRAH 2

(THE HEIFER)
THE COW (Baqara)
(Revealed at Medina)

In the name of Allah, the Beneficent, the Merciful.

(2:1) Alif. Lâm. Mîm.

A.J. Arberry also includes this in his opening translation, while Abdullah Yusuf Ali uses the three letters "*A.L.M.*"

There is a lot of debate and many, various explanations among Muslim scholars regarding what this verse means; however, we are unable to cite a reliable source that can give us a satisfactory, contextual translation with irrefutable evidence for the meaning of *Alif* (ﺍ). *Lâm* (ﻝ). *Mîm* (ﻡ). Marmaduke Pickthall states that they are three letters from the Arabic alphabet. These three words are also the names of three Hebrew letters, *Alif (א). Lam (ל). Mim (מ).*

(2:2) *This is the Scripture whereof there is no doubt, a guidance unto those who ward off (evil).*

A half a millennium before the writing of the Koran, the Bible also made this claim when referring to itself; thus, no other books were needed:

All Scripture is given by inspiration of God and is profitable for doctrine, for reproof, for correction, for instruction in righteousness: That the man of God may be perfect, thoroughly furnished unto all good work (2 Timothy 3: 16-17).

(2:3) Who believe in the unseen [spirit], and establish worship, and spend of that We have bestowed upon them (bracketed clarification mine);

Gabriel is continuing from his run-on sentence in the previous verse when he states, *"[For those] Who believe in the unseen [spirit]"...and establish worship, and spend of that We have bestowed upon them (bracketed clarifications mine).*

(2:4) And who believe in that which is revealed unto You (Muhammad) and that which was revealed before You, and are certain of the Hereafter.

Gabriel is referring to both the Koran and the Bible with the assumption that the "People of the Book" (as the Koran refers to Christians and Jews) will be equally accepting of the koranic revelations (which we are led to believe is in perfect harmony) alongside the Bible, thus assuring them a place in Heaven.

(2:5) These depend on guidance from their Lord. These are the successful.

This verse is referring to the "People of the Book" who also embrace the Koran and Islam. We see this type of compromise in today's society with the apostate teaching of Chrislam (Christian + Islam, possibly the one-world religion that is prophesied in Revelation 13:12 when the antichrist [denier of Christ's Divinity] forms his religion).

(2:6) As for disbelievers, whether You warn them or You warn them not it is all one for them; they believe not.

When we read the Bible, we are to interpret Scripture by using Scripture. The meaning of this passage from the Koran might be a bit confusing, leaving some readers to wonder if the people who are offered Islam are incapable of believing it, regardless of whether or not they have been approached about the Muslim faith. We can apply the same method we use to interpret Scripture to interpret the Koran, so we will use another verse from the Koran to help clarify the meaning of this verse:

> We sent not an apostle except (to teach) in the language [Arabic] of his (own) people, in order to make (things) clear to them. Now God (Allah) leaves straying [those who are lost] Those whom He pleases: And guides [saves] whom He pleases: And is Exalted in Power, Full of Wisdom (Sûrah 14:4, Abdullah Yusuf Al, bracketed clarifications mine).

It appears that Allah influences those he wants to accept Islam, thus allowing some to go to Heaven while rejecting others and sending them to Hell. He makes the choice. Conversely, the Bible teaches that the God of the Bible is not desirous that any should perish (2 Peter 3:9).

(2:7) Allah has sealed their hearing and their hearts, and on their eyes there is a covering. Theirs will an awful doom.

Keep this verse in mind as you study the Koran because right at the outset, Gabriel tells us that Allah deliberately causes some to reject both himself and Islam; yet in other verses we read:

> But as for him who shall repent and believe and do right, he haply [by chance] may be one of the successful (Sûrah 28:67).

This theme is repeated over and over again throughout the Koran, yet in other verses, Allah contradicts himself when he prevents others from accepting Islam. Which is it?

Later, in Sûrah 9:5, Allah instructs Muslims to kill or enslave all who reject Islam. This is very disturbing because if Allah preordained them to reject him, it is not their fault if they do not convert. It is even more troubling that Allah preordains them to be slaughtered!

> Then, when the sacred months have passed, slay the idolaters wherever you find them, and take them (captive), and besiege them, and prepare for them each [an] ambush. But if they repent and establish worship [to Allah] and pay the poor-due, then leave

their way free. Look! Allah is Forgiving, Merciful (Sûrah 9:5, bracketed clarifications mine).

(2:8) And of mankind are some who say: "We believe in Allah and the Last Day, when they believe not."

This passage seems to be referring to polytheists because—unlike the Judeo-Christian religions—we cannot find any reference to any Pagan religions which refer to the "Last Day;" however, this might include Christians and Jews who perhaps—for the sake of safety—give lip service to Allah and the Islamic "Last Day," but in actuality reject it because of Islam's many conflicts with biblical doctrine. It seems, in an effort to appease or to have their lives spared, Pagans, Jews, and Christians are condemned for doing what Muslims themselves are told to do in Sûrah 3:28: When they find themselves in the minority and fear the "People of the Book," they are supposed to lie (i.e., *taqiyya*) to protect themselves.

(2:9) They think to beguile [deceive] Allah and those who believe, and they beguile none save [except] themselves; but they perceive not (bracketed clarifications mine).

This is a little confusing because Allah tells Muslims in verse 7 that he is the author of the disbelief among non-Muslims. The Koran's readers are justified if they are confused by that statement, which is repeated again in Sûrah 14, where it clearly states, "...*Then Allah sendeth whom He will astray, and guideth whom He will. He is the Mighty, the Wise*" (Sûrah 14:4).

(2:10) In their hearts is a disease; and Allah increases their disease. A painful doom is theirs because they lie.

The God of the Bible does not seek to increase a person's sin, but He will not stop their choice to keep sinning. Consider how God gave the land of Canaan to Abraham, then told him he would not see it come to fruition in his lifetime because the people of the land (Amorites) had not yet reached a lifestyle of sin that would justify a righteous God to punish them (Genesis 15:12-16). God did not cause the Amorites to continue sinning. Instead; He stood aside and allowed them to grow in their own depravity—it was their choice.

(2:11) And when it is said unto them: "Make not mischief in the earth," they say: "We are peacemakers only."

Besides Arab polytheists, we can see how this could also refer to Jews and Christians, especially in light of the Bible because of its content. This verse claims that non-Muslims are lying because they make trouble when they claim, *"We are peacemakers only."* Yet the Bible teaches Christians and Jews to be peacemakers: "Deceit is in the heart of them that imagine evil: but to the counselors of peace is joy" (Proverbs 12:20), and "Blessed are the peacemakers: for they shall be called the children of God" (Matthew 5:9). If Jews and Christians actually admit that they follow these biblical directives, why should they be accused of lying?

(2:12) Are not they indeed the mischief-makers? But they perceive not.

> *Do the Pagans, and the "People of the Book" [Bible] cause Muslims trouble? Yes, because they do not understand or accept that the Koran is the final revelation from God (paraphrase and bracketed clarification mine).*

Those who might point out the inconsistencies between the Koran's version of biblical stories and the actual stories found in the Bible are *"mischief-makers."* Other *"mischief-makers"* are those who try to evangelize Muslims or will not give up their Pagan gods.

(2:13) And when it is said unto them: Believe as the people believe, They say: "Shall we believe as the foolish believe?" Are not they indeed the foolish? But they know not.

In the last three verses (2:11-13), it appears that the Koran is saying this because the Pagans, particularly the Christians and Jews, will not accept Allah and Islam (due to the many differences between the two); therefore, they are the fools. From the Koran's point of view, this is the reason Christians and Jews are causing problems—which renders them evil malcontents and troublemakers.

(2:14) And when they fall in with those [Muslims] who believe, they say: "We believe;" but when they go apart to their devils [jinns posing as pagan deities], they declare: "Look! We are with you; verily [truly] we did but mock" (bracketed clarifications mine).

Many Christians and Jews, as well as Pagans, might have sought to live in harmony with Muslims by trying to patronize them; however, according to Allah, when they are alone, they become demonically influenced by Satan and other jinns. Possibly, they are admitting to each other that they are only fooling their Muslim neighbor when the actuality is that they reject Islam; perhaps they see the many discrepancies between the Bible and the Koran), or maybe they prefer to remain who they are—Pagans, Christians, or Jews.

(2:15) Allah (Himself) does mock them, leaving them to wander blindly on in their contumacy [refusal to accept and obey]. (Bracketed clarification mine.)

In other words, Gabriel is saying Allah makes fun of the Christians, Jews, and Pagans because Allah is who allows them to wander in ignorance and not accept Islam.

Jews and Christians especially should recognize the truth because the Koran is flavored with many Bible stories containing biblical themes, which Allah claims he also shared in the Bible; consequently, if they choose to ignore the truth of the Koran, then they are just fools!

OBSERVATION: These statements should be kept in mind as the Koran waffles back and forth between Allah wanting or not wanting Christians and Jews to convert to Islam. Remember, the Koran also teaches that Allah determines who becomes converts and who doesn't. Wanting something and controlling something are two different things. Evidently, Allah is able to have it both

(2:16) These are they who purchase error at the price of guidance, so their commerce does not prosper, neither are they guided.

Gabriel says that people who "buy into" polytheism or the Judeo-Christian traditions—while passing over the teachings of Islam—will not attain blessings from Allah, nor will they be blessed because they are misled.

CONSIDER: Based on the last several verses we have read, you can decide whether or not the Christians and Jews being referred to were misled by their own choice or something more sinister

(2:17) Their likeness is as the likeness of one who kindles [starts a] fire, and when it sheds its light around him Allah takes away their light and

leaves them in darkness, where they cannot see (bracketed clarification mine).

To those who refuse to accept Islam, Allah removes the light so they cannot see; therefore, when they hear Muhammad's teachings and become excited by what they hear, they have second thoughts and reject it.

CONSIDER: If Allah prevents the seeker of truth from receiving it, why does he tell Muhammad to continue to preach the message of Islam to Christians, Jews, and Pagans? This is

(2:18) Deaf, dumb and blind; they return not [to the truth of Islam]. (Bracketed clarification mine.)

Combined with the previous verse, it is because Allah renders hypocrites as *"deaf, dumb and blind"* to the truth of Islam. Like a bright light, they are exposed to Islam but refuse to recognize the truth, so Allah removes the light, leaving them in the dark and never able to return to the truth of Islam again.

(2:19) Or like a rainstorm from the sky, wherein is darkness, thunder and the flash of lightning. They thrust their fingers in their ears by reason of the thunder-claps, for fear of death. Allah encompasses the disbelievers (in His guidance).

They are fools who refuse to accept the truth of Islam, even though they are completely surrounded by its truth, and its "blessed message" falls on them like rain from the sky. When the truth of Islam thunders at them, they plug up their ears so they will not have to hear it. They fear death, but reject the teaching that would secure a wonderful afterlife. Consequently, Allah is watching and knows it is their own fault; they do not accept the truth.

Again, the Koran presents us with a twofold explanation of why people do not accept Islam. Verse 18 tells us Allah leaves them *"deaf, dumb, and blind,"* while verse 19 tells us the disbelievers refuse to hear. One could not be faulted for asking Allah, "Which is it?" In the Bible, James 1:8 says, "A double-minded man is unstable in all his ways."

(2:20) The lightning almost snatches away their sight from them. As often as it flashes forth for them they walk therein, and when it darkens against them they stand still. If Allah willed, He could destroy their hearing and their sight. Look! Allah is able to do all things.

This is a repeat of verses 17 and 19, but with a different consequence: *"If Allah willed, He could destroy their hearing and their sight,"* although as we previously stated, we read in verse 18, *Allah did will that they be* "deaf, dumb and blind. "

In Sûrah 2:17-20, for those who do not believe in Islam and are led astray, Allah is the one who allows it. As we previously read, Allah determines who becomes converts and who does not. Otherwise, how could some people be so "deaf, dumb and blind" (Sûrah 2:18a)? If this is the case, then even more questions are raised regarding the fairness of condemning those who will not convert. The Bible teaches the following in 2 Peter and Romans 3 and 6.

...God is not desirous that any should perish... (2 Peter 3:9).

For all have sinned and fall short of the glory of God (Romans 3:23).

For the wages of sin is death; but the gift of God is eternal life through Jesus Christ our Lord (Romans 6:23).

(2:21) O mankind! Worship your Lord, Who has created you and those before you, so that you may ward off (evil).

Gabriel tells the people everywhere they should accept the teachings of the Koran, which teaches Allah is their god because he is the one who created them and gave them the ability to reject evil.

(2:22) Who has appointed [made] the earth a resting-place for you, and the sky a canopy; and caused water to pour down from the sky, thereby producing fruits as food for you. And do not set up rivals [the Trinity] to Allah when you know better (bracketed clarifications mine).

Gabriel is telling Muhammad that believers should know who appointed a resting place for them and, therefore, they should realize he made every good thing that comes from the beautiful earth and sky. The gentle rain provides for their crops and water to drink, so they should reject the Jesus of Christianity and accept the *Isa* (Arabic name for Jesus) of Islam. As we read in this verse, "And do not set up rivals to Allah." Once again, we see the underlying theme of the Koran—its ongoing attacks on the Divinity of Jesus and the Trinity.

(2:23) And if you are in doubt concerning that which We reveal unto Our slave (Muhammad), then produce a sûrah of the like thereof, and call your witnesses beside Allah if you are truthful.

If there is any doubt concerning what Muhammad is teaching, the unbeliever is told to produce a sûrah(s) or other documentation and bring a witness to prove they are truthful.

45

OBSERVATION: Christians do have such a document—it is called the Bible, and its witness is the Triune God therein. Proof that the Bible is the inerrant Word of God is manifested through predictions of future events—sometimes hundreds, or even thousands of years in the future—which only God knows about before they happen. God is not stingy with His prophecies since the Bible is over 25% prophecy, unlike the Koran, which contains no prophecy. Many of the Bible's prophecies have been fulfilled, some are being fulfilled today, and some are yet to be fulfilled.

Jews and Christians have a Bible filled with prophecy, which acts as God's personal endorsement throughout the Scriptures. Some might argue that Satan can also predict future events that he plans to bring about. We have no argument with that, but one thing is for certain, while Satan knows what he plans to do at some point in the future, only God is capable of knowing the outcome of those future events. (NOTE: There are no prophecies in the Koran, other than self-fulfilling ones.)

(2:24) And if you do it not—and you can never do it—[produce such proof] then guard yourselves against the fire [Hell] prepared for disbelievers [in Islam], whose fuel is of men and stones (bracketed clarifications mine).

Gabriel is saying that Allah created Hell-fire for those people who reject Islam, but the God of the Bible teaches that Hell was originally created for the devil and his angels:

Then shall He say also unto them on the left hand, "Depart from me, you cursed, into everlasting fire, prepared for the devil and his angels" (Matthew 25:41).

(2:25) And give glad tidings (O Muhammad) unto those who believe and do good works; that theirs are the Gardens underneath which rivers flow; as often as they are regaled with food of the fruit thereof; they say: "This is what was given us aforetime; and it is given to them

in resemblance. There for them are pure companions [dark eyed full breasted virgins]; there for them ever they abide [to enjoy for eternity]." (Bracketed clarifications mine.)

Muhammad Habib Shakir translates *"pure companions"* as *"pure mates."* Unlike the Bible, which teaches regarding the afterlife, "For in the resurrection they neither marry, nor are given in marriage, but are as the angels of God in Heaven" (Matthew 20:30). However, Islam is a very lustful religion with evidently a lot of sex in Muslim Heaven (Sûrah 56:1-38; 52:20; 78:31-33).

The premise at the beginning of this verse, "... who believe and do good works ... " is biblically incorrect since the Bible teaches:

> For by grace [undeserved gift] are you saved through faith; and that not of yourselves: it is the gift of God not of works, lest any man should boast (Ephesians 2:8-9, bracketed clarification mine).

Before Christ died on the cross for us, only the blood of an animal offered a temporary covering of the sins of the people until the next time they sinned, which was probably almost immediately. It took the ultimate blood sacrifice of Jesus on the cross—once and for all time—for the remission of sins. This divine gift of salvation is only available to those who accept Jesus as their Lord and Savior.

As the Bible states:

> But after that the kindness and love of God our Savior toward man[kind] appeared, Not by works of righteousness, which we have done, but according to His [God the Fathers] mercy He [God the Father] saved us, by the washing of regeneration, and renewing of the Holy Ghost; Which He [God the Father] shed on us abundantly through Jesus Christ our Savior; That being justified by His grace, we should be made heirs according to the hope of eternal life (Titus 3:4-7, bracketed clarifications mine).

The last part of this koranic verse, along with other repeated Sûrahs below, appeals to lustful rewards for those Allah allows in heaven by stating:

> And (there are) fair ones with wide, lovely eyes (Sûrah 56:22)

A more accurate translation of this passage can be found in A.J. Arberry's translation, which reads:

> And maidens with swelling breasts, like of age, and a cup overflowing (Sûrah 56:22, Arberry).

This theme is repeated again in Sûrah 78:

> There for them are pure companions for them ever they abide; And (there are) fair ones with wide, lovely eyes (Sûrah 56:22) And voluptuous women of equal age (Sûrah 78:33).

As we previously stated, Shakir's translation of *"pure mates"* is *"wives/concubines."* This is contrary to biblical teaching, which teaches that there is no marriage or marital relationship after you die (Matthew 22:23-30).

(2:26) Look! Allah disdains not to coin [create] the similitude [similarity] even of a gnat. Those who believe know that it is the truth from their Lord; but those who disbelieve say: "What does Allah wish (to teach) by such a similitude [similarity]? He misleads many thereby, and He guides many thereby; and He misleads thereby only miscreants [trouble-makers"] (bracketed clarifications mine).

This concept is not in the Bible. Muhammad Habib Shakir's translation is a little easier to understand:

> Surely Allah is not ashamed to set forth any parable—(that of) a lowest or anything above that; then as for those who believe, they know that it is the truth from their Lord, and as for those who disbelieve, they say: "What is it that Allah means by this parable: He causes many to err by it and many He leads aright [correctly] by it! but He does not cause to err by it (any) except the transgressors" (bracketed clarification mine, quotations added).

The God of the Bible does not lead people astray. He gives us free will to accept or reject His plan for our lives. Shakir's last sentence is similar to other translations of the Koran:

... but Allah does not cause (any) to stumble by it except the sinners whom Allah will lead (paraphrase mine).

On the contrary, the God of the Bible is not the father of sin or wickedness. That is left up to Satan, and the choices people make.

You are of *your* father the devil, and the desires of your father you want to do. He was a murderer from the beginning, and does not stand in the truth, because there is no truth in him. When he speaks a lie, he speaks from his own *resources,* for he is a liar and the father of it (John 8:44, NKJV).

In fact, the God of the Bible does not mislead people:

The Lord is not slack concerning *His* promise...but is longsuffering toward us, not willing that any should perish but that all should come to repentance (2 Peter 3:9, NKJV).

(2:27) Those who break the Covenant of Allah after ratifying it, and sever that which Allah ordered to be joined, and (who) make mischief in the earth: Those are they who are the losers.

Islam converts who leave the faith are the losers because Allah commands them to be killed, as we can see when we use the Koran to interpret the Koran by citing Sûrah 4:89:

They [Muslim converts who renounce their conversion] desire that you [Muslim believer] should disbelieve as they have disbelieved, so that you might be (all) alike; therefore take not from among them friends until they fly [leave] (their homes) in Allah's way [to fight the infidels]; but if they turn back [and refuse to fight for Islam], then seize them and kill them wherever you find them, and take not from among them a friend or a helper (Sûrah 4:89, Muhammad Habib Shakir, bracketed clarifications mine).

49

The killing of Muslims who leave the faith (apostates) is also encoded in the Hadith:

> Narrated [by] 'Ikrima:
>
> *... The Messenger of Allah said, "Whoever changes his (Islamic) religion, kill him."*[1]

Abd-Allah ibn Masood (sometimes spelled "Masud") expands on this Hadith:

> *The Messenger of Allah said: "It is not permissible to shed the blood of a Muslim who bears witness that there is no god except Allah and that I am the Messenger of Allah, except in one of three cases: a soul (in case of murder); a married person who commits adultery; and one who eaves his religion and separates from the main body of Muslims" (emphasis added).*[2]

(2:28) How disbelieve you in Allah when you were dead and He gave life to you! Then He will give you death, then life again, and then unto Him you will return.

This is passage is biblically inaccurate and unclear. Who was dead and is now alive?

Possibly the first death spoken about was the non-existent time before they were conceived in their mother's womb, or as some believe, their spirit existed before the human body did. They were then conceived born, and eventually died of natural or unnatural causes. Finally, they were resurrected spiritually and brought before Allah. This, of course, does not preclude the bodily resurrection (1 Thessalonians 4:17; 5:1-8; 1 Corinthians 15:52), which will occur for Christians at some future point.

Perhaps Abdullah Yusuf Ali's translation makes this passage more understandable:

> *How can you reject the faith in God [Allah]?—seeing that you were without life, and He gave you life; then will He cause you to die, and will again bring you to life; and again to Him will you return (bracketed clarification mine).*

Nonetheless, regarding the biblical resurrection, the Bible tells us, "Jesus said … 'I am the resurrection and the life …' " (John 11:25).

In context, we read:

Martha said to Him, "I know that he will rise again in the resurrection at the last day."

Jesus said to her, "I am the resurrection and the life. He who believes in Me, though he may die, he shall live. And whoever lives and believes in Me shall never die. Do you believe this?"

She said to Him, "Yes, Lord, I believe that You are the Christ, the Son of God, who is to come into the world (John 11:24-27).

Notice how Martha acknowledged that Jesus is the Son of God (which Islam strongly denies), and He did not correct her, but accepted her proclamation of His Divinity!

(2:29) He it is Who created for you all that is in the earth. Then turned He to the heaven, and fashioned it as seven sevens. And He is Knower of all things.

Arberry and Shakir also translate Heaven as *"seven heavens,"* while Ali translates this passage as "seven firmaments." This verse is also biblically inaccurate. The Bible records that God first created the Heavens in which we are told there are three, not seven, and then the earth in that order (Genesis 1:1). The first Heaven is the gaseous atmosphere, which envelops the earth. The second Heaven is known as the "universe." The third Heaven is the abode of God, probably in a different dimension (2 Corinthians 12:2; Revelation 8:10, 12:4). (The Koran teaches, in addition to Allah having created seven heavens, he also created seven earths, Sûrah 65:12.)[3]

(2:30) And when your Lord said unto the angels: "Look! I am about to place a viceroy in the earth," they said: "Will you place therein one who will do harm therein and will shed blood, while we, we hymn your praise and sanctify You?" He said: "Surely I know that which you know not."

This seems to indicate that angels, like God, can see into the future and predict coming events. Satan, who is an angel (albeit a fallen one), cannot predict the future, other than those events he or any other angel might *cause* to happen at some future date; yet, as we stated previously, *only God knows the results*. Therefore, angels would not have any knowledge of what mankind might do, especially at the time of their creation and earthly commission before Adam and Eve had sinned. The angels had no reason to believe humans would shed blood if the angels were busy singing hymns to the Lord because the humans would probably join them in singing. The problem here is that after God created everything, including man, the Bible tells us, "And God saw everything that He had made, and, behold, it was very good. And there was evening, and there was morning—the sixth day" (Genesis 1:31, NIV); therefore, if everything was not just good but *very good,* having the angels suggesting, at that point in time, that humans were potentially bad is not only illogical, it also unbiblical.

(2:31) And He taught Adam all the names, then showed them to the angels, saying: "Inform me of the names of these, if you are truthful."

This is another biblically inaccurate verse. God did not teach Adam the names of the animals; He gave that job to Adam:

> Out of the ground the LORD God formed every beast of the field and every bird of the air, and brought *them* to Adam to see what he would call them. And whatever Adam called each living creature, that *was* its name. So, Adam gave names to all cattle, to the birds of the air, and to every beast of the field. But for Adam there was not found a helper comparable to him (Genesis 2:19-20, NKJV).

In the spirit of fairness, Pickthall does provide us with a footnote as to whom the names mentioned here might be referring:

> *Some, especially Sûfîs, hold "the names" to be the attributes of Allah; others, the names of animals and plants.*

However, if this "creation story" is an effort to parallel the biblical story found in Genesis 2:19, then the names are most likely referring to the animals and not the 99 names for Allah. The Bible never mentions the 953 names and titles of God in the creation story.

52

(2:32) They said: "Be glorified! We have no knowledge saving that which You have taught us. Look! You, only You are the Knower, the Wise."

The Koran contradicts itself again because now the angels say they do not have the knowledge, other than what Allah gave them, to believe that Adam would cause trouble and shed blood on the earth. They stated that just two verses earlier (verse 30) when they predicted that Adam and his family would do harm and shed blood. Now the angels are stating that only Allah could have known that was going to happen.

(2:33) He [Allah] said, "O Adam! Inform them of their names", and when he had informed them of their names, He said: "Did I not tell you that I know the secret of the heavens and the earth? And I know that which you disclose and which you hide" (bracketed clarification mine).
Allah is telling Adam to inform the angels what the names of the animals are and then brags to the angels that he knew the animal's names even before Adam told them their names. After all, according to the Koran, Allah knows everything:

> *He [Allah] said, Watch out, Adam! I also know your mind and what you are going to do even before you think of doing it! (Sûrah 2:33, paraphrase mine.)*

This was also a lesson to the angels that Allah was able to place on his earthly overlord, Adam, limited authority, and wisdom over the earth.

(2:34) And when We said unto the angels: "Prostrate yourselves before Adam," they fell prostrate, all save Iblîs [Satan, chief of the jinn]. He demurred [protested] through pride, and so became a disbeliever (bracketed clarifications mine).

There is nothing biblical about verses 32-34, and they appear to be koranic embellishments. To prostrate oneself before something or somebody is a form of worship and submission. Angels do not submit to the authority of people, nor do they worship people. People do not bow down to angels and worship them either because, like us, they are fellow servants of God (Revelation 22: 8-9). Mankind was crowned with glory and honor and made a little lower than the angels (Psalm 8:4-5; Hebrews 2:7), thus negating the need for angels to worship any human.

Also, why did Satan become a disbeliever—a disbeliever in what? Contrary to this koranic verse, the angels (like humans) were created to only worship God and be His messengers (angel means "messenger").

(2:35) And We said: "O Adam! Dwell you and your wife in the Garden, and eat you freely (of the fruits) thereof where you will; but come not nigh [near] this tree lest you become wrongdoers" (bracketed clarification mine).

While this koranic passage is similar to one in the Bible, it still misses the point that if they ate from the special tree of *the knowledge of good and evil,* they would not just be *naughty*, they would die:

And the LORD God commanded the man, saying, "Of every tree of the garden you may freely eat:

"But of the tree of the knowledge of good and evil, you shall not eat of it: for in the day that you eat thereof you shall surely die" (Genesis 2: 16-17).

God prohibited Adam and Eve from eating from that particular tree not because they would innocently become wrongdoers, but because they would *know* what it would *mean* to be a wrongdoer (knowing good and evil) and thus lose their innocence.

When Adam and Eve were in a child-like state of innocence, they could not be held accountable for their actions, but once they knew the difference between good and evil, they became like children when they reached an age of accountability. Their actions caused them to realize what it meant to disobey God. They instantly knew they were naked and had just committed a sin by eating from the forbidden tree!

(2:36) But Satan caused them to deflect therefrom and expelled them from the (happy) state in which they were; and We said: "Fall down, one of you a foe unto the other! There shall be for you on earth a habitation and provision for a time."

A.J. Arberry translates this:

> Then Satan caused them to slip therefrom [a good relationship with Allah] and brought them out of that they were in; and We [Allah] said, "get you all down, each of you an enemy of each other; and in the earth a sojourn shall be yours, and enjoyment for a time" (bracketed clarification mine).

We are told here that it was Satan who expelled humans from His Islamic heaven: *"But Satan caused them to deflect therefrom and expelled them from the (happy) state in which they were."* While Satan did cause the humans to fall from grace into sin (Genesis 3:1-17), humans did not fall from Heaven (there were only two humans at that time, Adam and Eve) and became exiled from Islamic Heaven to the earth. In the Bible, God created man from and on the earth (Genesis 1:24-28; 2:5-7), and was exiled by God from the Garden of Eden, which was also on earth (Genesis 2:8).

And the LORD God said, "Behold, the man is become as one of us, to know good and evil: and now, lest he put forth his hand, and take also of the tree of life, and eat, and live forever:" Therefore the LORD God sent him forth from the garden of Eden, to till the ground from whence he was taken. So he drove out the man; and he placed at the east of the garden of Eden *Cherubims*,[4] and a flaming sword which turned every way, to keep the way of the tree of life (Genesis 3:22-24, bracketed emphasis added).

"Fall down, one of you a foe unto the other!" means that Satan and his jinn (demonic angels) would be constantly at war with the humans.

(2:37) Then Adam received from his Lord words (of revelation), and He relented toward him. Indeed! He is the Relenting, the Merciful (bracketed clarification mine].

Allah revealed to Adam (who was originally created immortal) what he had just done was wrong, which caused Adam to confess his wrongdoing. Then Allah forgave him. Notice there are no consequences for Adam's sin against Allah, unlike the Bible (Genesis 3:17-19).

... Because you have...eaten from the tree of which I commanded you, saying, "You shall not eat of it...." Cursed *is* the ground for your sake; In toil you shall eat *of* it All the days of your life....Till you return to the ground, For out of it you were taken; For dust you *are,* And to dust you shall return(Genesis 3:17-19, NKJV).

(2:38) We said: "Go down, all of you, from here; but truly there will come unto you from Me a guidance; and whoso follows My guidance, there shall no fear come upon them neither shall they grieve."

This is both a biblical and koranic foreshadowing. Speaking for Allah, Gabriel is telling them (Adam, Eve, and possibly some of their descendants) they have to leave heaven and go to earth, but Allah will send them guidance (through prophets along with the Bible and the Koran) to bring them comfort. While this could be called a koranic prophecy, it is a self-fulfilling one placed into a revisionist version of Genesis after the fact.

(2:39) But they who disbelieve [Arab polytheists, Christians and Jews], Our revelations, such are rightful owners of the Fire. They will abide therein" (bracketed clarification mine).

If one rejects Allah's teachings, they will be cast into Hell-fire. In Islam, no one, including Muhammad (Sûrah 46:9), is ever assured of their salvation unless they die in a jihad for Allah.

> *Those whom Allah (in His plan) wills to guide—He opens their breast to Islam; those whom He wills to leave straying—He makes their breast closed and constricted, as if they had to climb up to the skies: thus does Allah (heap) the penalty on those who refuse to believe (Sûrah 6:125).*

The above verse and the one below confirms there is no free will in salvation, yet the only guarantee of paradise is dying in a jihad:

> *And if you are slain, or die, in the way of Allah, forgiveness and mercy from Allah are far better than all they could amass [gain on earth] (Sûrah 3:157, bracketed clarification mine).*

Fighting is prescribed for you, and you dislike it. But it is possible that you dislike a thing which is good for you, and that you love a thing which is bad for you. But Allah knows, and you know not (Sûrah 2:216).

See! Allah has brought from the believers their lives and their wealth because the Garden will be theirs: they shall fight in the way of Allah and shall slay and be slain. It is a promise, which is binding on Him in the Torah, the Gospel and the Qur'an. Who fulfills His covenant better than Allah? Rejoice then in your bargain that you have made, for that is the supreme triumph (Sûrah 9:111, emphasis added).

OBSERVATION: In Sûrah 9:111, we read that those who "shall slay or be slain" for Allah will gain heaven. Why would a god encourage that? The last half of verse 111 is unbiblical; it claims the "Torah and the Gospel" teach the same koranic promise of paradise for those who fight and die for God as a means of salvation. Such a passage is not found anywhere in the Torah, gospel(s), or anywhere else in the Bible for that matter. Ephesians 2:89 teaches just the opposite. We can also see in the Gospel of Matthew what Jesus taught: "You have heard that it was said, 'You shall love your neighbor and hate your enemy.' But I say to you, 'love your enemies, bless those who curse you, do good to those who hate you and pray for those who spitefully use you and persecute you' " (Matthew 5:43, NKJV). This verse provides even more proof that the God of the Bible and Allah (the god of the Koran) are not the same.

As for those *"...who disbelieve [Arab polytheists, Christians, and Jews], Our revelations, such are rightful owners of the Fire" (Sûrah 2:39, bracketed clarification mine),* the Bible discusses Hell and assures us that if our names are written in the Book of Life, we will avoid it:

And the sea gave up the dead which were in it; and death and Hell delivered up the dead which were in them: and they were judged every man [people] according to their works.

And death and Hell were cast into the lake of fire.

This is the second death. And whosoever was not found written in the book of life was cast into the lake of fire (Revelation 20:13-15, bracketed clarification mine).

Jesus instructs us how a person can escape the horrible eternal fire, and if Jesus *(Isa)* were an Islamic prophet as the Koran claims He is, it would be improper for Him to lie. This being the case, how do we deal with the following claim Jesus made about Himself?

For God so loves the world that He gave His only unique Son, that whoever believes in Him should not perish but have everlasting life. For God did not send His Son into the world to condemn the world, but that the world through Him might be saved (John 3:16-17).

Many translations read, "... His only begotten Son," which comes from the Greek word *monogenēs (*μονογενής*)* and means "one of a kind, unique." A new human body infused with the second member of a pre-existing Triune God and without the use of any form of sperm would definitely be one of a kind and *very* unique!

(2:40) O Children of Israel! Remember My favour wherewith I favored you, and fulfill your (part of the) covenant, I shall fulfill My (part of the) covenant, and [then you should] fear Me (bracketed clarification mine).

This sudden shift from disbelievers to Israelites, while confusing, is nonetheless typical of the way ideas are arranged in the Koran. Now we are addressing a biblical covenant, which might be referring to one made with Abram—the grandfather of Israel—at the time when God changed his name to Abraham:

No longer shall your name be called Abram, but your name shall be Abraham, for I have made you a father of many nations (Genesis 17:5, NKJV).

Following the name change, God established an everlasting covenant with Abraham:

I will make you exceedingly fruitful; and I will make nations of you, and kings shall come from you. And I will establish My covenant between Me and you and your descendants after you in their generations, for an everlasting covenant, to be God to you and your descendants after you. Also I give to you and your descendants after you the land in which you are a stranger, all the land of Canaan, as an everlasting possession; and I will be their God (Genesis 17:6-8, NKJV).

However, the continuation of this covenant is troubling to Muslims because it gives preference to Abraham and Sarah's son, Isaac, who—even though he would be Abraham's second son—he was designated by God to be the son of promise over Ishmael. Ishmael was the only son Abraham had known, so he was content with having only one son because by then, Sarah was very old at the age of 90. How could she hold up under the strains of childbirth? Therefore, Abraham asked God if perhaps Ishmael could be given the covenant, even though he was only half of Abraham's family. (Sarah was also from Abraham's bloodline because she was his half-sister):

... Then God said: "No, Sarah your wife shall bear you a son, and you shall call his name Isaac; I will establish My covenant with him for an everlasting covenant, *and* with his descendants after him" (Genesis 17:19, NKJV, emphasis added).

God also honored Abraham's request for Ishmael to be blessed:

And as for Ishmael, I have heard you. Behold, I have blessed him, and will make him fruitful, and will multiply him exceedingly. He shall beget twelve princes, and I will make him a great nation (Genesis 17:20, NKJV).

Nevertheless, God repeated that His covenant would be solely given to Isaac and passed down exclusively through his descendants, which includes all the tribes of Israel:

> But *My covenant I will establish with Isaac*, whom Sarah shall bear to you at this set time next year (Genesis 17:21, NKJV, emphasis added).

It is interesting to note that Muslims conveniently avoid another covenant that was also promised to the children of Israel by the prophet, Jeremiah:

> Behold, the days come, saith the LORD, that I will make a new covenant with the house of Israel, and with the house of Judah Not according to the covenant that I made with their fathers in the day that I took them by the hand to bring them out of the land of Egypt; which my covenant they brake, although I was an husband unto them, saith the LORD:
>
> But this shall be the covenant that I will make with the house of Israel; After those days, saith the LORD, I will put my law in their inward parts, and write it in their hearts; and will be their God, and they shall be my people. (Jeremiah 31:31-33).

The covenant directed toward Isaac's descendants came to fruition around 500 years after Jeremiah gave that prophecy through the Messiah, Jesus. Christians refer to the new covenant in Jeremiah 31:31 as the New Testament. It is further explained in the biblical book of Hebrews:

> For if that first *covenant* had been faultless, then no place would have been sought for a second [*covenant*] because finding fault with them, He said: "Behold, the days are coming," says the LORD, "when I will make a new covenant with the house of Israel and with the house of Judah" (Hebrews 8:7-8, NKJV).

 "For I will be merciful to their unrighteousness, and their sins and their lawless deeds I will remember no more." In that, He says, "A new *covenant*;" He has made the first obsolete. Now what is becoming obsolete and growing old is ready to vanish away (Hebrews 8:12-13, NKJV, Ref. Jeremiah 31:31).

 And to Jesus the mediator of the new covenant, and to the blood of sprinkling, that speaks better things than that of Abel (Hebrews 12:24, NKJV).

(2:41) And believe in that which I reveal [in the Koran], confirming that which you possess already (of the Scripture), [in the Bible] and be not first to disbelieve therein, and part not with My revelations [in the Koran] for a trifling price, and keep your duty unto Me (bracketed clarifications mine).

Allah is attempting to validate the Koran by implying that he was the one who gave the Bible to Christians and Jews. Because they accept the Bible, he is suggesting they should also accept the Koran. He believes the Koran and Bible are in perfect harmony with each other, yet just in this short exploration of the second sûrah, as we have seen, we have already found many troubling discrepancies. Nevertheless, once again, Allah claims that he is the author of both books, saying that the Christians and Jews have no reason to reject him as the God of the Bible just because he has an Arabic name. His new revelation is presented by the last and greatest prophet—not from the House of Israel—but from the House of Ishmael. This, too, is problematic for Bible-believing Jews and Christians because Muhammad is a son of Ishmael, and the god of the Koran comes out of the land of Arabia.

The Bible clearly states:

 What advantage then has the Jew, or what is the profit of circumcision? Much in every way! Chiefly, because to them were committed the oracles [prophets who revealed the Bible] of God (Romans 3:1-2, NKJ, bracketed clarification mine).

As seen in the previous verse, the Bible makes it clear Scripture is only given through Israel (Jacob), not Ishmael, because God made His covenant with Abraham through his ancestral bloodline. That bloodline included Sarah because she was Abraham's half-sister, so the bloodline continued unabated through their son, Isaac, and Isaac's son, Jacob (Israel), who also married their close cousins.[5]

God still honored Abraham's love for Ishmael and promised very generous blessings for him and his descendants; however, there was never an amicable relationship between the two boys and their descendants. To this day, their family connection remains strained.

We read about that hostility when Nehemiah was allowed to return to Jerusalem and rebuild what Nebuchadnezzar damaged. When the people who had replaced the Israelites in the land of Israel, including Ishmael's descendants (Arabs), heard about Nehemiah and his plan to rebuild the city's walls and the Temple, Nehemiah observed, "They laughed us to scorn ..." (Nehemiah 2:19).

Family ties were always strained among the children of Ishmael and Isaac because Isaac's descendants—not Ishmael's—were the ones who received God's covenant blessing. Sadly, more often than not, Ishmael's descendants not only harbored resentment, but they also became enemies of Israel—just as they are today.

Continuing with the example of this animosity—in the story of Nehemiah—and his restoration of Jerusalem's Temple and the walls, Nehemiah explains:

> Now it happened when Sanballat, Tobiah, *Geshem the Arab*, and the rest of our enemies heard that I had rebuilt the wall and that there were no breaks left in it (though at that time I had not hung the doors in the gates), that Sanballat and Geshem sent to me, saying, "Come, let us meet together among the villages in the plain of Ono." But they thought to do me harm (Nehemiah 6:1-2, NKJV, emphasis added).

(2:42) Confound not truth with falsehood, not knowingly conceal the truth.

By denying acceptance of the Koran, Allah is accusing the Christians and Jews of rejecting the real *"truth."* By doing so, they are showing their willing ignorance. Even so, as we pointed out earlier, Allah told the Christians and Jews they should compare the Bible with the revelations of Muhammad (no disrespect intended, but Jews are typically savvy and literate—unlike Muhammad—when it comes to Scripture), so when they pointed out the many errors between Muhammad's revelations and the Bible, they had to be made to look like they were bearing false witness, as we read in this verse.

(2:43) Establish worship, pay the poor-due, and bow your heads with those who bow (in worship).

This verse is also reminiscent of a passage from the Bible:

Let us hold fast the profession of our faith without wavering (for He is faithful that promised); And let us consider one another to provoke unto love and to good works: Not forsaking the assembling of ourselves together, as the manner of some is; but exhorting one another: and so much the more, as you see the day approaching (Hebrews 10:23-25).

(2:44) Enjoin [teach] your righteousness upon mankind while you yourselves forget (to practice it)? And you are readers of the Scripture! Have you then no sense? (Bracketed clarification mine.)

We know the Law was passed down to humanity through the Ten Commandments, which were given to Moses on Mount Sinai, but in this verse, Gabriel is accusing the Jews and Christians of breaking those laws (as many of us still do intentionally or inadvertently). Apparently, the "People of the Book," while able to acknowledge biblical Scripture, are too stupid to accept the teachings of Muhammad, yet—as we have read—Allah is the one who claims to cause people to accept or reject him, which is contradictory at best.

(2:45) Seek help in patience and prayer; and truly it is hard save [except] for the humble-minded (bracketed clarification mine).

In context, we read:

> Enjoin [teach] your righteousness upon mankind while you yourselves forget (to practice it)? And you are readers of the Scripture! Have you then no sense? Seek help in patience and prayer; and truly it is hard save for the humble minded (Sûrah 2:44-45, bracketed clarifications mine).

Presumably, those who are "humble-minded" might also be those who are ignorant and, therefore, less likely to be aware of the conflicts between the Bible and the Koran.

The Bible also teaches that we should be humble "... but in lowliness of mind let each esteem others better than themselves" (Philippians 2:3b). Still, this would not have any bearing on accepting a religious system that conflicts with the teachings of the Bible.

(2:46) Who know that they will have to meet their Lord and that unto Him they are returning.

Muhammad admitted that he had no assurance of what Allah would do with him after he died (Sûrah 46:9). We can gather by this passage that we should all have a humble attitude and prepare for the day—which will surely happen to all of us—when we will die and have to stand in the presence of Allah. This is reminiscent of Ecclesiastes:

Then shall the dust return to the earth as it was: and the spirit shall return unto God who gave it (Ecclesiastes 12:7).

(2:47) O Children of Israel! Remember My favour wherewith I favoured you and how I preferred you to (all) creatures.

Muhammad sought early on to bring the Jews into his new religion of Islam. This verse is little patronizing and a part of that effort.

(2:48) And guard yourselves against a day when no soul will in aught [anything] avail [benefit] another, nor shall intercession be accepted from it [Israel], nor will compensation be received from it, nor will they be helped (bracketed clarifications mine).

Unlike our other two translators, Abdullah Yusuf Ali translates this passage using the word "her" in place of "it" implying that the Israelites believed salvation came to them because of the prophets who came from among them; therefore, God would give them special favor and permit them into Heaven. But that seems a bit of a stretch when compared with the translations of Arberry, Shakir, and Pickthall, where the word "it" appears to stand for "soul" and not "her."

(2:49) And (remember) when We did deliver you from Pharaoh's folk, who were afflicting you with dreadful torment, slaying your sons and sparing your women: That was a tremendous trial from your Lord.

Again, here is another confusion of biblical Scriptures. The Hebrew people were not undergoing a trial in the sense God was trying to teach them something or that they had done anything wrong. On the contrary, God was using the Egyptians to delay the Hebrews from returning and claiming the land of Canaan He had promised to them because the sins of the Amorites had not risen to a level to justify their destruction by a just God (Genesis 15:13-16), as we will read later. By tolerating this repression, God was assuring the Hebrews they would be more than ready to leave Egypt and return to the land of Canaan when the time was right. It was the Egyptians who were punished for enslaving the children of Israel (Genesis 15:14). Second, the Egyptians were using the Hebrew men to help with building projects, so why would Pharaoh kill the strong male workforce he depended on and allowed only the weaker sex to survive?

In fairness, by the time Moses was born, Pharaoh had ordered post-birth abortions for every Hebrew male baby (Exodus 1:15-16). This was a means of population control to prevent the Hebrew slaves from overpowering the Egyptians. Pharaoh did not want a Hebrew male population to grow beyond what was needed for the workforce because he feared it would embolden the Hebrew slaves to rise up against him and perhaps take over his kingdom (Exodus 1:10).

Some four hundred years before Moses and his people were slaves in Egypt, God had warned Abraham about his descendants' captivity and why they would be held there:

Now when the sun was going down, a deep sleep fell upon Abram; and behold, horror *and* great darkness fell upon him. Then He said to Abram: "Know certainly that your descendants will be strangers in a land *that is not theirs,* and will serve them, and they will afflict them four hundred years And also the nation whom they serve I will judge; afterward they shall come out with great possessions. Now as for you, you shall go to your fathers in peace; you shall be buried at a good old age. But in the fourth generation they shall return here, for the iniquity of the Amorites *is* not yet complete" (Genesis 15: 12-16, NKJV, emphases added).

DEALING WITH BIBLICAL GENERATIONS

Some have reasoned that a generation is 40 years based on this passage from the Bible: "And the LORD'S anger was kindled against Israel, and he made them wander in the wilderness forty years until all the generation that had done evil in the sight of the LORD was consumed" (Numbers 32:13, emphasis added). The Bible is referring to children who had reached the age of accountability and adults who refused to go into Canaan and possess the land. The generation who would not enter the Promised Land were family members of various ages, from older children, teenagers, and adults to the very old. (Moses was around 80 years old, and Joshua was 40 years old at the time God passed that judgment on the Israelites).

After the flood of Noah, the life span of people began to decrease; however, in Genesis, a time close to the flood, the life span was 120 years: "And the LORD said, My spirit shall not always strive with man, for that he also *is* flesh: yet his days shall be an hundred and twenty years" (Genesis 6:3).

The Israelites were in Egypt 430 years (Exodus 12:40), approximately 50 years shy, but well into the fourth generation, which was a generality as some might have lived a little longer than others. Abraham lived to be 175 years old (Genesis 25:7). During the time of King David, up to and including today's generation, we live on an average of threescore and ten or fourscore if one is very healthy

(Psalm 90:10). A score is twenty years, so threescore and 10 is equal to 20 X 3 = 60 + 10 = 70 years or 20 X 4 = 80 years if a person is healthy.

(2:50) And when We brought you through the sea and rescued you, and drowned the folk [army] of Pharaoh in your sight (bracketed clarification mine).

This is a koranic likeness of Exodus 14:21-22 when the Israelites crossed the Red Sea on dry land, followed by the drowning of Pharaoh's army (Exodus 14:23-28).

(2:51) And When We did appoint for Moses forty nights (of solitude), and then you chose the calf, when he had gone from you, and were wrongdoers.

The forty nights of solitude is when Moses went up to the Mountain of God (Mount Sinai) in Exodus 24:18 and 34:28. This also refers to the golden calf mentioned in Exodus while Moses was on the mountain conversing with God:

Now when the people saw that Moses delayed coming down from the mountain, the people gathered together to Aaron, and said to him, "Come, make us gods that shall go before us; for *as for* this Moses, the man who brought us up out of the land of Egypt, we do not know what has become of him."

And Aaron said to them, "Break off the golden earrings which *are* in the ears of your wives, your sons, and your daughters, and bring *them* to me." So all the people broke off the golden earrings which *were* in their ears, and brought *them* to Aaron. And he received *the gold* from their hand, and he fashioned it with an engraving tool, and made a molded calf.

Then they said, "This *is* your god, O Israel, that brought you out of the land of Egypt!"

So when Aaron saw *it,* he built an altar before it. And Aaron made a proclamation and said, "Tomorrow *is* a feast to the LORD." Then they rose early on the next day, offered burnt offerings, and brought peace offerings; and the people sat down to eat and drink, and rose up to play (Exodus 32:1-6, NKJV).

(2:52) Then, even after that, we pardoned you [children of Israel] in order that you might give thanks (bracketed clarification mine).

The Bible explains it differently. When God told Moses how the children of Israel had turned against Him and were worshipping the molten calf, He was not in a forgiving mood! He told Moses He was going to destroy them and start all over again with Moses and his house (Exodus 32:7-10); however, Moses pleaded for the people, so God relented and forgave them (Exodus 32:11-14).

(2:53) And When We gave unto Moses the Scripture and the criterion of right and wrong), that you might be led aright [in the right way] (bracketed clarification mine)

This seems to be referring to Exodus 32:15-16 when God gave Moses the two tablets containing the Ten Commandments that were in Moses' possession on his way back down from Mount Sinai; nevertheless, the knowledge of right (good) and wrong (evil) was received by mankind in the Garden of Eden when they listened to the Serpent who called God's Word into question and ate the forbidden fruit of the tree of knowledge of good and evil (Genesis 2:16-17), an act that caused humans to fall from grace (Genesis 3:1-7).

(2:54) And when Moses said unto his people: "O my people! You have indeed wronged yourselves by your choosing of the calf (for worship) so turn in penitence to your Creator, and kill (the guilty) [the wrong-doers] yourselves. That will be best for with your Creator and He will relent toward you. Look! He is the Relenting, the Merciful" (bracketed clarification mine).

Moses never cautioned the people to ask God's forgiveness, nor did he ask the people, in general, to *"...kill (the guilty) (the wrong-doers) yourselves;"* rather Moses asked for volunteers from his own family (Levites) to execute the wrong-doers:

And it came to pass, as soon as he came near unto the camp, that he saw the calf, and the dancing: and Moses' anger grew hot, and he cast the tables out of his hands, and broke them beneath the mount.

And he took the calf which they had made, and burnt it in the fire, and ground it to powder, and scattered it upon the water, and made the children of Israel drink of it.

And Moses said unto Aaron, "What did this people unto you, that you have brought so great a sin upon them?"

And Aaron said, "Let not the anger of my lord wax [grow] hot: you know the people that they are set on mischief."

For they said unto me, "make us gods, which shall go before us: for as for this Moses, the man that brought us up out of the land of Egypt, we know not what is become of him."

And I said unto them, "Whosoever has any gold, let them break it off." So they gave it me: then I cast it into the fire, and there came out this calf.

And when Moses saw that the people were naked (for Aaron had made them naked unto their shame among their enemies).

Then Moses stood in the gate of the camp, and said, "Who is on the LORD's side? let him come unto me." And all the sons of Levi gathered themselves together unto him.

And he said unto them, "Thus says the LORD God of Israel, 'Put every man his sword by his side, and go in and out from gate to gate throughout the camp, and slay every man his brother, and every man his companion, and every man his neighbor.' "

And the children of Levi did according to the word of Moses: and there fell of the people that day about three thousand men (Exodus 32:19-28, bracketed clarification mine).

(2:55) And when you said: "O Moses! We will not believe in you till we see Allah plainly" and even while you gazed the lightning seized you.

We will first address the initial part of this interesting verse. Regarding the statement, *"O Moses! We will not believe in you till we see Allah plainly"* (2:55a), it appears to be out of sequence since the people never made this request at Mount Sinai. They had already seen God's manifestation in their midst before the events on Mount Sinai took place.

And the Lord went before them by day in a pillar of a cloud, to lead them the way; and by night in a pillar of fire, to give them light; to go by day and night (Exodus 13:21).

We will refer to the Scripture regarding the event among God, Moses, and the people on Mount Sinai in Exodus 24:

And He said unto Moses, "Come up unto the LORD, you, and Aaron, Nadab, and Abihu, and seventy of the elders of Israel; and worship you afar off. And Moses alone shall come near the LORD: but they shall not come nigh; neither shall the people go up with him" (Exodus 24:1-2).

The Bible does not record the people telling Moses, *"O Moses! We will not believe in you till we see Allah plainly."* Some did see God, but it was before the rebellion, not after it—and it was at His invitation—not because the people demanded it, as we will read in the next four verses:

Then went up Moses, and Aaron, Nadab, and Abihu, and seventy of the elders of Israel: And they saw the God of Israel: and there was under His feet as it were a paved work of a sapphire stone, and as it were the body of Heaven in His clearness. And upon the nobles of the children of Israel He laid not His hand: also they saw God, and did eat and drink. And the LORD said unto Moses, "Come up to me into the mount, and be there: and I will give you tables of stone, and a law, and commandments which I have written; that you may teach them" (Exodus 24:9-12).

The Bible refers to lightning on Mount Sinai, but the lightning never touched Moses in any way. The following passage is basically all the Bible has to say regarding the lightning on the mountain:

> On the morning of the third day, there was thunder and lightning, with a thick cloud over the mountain, and a very loud trumpet blast (Numbers 11:16).

In the second part of this koranic verse, there is nothing even remotely similar in the biblical record which states, "—*the lightning seized you [Moses]*" (Sûrah 2:55b, bracketed clarification mine), which resulted in his death as we will see in the next verse.

(2:56) Then We revived you after your extinction [death], that you might give thanks (bracketed clarification mine).

In light of the Bible, this is simply another koranic embellishment with no basis in fact. Consider: When a man of God dies, he goes immediately to a wonderful place of peace and tranquility (2 Corinthians 5:8), so why would he be thankful to be returned to a life subjected to betrayal, sickness, and pain? What in the world is Gabriel talking about? The Bible, nor any other historical account we are aware of, ever recorded Moses' death by lightning, much less revived again by God. The Koran is confusing stories—yet again. Deuteronomy records that approximately 40 years after Moses went up to Mount Sinai, he went to Mount Nebo/Pisgah, where he died a natural death.

> And Moses went up from the plains of Moab unto the mountain of Nebo, to the top of Pisgah that is over against Jericho. And the LORD showed him all the land of Gilead, unto Dan.... And the LORD said unto him, "This is the land which I swore unto Abraham, unto Isaac, and unto Jacob," saying, "I will give it unto your seed: I have caused you to see it with your eyes, but you shall not go over there." So Moses the servant of the LORD died there in the land of Moab, according to the word of the LORD. And he buried him in a valley in the land of Moab, over against Beth Peor: but no human knows of his sepulcher [where he is buried] unto this day (Deuteronomy 34:1-6, bracketed clarification mine).

(2:57) And We caused the white cloud to overshadow you and sent down on you the manna and the quails, (saying): "Eat of the good things wherewith We have provided you"—We wronged them not, but they did wrong themselves.

The *"white cloud"* described here is linked with the quail story in Exodus 16:13. A white cloud is not a rain cloud, which is generally darker. Some Muslim scholars suggest the white cloud provided the Israelites with shade while traveling in the Sinai desert, although that cannot be found in the Bible. It seems more likely that the Koran is confusing the *"white cloud"* with the pillar of smoke by day and the pillar of fire by night during the same period:

> And the LORD went before them by day in a pillar of a cloud, to lead them the way; and by night in a pillar of fire, to give them light; to go by day and night: He took not away the pillar of the cloud by day, nor the pillar of fire by night, from before the people (Exodus 13:21-22).

As we can see in the following biblical account, the story of quail and manna was not connected to a cloud in any way:

> And the LORD said to Moses, saying, "I have heard the complaints of the children of Israel. Speak to them, saying, 'At twilight you shall eat meat, and in the morning you will be filled with bread. And you shall know that I *am* the LORD your God.' "

So it was that quails came up at evening and covered the camp, and in the morning the dew lay all around the camp. And when the layer of dew lifted, there, on the surface of the wilderness, was a small round substance, as fine as frost on the ground. So when the children of Israel saw it, they said to one another, "What is it?" [Strong's Hebrew word #3131 *Manna* means, "What is it?"] For they did not know what it was.

And Moses said to them, "This *is* the bread which the LORD has given you to eat" (Exodus 16:11-15, NKJV, bracketed clarification mine).

(2:58) And remember We said: "Go into this township and eat freely of that which is therein, and enter the gate prostrate and say: 'Repentance. We will forgive you our sins and will increase (reward) for the right-doers'".

This is another koranic improvisation. The Bible never recorded the Israelites traveling and eating in any town during their desert wanderings. They were never told that bowing down when entering an unspecified town—or any town for that matter—would allow their sins or the sins of the inhabitants of any town to be forgiven. During the time of the Exodus, sins could only be covered through the offering of a blood sacrifice to God (Leviticus 17:11; Hebrews 9:22).

(2:59) But those who did wrong changed the word which had been told them for another saying, and We sent down upon the evil-doers wrath from Heaven for their evildoing.

If this verse is suggesting that the Bible was rewritten, as we discussed in Volume I *of Islam Exposed: A Simple Crash Course on Islam* in Chapter 5 regarding *"...those who did wrong changed the word ...,"* this charge is historically inaccurate and—as we explained in that chapter—has been disproved through archaeology. If the Koran is suggesting Christians profess a Trinity and, therefore, have added something not found in the Old Testament, that is also incorrect. The Old Testament not only mentions God's Son in Proverbs 30:4, but it also remarks about the Trinity in Isaiah 48:16, which we will address later in Volume III, Chapter 8 of our three-volume series, *Islam Exposed, Islam: Science-Bible-Archaeology and Myths.*

(2:60) And when Moses asked for water for his people, We said: "Smite with your staff the rock." And there gushed out therefrom twelve springs (so that) each tribe knew their drinking-place. "Eat and drink of that which Allah has provided, and do not act corruptly, making mischief in the earth."

Once more, we have a different rendition of what happened when Moses hit the stone and brought forth the water. There are two accounts of this story in the Bible. The first one is when Moses struck the stone (Exodus 17:6). The second is when Moses was told to speak to the stone (Numbers 20:8). This does not mean the Bible contradicts itself; rather, the Exodus version is a brief description of what happened. In a more detailed account in Numbers, Moses did, in fact, strike the stone; nevertheless, God told Moses to strike the stone only once, but Moses disobeyed and struck the stone twice in anger. Neither story spoke of twelve separate springs. It is peculiar the Koran would address the miracle of water from a stone while ignoring the very strict punishment given to one of the Bible's greatest prophets who it also claims as an alleged prophet of Islam:

Then the LORD spoke to Moses, saying, "Take the rod; you and your brother Aaron gather the congregation together. *Speak to the rock* before their eyes, and it will yield its water; thus you shall bring water for them out of the rock, and give drink to the congregation and their animals." So Moses took the rod from before the LORD as He commanded him.

And Moses and Aaron gathered the assembly together before the rock; and he said to them, "Hear now, you rebels! *Must we* bring water for you out of this rock?" Then Moses lifted his hand and *struck the rock twice* [not once as God had instructed him to do] with his rod; *and water came out abundantly*, and the congregation and their animals drank.

Then the LORD spoke to Moses and Aaron, "Because you did not believe Me, to hallow Me in the eyes of the children of Israel, therefore you shall not bring this assembly into the land which I have given them" (Numbers 20:7-12, NKJV, bracketed clarifications mine, emphases added).

(2:61) And when you [Israelites] said, "O Moses! We are weary of one kind of food; so call upon your Lord for us that he bring forth for us of that which the earth growth—of its herbs and its cucumbers and its corn and its lentils and its onions." He said: "Would you exchange that which is higher for that which is lower? Go down to settled country, thus you shall get that which you demand." And humiliation and wretchedness were stamped upon them and they were visited with wrath from Allah. That was because they disbelieved in Allah's

revelations and slew the prophets wrongfully. That was for their disobedience and transgression [sin]." (Bracketed clarifications mine.)

This verse is not only disjointed, but it is also an anachronistic passage (something placed in a time where it did not exist) because it goes from a discussion regarding the desire to have a variety of foods to the killing of biblical prophets. Historically, by the time of Moses, no Hebrew prophets had been killed. That came much later, after the time of Moses (thus the anachronism).

As for the people requesting Moses to ask the Lord *"to bring forth for us of that which the earth growth—of its herbs and its cucumbers and its corn and its lentils and its onions,"* that is a perversion of what the Jews were lamenting about. The Hebrews never asked Moses to intercede with God for them to have the dessert grow the types of food they had in Egypt; however, the Bible does tell us the children of Israel were grumbling because they wanted to return to Egypt where they had that food rather than die in the desert. It was God who came alongside Moses and said He would provide them with bread and meat—not the other way around:

And the whole congregation of the children of Israel murmured against Moses and Aaron in the wilderness:

And the children of Israel said unto them, "Would to God we had died by the hand of the LORD in the land of Egypt, when we sat by the flesh [stew] pots, and when we did eat bread to the full; for you have brought us forth into this wilderness, to kill this whole assembly with hunger."

Then said the LORD unto Moses, "Behold, I will rain bread from Heaven for you; and the people shall go out and gather a certain rate every day, that I may prove them, whether they will walk in my law or not" (Exodus 16:2-4, bracketed clarification mine).

As for the last part of Sûrah 2:261, which states, *"And humiliation and wretchedness were stamped upon them and they were visited with wrath from Allah,"* Allah appears to be vindictive while—conversely—the God of the Bible is more measured.

God showed His patience and tolerance when He said in Exodus 16:4 that He would "... rain bread down from Heaven ..." for them and the people would be able to go out and gather enough of it every day. The God of the Bible wanted to prove to them He was a caring God— whether they walked in His law or not. Likewise, God never told the wandering Hebrews to get the food they wanted by going to town. Villages were far and few between in the desert, and during their forty years of wandering, there is no record of Hebrews interacting commercially with any villagers or caravans.

(2:62) Look! Those who believe (in that which is revealed until you, Muhammad), and those who are Jews, and Christians, and Sabaeans[6]—whoever believes in Allah and the Last Day and does right—surely their reward is with their Lord, and there shall no fear come upon them neither shall they grieve.

Jews and Christians believe in one God and the Last Days' scenario, unlike the Pagans. This is not only another clever way to identify with them, but it is also meant to suggest that Allah is just another name for the God of the Bible, thus hoping to make Islam more appealing. Regardless of this, this verse contains some problems.

The Koran has Jews, Christians, and people from Sheba (Sabaeans) together as a group. Of course, the Jews (descendants of Judah) are only one of the twelve Hebrew tribes, and Christians might include anyone from any nationality who believes in Jesus, the Son of God; therefore, the Jews and Christians are considered the "People of the Book" by Muslims. (Anyone may become a believer in the "Jewish" faith as well—but unlike Christians—Jews do not seek converts to their religion, as Judaism is a tribe, a faith, and a nationality.)

There is also some controversy regarding the Sabaeans (people allegedly descended from the land of Sheba). Many believe they are probably African people (Ethiopians) associated with the biblical story of Solomon and the Queen of Sheba, but in this case, they probably came from the Arabian Peninsula (Yemen) and were associated with the Arab Polytheists. As for the Koran, including the Sabeans[7] with the Christians and Jews as "People of the Book," it is believed that the Queen of Sheba came to believe in the Hebrew God as suggested in

Scripture (I Kings 10:1-13). Many of her people did embrace the Hebrew religion and migrated to Israel during the twentieth century, where their living descendants can still be found today.

Another problem with this koranic verse is the admonition that belief in Allah, with accompanying good works, brings salvation. That is just the opposite of the gospel teachings and ignores the fact the Bible teaches that salvation is a gift, even for those Jews of the first century who did not participate in the crucifixion of Jesus. For it is only through faith in Jesus *(Isa)* that we are saved and is something that cannot be earned:

> let it be known to you all, and to all the people of Israel, that by the name of Jesus Christ of Nazareth, whom you crucified, whom God raised from the dead.... nor is there salvation in any other, for there is no other name under Heaven given among men by which we must be saved (Acts 4:10, 12, NKJV).

> So too, at the present time there is a remnant [of Hebrews] chosen by grace, And if by grace, then it cannot be based on works; if it were [through works], grace would no longer be grace [i.e., an undeserved gift from God]. (Romans 11: 5-6, bracketed clarifications mine.)

(2:63): And (remember, O children of Israel) when We made a covenant with you and caused the Mount to tower above you (saying):"Hold fast that which We have given you, and remember that which is therein, that you may ward off (evil)."

This verse is a bit curious. It seems to imply that Allah created Mount Sinai by making it grow into a mountain in the presence of the Hebrews. The other three translators, Arberry, Ali, and Shakir, basically say the same thing as well. This would have been a momentous event, and if such a miraculous event had occurred, why was it not recorded in the Bible?

Because this verse refers to Mount Sinai, the *"covenant"* it mentions is probably the Ten Commandments since that is the only covenant given at the time of the described event.

(2:64) Then, even after that, you turned away, and if it had not been for the grace of Allah and His mercy you [would] had been among the losers (bracketed clarification mine).

In context, this is a summary of the events at Mount Sinai. The children of Israel actually rebelled before Moses gave them the Ten Commandments. Because of their treachery, God wanted to destroy them all and not show them any mercy (Exodus 32:9-10) while Moses was still on top of Mount Sinai; however, Moses interceded on their behalf, so God relented (Exodus 32:14). As for the rebels, Moses had them executed (Exodus 32:27-28).

(2:65) And well you knew those amongst you who transgressed in the matter of the Sabbath: We said to them [the Hebrews]: "Be you apes, despised and hated" (bracketed clarification mine).

This too, is a bit disjointed as the Koran jumps to another subject—the breaking of the Sabbath—which was never the problem at Mount Sinai. Many Muslims who quote this passage (or other similar koranic passages found in Sûrahs 5:60 and 7:166) have been unfairly accused of being politically incorrect and identified as using hate speech. Even so, this is another instance—in light of the New Testament—where the Koran stands in direct conflict with biblical teachings:

So let no one judge you in food or in drink, or regarding a festival or a new moon or *Sabbaths*, which are a shadow of things to come, but the substance is of Christ (Colossians 2:16-17, NKJV, emphasis added).

The ones spoken about in Sûrah 2:65, who are alleged to have broken the Sabbath, might be confusing the Messianic Jews (Christians) who, in the first century, observed Saturday worship, but also gathered for Sunday worship and fellowship—the day Jesus rose from the dead—with the seventh-century Christians who observed Sunday as the Sabbath.

After the first century, Sunday also became known as the Lord's Day and, eventually, the Christian Sabbath; however, every day is a good day to worship God! The term, *"Be you apes ...,"* has despicably been applied primarily to the Jews as we will observe in Sûrah 5:60—where Allah condemns Jews and Christians for rejecting Muhammad and his koranic teachings—or for those who just reject his warnings as repeated again in Sûrah 7:

> *So when they took pride in that which they had been forbidden, We said unto them: "Be you apes despised and loathed!" (Sûrah 7:166, emphasis added.)*[8]

We will pause here to mention that Muslims also left the biblical Sabbath of Saturday (the seventh day when God rested from the six days of creation) to celebrate their Sabbath day on Friday.

As for the references to people turned into animals, this commentary is also exclusive to the Koran and Islam. There is no place in biblical Scripture where Jews, Christians, or any other ethnic group are referred to—or turned into—apes, pigs, or any other animal for that matter. In fact, the God of the Bible never uses such derogatory remarks when referring to His people. Apes are only mentioned in two places in the entire Bible (both referring to the same event) as we read in 1 Kings and 2 Chronicles:

The king had a fleet of trading ships at sea along with the ships of Hiram. Once every three years it returned, carrying gold, silver and ivory, and apes and baboons (1 Kings 10:22).

For the king's ships went to Tarshish with the servants of Huram: every three years once came the ships of Tarshish bringing gold, and silver, ivory, and apes, and peacocks (2 Chronicles 9:21).

(2:66) And We made it an example [warning] to their own and to succeeding generations, and an admonition to the Allah-fearing (bracketed clarification mine).

This verse is a continuation of the previous one and is unique to the seventh-century Koran. This is reinforcing Allah's condemnation of the Christians and Jews who had fallen out of favor with Allah. They were cursed to be as apes—and even worse, pigs—as revealed in Sûrah 5:60, yet such a horrific curse on anyone is not supported in the Bible.

(2:67) And when Moses said unto his people: "Look! Allah commands you that you sacrifice a cow," they said: "Do you make game of us [are you kidding us]?" He answered: "Allah forbid that I should be among the foolish!" (Bracketed clarification mine.)

It seems that the Koran is referring to Chapter 19 in the Book of Numbers where a red heifer, who had never been worked and was in perfect health without blemish (verse 2), was sacrificed as a burnt offering (verse 5), and its ashes were mixed with water and kept as a purification drink (verse 9). It is not clear why sacrificing an animal, which was not unusual in that day, seemed so funny.

(2:68) They said: "Pray for us unto your Lord that He make clear to us what (cow) she is." (Moses) answered: "Look!" He says, "Verily [truly] she is a cow neither with calf nor immature; (she is) between the two conditions; so do that which you are commanded" (bracketed clarification mine).

This is unique to the Koran. It is not reflected anywhere in the Bible. The children of Israel never asked God—when told to sacrifice an animal, in this case, a cow—what His preference regarding the type of cow it should be. This is simply another koranic, biblical embellishment. As for the statement, *"Verily [truly] she is a cow neither with calf nor immature,"* it simply means she is a heifer, which is a cow that is not a baby anymore, but also not old enough to be mated. This is in agreement with the biblical teaching regarding the cow's age by referring to it as a heifer (Numbers 19:2, bracketed clarification mine).

(2:69) [again] They said: "Pray for us unto your Lord that He make clear to us of what colour she is." (Moses) answered: "Look!" He says: "Verily [truly] she is a yellow cow. Bright is her colour, gladdening beholders" (bracketed clarifications mine).

Once more, this appears to be referring to the biblical red heifer found in the book of Numbers, Chapter 19.

Abdullah Yusuf Ali says the color is a "fawn-color," while Muhammad Habib Shakir agrees with Marmaduke Pickthall that the color of the cow is "yellow," yet A.J. Arberry uses the color "golden" in place of yellow.

(2:70) [Repeating themselves again] They said: "Pray for us unto your Lord that He make clear to us what (cow) she is. Look! cows are much alike to us; and Lo! if Allah wills, we may be led aright" (bracketed clarification mine).

This is an interesting passage considering the similar, preceding verses. There is no mention in the Bible where anyone showed curiosity about the color of people or animals; however, the Bible does comment on the colors of animals from time-to-time, such as the story of Jacob's scheme to multiply spotted sheep (Genesis 30:25-43) and this story regarding a red heifer. But in the Bible, it was God who brought up the subject of what color the special heifer should be (Numbers 19).

(2:71) (Moses) answered: "Look!" He said: "Verily [truly] she is a cow unyoked; she ploughed not the soil nor watered the tilth [fertile soil]; [she will be] whole and without mark." They said: "Now you brings the truth. So they sacrificed her, though almost they did not" (bracketed clarifications mine).

This summary in verse 71 is in line with chapter 19 in the biblical Book of Numbers regarding the red heifer, although the last part of the passage which reads, *"So they sacrificed her, though almost they did not"* appears to be another koranic improvisation because the Koran's suggestion that the Hebrews hesitated to obey God in performing this sacrifice is not even suggested in the Bible.

(2:72) And (remember) when you slew a man [Moses] and disagreed concerning it and Allah brought forth that [dead body] which you were hiding (bracketed clarifications mine).

81

This is a reinforcement of the uniquely koranic story regarding the man Moses killed (Exodus 2:11-15). When confronted with the murder, Moses denied he had killed anyone and caused an argument among the Hebrews as to who had killed the man. According to this verse, Allah used the murdered man to expose Moses. This story should not be confused with anything remotely similar in the Bible because it is purely another creative koranic embellishment.

(2:73) So We said: "Strike the (body) with a piece of the (heifer)." Thus Allah bringeth the dead to life and showed you His Signs: [so that] Perchance [by chance] you may understand (bracketed clarifications mine).

It might be enlightening to see how A. J. Arberry deals with these passages in context regarding the cow (Sûrah 2:71-73):

> He [Moses] said, [referring to Allah] "He says she shall be a cow not broken to plough the earth or to water the tillage, one kept secure, with no blemish on her." They said, "Now you have brought the truth;" and therefore they sacrificed her, a thing they had scarcely [unwillingly] done. "And when you killed a living soul [going back to an earlier time in Egypt], and disputed thereon—and God disclosed what you were hiding—so We said, 'Smite him [the dead Egyptian] with part of it' ["it" being a part of the Koran's erroneous yellow cow sacrificed during the 40 years of desert wandering]; even so God brings to life the dead, and He shows you His signs, that haply [by chance] you may have understanding" (Arberry, Sûrah 2:71-73 bracketed clarifications mine).

Verse 73 is saying that Allah arranged for the murdered man to be brought back to life in order to identify Moses as his murderer. Consider that Moses is believed to have been over 80 years old (Exodus 7:7) when he returned to Egypt, which was just before Pharaoh let the people and Moses leave (Exodus 13:17) and began their 40 years of wandering in the desert (Numbers 14:20-35); but in this koranic version, it was only six verses ago in the Koran when Allah introduced a special cow for the first time during the Exodus event.

In an almost dream-like sequence, the Koran leaves the Exodus event and travels decades back in time to when Moses was still a prince of Egypt—and as if by magic—the cow mysteriously appeared again, but this time it is in the story of Moses killing the Egyptian, probably an Egyptian soldier or overseer, who was beating a Hebrew slave. Moses reacted violently because the Hebrew slave was from the same people as Moses, thus the reason for Moses' intervention (Exodus 2:11-15). In this verse, we are now told that Allah instructed Moses to hit the dead man with a part of the cow, which brought the dead Egyptian back to life—and this from a cow who hadn't been born yet!

To summarize, historically, it was during the time of wandering of the children of Israel in the Sinai desert when God first introduced the Red Heifer—not before this event (Numbers 19:1-3).

The Koran's version is out of chronological order because it transports us back almost a half a century to the time when Moses killed the Egyptian:

Now it came to pass in those days, when Moses was grown, that he went out to his brethren and looked at their burdens. And he saw an Egyptian beating a Hebrew, one of his brethren. So he looked this way and that way, and when he saw no one, he killed the Egyptian and hid him in the sand. (Exodus 2:11-12, NKJV)

Once again, we are presented with a very peculiar, reconstructed Bible story where we are left scratching our heads and wondering from where this story came.

In summary of this verse, it appears that the order presented here is intentional in all translations of the Koran we accessed. First, Allah describes the cow to Moses during the time when Israel was undergoing the 40 years of wandering in the desert, where the children of Israel were told to sacrifice a heifer. Next, we are told that part of that same cow is used in an earlier story to expose the younger Moses regarding his killing of one of the men who were fighting:

83

Again, something created in the future cannot exist in the past unless you have a time machine, but the Koran does not make that claim. For a reader of the Bible, this is very confusing, to say the least, and can only be explained by this fact—this is another koranic anachronism.

(2:74) Then, even after that, your hearts were hardened and became as rocks, or worse than rocks, for hardness. For indeed there are rocks from out which rivers gush, and indeed there are rocks which split asunder so that water flows from them. And indeed there are rocks which fall down for the fear of Allah. Allah is not unaware of what you do.

This verse is an abrupt transitional verse where we are redirected to a comparison of rocks: "... *For indeed there are rocks from out which rivers gush, and indeed there are rocks which split asunder so that water flows from them ....*" This was probably aimed at the Jewish tribes of Medina, as well as some of the Christians in the area who might have converted to Islam for a time but found problems with its biblical references. This verse is going back 14 verses and picking up from where verse 60 left off. Once again, the Koran is confusing Bible stories by merging separate incidents into one event by blending the first part of this verse, which refers to the Old Testament story of Moses striking the rock in Exodus 17:6 and the last part of this verse which states, *And indeed there are rocks which fall down for the fear of Allah.*" This is reminiscent of the New Testament event found in Luke 19 when Jesus entered the city of Jerusalem, and His disciples began rejoicing and praising Him:

"Blessed *is* the King who comes in the name of the LORD! Peace in heaven and glory in the highest!" And some of the Pharisees called to Him from the crowd, "Teacher, rebuke Your disciples."

But He answered and said to them, "I tell you that if these should keep silent, *the stones would immediately cry out*" (Luke 19:38-40, NKJV, emphasis added).

In light of this biblical passage from the Gospel of Luke, we can see how the last part of Sûrah 2:74, which Pickthall translates, "... *And indeed there are rocks which fall down for the fear of Allah,*" might be confused with the passage from Luke where Jesus claimed, "*the stones* would immediately cry out." This not only shows rocks with emotions incorporated into this koranic verse, but also an allegorical substitution using Allah's name in place of Jesus. "*And indeed there are rocks which fall down [which would call out] for the fear [for the love] of Allah [Jesus].*" Other than this passage, the Bible is silent about rocks being afraid or responding to God in any way.

(2:75) Have you any hope that they [Jews and Christians] will be true to you when a party of them used to listen to the Word of Allah, then used to change it, after they had understood it, knowingly? (Bracketed clarification mine.)

With the previous verse 74, the Koran abruptly abandons the Exodus story and continues in a different direction. It implies that because there are many conflicting, historical events, and passages between the Bible and the Koran, it is because the Jews and Christians rewrote, twisted or incorrectly remembered what was originally given to them in the Bible by Allah; thus, the reason they will not heed what Muhammad is trying to teach them, or they have changed their minds about being a Muslim. However, archaeology and earlier documentation tell us otherwise—the Bible has been very consistent throughout the ages, and its followers have faithfully kept its doctrines (the apostate Gnostic gospels excepted).

(2:76) And when they fall in with those who believe, they say: "We believe." But when they go apart one with another they say: "Prate [disparage] you to them of that which Allah has disclosed to you that they may contend with you before your Lord concerning it? Have you then no sense?"

Abdullah Yusuf Ali's translation is easier to understand:

> *Behold! when they meet the men of Faith [believers in the Prophet Muhammad], they say: "We believe": But when they meet each*

other in private, they say: "Shall you [fellow Jews and Christians] tell them [Muslims] what Allah has revealed to you [in the Bible], that they may engage you in an argument [and use against you what the Bible has to say] about it before your Lord?- Do you not understand (their aim)? (Bracketed clarification mine.)

Simply put, Christians and Jews are two-faced when they patronize Muslims saying they believe in Muhammad's teachings when they admit among themselves that they are afraid Muslims might use their own Bible against them because they are really ignorant about what their Bible really teaches.

(2:77) Are they then unaware that Allah knows that which they keep hidden and that which they proclaim?

Again, this indicates Christians and Jews might be fooling some Muslims—but not Allah. Allah knows the Jews and Christians, out of fear, do not want to debate the Muslims because they know they have perverted the Bible, and it is the Muslims who have the true Scriptures.

(2:78) Therefore woe be unto those who write the Scripture with their hands and then say, "This is from Allah," that they may purchase a small gain therewith. Woe unto them for that their hands have written, and woe unto them for that they earn thereby.

A. J. Arberry's translation:

And some there are of them that are common folk not knowing the Book [Bible], but only fancies and mere conjectures (bracketed clarification mine).

Because the Koran is challenged regarding its conflicts with the Bible, some of Muhammad's Arab followers, who hear the questioning by the Jews and are beginning to doubt what he is telling them, are told by Muhammad that the Jews are illiterate and cannot read nor write. However, the opening of this verse seems to contradict that theory as it begins, *"Therefore woe be unto those who write the Scripture with their hands and then say, 'This is from Allah.' "* This suggests that the

Bible is a fabrication and what Jews and Christians claim to be disagreements between the Koran and the Bible are actually corrupted biblical stories created to challenge the Koran's truths. To be even-handed, it is possible many Arab Christians were illiterate like the Pagan Arabs were because the dawn of Islam was also the dawn of the Dark Ages;[9] however, Jews, by their very cultured upbringing, have always placed a high priority on literacy. Surprisingly, oral traditions, like those written down in the Hebrew Mishnah (Mishna) around the second to fourth century A.D. and the later Talmud compiled around 500 A.D., are transmitted incredibly accurate and have been proven to leave no room for heresy to creep in. Consider: If this were not true, then the accuracy of the koranic transmission could also be questioned.[10]

(2:79) Therefore woe be unto those who write the Scripture with their hands and then say, "This is from Allah," that they may purchase a small gain therewith. Woe unto them for that their hands have written, and woe unto them for that they earn thereby.

Gabriel says that Allah will deal harshly with those (rabbis and scribes) who unscrupulously create counterfeit texts along with false marginal notes (comments) and claim them as Bible verses from Allah, as well as sell them for profit to unsuspecting Jews and Christians.

Abdullah Yusuf Ali, A.J. Arberry, and Muhammad Habib Shakir use the term *"Book;"* Pickthall chooses to use the word *"Scripture"* which, in this case, is also used to refer to the Bible.

Primarily, this verse is referencing the commentaries the rabbis and scribes wrote to accompany the Scriptures of the Torah, which are sometimes read in the marginal notes in the Bible. This verse, which makes it seem like the rabbis and scribes rewrote the Torah, and other biblical books, is an attack on the Bible and its commentaries. It suggests that Muhammad was hoping to convince the gullible Jews and Christians, who thought their Bibles were purposefully corrupted, in an effort to justify the many discrepancies between the Bible and the Koran. (We explore the accuracy of the Bible further in *Volume I* of *Islam Exposed: A Simple Crash Course on Islam,* where we show that the false charge of corruption, as alluded to in this verse, has been disproven by archaeologists using the Dead Sea Scrolls and other sources of documentation).

(2:80) And they say: "The Fire (of punishment) will not touch us save for a certain number of days. [in purgatory]:" Say: "Have you received a covenant from Allah—truly Allah will not break His covenant—or tell you concerning Allah that which you know not?" (Bracketed clarification mine.)

This first part of this verse, which reads, *"And they say: 'The Fire shall not touch us but for a few numbered days ...' "* is aimed at the unbiblical concept held by some early Christians and current Roman Catholics. When souls die, they go through a purging (purgatory) where they can be *prayed out of*[11] as a prelude to being allowed entrance into paradise. This is not found in either the Old or New Testaments of the Bible, but praying for the dead was mentioned in the historical Apocrypha book of 2 Maccabees[12] in Chapter 2, verses 39-45. While not considered canon (the list of the godly inspired books of the Bible), Maccabees is included in the Roman Catholic Bible. Martin Luther, in his *Ninety-five Theses* (sometimes written as *95 Theses)*, claimed in #29, "Who knows whether all souls in purgatory wish to be redeemed, since we have exceptions in St. Severinus and St. Paschal), as related in a legend."[13] In other words, he said purgatory (limbo) cannot be proven from Scripture. Although Luther personally believed in purgatory, he took issue with the Church putting themselves above God as the decision-maker regarding one's length of stay in purgatory. Maccabees also provided for the Church to allow a sinner to pay money for an indulgence (a pardon or absolution from God's wrath) for their (or someone else's) time off in purgatory. They could even buy a "get out of jail card" called a plenary (total) indulgence based on this passage from 2 Maccabees which was dealing with the dead: "He [Judas Maccabee] also took up a collection, man by man, to the amount of two thousand drachmas of silver, and sent it to Jerusalem to provide for a sin offering" (2 Maccabees 2:43, bracketed clarification mine). To sum it up, Martin Luther took issue with the Church allowing you to buy a "get out of limbo card" or even a quick bypass out of purgatory by purchasing an indulgence.

From the time of Luther's posting of his 95 Thesis until the Council of Trent, It took the Church 46 years to condemn "all base gain for securing indulgences" in 1563. That was followed by Pope Pius V, four years later, in 1567, formalizing the end of purchasing indulgences. The Bible assures us:

We are confident, I say, and willing rather to be absent from the body [through death], and to be [immediately] present with the Lord [in Heaven] (2 Corinthians 5:8, bracketed clarifications mine).

Jesus made the following promise to the thief on the cross as they were dying:

And Jesus said unto him, "Truly I say unto you, Today shall you be with me in paradise" (Luke 23:43).

OBSERVATION: Some Islamists might question that because the Bible says Jesus was on the earth forty days after His Resurrection (Acts 1:3), how could He have kept His promise to the criminal on the cross when He told him He would be with him in Heaven that very day? They might argue that is proof the Bible is corrupted, and that Jesus was never crucified; nevertheless, the answer is very simple to anyone who is familiar with the Scriptures. Jesus was referring to that same day in Heaven, and Heaven's day is different than the 24-hour solar day we have here on earth, as we will see below.

To begin with, both the Old and New Testaments validate, "A day in Heaven is a thousand years on earth …" (Psalm 90:4; 2 Peter 3:8); therefore, a year on earth amounts to about one minute and forty seconds in Heaven. That being the case, even though Jesus' remained on earth for forty days after His resurrection and before He ascended into Heaven, His time on earth would have been around ten seconds in Heaven's time; consequently, Jesus and the criminal on the cross would not only have been in Heaven on the same day—as Jesus promised— but their arrival in Heaven would have been separated by only a few seconds! Another point to consider is that during the time Jesus was in the grave for three days followed by His resurrection, He had not (according to His own words) gone to be with the Father in Heaven yet (John 20:17).

(2:81) Nay, but whosoever has done evil and his sin surrounds him; such are [the] rightful owners of the Fire [of Hell]; they will abide therein (bracketed clarifications mine).

In Islam, sinners and unbelievers will go straight to Hell. Even more astonishing is that in Islam, there is no Savior or guarantee of salvation in Islam. Even Muhammad had no assurance whether he would be sent to Heaven or Hell (Sûrah 46: 8-9; (*Sahih al-Bukhari*, Volume 5, Book 58, Number 266).

(2:82) And those who believe [in Islam] and do good works: such are rightful owners of the Garden. They will abide therein (bracketed clarification mine).

Sûrah 2:81-82 continues the koranic view of works-oriented salvation, which is shared with all other religions except Christianity.

In Islam, it is *what you can do for God*; in Christianity, it is *what God has done for you* (John 3:16-17; Peter 3:9).

(2:83) And (remember) when We made a covenant with the Children of Israel, (saying): Worship none save Allah (only), and be good to parents and to kindred [relatives] and to orphans and the needy, and speak kindly to mankind; and establish worship and pay the poor-due. Then, after that, you slid back, save a few of you, being averse.

While reflecting on Allah's alleged interaction with the Jews, it seems that he is taking issue with them for having been given the Scriptures and Laws of Moses, only to turn their backs on them. We are told that rejection of the Scriptures by the Jews is an ongoing thing with only a few remaining true believers. This, of course, is far from historical or theologically accurate. History records the millions of millions of Jews who paid with their lives for their unwavering devotion to God. Perhaps this is meant to establish for Muhammad's followers why the "People of the Book," who Allah says would find no difference between the Bible and Koran (Sûrah 5:47), are not jumping at the opportunity to follow Muhammad and his alleged final revelation from their God.

Conceivably, this could give his followers a reason why the Jews are not accepting the Koran, and that is why Allah is accusing the Jews of continuing this heresy right up to this very day.

(2:84) And when We made with you a covenant (saying): Shed not the blood of your people nor turn (a party of) your people out of your dwellings. Then you ratified (Our covenant) and you were witnesses (thereto).

This seems a bit vague. We know that many of the Hebrew Prophets were killed by the people, but an ongoing wholesale eviction and slaughter of their neighbors or ongoing intertribal warfare is not something we are able to document, through research, as a Hebrew practice in the Bible. However, it is true that Arab tribes fought continually against each other.

(2:85) Yet you it is who slay each other and drive out a party of your people from their homes, supporting one another against them by sin and transgression?—and if they came to you as captives you would ransom them, whereas their expulsion was itself unlawful for you — Believe you in part of the Scripture and disbelieve you in part thereof? And what is the reward of those who do so save ignominy [disgrace] in the life of the world, and on the Day of Resurrection they will be consigned to the most grievous doom [judgment]. For Allah is not unaware of what you do (bracketed clarifications mine).

As stated on the previous page, some Hebrews did kill many of the prophets, yet not every prophet was murdered, nor was there a wholesale slaughter between the Hebrew tribes. We read in I Kings 18:13 that Queen Jezebel was a Pagan, not a Hebrew, who worshipped Ba'al. She was the daughter of the Phoenician priest-king, Ethba'al, who ruled both Tyre and Sidon, located in what is now Lebanon. She had many unnamed prophets of Israel killed during her reign. Consider: What society does not have any people who commit murder?

Perhaps the accusation here is directed toward the Jews and Christians as adversaries who ransom each other for money as an ongoing practice between either Jews and Christians or between the tribes of Israel. That is not something we would find in Scripture. It was more in line with the warring Muslim sects who continue that tradition to this very day.

On the Arabian Peninsula, historically, there was continual intertribal warfare. Even today, throughout the Muslim world, tribes continue to war among themselves as we have seen with the Sunnis vs. Shi'ites and ISIS, who are seeking domination, enslavement, and booty over everyone not associated with them. In fairness, can we really fault Muslims when they follow their role model, "The Prophet of the Sword," Muhammad, who also attacked other Arabian tribes and forced them to pay up and/or convert to Islam?

(2:86) Such are those who buy the life of the world at the price of the Hereafter. Their punishment will not be lightened, neither will they have support.

This verse echoes the words of Jesus when He says:

For what is a man profited, if he shall gain the whole world, and lose his own soul? [or what shall a man sell his immortal soul for?] (Matthew 16:26, bracketed clarification mine.)

(2:87) And verily [truly] We gave unto Moses the Scripture and We caused a train of messengers to follow after him, and We gave unto Jesus, son of Mary, clear proofs (of Allah's sovereignty), and We supported him with the Holy spirit. Is it ever so, that, when there cometh unto you a messenger (from Allah) with that which you yourselves desire not, you grow arrogant, and some you disbelieve and some you slay? (Bracketed clarification mine.)

Observation: Notice the reference to Allah sending "the Holy spirit" to Jesus, which is mentioned in all four of the translations we referenced. The third member of the Trinity is not acknowledged in Islam so we must ask, "Who is *the 'Holy spirit' mentioned here?*" In a foot note, Pickthall claims the Holy spirit is the angel, Gabriel. If so, why didn't Gabriel, who is telling this story, inform us it was him? He uses the term "angels" in the Koran (Sûrah 35 is ملائكة, "the Angels," so why not "the holy Spirits, plural." For example, Sûrah 2:87 refers to two angels, not two Holy Spirits, and we are to believe that Holy Spirit (initial caps) and angel (not initial caps) are the same? If Gabriel is the "holy spirit" of the Koran, then we have another conspicuous discrepancy between the Koran and the Bible, of which Allah claims he is the author. Perhaps mentioning the Holy Spirit is only "koranic Bible-speak" used in order to make the Koran sound more acceptable to Christians.

Once again, the Koran seems to be addressing the people of the Bible. This echoes the words of Jesus when, approximately seven hundred years earlier, He said:

"O Jerusalem, Jerusalem, which kills the prophets, and stones them that are sent unto you; how often would I have gathered your children together, as a hen does gather her brood under her wings, and you would not!" (Luke 13:34.)

According to one Islamic source, we are told this verse "... also denotes the Holy Spirit of Jesus, the spirit which God had endowed with angelic character." This source also goes on to say: "The expression *'clear proofs'* refers to those signs which are likely to convince a truth-seeking and truth-loving person that Jesus is [only] a prophet of God."[14] When Allah makes the claim, "...*and We supported him with the Holy spirit,*" it seems apparent that it is a Spirit that is separate from Allah and from

Jesus, but not the Holy Spirit of the Bible. Biblically, it is necessary to also ask, "Who did the 'Son of Mary' consider Himself to be?" The answer (among other passages of Scripture) can be found in the dialogue between Jesus and the Apostle Peter:

> When Jesus came into the region of Caesarea Philippi, He asked His disciples, saying, "Who do men say that I, the Son of Man, am?"

> So they said, "Some *say* John the Baptist, some Elijah, and others Jeremiah or one of the prophets."

> He said to them, "But who do you say that I am?"

> Simon Peter answered and said, "You are the Christ, the Son of the living God."

> Jesus answered and said to him, "Blessed are you, Simon Bar-Jonah, for flesh and blood has not revealed *this* to you, but My Father who is in Heaven" (Matthew 16: 13-17, NKJV).

In light of this koranic passage—compared to the words of Jesus in the Bible—we are once more presented with another troubling conflict. Jesus did not accept the description given to Him as one of the prophets, as the Koran teaches later in verse 136 and again in Sûrahs 3:84; 4:157, etc.) but agreed with Peter that, while He does prophesy, He is more than a prophet; He is the "Son of the living God."

(2:88) And they say: "Our hearts are hardened." Nay, but Allah has cursed them for their unbelief. Little is that which they believe.

Who *"they"* are is a little confusing, but perhaps—in light of the previous verse—"they" are the Christians and Jews who are offering the excuse that the reason they have not accepted Islam is that their hearts are closed to Islam. Gabriel insists that Allah is cursing them because they refuse to believe on their own without Allah's intervention and, therefore, they bring Allah's curse on themselves. This verse contradicts Sûrah 10:25, which states:

But God [Allah] does call [whom he will] to the Home of Peace [Dar al-Islam]: He does guide whom He pleases to a way that is straight (Sûrah 10:25, Abdullah Yusuf Ali, bracketed clarifications mine).

Why would Allah harden his heart toward those who do not accept him if he caused their disbelief in the first place?

(2:89) And when there comes unto them a Scripture from Allah, confirming that in their possession—though before that they were asking for a signal triumph over those who disbelieved—and when there come unto them that which they know (to be the truth) they disbelieve therein. The curse of Allah is on disbelievers.

And when there comes unto them the Koran from Allah, confirming the Bible which they had in their possession—in answer to their request for a miraculous sign to prove to those who disbelieved—so we sent them, Muhammad and the Koran which they know (to be the truth), but wouldn't accept it. The curse of Allah is on disbelievers (paraphrase mine).

According to this passage, before Muhammad appeared, the Jews had been looking for a sign to defend against those who challenged their belief in only one God, so Allah sent them the Koran. We are told that the Jews who asked for a miraculous sign rejected it once it came, even though the Bible confirmed it was accurate, and thus, brought the wrath of Allah on them.

(2:90) Evil is that for which they sell their souls: that they should disbelieve in that which Allah had revealed [through Muhammad and the Koran], grudging that Allah should reveal of His bounty unto whom He will of His bondmen [servants]. They have incurred anger upon anger. For disbelievers is a shameful doom (bracketed clarification mine).

This is a not-so-veiled threat against the "People of the Book" who reject the alleged authenticity of the teachings contained in the Koran.

(2:91) And when it is said unto them: "Believe in that [the Bible]," which Allah hath revealed, they say: "We believe in that which was revealed unto us." And they disbelieve in that [the Koran] which cometh after it, though it is the truth confirming that which they possess. Say (unto them, O Muhammad): "Why then slew you the prophets of Allah aforetime [before], if you are (indeed) believers?" (Bracketed clarification mine.)

We see this concept repeated in the next chapter, Sûrah 3:

He has revealed unto thee (Muhammad) the Scripture [Koran] with truth, confirming that which was (revealed) before it, even as He revealed the Torah and the Gospel (Pickthall, Sûrah 3:3).

This verse acknowledges that Christians and Jews believe in the Bible, whose authorship Allah claims as his. Then Allah asks the rhetorical question, *"Why then slew you the prophets of Allah aforetime [before]?"* or to paraphrase it, *"Why did the 'People of the Book' kill their prophets if they believe in the words brought to them by those very same prophets?"* This implies, like the biblical prophets sent by Allah, that the Christians and Jews are also rejecting Muhammad. The reason that the prophets were killed was that they had prophesied some very unpopular things which caused some—not all—to silence them by murder; nevertheless, those unpopular prophecies *did* eventually prove correct and, therefore, they are included in the canon of Scripture!

Now ask yourself, "Why did the Jews and Christians refuse to accept the teachings of Muhammad?" That would be a reasonable question, and the answer is twofold: (1) Muhammad offered no words of a prophecy or miracles, which is how the prophets of the Bible proved God was speaking through them, and (2) when the Jews and Christians compared the Bible with the Koran, as they were challenged to do in Sûrah 4:82 and Sûrah 5:47, they found many discrepancies. Of course, the Jews who are spoken to here never killed any prophet; the last time that happened was seven hundred years before their time.

(2:92) And Moses came unto you with clear proofs (of Allah's Sovereignty), yet, while he was away, you chose the calf (for worship) and you were wrong-doers.

Gabriel is speaking directly to the Jews and reminding them about the events which took place in Exodus 32. If this seems like déjà vu, it is. See verse 54.

(2:93) And when We made with you a covenant [10 Commandments] and caused the Mount to tower above you, (saying): "Hold fast by that which We have given you, and hear (Our Word)," they said: "We hear and we rebel." And (worship of) the calf was made to sink into their hearts because of their rejection (of the covenant). Say (unto them): "Evil is that which your belief enjoins on you, if you are believers" (bracketed clarification mine).

CONSIDER: If, as the Koran states in this verse, that Allah, *"… caused the Mount to tower above you,"* it would have had to rise up all at once some 7,000 feet above the valley floor, which would have caused a huge earthquake throughout the Mediterranean and Red Sea region—even bigger than the volcanic eruption of Mount Vesuvius in 79 A.D. The earthquake would have resulted in major catastrophic destruction of buildings and cities. An event like that would have also produced tsunamis that would have wiped-out low-lying towns and villages. Such a horrific event would undoubtably have been recorded by the various countries surrounding the Mediterranean and Red Seas; yet, unlike the eruption of Mount Vesuvius, there is no such historical record of such an event.

While Verses 92 and 93 are comparatively biblical, they are still koranic embellishments. Notice the order of events in verse 93, which states, *"And when We made with you a covenant and caused the Mount to tower above you… And (worship of) the calf was made to sink into their hearts because of their rejection (of the covenant)."* It is important to realize that the ground did not rise up and form into a mountain before the children of Israel, and they did not reject the Covenant (Ten Commandments) because—as this passage incorrectly states—Moses had not yet gone up to the mountain and, therefore, the molten calf, which was created in his absence, could not have already sunk into their hearts.

In the verse preceding 93, the order suggests—contrary to this verse— that Moses did receive *"clear proofs"* (probably the Ten Commandments), and then goes on to state, *"While he was away, you chose the calf."* The reason given in this verse for the creation of the calf was because Allah caused the Jews to desire the calf, not of their own free will, but *"because of their rejection (of the covenant);"* within two verses, we have a conflicting order of events. Had they been reversed, it would have made more sense; nonetheless, God did not put the desire in the hearts of the "rebellious" Hebrews because the Koran states that Allah put it there.

But the Bible tells us:

And when the people saw that Moses delayed to come down out of the mount, the people gathered themselves together unto Aaron, and said unto him, "... Up, make us gods, which shall go before us; for as for this Moses, the man that brought us up out of the land of Egypt, we knew not what is become of him" (Exodus 32:1).

And he [Aaron] received them at their hand, and fashioned it with a graving tool, after he had made it a molten calf: and they said, "These [will] be your gods, O Israel, which brought you up out of the land of Egypt" (Exodus 32:4, bracketed clarifications mine).

And Moses turned, and went down from the mountain and the two tables of the testimony were in his hand: the tables were written on both their sides; on the one side and on the other were they written (Exodus 32:15).

God would remember the order of such important events, and even if He were feeble-minded, which is impossible, He has access to the Torah if he needs it.

(2:94) Say (unto them): If the abode of the Hereafter in the providence of Allah is indeed for you alone and not for others of mankind (as you pretend), then long for death (for you must long for death) if you are truthful.

This is still referring to the Jews and Christians who hold the biblical belief that they alone are able to be received into Heaven, and all Pagan worshipers will be sent to Hell; therefore, we see the sarcastic remark aimed at the "People of the Book" who reject Allah and his Prophet—that they should desire death because of their assurance of Heaven rather than suffer here on earth. (Islam offers no such assurance of salvation outside of dying in a jihad. A few examples are found in Sûrah 3:169-170; 52:46.)

While some Arabs were prosperous, many were nomadic; that, along with their intertribal warfare, kept them from acquiring great wealth. It was the Jews in the Arabian Peninsula who prospered the most. Perhaps these verses are motivated simply by Arab envy of the prosperous Jews.[15]

(2:95) But they will never long for it [death], because of [sins] that which their own hands have sent before them. Allah is aware of evil-doers (bracketed clarifications mine).

The claim made here is the "People of the Book" will never long for death because they have sinned and have no hope for redemption. This verse is very revealing because, in Islam, Muslims must give their son for Allah, while the gospels teach God gave His Son for you!

(2:96) And you will find them greediest of mankind for life and (greedier) than the idolaters. (Each) one of them would like to be allowed to live a thousand years. And to live (a thousand years) would be [by] no means remove him from the doom. Allah is Seer of what they do (bracketed clarification mine).

Because of the financial success of the Arabian Jews during the time of Muhammad and the vast political power of Christians throughout the Byzantine Empire during that time, it seems that Allah is belittling the Christians with an emphasis more toward the Jews, suggesting that they would love to live and wallow in their wealth for a thousand years. This verse serves to fan the flames of envy throughout the Arab world by implying that the blessings of God's chosen people were acquired by swindling the Arabs, whose lot in life was not as good as the lives of the Christians and Jews.

(2:97) Say [Muhammad]: Whoever is an enemy to Gabriel-for he brings down the (revelation) [of the Koran] to your heart by Allah's will, a confirmation of what went before [in the Bible], and guidance and glad tidings for those who believe (bracketed clarifications mine)

Gabriel is asking Muhammad why anyone would be against him when he is the one relating the words to Muhammad on behalf of Allah. This verse also assumes that Gabriel was instrumental in giving the biblical revelations; however, the Koran contradicts itself in Sûrah 16, where we read it is the Holy Spirit who reveals the Koran to Muhammad:

> *Say [Muhammad]: "The Holy Spirit has delivered it from your Lord with truth, that it may confirm (the faith of) those who believe, and as guidance and good tidings for those who have surrendered (to Allah)" (Sûrah 16:102, bracketed clarification mine).*

The interesting thing about this is that while denying the Trinity, the Koran keeps acknowledging the third member of the Trinity, the Holy Spirit. The Holy Spirit is not Allah, nor can He be Gabriel because Gabriel is an angel.

(2:98) Who is an enemy to Allah, and His angels and His messengers, and Gabriel and Michael! Then, lo! Allah (Himself) is an enemy to the disbelievers.

The structure of this passage is a little redundant where we read, *"... His angels and messengers, and Gabriel and Michael ..."* because everyone mentioned in this passage is an angel. "Angel" in Greek is *"angelos"* (ἄγγελος), which means "messenger." Perhaps Allah (always speaking through the angel Gabriel) is referring to his prophets, but if this is the case, we might wonder why Allah did not say so. Certainly, he knows that using the words "angels" and "messengers" is redundant and could be misunderstood in this type of context. It is also translated the same way in the other translations of the Koran. A.J. Arberry, Abdullah Yusuf Ali, and Muhammad Habib Shakir; however, in translating verse 101, translated it as a "prophet messenger." Still, it could be referring to Gabriel himself, who spoke on Allah's behalf when he gave the Koran to Muhammad. This is not important as far as content is concerned, but it is a little confusing.

NOTE: In this verse, Gabriel is being referred to as an angel (not capitalized) as opposed to being referred to as the Holy Spirit (Capitalized). Is this an inconsistency, or does this prove that Gabriel is really just an angel and not the Holy Spirit?

(2:99) Verily [truly] We have revealed unto you clear tokens, and only miscreants [troublemakers] will disbelieve in them (bracketed clarifications mine).

Christians and Jews with biblical knowledge would not be inclined to accept the Koran's passages, which either conflict with or radically embellish the Scriptures. The results of such rejections are manifested themselves through the Koran's dealing with the "People of the Book"—not on an intellectual basis by using counter-arguments—but by belittling and calling them perverse, transgressors, troublemakers, and more.

(2:100) Is it ever so [has always been] that when you [people] make a covenant a party [group] of you set it aside? The truth is, most of them believe not (bracketed clarifications mine).

This is a koranic generalization implying that if Christians and Jews do not accept the teachings of the Koran, it is because they also reject the covenant between God and themselves as found in the Old and New Testaments. This claim is not biblically provable; on the contrary, the reason for their rejection of the Koran's teachings is because it does *not* align itself with the Bible, which the "People of the Book" accept as truth.

(2:101) And when there comes unto them a messenger from Allah, confirming that which they possess [Bible], a party of those who have received the Scripture [Bible] fling [toss] the Scripture [Koran] of Allah behind their backs as if they knew not [what it contained] (bracketed clarifications mine).

Verses 98-101 reveal a slight frustration regarding the "People of the Book's" refusal to accept what Allah is claiming to be post-biblical enlightenment from God. One of the reasons why the "... *party of those who have received the Scripture [Bible] fling [toss] the Scripture [Koran] of Allah* " is because the Koran not only uses scriptural embellishments, it also mixes stories and events with places and people that are either not in the correct time sequence or geographically incorrect.

(2:102) And follow that which the devils falsely related against the kingdom of Solomon. Solomon disbelieved not [i.e., he believed]; but the devils disbelieved; teaching mankind magic and that which was revealed to the two angels in Babel, Hârût and Mârût. Nor did they (the two angels) teach it to anyone till they had said: "We are only a temptation, therefore disbelieve not [don't believe] (in the guidance of Allah)". And from these two (angels) people learn that by which they cause division between man and wife; but they injure [harm] thereby no-one save [except] by Allah's leave [permission]. And they learn that which harms them and profits them not. And surely they do know that he who trafficks [deals] therein will have no (happy) portion in the Hereafter; and surely evil is the price for which they sell their souls, if they but knew (bracketed clarifications mine).

Yet again we have another passage unique to the Koran. Neither this story nor these particular koranic angels are reflected in the Bible. The so-called angels mentioned here, Hârût and Mârût, are probably the Arabic mythological jinns[16] (Christians refer to them as fallen angels) asked Allah's permission to visit earth, but they became enamored with the temptations of the worldly life, so they were hung upside down by their feet in the city of Babylon.[17]   These mischievous, spiritual creatures work magic like the "jinns" or "genies," as they are referred to in the story of *Aladdin and the Magic Lamp*. Whether they are called "devils," "jinns," or "genies" the reference to Hârût and Mârût does not exist in the Bible.

(2:103) And if they had believed and kept from evil, a recompense from Allah would be better, if they only knew.

Basically, in context, we are told that Christians and Jews are missing out on something good instead of the inevitable punishment they will receive for rejecting Allah, which is spoken about in the next verse.

(2:104) O you who believe, say not (unto the Prophet): "Listen to us" but say "Look upon us," and be you listeners. [Because] For disbelievers [there] is a painful doom (bracketed clarifications mine).

Essentially, we are advised to be quiet and listen to Muhammad because his words are for our benefit. In other words, "Be still and learn!" Otherwise, yours "*is a painful doom.*"

(2:105) Neither those who disbelieve among the people of the Scripture nor the idolaters love that there should be sent down unto you any good thing from your Lord. But Allah chooses for His mercy whom He will, and Allah is of Infinite Bounty.

This verse claims that Christians, Jews, and Pagans want bad things for Muhammad, but that shouldn't bother him because, as we are told: *"But Allah chooses for His mercy whom He will,"* which is also an often-repeated subject of the Koran. If Muslims take the Koran literally like Jews and Christians do their Bible, this verse means that people do not have free will and are at Allah's special mercy; therefore, for those watching Muhammad who might think it is his fault when some people are not accepting Islam, they couldn't be more wrong. Allah rejects whom he will and allows them not to believe Muhammad's teachings. Thereby, they are already condemned to Hell by Allah despite the efforts of Muhammad.

(2:106) Such of our revelations as We abrogate [replace] or cause be forgotten, we bring (in place) one better or the like thereof. Know you not that Allah is Able to do all things? (Bracketed clarification mine.)

Changing Allah's mind for something better seems a little contrived, and to *"...bring (in place) one better or the like thereof,"* is subjective at best, although it always worked out well for Muhammad.

CONSIDER: According to Muslim tradition, the Koran has existed since the beginning of time.[18] If Allah is God and has known all things (omnificent) from the beginning of time until the End of the Age, why would he have to *fix* a mistake in the Koran or change his mind? Surely, he would have known in advance what the outcome of his decrees would be before he made them and, therefore, be able to head off any demon who would try to fool his prophets; so why would Allah need to change any of it? This is called the "doctrine of abrogation" or the "doctrine of repeal." It is another way of saying that Allah can go back on his word and thereby not honor it (lie).

The Bible says that God not only knows who we are before we even exist, but He also knows how many days we will live on earth and, presumably, what we do before we even do it, as we see in the following Scripture:

Your eyes saw my unformed body; all the days ordained for me were written in Your book before one of them came to be (Psalm 139:16, NIV)

Verse 106 is a very troubling passage. Gabriel is suggesting that Allah can abrogate his decrees (change, revoke, or go back on a promise) for the better. The mincing of words still allows for voiding an original proclamation by Allah and replacing it with something else—supposedly "something better." Still, it was usually done to give Muhammad cover, as Muhammad's child bride, Aisha, alluded to in sûrah 19:21 when she said, "I believe your Lord can deny you nothing." Make no mistake; the Koran is saying that when Allah rules on something, it can be altered! Putting it another way, Allah can change his mind and go back on something he once passed judgment on, which is a roundabout way of saying that if Muslims believed in something Allah had decreed, they could never be sure if it would be modified or changed again.

The Koran also teaches that Allah can deceive:

> And they (the disbelievers) schemed, and Allah schemed (against them): and Allah is the best of schemers [i.e., deceivers]. (Pickthall, Sûrah 3:54, bracketed clarification mine.)

These are some of the many instances where the God of the Bible is vastly different from the Koran's author.

The Bible teaches that God cannot lie and never changes:

God is not human, that He should lie, not a human being, that He should change His mind. Does He speak and then not act? Does He promise and not fulfill? (Numbers 23:19, NIV.)

On the other hand, "People swear by someone greater than themselves, and the oath confirms what is said and puts an end to all argument" (Hebrews 6:16, NIV).

Because God wanted to make the unchanging nature of His purpose very clear to the heirs of what He promised, He confirmed it with an oath. God did this so that, by two unchangeable things in which—it is impossible for God to lie—we who have fled [to Him] to take hold of the hope set before us may be greatly encouraged (Hebrews 6:17-18, NIV, bracketed clarification mine).

In hope of eternal life which God, who cannot lie, promised before time began (Titus 1:2, NKJV).

He who is the Glory of Israel does not lie or change His mind; for He is not a human being, that He should change His mind (1 Samuel 15:29).

"For I *am* the LORD, I do not change; Therefore you are not consumed, O sons of Jacob" (Malachi 3:6, NKJV, emphasis added).

I have sworn by Myself; The word has gone out of My mouth *in* righteousness, And shall not return, That to Me every knee shall bow, Every tongue shall take an oath (Isaiah 45:23, NKJV, emphasis added).

For when God made promise to Abraham, because He could swear by no greater, He swore by Himself (Hebrews 6:13, NKJV).

However, this matter of koranic abrogation might be even more sinister. At the beginning of his ministry, Muhammad made every effort to pacify Christians and Jews in order to convert them to his new religion. Having failed at that, the revelations he received became more and more hostile toward them—*"Make no friends of Christians and Jews"* (Sûrah 5:51). The problem for Muhammad then became how to gloss over his earlier courting of the "People of the Book" after he displayed his hostility toward them. The answer was simple: Allah could have abrogated (changed) it by offering the Muslims a newer and better revelation, which would have made all previous revelations null and void. In his book *MUHAMMAD AND HIS RELIGION,* Arthur Jeffery explains:

> The Qur'an is unique among sacred Scriptures in teaching a doctrine of abrogation according to which later pronouncements of the Prophet abrogate [i.e., declare null and void] his earlier pronouncements. The importance of knowing which verses abrogate others has given rise to the Qur'anic science known as Nasikh wa Mansukh (bracketed clarification mine).[19]

Volume II of the Koran contains the first koranic revelations, which, for the most part, were short, peaceful, and tolerant toward Christians and Jews. As Muhammad became more prolific, the sûrahs became longer and more involved. The Koran's first volume consists of Muhammad's last revelations, which replaces or abrogates any conflicting verses in Volume II. If a new convert wonders why the Koran says one thing in one place only to contradict itself in another, they would be told that they are to go by the last thing the prophet said regarding the matter; therefore, where the Koran is concerned, the last revelations are in the first volume, and the first revelations are in the last volume.

(2:107) Know you not that it is Allah unto Whom belongs the Sovereignty of the heavens and the earth; and you have not, beside Allah, any guardian or helper?

Where we read in the above verse, "...*you have not, beside Allah, any guardian or helper...*" refers to Jesus and His mother, Mary (Islam's misinformed version of the Trinity), so once again, the Koran continues its assault on the Divinity of Christ.

My little children, these things write I unto you, that you sin not. And if any man sin, we have an advocate [intercessor] with the Father, Jesus Christ the righteous (1 John 2:1, bracketed clarification mine).

What then shall we say to these things? If God *is* for us, who *can be* against us? He who did not spare His own Son, but delivered Him up for us all, how shall He not with Him also freely give us all things? Who shall bring a charge against God's elect? *It is* God who justifies. Who *is* he who condemns? *It is* Christ who died, and furthermore is also risen, who is even at the right hand of God, *who also makes intercession for us* (Romans 8:31-34, NKJV, emphases added).

Now there have been many of those priests, since death prevented them from continuing in office, but because Jesus lives forever, He has a permanent priesthood. Therefore He is able to save completely those who come to God through Him, because He always lives to intercede for them (Hebrews 7:23-25, NIV).

(2:108) Or would you question your messenger as Moses was questioned aforetime? He who chooses disbelief instead of faith, verily [truly] he has gone astray from a plain road (bracketed clarification mine).

Yusuf Ali's translation of this verse:

Would you question your Messenger [Muhammad] as Moses was questioned of old? but whoever changes from Faith [Islam] to Unbelief, Has strayed without doubt from the even way (bracketed clarification mine).

Based on the previous verse (2:107)—which denies the gospel (i.e., Good News of Christ) as the intercessor for Christians and this verse—we disbelievers are challenged to embrace the teachings of Islam by embracing the Koran's misconception of the Gospel of Jesus. We must reject the Good News that Jesus is the Savior of mankind and not question the teachings of Muhammad or the Koran

As we have been forced to do repeatedly, once again we have to counter the continued onslaught against the gospel message by explaining that the Good News is how God came to earth by taking the body of a man so that He could be the final, perfect sacrifice whose shed blood would atone for our sins. By rejecting this gospel for another "gospel"—in this case—it is the gospels that Allah allegedly "taught" Jesus (Sûrah 3:47-48). With that in mind, the gospels were not produced and given to us until years after Jesus was no longer on the earth. The truth is that it was Jesus—God incarnate—who came to earth; that is the Good News or as we say in Greek, *"evangelium"* (εὐαγγέλιον) translated in the Old English as gospel (*god* meaning "good" and *spel* meaning "news"). This koranic misunderstanding of what the gospel means confirms—that the God of the Bible and His Son are not the god of Islam and, therefore, the teachings of Muhammad are to be rejected:

But even if we, or an angel from heaven, preach any other gospel to you than what we have preached to you, let him be accursed.

As we have said before, so now I say again, "if anyone preaches any other gospel to you than what you have received, let him be accursed" (Galatians 1:8-9).

NOTE: When the Bible repeats anything, it is to be understood that what is being said is exceptionally important.

(2:109) Many of the people of the Scripture long to make you disbelievers after your belief [conversion to Islam], through envy on their own account, after the truth hath become manifest unto them. Forgive and be indulgent (toward them) until Allah give command. See! Allah is Able to do all things (bracketed clarification mine).

The beginning of this verse seems to imply that Christians and Jews want Muslims to lose faith in Islam because they are jealous of them. This alleged and supposed envy by Christians and Jews appears to be Gabriel's attempts to strengthen a Muslim's resolve to stay in the faith. Islam is a faith that only guarantees salvation if you sacrifice your life in a jihad for Allah. Why would any Bible believer be envious of that?

As for trying to get Muslims to leave their faith, Christians would love for everyone to be saved through the real gospel message, which is that God sent His Son to earth, that whosoever believes in Him will be saved from the fires of Hell and have everlasting life (John 3:16). Christians also believe the Bible over the Koran because, unlike the Koran, the Bible validates itself through over 25% prophecy, of which many prophecies have already been fulfilled, some are currently being fulfilled, and some prophecies that will be fulfilled at some point in the future.

One example of the many far-reaching biblical prophecies that were waiting to be fulfilled during the time of Muhammad was the restoration of the nation of Israel, which had not existed for 1,200 years, nor would it exist for approximately another fourteen centuries after the time of Muhammad. Yet, the Bible talked of a restored Israel in the latter days, and against all the odds, Israel would be reborn in a day—in an hour just as predicted by the prophet, Isaiah (Isaiah 66:8), and it was—on May 14, 1948!

The Koran has not revealed God's imprimatur through the prophetic Word as the Bible does; therefore, Bible-believing Christians and Jews reject Islam. That being said, unlike the Koran, Jesus instructed Christians not to force conversion on anyone:

> And whosoever shall not receive you, nor hear your word [regarding the gospel], when you depart out of that house or city, shake off the dust of your feet (Matthew 10:14, bracketed clarification mine).

Nevertheless, at the end of verse 109, Muslims are told to *"Forgive and be indulgent (toward them)"* until Allah commands differently, for Allah has power over all things."

(2:110) Establish worship, and pay the poor-due; and whatever of good you send before (you) for your souls, you will find it with Allah. Look! Allah is Seer of what you do.

Once more, we see a works-centered faith, which promises that it will be good for the believer's soul if they worship Allah and are charitable; which is not a bad work, we would agree. On the other hand, the motivation in Islam for doing well is done with the hope of entrée into heaven, and not so much charity (love) for charity's (love's) sake. Christians are motivated to love God first, then their neighbor. If they do this, then everything else will flow out of that love (Matthew 6:33).

Jesus was asked:

> "Master, which is the great[est] commandment in the law?" Jesus said unto him, "You shall love the Lord your God with all your heart, and with all your soul,

110

and with all your mind. This is the first and great commandment. And the second is like unto it, you shall love your neighbor as yourself." On these two commandments hang all the law and the prophets (Matthew 22:36-40).

[Jesus said] "By this everyone will know that you are my disciples, if you love one another" (John 13:35, bracketed clarification mine).

(2:111) And they say: "None entereth paradise unless he be a Jew or a Christian." These are their own desires. Say: "Bring your proof (of what you state) if you are truthful."

This verse asks for proof if there is another way to attain paradise besides Allah's way. The requested proof is given in the gospel, which Allah claims he authored:

Jesus says unto him, "I am the way, the truth, and the life: no man comes unto the Father, but by me" [not by Buddha, not by Muhammad, not by the Rev. Sun Myung Moon, not by Hari Krishna, or not by the Dalai Lama, etc.] (John 14:6, bracketed commentary mine.)

When speaking to Nicodemus, Jesus also made it clear that the only way to paradise was to be born again by accepting Jesus as Lord:

Jesus answered and said unto him, "Truly, truly, I say unto you, except a man be born again [through the Spirit], he cannot see the kingdom of God. That which is born of the flesh is flesh; and that which is born of the Spirit is spirit" (John 3:5-6, bracketed clarification mine).

For God so loves the world, that He gave His only begotten [Greek, monogenés or unique] Son, that whosoever believes in Him should not perish, but have everlasting life (John 3:16).

(2:112) Nay, but whosoever surrenders his purpose [life] to Allah while doing good, his reward is with his Lord; and there shall no fear come upon them neither shall they grieve (bracketed clarification mine).

Again, we have a works-oriented religion with a reward for doing well, as opposed to the gospel message of the Bible. Gabriel is saying to be good (do good works) and accept Allah, while the Bible teaches that if we accept Jesus as our Lord, we will naturally desire to do good because we cherish His love for us and we desire to share His love:

Therefore if *there is* any consolation in Christ, if any comfort of love, if any fellowship of the Spirit, if any affection and mercy, fulfill my joy by being like-minded, having the same love, *being* of one accord, of one mind. *Let* nothing *be done* through selfish ambition or conceit, but in lowliness of mind, let each esteem others better than himself. Let each of you look out not only for his own interests, but also for the interests of others (Philippians 2:1-5, NKJV).

(2:113) And the Jews say the Christians follow nothing (true), and the Christians say the Jews follow nothing (true); yet both are readers of the Scripture. Even thus speak those who know not. Allah will judge between them on the Day of Resurrection concerning that wherein they differ.

Muhammad Habib Shakir translates it this way:

And the Jews say: "The Christians do not follow anything (good)" and the Christians say: "The Jews do not follow anything (good) while they recite the (same) Book." Even thus say those who have no knowledge, like to what they say; so Allah shall judge between them on the day of Resurrection in what they differ.

To begin with, Jews and Christians do not read the same Bible, as this verse implies. While Jews have the Tanakh (Old Testament), Christians have the Tanakh as well, plus what is referred to as the New Testament (see Jeremiah 31:31). Jews do not include the New Testament in their Bible because they do not accept Jesus as their Messiah. Surely Allah would know that.

The problem with Sûrah 2:112-113 is the premise; however, the apparent biblical enigma Allah is confused about, concerning Jews and Christians arguing over their Bibles, is easily explained. The Old Testament is the New Testament concealed, and the New Testament is the Old Testament revealed. The basic law is the same for both books; only the New Testament, as we just explained, is the fulfillment of the Old Testament's prophesied Messiah, Jesus, who is also known as Yeshua bar Abba or Jesus, Son of the Father.

(2:115) Unto Allah belong the East and the West, and whithersoever you turn, there is Allah's Countenance [face]. Look! Allah is All-Embracing, All-Knowing (bracketed clarification mine).

According to this verse, Allah is *omnipresent* (everywhere at once throughout the cosmos).

(2:116) And they say: "Allah has taken unto Himself a son. Be He [Allah] glorified! Nay, but whatsoever is in the heavens and the earth is His. All are subservient unto Him" (bracketed clarification mine).

Since Allah claims to be the same person as the God of the Bible, we have a serious conflict with the Koran and Bible's uniformity, especially in light of the repetitive attacks against the Divinity of Jesus.

(2:117) The Originator [Creator] of the heavens and the earth! When He decrees a thing, He says unto it only: Be! and it is (bracketed clarification mine).

Here we see Allah referred to as *"The Originator [Creator] of the heavens and the earth!"* This is a serious departure from the Bible (by which we are to judge the Koran as decreed in Sûrahs 5:47 and 10:94). According to the Bible, all things were created through the reasoning (*logos*) of God (also known as Jesus [John 1:1]), whose Divinity is constantly attacked in the Koran, as we just saw once again in the previous verse.

For in Him [Jesus] all things were created: things in Heaven and on earth, visible and invisible, whether thrones or powers or rulers or authorities; all things have been created through Him [Jesus] and for Him. He is before all things, and in Him all things hold together (Colossians 1:16-17, NIV, bracketed clarification mine).

Some may point out that in Genesis 1:1, the Bible states, "In the beginning God created the heaven and the earth." The singular word "God" is not present in the original Hebrew. The word in Hebrew is "Elohim," and whenever we see "im" at the end of a Hebrew word, it is the equivalent of an "s" at the end of a word in English, which makes the word plural. In other words, Genesis 1:1 could be translated, "In the beginning Gods created...."

(2:118) And those who have no knowledge say: "Why doesn't Allah speak unto us, or some sign [miracle] come unto us?" Even thus, as they now speak [others], spoke [like] those (who were) before them. Their hearts are all alike. We have made clear the revelations for people who are sure (bracketed clarifications mine).

Muhammad Habib Shakir translates this passage:

And those who have no knowledge say: "Why does not Allah speak to us or a sign come to us?" Even thus said those before them, the like of what they say; their hearts are all alike. Indeed We have made the communications clear for a people who are sure.

The answer regarding why there are no signs and wonders in the Koran is explained in Sûrah 41, where we read:

Had We sent this as a Qur'an (in the language) other than Arabic, they would have said: "Why are not its verses explained in detail? What! (a Book) not in Arabic and (a Messenger) an Arab?" Say: "It is a Guide and a Healing to those who believe; and for those who believe not, there is a deafness in their ears, and it is blindness in their eyes: They are (as it were) being called from a place far distant!" (Sûrah 41:44, Abdullah Yusuf Ali.)

114

Some of the people are questioning why Allah has not spoken to them or given them a miraculous sign like the biblical prophets of old, but Allah says that it was offered to them by a fellow Arab in the form of the Koran. That—in and of itself—is a miracle; however, they were not able to recognize or receive it as a miracle.

It seems as though Sûrah 41:44 was given to Muhammad to side-step the reason he did not validate that he was a prophet from God by performing miracles like Jesus and the other prophets in the Bible had done.

(2:119) Look! We have sent you (O Muhammad) with the truth, a bringer of glad tidings and a warner. And you will not be asked about the owners of hell-fire.

A.J. Arberry's translation:

> *We have sent you with the truth, good tidings to bear, and warning. You shall not be questioned touching the inhabitants of Hell.*

Gabriel is explaining that Allah sent Muhammad to bring the message of Islam, but for whatever reason, in this passage, he will not be allowed to address those who are going to Hell.

(2:120) And the Jews will not be pleased with you, nor will the Christians, till you follow their creed. Say: "Look! the guidance of Allah (Himself) is Guidance. And if you should follow their desires after the knowledge which has come unto you, then would you have from Allah no protecting guardian nor helper."

It appears that the Koran's Gabriel is telling Muhammad that the Christians and Jews will not accept him unless Muhammad accepts their religions, but Gabriel tells readers of the Koran in Sûrah 3:3 that Allah says he is the author of both the Bible and Koran, and that this is the final revelation from him; therefore, they should accept Islam because if they do not, it will be too late, and they will have no helper or savior to defend them at the Judgment.

(2:121 Those unto whom We have given the Scripture [Koran], who read it with the right reading, those believe in it. And whoso disbelieves in it, those are they who are the losers.

This verse appears to suggest that if one reads the Bible correctly, the transition to Islam would naturally follow, but if they do not accept the Koran as the word of god, they are the losers. (Remember, according to the Koran, Sûrah 14:4, Allah determines whether or not someone accepts Islam). Many warnings are given in the Bible against accepting conflicting and intimidating revelations from other sources.

Beloved, do not believe every spirit, but test the spirits, whether they are of God; because many false prophets have gone out into the world. By this you know the Spirit of God: Every spirit that confesses that Jesus Christ has come in the flesh is of God, and every spirit that does not confess that Jesus Christ has come in the flesh is not of God. And this is the *spirit* of the Antichrist, which you have heard was coming, and is now already in the world. (1 John 4:1-3, NKJV).

(2:122) O Children of Israel! Remember My favour wherewith I favoured you and how I preferred you to (all) creatures.

Here we shift to-a new subject of how Allah appointed the "Children of Israel" to continue carrying the message of Islam taught by their father, Abraham. Islamic scholars allege that Adam, Enoch, Noah, and Abraham were all early Prophets of Islam.

This is the biblical promise to Israel referred to in this verse:

Now the LORD had said unto Abram, "Get you out of your country, and from your kindred [relatives], and from your father's house, unto a land that I will show you: And I will make of you a great nation, and I will bless you, and make your name great; and you shall be a blessing: And I will bless them that bless you, and curse him that curses you: and in you shall all families of the earth be blessed" (Genesis 12:1-3).

This prophecy, where "all families of the earth be blessed," is again repeated in Genesis 28:14, which was fulfilled through Jesus Christ.

(2:123) And guard (yourselves) against a day when no soul will in aught [not] avail another, nor will compensation be accepted from it, nor will intercession be of use to it; nor will they be helped.

There will be a time when people die and, therefore, will no longer be able to get help from others. With death, there is no intercessor (Jesus), and there is no hope if they do not accept Allah's message. The Bible teaches otherwise:

My little children, these things write I unto you, that you sin not. And if any man sin, we have an advocate with the Father, Jesus Christ the righteous: And He is the propitiation [appeasement] for our sins: and not for ours only, but also for the sins of the whole world (1 John 2:1-2, bracketed clarification mine).

(2:124) [Gabriel said] And (remember) when his [Abraham's] Lord tried [tested] Abraham with (His) [Allah's] commands, and he [Abraham] fulfilled them, He [Allah] said: "Look! I have appointed you a leader for mankind." (Abraham) said: "And of my offspring (will there be leaders)?" He [Allah] said: "My covenant includes not wrong-doers" (bracketed clarifications mine).

Yusuf Ali has an almost different translation:

And remember that Abraham was tried by his Lord with certain Commands, which he fulfilled: He said: "I will make you an Imam to the Nations." He pleaded: "And also (Imams) from my offspring!" He answered:" But My Promise is not within the reach of evil-doers."

Let's first address the first part of this verse where Allah says, *"I have appointed you a leader...."* A.J. Arberry also says, *"leader,"* and Muhammad Habib Shakir says, *"Imam."* While imam can mean leader, it is more closely associated with the Shia religious leaders, who were not on the scene for thousands of years after Abram; therefore, we will go with the word *"leader"* instead of *"imam."*

As for the first part of this passage, Abraham's first test was his willingness to leave his home and go to the land God had promised him. (Genesis 12:1-2). (Note: God later changed Abram's name to Abraham in Genesis 17:5.) Abraham's second test was his belief that he and Sarah would have a son—but when she reached the age of 76, and Abraham was 86, they still remained childless. They both began to doubt God's promise of her bearing Abraham a son. That is why Sarah gave her maidservant, Hagar, to Abraham so she would bear him a child (Ishmael) on Sarah's behalf, a custom of that day (Genesis 16:16). The miracle happened when Sarah was around 91, and Abraham was around 100; she bore him a son, Isaac (Genesis 17:17).

NOTE: The birth of Ishmael to Hagar was not a miracle; Abraham and Sarah were disobedient because they were not willing to wait for God to choose the time for Sarah to become pregnant. Conceiving a child at approximately 91 years of age, long after menopause, would take a miracle, just like a virgin getting pregnant without a man would be a miracle. Thus, both the birth of Isaac—the biblical beginning of God's people—and the birth of Jesus—the biblical final chapter regarding God's people—involved women for whom it would be impossible to bear a child, making both conceptions miraculous.

According to the Bible (Genesis 22:1-12), the most challenging test for Abraham occurred after Abraham and Sarah's son was born, when God challenged Abraham to sacrifice Isaac (*not* Ishmael, Hagar's son, as the Koran states in Sûrah 37:100-112).

Nevertheless, Muslim scholars will argue that it was the final test for Abraham to see if he was willing to sacrifice Ishmael before Isaac was even born:

And when (his son) was old enough to walk with him, (Abraham) said: "O my dear son [no name given], I have seen in a dream that I must sacrifice you. So look, what think you [what do you think]?" He said: "O my father! Do that which you are commanded. Allah willing, you shall find me of the steadfast [devoted]." Then, when they had both surrendered (to Allah), and he had flung him down upon his face, We called unto him: "O Abraham! You have already fulfilled the vision. Look! thus do We reward the good. Look! that verily [truly] was a clear test" (Sûrah 37:102-106, bracketed clarifications mine).

(2:125) And when We made the House [the Ka'aba] (at Mecca) a resort for mankind and sanctuary, (saying): "Take as your place of worship the place where Abraham stood (to pray)." And We imposed a duty upon Abraham and Ishmael, (saying): "Purify My house for those who go around and those who meditate therein and those who bow down and prostrate themselves (in worship)." (Bracketed clarification mine.)

We will first address the part in this verse where it states, *"Take as your place of worship the place where Abraham stood (to pray)." And We imposed a duty upon Abraham and Ishmael.* It alludes to the Muslim belief that Abraham and Ishmael built the Ka'aba as a place of worship for Allah, as we will see in verse 127. Where we read, *"Purify My house for those who go around…,"* deals with one of the aspects of worshiping at the Ka'aba in Mecca. Because of the alleged connection of Abraham and Ishmael to Mecca and the Ka'aba, Muslims are required to make a pilgrimage (e.g., Hajj) to Mecca at least once in their lifetime and participate in several required rituals. One of those ritual events is the *tawaf* (ظَوَاف) (e.g., circumambulation), which consists of Muslim believers walking in a great circle seven times around the Kaaba.

The second problem found in this verse is that—outside of the Koran of the seventh century A.D. (written almost three millenniums after the time of Abraham)—there are no references or suggestions that Abraham was ever in the Arabian Peninsula. The Bible tells us Abram [God changed Abram's name to Abraham when Abram was 99 years old, long after he first left the land of Ur (Genesis 17:5)] avoided Arabia by following the northern route along the Fertile Crescent, which is the territory between the Tigris and Euphrates Rivers (east of Arabia). He then headed southwest to the land of Canaan, which is north of Arabia, bordering on the Mediterranean Sea.

Chart 2. Abraham's Travels

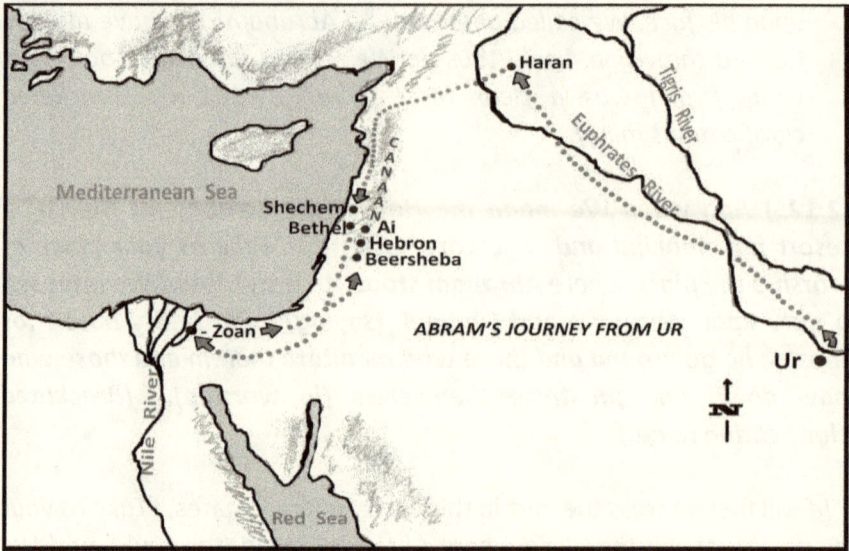

Abram then stopped at Shechem before moving south-west to an area between Beth-el and Ai (Genesis 12:8-9; Genesis 12:6). Because of a drought, Abram took his family and traveled southwest into Egypt (Genesis 12:12:10-20). After the drought was over, he turned around and headed northeast again, returning to the land of Canaan. There, he settled in the Judean hill country near Bethel (Genesis 13:1-9).

Evidently, Islam needed a historically revised story to give the Arabian people a reason to justify Muhammad's claim that he was a descendant of a prophet named Ishmael. If that were true, it would make him the benefactor of an alleged Arab prophetic holy dynasty. For that to have occurred, Ishmael would have had to be the child of sacrifice. As we have discussed, Allah claims he authored both the Bible (Sûrah 3:3) and the Koran, but for Ishmael to be the child of sacrifice, the Bible would have to have been tainted. If that were possible, then Allah would not have been able to protect the Bible from corruption.

This creates an enigma for Muslims: *"If Allah cannot protect the Bible, then how is he able to protect the Koran (Sûrah 15:9)?"* We must also ask, "How do we know Muslims believe that it was Ishmael and not Isaac, who was the child of sacrifice?" To find the answer, we have to look at Islam's holy days. Muslims have two holy days, one beginning and the other ending their holy season of Ramadan. The first one is Eid al-Fitr ("Festival of Breaking the Fast"), and the second is Eid al-Adha (the "Festival of Sacrifice"), which commemorates the time Abraham prepared to offer Ishmael as a sacrifice to Allah in Mecca.

It should be pointed out that the Koran does not give the name of the son who Abraham offered as the sacrifice. However, it can be argued that it was Ishmael because after Allah prevented Abraham from completing the sacrifice, he promised Abraham another son who would be a great prophet (Sûrah 37:99-113). Therefore, if Isaac had not been born yet and Abraham had just attempted to offer his first son as a sacrifice, then the sacrificial son, according to the Koran, had to be Ishmael:

> And [because of his willingness to sacrifice his son] we gave him [Abraham] tidings of the birth of Isaac, a prophet of the righteous (Sûrah 37:112, bracketed clarifications mine).

NOTE: The problem is two-fold. (1) There is no historical or biblical evidence mentioned outside the Koran regarding Abram (Abraham) having ever traveled to Arabia during the 2,500 years preceding the onset of Islam in the seventh century A.D., and (2) there is no historical or biblical evidence of Abraham offering his son, Ishmael to Allah in Mecca, but there is archaeological evidence of Abraham's presence in Canaan (Genesis 23:9). We know the burial place of Abraham and Sarah, known as the Cave of Machpelah (Genesis 23:9) is in Hebron (see map).

The Koran also states that Ishmael was a prophet of God, just like Abraham was, which is also contrary to Scripture. When the prophet, Moses, said that one greater than him would be revealed at some point in the future, Muslims insist that Moses was referring to the future Arabian, Muhammad; however, that would be in direct conflict with the Bible's revelation that God's covenant would pass through the descendants of Isaac—not Ishmael (Genesis 17:19; 21).[20] The Bible records Moses telling the children of Israel:

> The LORD your God will raise up unto you a Prophet from the midst of you, of your brethren, like unto me; unto him you shall hearken [listen] (Deuteronomy 18:15, bracketed clarification mine.)

Now we must ask, "Who were Moses' brothers?" The answer is the children of Israel—his fellow Hebrews! Therefore, we know the greatest Prophet—as well as all prophets—have to come from the house of Israel as taught in the Bible, not from Arabia:

> What advantage then has the Jew? or what profit is there of circumcision?
>
> Much [in] every way: chiefly, because that unto them were committed the oracles [words] of God [which revealed the books of the Bible] (Romans 3:1-2, bracketed clarifications mine).

Therefore, in light of biblical Scriptures, it appears that Allah continues to take liberties with history, which is not surprising since we read only twenty verses ago where Allah confessed the following:

> *None of Our revelations [even a single verse] do we abrogate [change] or cause to be forgotten [erased], but We substitute something better or similar: Know you not [do you not know] that Allah has power over all things? (Sûrah 2:106, Abdullah Yusuf Ali, bracketed clarifications mine.)*

(2:126) And when Abraham prayed: "My Lord! Make this a region of security and bestow upon its people fruits, such of them as believe in Allah and the Last Day," He answered: "As for him who disbelieves, I shall leave him in contentment for a while, then I shall compel him to the doom of Fire—a hapless [horrible] journey's end!" (Bracketed clarification mine.)

This takes place in Mecca, where Abraham is supposedly offering Ishmael as a sacrifice. In this verse, Abraham is allegedly asking Allah to "... *Make this a region of security....*" Arberry refers to *"region"* as *"land,"* and Shakir and Ali refer to *"region"* as a *"city"*).

Biblically, it was on Mount Moriah (2 Chronicles 3:1), where the real city of peace is, Jerusalem. The Bible records that Abraham offered Isaac on Mount Moriah as a sacrifice to the God of the Bible. The meaning of the name of Mecca is obscure, but the name "Jerusalem" means "City of Peace."

This verse is a bit disjointed as the Koran goes from Abraham asking Allah to make the region of Mecca a city of peace to Allah to telling us he will allow sinners to enjoy the fruits of their sin for a while before he sends them into Hell.

(2:127) And when Abraham and Ishmael were raising the foundations of the House [Ka'aba], (Abraham prayed): "Our Lord! Accept from us (this duty). Behold! You, only You, art the Hearer, the Knower" (bracketed clarification mine).

This is another koranic anachronism (refer to the NOTE insert above for verse 125). The Abraham of the Bible never set foot in Mecca, nor was Ishmael ever recorded as participating in the construction of anything in Arabia, the land of Canaan, or Egypt, where Abram and Sarai visited (Genesis 12:10) and where Abram and Sarai acquired Hagar, Ishmael's mother (Genesis 12:16).

OBSERVATION: As previously stated Islamic tradition teaches that the child of sacrifice was Ishmael in Mecca, not Isaac at Jerusalem's Mount Moriah (Genesis 22:2). It also teaches that Ishmael and his father, Abraham, purified the Ka'aba (verse 125) and, as we see in this verse, they were responsible for building it.[21] This story is a rewrite of the biblical story, which states that Abraham prepared to offer Isaac on Mount Moriah where the Temple stood and where the Dome of the Rock—the rock being the place of sacrifice—now stands (Genesis 22:9-12; Hebrews 1:17-18). We cannot find any historical, biblical, or archaeological mention—outside of the Koran and Hadith— that Abraham was ever in Arabia.

In addition, we are unable to find in the Koran or any of the Hadiths, with the possible exception of some commentaries later added, the evolving concept that mimics the biblical story of Abraham, Isaac, and the Mount Moriah incident—which Muslim revisionists claim took place in Mecca. Neither could we find anywhere in the Koran or Hadiths where the name of the son Abraham offered for sacrifice was Ishmael—or Isaac, for that matter. However, the Koran tells us that after Abraham offered his son as a sacrifice, he was rewarded with another son named Isaac (Sûrah 37:112). Since Abraham only had two sons, the first child mentioned—who Muslims insist was offered as a sacrifice—had to be Ishmael.

It should also be pointed out again that the Muslim Festival of Eld-ul-Adha commemorates the Muslim tradition of Abraham's willingness to sacrifice his son, Ishmael, to Allah—in Mecca—as Allah had commanded; nevertheless, it seems more likely that this verse is simply referring to Abraham and Ishmael building the Ka'aba.

Abraham continues his prayer:

(2:128) "[Hear] Our Lord! And make us submissive unto You and of our seed a nation submissive unto you, and show us our ways of worship, and relent toward us. Look! You, only You, are the Relenting, the Merciful" (bracketed clarification mine).

Abraham continues asking Allah to make him and his son, along with their future followers, a nation submissive to him and how he should be worshipped.

(2:129)" [Hear] Our Lord! And raise up in their midst a messenger from among them who shall recite unto them Your revelations, and shall instruct them in the Scripture and in wisdom and shall make them grow. Behold! You, only You, are the Mighty, Wise" (bracketed clarification mine).

When we read this passage, it appears that Muhammad is creating a prophetic endorsement of himself by having Abraham ask Allah to send a future "messenger" (prophet) to the descendants of Ishmael (Ishmaelites and Arabs) because he couldn't read:

[Hear] Our Lord [ALLAH]! And raise up in their midst a messenger from among them [Muhammad] who shall recite unto them Your revelations, and shall instruct them in the Scripture and in wisdom (bracketed clarifications mine).

124

NOTE: Some Muslims suggest that this passage might have also established the Muslim Feast of Id-al-Adha (see commentary for verse 124), which celebrates the willingness of Abraham to sacrifice his son, Ishmael, as Allah had commanded. Other Muslim scholars suggest that this is one of the koranic passages which attempts to prove Muhammad is the prophet like Moses, who was foretold about in the Bible).

(2:130) And who forsakes the religion of Abraham save him who befools himself? Verily [truly] We chose him in the world, and look! in the Hereafter he is among the righteous (bracketed clarifications mine).

All the Koran translations we referenced were just as confusing as Pickthall's translation, so we researched several other versions and found that Muhammad Asad's version of the Koran offers the most understandable translation of this verse:

And who, unless he be weak of mind, would want to abandon Abraham's creed, seeing that We have indeed raised him high in this world, and that, verily, in the life to come he shall be among the righteous? (Sûrah 1:130, Muhammad Asad[22], bracketed clarification mine).

It is interesting to reflect here how the Koran teaches that the religion of Abraham was Islam, which (as it also claims) would make Abraham a Muslim prophet, although biblically and historically, that would be impossible. There are no documented pieces of evidence of a religion calling itself Islam existing before the seventh century A.D., and the name Allah is nowhere to be found in Judeo-Christian Scriptures.

(2:131) When his Lord said unto him: "Surrender!" he said: "I have surrendered to the Lord of the Worlds."

The Bible records Abraham's relationship with God:

And the Scripture was fulfilled which says, "Abraham believed God, and it was imputed [credited] unto him for righteousness: and he was called the Friend of God" (James 2:23, bracketed clarification mine).

(2:132) The same did Abraham enjoin upon his sons, and also Jacob, (saying): "O my sons! Look! Allah has chosen for you the (true) religion; therefore die not save as men who have surrendered (unto Him)."

As we previously stated, the Koran's verses 128-132 are mostly generalities; however, Genesis 17:19-21 gives us the facts regarding God's plans for the sons of Abraham, Isaac, and Jacob:

And God said, "Sarah your wife shall bear you a son indeed; and you shall call his name Isaac: and I will establish my covenant with him for an everlasting covenant and with his seed after him.

"And as for Ishmael, I have heard you: Behold, I have blessed him, and will make him fruitful, and will multiply him exceedingly; twelve princes shall he beget, and I will make him a great nation.

"But my covenant will I establish with Isaac, which Sarah shall bear unto you at this set time in the next year" (Genesis 17:19-21).

Isaac's sons were Jacob and Esau. As the oldest son, Esau sold his birthright (Genesis 25:31-34), so the covenant was passed down through Jacob.

(2:133) Or were you present when death came to Jacob, when he said unto his sons: "What will you worship after me?" They said:
We shall worship your God, the God of your fathers, Abraham and Ishmael and Isaac, One God, and unto Him we have surrendered."

While sounding biblical, this conversation was never recorded in Scripture, and when one reads about the death of Jacob in the Bible, Ishmael and Allah are never mentioned:

And Jacob called unto his sons, and said, "Gather yourselves together, that I may tell you that which shall befall you in the last days. Gather yourselves together, and hear, you sons of Jacob; and hearken unto Israel your father" (Genesis 49:1).

Jacob then prophesied individually over each son (Genesis 49:2-32).

...And when Jacob had made an end of commanding his sons, he gathered up his feet into the bed, and yielded up the ghost, and was gathered unto his people (Genesis 49: 33).

(2:134) Those are a people who have passed away [Abraham, Ishmael, Isaac and Jacob]. Theirs is that which they earned, and yours [non-believers] is that which you earn. And you will not be asked of what they used to do (bracketed clarifications mine).

Regarding Abraham, Ishmael, Isaac, and Jacob, the Koran tells us, *"Theirs is that which they earned;"* because of their merits (i.e., works), they earned a place in heaven, *"and yours [non-believers] is that which you earn"* [which is a place in Hell]. (Bracketed clarification mine.)

Abraham, Ishmael, Isaac, and Jacob allegedly worshiped Allah and were rewarded for it, while the stiff-necked Jews and Christians who refused to do so would suffer for it! (Bracketed clarification mine.)

Biblically, Islam is a works-based religion, which is one of the reasons Islam is not the way to Heaven. The Bible, which does not teach a works-based religion, provides that accepting God's Son, Jesus, as your personal Savior is the only way of attaining Heaven:

But after that the kindness and love of God our Savior toward man[kind] appeared,

127

Not by works of righteousness which we have done, but according to His mercy He saved us, by the washing of regeneration, and renewing of the Holy Ghost;

Which He shed on us abundantly through Jesus Christ our Savior; That being justified by His grace [unearned gift from God], we should be made heirs according to the hope of eternal life (Titus 3:4-7, bracketed clarifications mine, emphasis added).

(2:135) And they say: "Be Jews or Christians, then you will be rightly guided." Say (unto them, O Muhammad): "Nay, but (we follow) the [Muslim] religion of Abraham, the upright, and he was not of the idolaters" (bracketed clarification mine).

The last part of this verse, where we read, *"...and he was not of the idolaters,"* is clarified by Yusuf Ali: *"...and he joined not gods with Allah,"* which makes this another example of the Koran's numerous and ongoing attacks on the Divinity of Christ.

The Koran is taking issue with Christians and Jews who do not follow Islam, a religion invented in the seventh century A.D. but claimed to be the alleged true religion of Abraham; however, the Bible says differently. It tells us the Jews are the children of Abraham, while the non-Jewish Christians are the spiritual children of Abraham:

Therefore, the promise comes by faith, so that it may be by grace and may be guaranteed to all Abraham's offspring—not only to those who are of the law [Hebrews] but also to those who have the faith of Abraham. He is the father of us all (Romans 4:16, NIV, bracketed clarification mine).

Even as Abraham believed God, and it was accounted to him for righteousness. Know you therefore that they which are of faith, the same are the children of Abraham.

And the Scripture, foreseeing that God would justify the heathen through faith, preached before the Gospel unto Abraham, saying, "In you shall all nations be blessed."

So then they which be of faith are blessed with faithful Abraham (Galatians 3:6-9).

(2:136) Say (O Muslims): "We believe in Allah and that which is revealed unto us and that which was revealed unto Abraham, and Ishmael, and Isaac, and Jacob, and the tribes, and that which Moses and Jesus received, and that which the prophets received from their Lord. We make no distinction between any of them, and unto Him we have surrendered."

This might seem biblically acceptable except for one very important detail—Jesus was never given the revelation of God because He IS the Revelation of God in the flesh:

Beware lest any man spoil you through philosophy and vain deceit, after the tradition of men, after the rudiments of the world, and not after Christ. For in Him dwells all the fullness of the Godhead bodily (Colossians 2:8-9).

He was in the world, and the world was made by Him, and the world knew Him not. He [Jesus] was in the world, and the world was made through Him, and the world did not know Him. He came to His own, and His own did not receive Him. But as many as received Him, to them He gave the right to become children of God, to those who believe in His name: who were born, not of blood, nor of the will of the flesh, nor of the will of man, but of God. And the Word became flesh and dwelt among us, and we beheld His glory, the glory as of the only begotten (Greek μονογενοῦς or monogenesis meaning "one of a kind") of the Father full of grace and truth (John 1:10-14, NKJV bracketed clarifications mine).

(2:137) *And if they believe in the like of that which you believe, then are they rightly guided. But if they turn away, then are they in schism [split off], and Allah will suffice thee (for defence) against them. He is the Hearer, the Knower (bracketed clarification mine).*

According to this verse, if the Christians and Jews believe in what Muhammad is teaching, all will go well for them. If not, Allah will condemn them; yet in another sûrah, we are taught that Allah decides who will believe and who won't:

> *Those whom Allah (in His plan) wills to guide, He opens their breast to Islam; those whom He wills to leave straying, He makes their breast close and constricted, as if they had to climb up to the skies: thus does Allah (heap) the penalty on those who refuse to believe (Sûrah 6:125, Abdullah Yusuf Ali).*

Make a mental note here because Sûrah 6:125 clearly states, *"Those whom Allah (in His plan) wills to guide, He opens their breast to Islam; those whom He wills to leave straying, He makes their breast close and constricted...."* There are other conciliatory verses in the Koran that allow people to have the choice of free-will. Those verses come in later sûrahs in the Koran. Although this was placed in the Koran as an early sûrah (6), it was actually received in the middle (i.e., the 55th sûrah) of the revelations received by Muhammad.

(2:138) *(We take our) color from Allah, and who knows better than Allah for coloring. We are His worshipers.*

Muhammad Habib Shakir clarifies the meaning of *"color"* in his translation as *"baptizing:"*

> *... the Baptism of Allah, and who is better than Allah in baptizing? And Him do we serve* Regarding verse 138, *"(Our religion is) the Baptism of Allah,"* the Bible provides us with the answer to the Koran's rhetorical question, *"...and who is better than Allah in baptizing"*:

And it came to pass, that, while Apollos was at Corinth, Paul having passed through the upper coasts came to Ephesus: and finding certain disciples,

He said unto them, "Have you received the Holy Ghost since you believed?" And they said unto him, "We have not so much as heard whether there be any Holy Ghost."

And he said unto them, "Unto what then were you baptized?" And they said, "Unto John's baptism."

Then said Paul, "John [the baptizer] truly baptized with the baptism of repentance, saying unto the people, that they should believe on Him which should come after him, that is, on Christ Jesus."

When they heard this, they were baptized in the name of the Lord Jesus (Acts 19:1-5, bracketed clarification mine).

> OBSERVATION: Have you ever heard of an emphasis on Muslim baptism? Certainly, the reason for baptism is lost on members of Islam. When Christians are baptized, they are identifying themselves with Christ's death on the Cross (which the Koran denies). His burial (which the Koran says never happened) is represented as Christians are submerged under the water, and His Resurrection (which the Koran also denies) is represented when they come up out of the water!

(2:139) Say (unto the People of the Scripture): "Dispute you with us concerning Allah when He is our Lord and your Lord? Ours are our works and yours your works. We look to Him alone."

Gabriel is telling Muhammad to tell the Bible believers the same idea that Muslims are still trying to *convince* Bible believers with today: "*Dispute you with us concerning Allah when He is our Lord and your Lord?*" Yet Christians believe that Jesus *(Isa)* is God (the Son), a fact Allah denies; therefore, in all honesty, Christians cannot agree that we believe in the same god as Muslims do. Regarding Jesus, the Bible teaches us Jesus received worship:

> And Thomas answered and said unto Him [Jesus], "My LORD and my God" (John 20:28, bracketed clarification mine).

The Bible also assures us:

> Whosoever shall confess that Jesus is the Son of God, God dwells [resides] in Him, and He in God (1 John 4:15, bracketed clarification min).

(2:140) Or say you that Abraham, and Ishmael, and Isaac, and Jacob, and the tribes were Jews or Christians? Say: "Do you know best, or does Allah?" And who is more unjust than he who hides a testimony which he has received from Allah? Allah is not unaware of what you do.

There are historical problems with verse 140. The first one is the quote, asking, *"Or say you that Abraham, and Ishmael, and Isaac, and Jacob, and the tribes were Jews or Christians?"*

Jews are one tribe, not several tribes that came *after* Isaac and Jacob. The Jews began with the birth of Judah (the patriarch of the tribe of Judah from whom the name "Jew" comes). Judah was one of the sons of Jacob (Israel), who was the patriarch of one of the twelve tribes of Israel (Genesis 49:1-28). All the sons of Jacob are called Hebrews, and they all believe in the God of the Bible, whose name is forever to be known as YHWH (Jehovah), never Allah (Exodus 3:13-15).

The statement, *"... and the tribes were Jews ..."* is not accurate and is, therefore, misleading. Surely, an omniscient God who was there when the sons of Israel—who became the patriarchs of the 12 tribes—were born (one of whom was named Judah from where the term "Jew" came) would have known that! During the first century, the citizens of Antioch who did not accept Christ as their Messiah applied the disparaging term "Christian"—a slur against those who had accepted Jesus (Hebrew, *Yeshua* [יְהוֹשֻׁעַ]); (Arabic *Isa* [عيسى]) as their Hebrew Messiah (Acts 11:26).

BACKGROUND: The Temple was in Jerusalem, which was in the tribal land of Judah. Under King David, Jerusalem became the capital of Israel until the split between Solomon's sons—who parted ways—and divided Israel into two kingdoms, the Northern Kingdom of Israel and the Southern Kingdom of Judah, which was the location of Jerusalem and the Temple. Later, in 135 A.D., the Roman Emperor, Hadrian, destroyed Judah and renamed the area *Syria-Palistinia* after Israel's old—and by then—extinct enemy, the Philistines. Hadrian then proceeded to disperse all the inhabitants of the Southern Kingdom, which were mostly from the large tribe of Judah and the priestly tribe of Levites, throughout Europe and the Roman Empire. Perhaps that is how the name for all Hebrews became "Jews" by default.

Unlike the claim in this koranic verse, which suggests that *"... the tribes were Jews or Christians,"* Christians are not tribes, nor were they ever considered one of a group of tribes. Christians are made up of people from every tribe and ethnic group who believe that Jesus is God in the flesh and lived among us (John 1:14). Possibly, Muhammad is confusing denominations with tribes (i.e., Greek Orthodox, Roman Orthodox, and Coptic Orthodox) or all Christians as "a tribe," in addition to the 12 Hebrew tribes.

(2:141) Those are a people who have passed away; theirs is that which they earned and yours that which you earn. And you will not be asked of what they used to do.

Does this verse seem like déjà vu? That's because it is almost identical to verse 134. This saying about what happened to others in the past remains in the past. The good and evil people have already received their eternal judgment, but those who are living today have the opportunity to travel down a new path, regardless of what those who went before them did.

(2:142) The foolish of the people will say: "What has turned them from the qiblah [the direction of prayer], which they formerly observed [faced]?" Say: "Unto Allah belong the East and the West. He guides whom He will unto a straight path" (bracketed clarification mine).

The first part of this passage deals with some confusion by the people when it asks the question, *"What has turned them from the qibla [the direction of Jerusalem], which they formerly observed [faced]?"* Yet it does not offer any explanation; rather, it simply states, *"Unto Allah belong the East (toward Egypt) and the West (toward Persia), He guides whom He will unto a straight path."* Historically, the children of Israel prayed toward Jerusalem as we can see in this passage of the exiled prophet, Daniel:

Now when Daniel learned that the decree had been published, he went home to his upstairs room where the windows opened toward Jerusalem. Three times a day, he got down on his knees and prayed, giving thanks to his God, just as he had done before (Daniel 6:10, NIV).

Finally, we are instructed at the end of this passage that people do not have free will because of Allah. *"He guides whom He will unto a straight path."*

(2:143) Thus We have appointed you a middle nation, that you may be witnesses against mankind, and that the messenger may be a witness against you. And We appointed the qiblah [direction of prayer] which you formerly observed only that We might know him who follows the messenger, from him who turns on his heels. In truth it was a hard (test) save for those whom Allah guided. But it was not Allah's purpose that your faith should be in vain, for Allah is Full of Pity, Merciful toward mankind (bracketed clarification mine).

The reference to a *"middle nation"* might have implied that the Jews and Christians were a community who followed the Torah and gospels, thus were an example to the Pagan world. According to this verse, they became corrupted when they refused to follow Muhammad, preferring instead their own agendas by rejecting him and the Koran. It was also a tradition for the "People of the Book" to bow in prayer toward Jerusalem when they prayed. Allah instructed Muhammad to abandon the Jews and Christians because they would not accept the Prophet of Islam's true teachings; rather, they insisted on remaining with their own tainted religious agendas.

Muhammad explained to his Muslim followers that Allah made him change the direction of prayer (using Allah's words), *"We might know him who follows the messenger...."* Yusuf Ali translates it to *"...test those who followed the Messenger."* The devoted Muslims would then pray toward (Mecca) where the Ka'aba was.[23.] For the "People of the Book" who had converted to Islam, that was a very difficult test because it meant "turning on their heels" away from Jerusalem.

(2:144) We have seen the turning of your face to heaven (for guidance, O Muhammad). And now verily We shall make you turn (in prayer) toward a qiblah which is dear to you. So turn your face toward the Inviolable [sacred] Place of Worship [the "Ka'aba in Mecca], and you (O Muslims), wheresoever you may be, turn your faces (when you pray) toward it. Look! Those who have received the Scripture know that (this revelation) is the Truth from their Lord. And Allah is not unaware of what they [the Bible believers] do (bracketed clarifications mine.)

Allah is confirming with Muhammad that he is pious because he always seeks guidance from above.

Muhammad has to acknowledge that the Jews and Christians have had the Bible long before the Koran, so he is making the claim that Allah was the one who gave them the Bible; therefore, the Bible endorses the Koran and what Muhammad is asking them to do.

Muhammad, referring to the Jews and Christians, states, *"Those who have received the Scripture know that (this revelation) is the Truth from their Lord."* It seems as if Muhammad hopes to place doubt in the ssumed illiterate minds of Bible believers, causing them to wonder if they should, in fact, change the direction they face when praying. For the undecided observer, this offers an explanation of why the "People of the Book" refuse to pray toward Mecca; it is because they are in rebellion against *"the Truth from their Lord."*

(2:145) And even if you brought unto those who have received the Scripture all kinds of portents [signs], they would not follow your qiblah [toward Mecca], nor can you be a follower of their qiblah [toward Jerusalem]; nor are some of them followers of the qiblah of others. And if you should follow their desires after the knowledge which has come unto you, then surely were you [were you] of the evildoers (bracketed clarifications mine).

Perhaps Muhammad needed an explanation as to why the Jews would only pray toward Jerusalem, not toward Mecca. We periodically see Bible believers asking why Muhammad has not provided miracles to prove he is a prophet from God. Here Allah helps Muhammad sidestep the issue by saying that even if Muhammad had provided them with *"portents [signs], they would not follow your qiblah [toward Jerusalem] ..."*

OBSERVATION: We see Allah's continuing disillusionment revealed with the followers of Scripture and their rejection of Muhammad's revisionist, biblical modifications. In fact, this verse condemns the thousands of years Hebrews have been in prayer facing toward Jerusalem because of the Jews' refusal to accept Islam. We see Allah giving Muhammad instructions for all Muslims to now face toward Mecca when praying.

(2:146) Those unto whom We gave the Scripture recognise (this revelation) as they recognise their sons. But look! a party of them knowingly conceal the truth.

This is suggesting that the Bible should convince the "People of the Book" to accept Islam. It implies that their lack of acceptance has nothing to do with the conflicts between the Bible and Koran because the "People of the Book" lie about what they know to be true in the Bible to fit their own evil agenda against the true revelations given to Muhammad—which harmonized with the ones found in the Scriptures which the angel, Gabriel, had previously given to Muhammad. Remember, as we discussed before, this should not be a problem for Allah because he is the one who causes people to either accept or reject the Koran (Sûrah 6:125).

(2:147) It is the Truth from your Lord (O Muhammad), so be not you of those who waver.

Since Muhammad cannot read, he is unable to verify the Koran's biblical accuracy; thus, Gabriel is encouraging him not to weaken or have any doubts because of the false challenges brought by the "People of the Book" against the new revelations he is receiving from Allah.

(2:148) And each one has a goal toward which he turns; so vie [strive] with one another in good works. Wheresoever you may be, Allah will bring you all together. Look! Allah is Able to do all things (bracketed clarification mine).

Simply put, because of the common faith shared by Muslims, they should strive for the common good and the Islamic cause together.

(2:149) And whencesoever [wherever] you come forth (for prayer, O Muhammad) turn your face toward the Inviolable [sacred] Place [the Ka'aba in Mecca] of Worship. Look! it is the Truth from your Lord. Allah is not unaware of what you do (bracketed clarifications mine).

Once more, the Koran attempts to give us more justification for the elevation of Muhammad's hometown, Mecca, as the holiest of all cities.

(2:150) Whencesoever [wherever] you come forth turn your face toward the Inviolable [sacred] Place of Worship [the Ka'aba in Mecca]; and wheresoever you may be (O Muslims) turn your faces toward it (when you pray) so that men may have no argument against you, save [except] such of them as do injustice—Fear them not, but

fear Me!—and so that I may complete My grace upon you, and that you may be guided (bracketed clarification mine).

By repeating verse 149 a second time with a little embellishment, Gabriel is really reinforcing the message of Muhammad's hometown [Mecca] as the holiest place on earth!

(2:151) Even as We have sent unto you a messenger from among you, who recites unto you Our revelations and causes you to grow, and teaches you the Scripture and wisdom, and teaches you that which you knew not.

Arabs are told to disregard what they might think they know about the scriptures; instead, listen to Muhammad and what he says the scriptures say because although they think they know it, they do not because only Muhammad knows the truth.

The key words at the end of this passage are *"... teaches you that which you knew not."* Remember, Allah can change his mind (Sûrah 2:106), which is one of the many reasons why the Koran appears to be in conflict with the Bible. The Bible is God's Word; it never changes (Malachi 3:6), and God cannot lie [Titus 1:2].

(2:152) Therefore remember Me, I will remember you. Give thanks to Me, and reject not Me.

Gabriel is telling Muslims not to reject Allah for any reason, and by extension, this would include biblical/koranic discrepancies.

(2:153) O you who believe! Seek help in steadfastness [being devoted] and prayer. Look! Allah is with the steadfast [devoted].

Muslims are advised that if they start doubting what has been revealed, they have to ignore their doubts and faithfully pray to be strengthened by Allah's revelations.

(2:154) And call not [don't say] those who are slain in the way of Allah "dead." Nay, they are living, only you perceive [it] not (bracketed clarifications mine).

Gabriel is reassuring Muslims not to be discouraged when their friends are killed in a jihad (holy war) since they are now living in an incredible spiritual paradise, even though they can no longer be seen.

CONSIDER: The purpose of this verse is to encourage Muslims that dying in the cause for Allah is a guarantee of admittance into heaven Pope Leo IV, wondered why the Muslims seemed to not fear death and when he found out used their concept of earning heaven if they die in war to encourage his troops to fight against the Muslims attacking Europe. This unbiblical promise of Pope Leo IV was also used later by Pope Urban II, and other popes in encouraging soldiers to join the Crusades.

(2:155) Be sure, and surely We shall try you with something of fear and hunger, and loss of wealth and lives and crops, but give glad tidings [advice] to the steadfast [devoted] (bracketed clarification mine).

Muslims should expect trouble ahead and embrace a Spartan warrior lifestyle as opposed to a peaceful and comfortable one.[24]

(2:156) Who say, when a misfortune strikes them: Surely we are Allah's and behold! unto Him we are returning.

This short verse appears simple when we first read it, but further study of it, within its context, indicates it might be preparing Muslims for verse 216, which discusses a Muslim's obligation to participate in holy wars (jihads). This attitude of "toughening it out" was the same rigid worldview of the ancient Greeks' Spartan society. Notice that the promise, *"...when a misfortune strikes...we are Allah's,"* assures a Muslim they will return to Allah in paradise (bracketed clarification mine).

139

(2:157) Such are they on whom are blessings from their Lord, and mercy. Such are the rightly guided.

The commitment to Islam (i.e., "submission") is demanding, but according to this verse, it has its rewards as well.

(2:158) Look! (the mountains) As-Safa and Al-Marwah are among the indications of Allah. It is therefore no sin for him who is on pilgrimage to the House [Ka'aba] (of Allah) or visits it, to go around them (as the pagan custom is). And he who does good of his own accord, (for him) look! Allah is Responsive, Aware (bracketed clarification mine).

Again, we unexpectedly shift to other subjects as we read, *"...It is therefore no sin for him ..."* which refers to the tradition of the Pagan Arabs who paraded around the Ka'aba when it housed other Arab idols. However, when Muhammad conquered Mecca, he agreed to allow the continuation of the very profitable pilgrimage to the Kaaba and its traditional rituals with one exception; it had to be purged of all Pagan idols and rededicated solely to the worship of Allah; thus, it was the Muslim ceremony of walking around the two small hills named "Safa" and" "Marwah" (which are approximately 450 meters or about a quarter of a mile apart), as well as circling the Ka'aba, that was rededicated and replaced as a Muslim ritual.[25]

Safa and Marwah are located near the Ka'aba in Mecca and believed to be where Hagar, Ishmael's mother, ran between them looking for water. They are commemorated during the Muslim's annual Hajj (pilgrimage).[26]

(2:159) Look! Those who hide the proofs and the guidance which We revealed, after We had made it clear to mankind in the Scripture [Bible]: such are accursed [doomed] of Allah and accursed of those who have the power to curse (bracketed clarifications mine).

This is a curse from Allah that is aimed at biblical scholars—rabbis and scribes—for keeping the "clear (signs)" of Scripture to themselves, therefore, people are unable to compare the Bible to the Koran to see that the teachings of Muhammad are true. They are doomed by Allah, his angels, other Christians, and Jews who know Islam is true, as well as by Muslims, all who have the power to curse them.

(2:160) Except those who repent and amend and make manifest (the truth). These it is toward whom I relent. I am the Relenting, the Merciful.

This is not actually a new verse, but the completion of the previous verse. It concludes with a promise to those who relent and make amends by revealing that the Bible and the Koran are compatible. Allah promises he will forgive them.

(2:161) Look! Those who disbelieve [in Islam], and die while they are disbelievers; on them is the curse of Allah and of angels and of men combined (bracketed clarification mine).

This verse is unique to the Koran since we do not find anywhere in the Bible a triune curse from God, angels, and people manifested against anyone. The Bible instructs us to "love your enemies, do good toward those who hate you" (Luke 6:27), and "... love your enemies, bless those who curse you, do good to those who hate you, and pray for those who spitefully use you and persecute you" (Matthew 5:44, NKJV).

Neither can we find anywhere in the Bible an instance where an angel formally pronounced a curse on anyone or anything. Generally, people bring curses upon themselves by offending the one who curses them. For example, God cursed Satan (Genesis 3:14) because he called God's Word into question. That was followed by God's curse of pain for women in childbearing because of Eve's sin (Genesis 3:16) when she listened to Satan, who lured her into eating from the forbidden tree after God told her not to. Another example was when God cursed the earth because of Adam's sin (Genesis 3:17). Nevertheless, devils can and do tempt and torment people.

(2:162) They ever dwell therein. The doom will not be lightened for them, neither will they be reprieved.

This passage is meant to scare unbelievers into accepting Allah and his teachings or face the horrible consequences.

(2:163) Your Allah is One Allah; there is no God save Him, the Beneficent, the Merciful.

It appears this concept is taken directly from the Hebrew Shema (the central prayer in the Jewish prayer book), which proclaims, "Hear, O Israel: The LORD our God is one LORD ..." (Deuteronomy 6:4).

(2:164) Look! In the creation of the heavens and the earth, and the difference of night and day, and the ships which run upon the sea with that which is of use to men, and the water which Allah sends down from the sky, thereby reviving the earth after its death, and dispersing all kinds of beasts therein, and (in) the ordinance of the winds, and the clouds obedient between heaven and earth: are signs (of Allah's Sovereignty) for people who have sense.

This koranic verse reflects many passages of Scripture: (1) Creation (Genesis 1:1); (2) day and night; (Genesis 1:3); (3) sailing of ships (Genesis 6:14-16); (4) currents in the sea; (Psalm 8:8); (5) rain (Joel 2:23, Matthew 5:45), and (6) the creation of animals (Genesis 1:20-25).

The idea behind this creation passage is similar to that found in Romans where we are told that God reveals Himself through His creation, and those who ignore Him will have no excuse for doing so:

Because that which may be known of God is manifest in them; for God hath shown it unto them. For the invisible things of Him from the creation of the world are clearly seen, being understood by the things that are made, even His eternal power and Godhead [Trinity]; so that they are without excuse (Romans 1:19-20, bracketed clarification mine).

Regarding the latter part of 2:164 which talks about states, *"...the ordinance of the winds, and the clouds obedient between heaven and earth,"* one particularly relevant passage of Scripture from Proverbs comes to mind:

Who has ascended up into Heaven, or descended? Who has gathered the wind in His fists? Who has bound the waters in a garment? who has established

142

all the ends of the earth? what is His name, and what is His Son's name, if you can you tell? (Proverbs 30:4.)

Does the name Jesus *(Isa)* come to mind?

(2:165) Yet of mankind are some who take unto themselves (objects of worship which they set as) rivals to Allah, loving them with a love like (that which is the due) of Allah (only)—those who believe are stauncher in their love for Allah—Oh, that those who do evil had but known, (on the day) when they behold the doom, that power belongs wholly to Allah, and that Allah is severe in punishment!

In the Arabian, polytheistic society of Muhammad's day, there were many Pagan gods who were objects of worship. We addressed one of the objects of worship in our previous discussion about the black stone in the Eastern corner of the Ka'aba in Mecca, which is still held in reverence by Muslims today. However, people can also be objects of worship. Therefore, when we read at the beginning of this passage, *"...mankind are some who take unto themselves (objects of worship which they set as) rivals to Allah..."* could also be applied to the Koran's concept of the Trinity. (By now, you should be familiar with the Koran's ongoing attack against the Trinity but not against the Cherub, which is an angel made up of not three but four entities [Ezekiel 10:14].) We are able to observe confirmation of the Trinity in this passage from the Old Testament, which is also a foreshadowing of who the members are:

Come you near unto me (Jesus), hear you this; I have not spoken in secret from the beginning (of creation); from the time that it was, there am I: and now the Lord GOD (the Father), and His Spirit (the Holy Spirit), have sent me (Isaiah 48:16).

(2:166) (On the day) when those who were followed disown those who followed (them), and they behold the doom [judgment], and all their aims collapse with them.

This passage is not clear. *"(On the day) when those who were followed..."* is in reference to two groups: (1) Religious leaders *(i.e.,* priests and rabbis) who use their positions of authority to misinform their congregants, and (2) *"...those who followed (them)...."* refers to the members of the congregation who sit under the leadership and instruction of the priests and rabbis who will, for whatever reason, be rejected by their teachers; in the end, all will be punished.

(2:167) And those who were but followers will say: "If a return were possible for us, we would disown them even as they have disowned us." Thus will Allah show them their own deeds as anguish for them, and they will not emerge from the Fire.

This is a warning to those who had followed religious leaders who lead them away from Islam and now realize that they await a bitter end. This also addresses leaders who deny Allah by following false gods or assigning others to Allah (Trinitarians); they will be severely dealt with. The faithful are to always be on guard against those "apostate religious" leaders who have led whole nations astray (Byzantium and Rome). They should be careful not to allow unscrupulous rabbis, priests, or Christian clergy to dupe them. In the end, Allah will send them—and those followers who believed them when they were told that they should reject the teachings of Muhammad—to Hell.

(2:168) O mankind! Eat of that which is lawful and wholesome in the earth, and follow not the footsteps of the devil. Look! he is an open enemy for you.

This verse is shifting our focus toward halal[27] foods, the Muslim equivalent of kosher foods. Perhaps this is an effort to prove that Allah is also the God of the Bible because of the similarity in what foods Muslims are allowed to eat compared with the diets of Jews. (We will discuss this in the commentary of the following verses). The second admonishment here is to avoid what Satan tempts the Muslims to eat.

(2:169) He enjoined upon you only the evil and the foul, and that you should tell concerning Allah that which you know not.

A Muslim cannot incorporate superstitious customs with Islam. This verse is also a set-up for the next verse by warning Muslims to beware of Satan's false doctrine.

(2:170) And when it is said unto them: "Follow that which Allah has revealed," they say: "We follow that wherein we found our fathers." What! Even though their fathers were wholly unintelligent and had no guidance?

Gabriel is complaining about those who have been given the revelations of Allah by Muhammad, but also try to blend Islam with their father's religious superstitions, which were based on myths and fables. Since the Koran is supposedly an extension of the Bible, this is probably referring to the Pagan Arab tribes. Allah is exasperated and calls them fools for following any religion but Islam. If one does not accept Islam to the exclusion of other faiths, they are labeled as stupid and without guidance; yet we have been told over and over again that Allah decides who accepts Islam.

NOTE: The Koran jumps back and forth a lot between Christians, Jews, and Pagans without any warnings or transitional phrases.

(2:171) The likeness of those who disbelieve (in relation to the messenger) is as the likeness of one who calls unto that which hears naught [nothing] except a shout and cry. Deaf, dumb, blind, therefore they have no sense (bracketed clarification mine).

Shakir and Ali say this verse is like a "parable," while Arberry's translation is closer to Pickthall's:

What? And if their fathers had no understanding of anything, and if they were not guided? The likeness of those who disbelieve I as the likeness of one who shouts to that which hears nothing, save [except] a call and a cry; deaf, dumb, blind—they do not understand (bracketed clarification mine).

To reduce this verse into simple terms, if people do not listen to Muhammad and accept his teachings, they are nothing more than dumb animals always following a leader without knowing why. They don't recognize or understand what's good for them when they hear Muhammad telling them the "truth." They hear the words, but to them, words are just sounds.

(2:172) O you who believe! Eat of the good things wherewith We have provided you, and render thanks to Allah if it is (indeed) He Whom you worship.

This is another *déjà vu* verse (see verse 168). While speaking of food, it can also imply that Allah's message is spiritually nourishing as much as food is nourishing to the body. They should reject that which was fed to them by their fathers, rabbis, priests, clergy, and even monks. They all appear to offer you nourishment, but will only feed you poison; therefore, you would be wise to turn to Allah, who is the best provider for your physical and spiritual well-being.

(2:173) He [Allah] has forbidden you only carrion [carcass], and blood, and swineflesh, and that which has been immolated [sacrificed] to (the name of) any other than Allah. But he who is driven by necessity, neither craving nor transgressing, it is no sin for him [to eat the unclean food]. Indeed! Allah is Forgiving, Merciful (bracketed clarifications mine).

This passage is forbidding the followers of Islam to eat certain foods, especially those animals slaughtered in any other name except Allah's. We agree that it is good advice not to eat unhealthy road kill or any other dead carcass (carrion); however, there is a provision given in this verse which allows a person who—for reasons beyond his control—might find himself in a desperate situation; in order to survive, he may be forgiven if he eats of the forbidden food.

We find some biblical agreement along with biblical conflict in this verse. The Bible says that the children of Israel were forbidden to eat any blood (Genesis 9:4; Leviticus 17:10; Deuteronomy 12:23) or swine/pork (Leviticus 11:7-8; Deuteronomy 14:8; Isaiah 66:17). In the Old Testament, only animals sacrificed to Pagan gods were to be avoided, suggesting a Hebrew tradition of not eating foods sacrificed to idols;

however, the New Testament releases Christians from that tradition. In fact, Jesus *(Isa)* declared:

So He said to them, "Are you thus without understanding also? Do you not perceive that whatever enters a man from outside cannot defile him, because it does not enter his heart but his stomach, and is eliminated, *thus* purifying all foods?" (Mark 7:18-19, NKJV.)

The Jerusalem Council urged Gentile converts not to eat meat that had been sacrificed to idols (Acts 15:29). God told the Apostle, Peter, that all foods were clean and could be eaten (Acts 10:15). The Apostle, Paul, provided an even more direct response concerning the matter:

So then, about eating food sacrificed to idols: We know an idol is nothing at all in the world and there is no God but one. For even if there are so-called gods, whether in Heaven or on earth (as indeed there are many "gods" and many "lords"), yet for us, there is but one God, the Father, from whom all things came and for whom we live; and there is but one Lord, Jesus Christ, through whom all things came and through whom we live.

But not everyone possesses this knowledge. Some people are still so accustomed to idols that when they eat sacrificial food, they think of it as having been sacrificed to a god, and since their conscience is weak, it is defiled. But food does not bring us near to God; we are no worse if we do not eat, and no better if we do (1 Corinthians 8:4-8, NIV).

Because Islam is a religion of abrogation (i.e., ongoing corrections of revelations), Allah abrogates the eating of meat sacrificed to idols, "*But he who is driven by necessity, neither craving nor transgressing, it is no sin for him [to eat the unclean food]*. Therefore, if a Muslim is starving and feels the need to eat—rather than starve to death—he/she may eat animals sacrificed to idols.

(2:174) Look! those who hide aught [anything] of the Scripture which Allah has revealed and purchase a small gain therewith, they eat into their bellies nothing else than fire. Allah will not speak to them on the

Day of Resurrection, nor will He make them grow. Theirs will be a painful doom.

This verse pertains to Jewish and Christian religious leaders who are allegedly hiding the truth found in the Bible. They keep their people deliberately ignorant of the compatibility of the Koran with the Bible by feeding them small amounts of false doctrine. By doing so, they will continue to feed on corrupted teachings. What they are really eating is fire! Because the religious leaders are purposefully ignoring the Koran, but accepting the Bible, they will suffer eternity Hell.

This is a repeat of what we read earlier in verse 166 in defense of why the Koran is not in agreement with the Bible, as Allah said it is. He is claiming that the rabbis and priests know that the Bible teaches exactly the same thing Muhammad taught, but they are lying to their illiterate flocks by insisting the Prophet of Islam was wrong.

(2:175) Those are they who purchase error at the price of guidance, and torment at the price of pardon. How constant are they in their strife to reach the Fire!

Since they will not accept Muhammad's teachings, they are in error and *"constant...in their strife,"* causing them to land in Hell for leading their congregations astray.

> NOTE: Remember, the Koran says that Allah guides whom he wants (Sûrah 24:46), thus, Allah, not the individual, chooses the path leading to Heaven or Hell. Still, Allah is offended by people who refuse Islam and for that reason, he sends them to Hell. This makes no sense, which is it?

(2:176) That is because Allah has revealed the Scripture with the truth. Look! those who find (a cause of) disagreement in the Scripture are in open schism [split] (bracketed clarification mine).

We are now informed, despite the fact that Allah revealed both the Bible and the Koran, that some will still not accept the koranic versions of the Bible. They will make the false claim they find inconsistencies between the Bible and Koran; thus, they are guilty of causing a split or open rebellion between Judaism, Christianity, and Islam. This is an example of why the formatting of the Bible, alongside the Koran's version of its Bible stories, needs to be compared in a neutral setting, which is what we have done with this book.

(2:177) It is not righteousness that you turn your faces to the East and the West; but righteous is he who believes in Allah and the Last Day and the angels and the Scripture and the prophets; and gives his wealth, for love of Him, to kinsfolk and to orphans and the needy and the wayfarer [wonderer] and to those who ask, and to set slaves free; and observes proper worship and pays the poor-due. And those who keep their treaty when they make one, and the patient in tribulation and adversity and time of stress. Such are they who are sincere. Such are the God [Allah]-fearing (bracketed clarification mine).

Basically, this verse is trying to show that just going through religious rituals is meaningless unless it is accompanied by good deeds. Bible believers would agree with much of this verse; however, pertaining to slavery, it is interesting to observe that throughout the Islamic world today, some Muslims still own slaves, but it is unusual for them to free a slave for the sake of doing a good deed. (Slaves brought to America were captured and sold by Muslims in Africa to the western slave traders.) Freedom is a commodity that is usually bought and paid for by another party, but as infrequent as it might be, a Muslim is not prohibited from freeing his slave out of the goodness of his heart.

(2:178) O you who believe! Retaliation is prescribed for you in the matter of the murdered; the freeman for the freeman, and the slave for the slave, and the female for the female. And for him who is forgiven somewhat by his (injured) brother, prosecution according to usage and payment unto him in kindness. This is an alleviation and a mercy from your Lord. He who transgresses after this will have a painful doom.

The Koran is echoing laws found in the Old Testament:

And he that kills a beast shall make it good; beast for beast. And if a man cause a blemish in his neighbor; as he has done, so shall it be done to him; Breach for breach, eye for eye, tooth for tooth: as he has caused a blemish in a man so shall it be done to him again. And he that kills a beast, he shall restore it: and he that kills a man, he shall be put to death (Leviticus 24:18-21).

Then shall you do unto him, as he had thought to have done unto his brother: so shall you put the evil away from among you. And those which remain shall hear, and fear, and shall henceforth commit no more any such evil among you. And your eye shall not pity; but life shall go for life, eye for eye, tooth for tooth, hand for hand, foot for foot (Deuteronomy 19:19-23).

Yet Jesus *(Isa)* made the Law stricter than the Koran's:

You have heard that it was said of them of old time, "Thou shall not kill; and whosoever shall kill shall be in danger of the judgment:"

But I say unto you, "That whosoever is angry with his brother without a cause shall be in danger of the judgment: and whosoever shall say to his brother, Raca [a contemptuous expression], shall be in danger of the council: but whosoever shall say, you fool, shall be in danger of Hellfire" (Matthew 5:21-22, bracketed clarification mine).

Jesus, unlike Allah of the Koran, encourages us to forgive because if we forgive, our God in Heaven will forgive us.

But to you who are listening I say: "Love your enemies, do good to those who hate you bless those who curse you, pray for those who mistreat you. If someone slaps you on one cheek, turn to them the other also. If someone takes your coat, do not withhold your shirt from them. Give to everyone who asks you, and if anyone takes

150

what belongs to you, do not demand it back. Do to others as you would have them do to you" (Matthew 7:12; Luke 6:13)

"If you love those who love you, what credit is that to you? Even sinners love those who love them. And if you do good to those who are good to you, what credit is that to you? Even sinners do that. And if you lend to those from whom you expect repayment, what credit is that to you? Even sinners lend to sinners, expecting to be repaid in full. But love your enemies, do good to them, and lend to them without expecting to get anything back. Then your reward will be great, and you will be children of the Most High, because he is kind to the ungrateful and wicked. Be merciful, just as your Father is merciful" (Luke 6:27-36, NIV).

(2:179) And there is life for you in retaliation, O men of understanding, that you may ward off (evil).

This verse is a continuation of the previous verse; together they mean, while it is good for Muslims to get even/take revenge *("...there is life for you in retaliation")* with those who have killed someone close to them, they should be careful not to "overkill," or as we are told here, *"... men of understanding, that you may ward off (evil),"* from continuing to take revenge on the offender's family." Once the offending person has been killed or has paid the "blood money," that should settle the matter.

Getting even/revenge to settle a score will avoid evil because the adversary is dead and can no longer do any harm. Again, this is the complete opposite of biblical Scripture, which teaches forgiveness:

Do not seek revenge or bear a grudge against anyone among your people, but love your neighbor as yourself. I am the LORD (Leviticus 19:18, NIV).

Jesus *(Isa)* echoes this wisdom when He is asked:

You have heard that it was said, "You shall love your neighbor and hate your enemy." But I say to you, "love your enemies, bless those who curse you, do good to those who hate you, and pray for those who spitefully use you and persecute you, that you may be sons of your Father in heaven; for He makes His sun rise on the evil and on the good, and sends rain on the just and on the unjust" (Matthew 5:43-45, NKJV).

CONSIDER: If you compare Sûrah 2:179 with Leviticus 19:18 and the Gospel of Matthew 5:43-45, do you believe they could come from the same author?

(2:180) It is prescribed for you, when one of you approaches death, if he leave[s] wealth, that he bequeath unto parents and near relatives in kindness. (This is) a duty for all those who ward off (evil). (Bracketed clarification mine.)

This verse is dealing with Sharia Law and is similar to Scripture in Proverbs and Numbers:

Say to the Israelites, "If a man dies and leaves no son, give his inheritance to his daughter. If he has no daughter, give his inheritance to his brothers. If he has no brothers, give his inheritance to his father's brothers. If his father had no brothers, give his inheritance to the nearest relative in his clan, that he may possess it." This is to have the force of law for the Israelites, as the LORD commanded Moses (Numbers 27:8-11, NIV).

A good man leaves an inheritance to his children's children: and the wealth of the sinner is laid up for the just (Proverbs 13:22).

(2:181) And whoso changes (the will) after he has heard it—the sin thereof is only upon those who change it. Lo! Allah is Hearer, Knower.

This verse is still discussing an individual's last will and testament. If anyone (e.g., the beneficiary, executor, etc.) changes another person's last will after he reads or hears it, he brings himself under Allah's condemnation.

(2:182) But he who fears from a testator [the person who has executed his Last Will and Testament] some unjust or sinful clause, and makes peace between the parties, (it shall be) no sin for him. Indeed! Allah is Forgiving, Merciful (bracketed clarification mine).

The Koran continues to address inheritance and commending the person who is estranged or brings estranged family members back to a semblance of restoration, even if it means—like in this particular instance—bypassing or mutually bringing about a settlement between the inheritors and allowing some amends to be made in the person's will. It will not be held against them.

(2:183) O you who believe! Fasting is prescribed for you, even as it was prescribed for those before you, that you may ward off (evil);

Gabriel is referring to the practice of sustaining from eating food as a means to subdue the flesh just as the Bible instructs the Christians and Jews to do.

Although Bible believers may use fasting as an aid to subdue the flesh, the main purpose of fasting is to focus on God's Word and draw closer to Him (Nehemiah 1:4; Acts 14:23, etc.).

(2:184) (Fast) a certain number of days; and (for) him who is sick among you, or on a journey, (the same) number of other days [should make up the missed days of fasting]; and for those who can afford it there is a ransom [an alternate by]: the feeding of a man in need— but whoso doeth good of his own accord, it is better for him: and that you fast is better for you if you did but know (bracketed clarifications mine).

This reinforces a works-based religion, including the prescription for charity (love) as a means to "buy" (ransom) Allah's favor by feeding the poor. The reader is told that goodness for goodness sake is ultimately the best way to go along with fasting.

(2:185) The month of Ramadân in which was revealed the Qur'ân, a guidance for mankind, and clear proofs of the guidance, and the Criterion (of right and wrong). And whosoever of you is present, let him fast the month, and whosoever of you is sick or on a journey, (let

him fast the same) number of other days. Allah desires for you ease; He desires not hardship for you; and (He desires) that you should complete the period, and that you should magnify Allah for having guided you, and that peradventure you may be thankful.

This redundant verbiage is a prescription of Sharia Law regarding the holy season of Ramadan. On the surface, it seems to invoke a severely long period of fasting: *"...let him fast the month...,"* but it is not as strenuous as it appears. Muslims fast from daybreak until evening, at which time a feast is prepared. It is the reverse of what we in the West call "breakfast" ("break" "fast"), which is observed the morning after a night's fasting while asleep.

However, if someone is sick during a journey and fasting would make them worse, the fast may be delayed until after Ramadan or their journey is over. Allah does not want his followers to be ill.

(2:186) And when My servants question thee concerning Me, then surely I am nigh [near]. I answer the prayer of the supplicant when he cries unto Me. So let them hear My call and let them trust in Me, in order that they may be led aright (bracketed clarification mine).

This verse, combined with the previous verses (vs. 184 and 185), assures the devout Muslim worshipper that Allah is paying attention to their prayers; even though they cannot see him, he is there and hears their cry. Nevertheless, in order for Allah to guide them accordingly, they are required to observe the time of fasting and prayer.

(2:187) It is made lawful for you to go in unto your wives on the night of the fast. They are raiment for you and you are raiment for them. Allah is Aware that you were deceiving yourselves in this respect and He has turned in mercy toward you and relieved you. So hold intercourse with them and seek that which Allah hath ordained for you, and eat and drink until the white thread becometh distinct to you from the black thread of the dawn. Then strictly observe the fast till nightfall and touch them not, but be at your devotions in the mosques. These are the limits imposed by Allah, so approach them not. Thus Allah expounds [expands] His revelation to mankind that they may ward off (evil) (bracketed clarification mine).

When this verse was written, apparently Muslim men were not abstaining from intimate relationships with their wives during the month of Ramadan, so Allah decided that it would be all right for them not to remain celibate during the night and *"to go into their wives."* It appears that Allah decided the most feasible option was to keep them happy rather than loose converts; nevertheless, they should abstain from sex during the day. It was expected that obedient Muslims would attend certain services in their mosques during Ramadan and abstain from fleshly desires on those occasions.

(2:188) And don't eat up all your property among yourselves in vanity, nor seek by it to gain the hearing of the judges that you may knowingly devour a portion of the property of others wrongfully.

Muhammad Habib Shakir translation is a little easier to understand:

And do not swallow up your property among yourselves by false means, neither seek to gain access thereby to [bribe] the judges, so that you may swallow up a part of the property of men wrongfully while you know [it's wrong] (bracketed clarification mine).

This is a warning to those whose egos demand that they create wealth at the expense of others by laying claim to another's land, knowing full well that their neighbor would have trouble proving ownership, despite the fact that his neighbor actually does own the land. The people are warned not to do such an evil thing. They are also warned not to bribe judges with favors or money in order to help them gain even more ill-gotten property from their struggling neighbors.

(2:189) They ask thee, (O Muhammad), of new moons, say: "They are fixed seasons for mankind and for the pilgrimage. It is not righteousness that you go to houses by the backs thereof (as do the idolaters at certain seasons), but the righteous man is he who wards off (evil). So go to houses by the gates thereof, and observe your duty to Allah, that you may be successful."

Like the Hebrews, Muslims used the lunar calendar to count months and holidays. This is an allegorical passage, which instructs all Muslims not to put on airs and attempt to look religious during holy days, nor should they do things not becoming of proper Islamic behavior when no one is looking. An obedient Muslim should be forthright and not a hypocrite because Allah is not fooled, so they are to act in a trustworthy manner.

As for the statement, *"It is not righteousness that you go to houses by the backs thereof,"* one superstition Muslims shared with Pagans was not to enter one's home through the door when in a state of consecration for a pilgrimage or when returning from a journey; instead,
they would leap over the back wall or climb through a window. Superstition was frowned on by Allah.

(2:190) Fight in the way of Allah against those who fight against you, but begin not hostilities. Lo! Allah loves not aggressors.

This is one of the "proof-texts" cited by Muslims and others to prove that Islam is a "religion of peace." On the surface, this seems to be a measured and prudent approach to dealing with potential adversaries; however, the Koran appears to be conflicted. On the one hand, Allah tells us that he loves non-aggressors and not to attack unless

attacked—fair enough. The problem is—just 26 verses later—Allah tells his followers:

> *Warfare is ordained for you, though it is hateful unto you; but it may happen that you hate a thing which is good for you, and it may happen that you love a thing which is bad for you. Allah knows, you know not (Sûrah 2:216).*

This verse tells Muhammad's followers not to begin hostilities, while verse 216 tells them, *"war is ordained for them."* Because verse 216 is a later revelation, it replaces (i.e., abrogates) this verse.

This is not the only verse that conflicts with other passages. Consider a few of the following commands from Allah to his followers:

> *Let those fight in the cause of God Who sell the life of this world for the Hereafter. To him who fights in the cause of God,—whether he*

is slain or gets victory—Soon shall We give him a reward of great (value). (Yusuf Ali Sûrah 4:74.)

It seems that this current conciliatory verse (Sûrah 2:190), which we are studying, abrogates Sûrah 4:74. However, a quick look at our chart at the beginning of this book regarding the order of the Koran's sûrahs, shows that Sûrah 2 was actually the 87th Sûrah revealed to Muhammad, while Sûrah 4 was the 92nd Sûrah revealed to him. That makes Sûrah 4:94 a replacement for Sûrah 2:190. An even more extreme verse can be found in Sûrah 5:51:

O you who believe! do not take the Jews and the Christians for friends; they are friends of each other; and whoever amongst you takes them for a friend, then surely he is one of them; surely Allah does not guide the unjust people (Sûrah 5:51, Muhammad Habib Shakir).

Sûrah 5:51 was, in fact, the 112th verse given to Muhammad out of 114 Sûrahs, and that's why it also replaces Sûrah 2:190. As if that's not enough, there is an even more violent verse:

When your Lord inspired the angels (saying): "I am with you. So make those who believe stand firm. I will throw fear [Arberry, Ali, and Shakir all use the word "terror"] into the heart of those who disbelieve. Then smite [behead] the necks and smite [chop off] of them [Christians, Jews, and Pagans] each finger."

That is because they opposed Allah and His messenger. Whoso opposes Allah and His messenger (for him) see! Allah is severe in punishment.
That (is the award), so taste it, and (know) that for disbelievers is the torment of the Fire.

O you who believe! When you meet those who disbelieve in battle, turn not your backs to them.

Whoso[ever] on that day turns his back to them, unless maneuvering for battle or intent to join a company, he truly has incurred wrath from Allah, and his habitation will be Hell, a hapless [horrible] journeys end.

You (Muslims) slew them not, but Allah slew them. And you (Muhammad) throwest not when you did throw, but Allah threw, that He might test the believers by a fair test from Him. See! Allah is Hearer, Knower (Sûrah 8:12-17, bracketed clarifications mine).

Yusuf Ali explains what was thrown: *"when you threw (a handful of dust), it was not your act, but God's."*

Sûrah 8:12-17 was the 88th sûrah given to Muhammad, while Sûrah 2:190 was the 87th; therefore, Sûrah 8:12-17 cancels Sûrah 2:190. Lest we become tiresome, we have yet another verse replacing this proof-text; that contradicts this passage that Muslims only fight when they are attacked, and they never start a fight because Islam is a "religion of peace:"

Then, when the sacred months have passed, then slay the idolaters wherever you find them, and take them (captive), and besiege them, and prepare for them each ambush. But if they repent and establish worship and pay the poor-due, then leave their way free. See! Allah is Forgiving, Merciful (Sûrah 9:5).

As with the other sûrahs, Sûrah 9:5 titled the "Verse of the Sword," was given as the 113th sûrah to Muhammad and was the next to the last sûrah received by him, which allowed Sûrah 9:5 to also cancel Sûrah 2:190!

The verses cited above also abrogate all the conciliatory verses we have seen so far in Sûrah 2, as well as the rest of the conciliatory verses that follow in this Sûrah.

As time advanced, Allah became more militant in the Koran and less accommodating toward Christians and Jews because they spurned his earlier conciliatory advancements; however, some people would confidently argue that an omniscient (all-knowing) God would not be taken by surprise with that rejection based on the conflicts between the Koran and the Bible because—being "god"—Allah should have already known that would happen. Besides, an all-knowing and powerful God would never have allowed the original Bible stories to be altered, knowing they would conflict with the same stories later retold in the Koran. Allah would have protected his work as He claimed he would (Sûrah 15:9). We have to also remember, as we have seen, the Koran repeatedly tells us Allah is who decides who will accept Islam and who will reject it.

The real question is this: If Allah is the author of the Bible and the author of the Koran, why would he not remember what he said in the Bible the first time (which he could easily refer to because it was all written down) when he repeated the same stories again in the Koran?

Three ways Muslims could respond to this enigma (mystery/paradox) is either: (1) Admit that the Koran is wrong—an option they are not allowed to consider; (2) try to convince the Jews and Christians that the Bible is corrupt which, for the Muslims, would explain why there are so many differences between the historical accounts contained in the Bible and the conflict with those corrupted Bible stories found in the Koran, or (3) simply kill anyone who questions the authority of the Koran and teachings of Muhammad.

(2:191) And slay them wherever you find them, and drive them out of the places whence they drove you out, for persecution is worse than slaughter. And fight not with them at the Inviolable [sacred] Place of Worship [the Ka'aba] until they first attack you there, but if they attack you (there) then slay them. Such is the reward of disbelievers (bracketed clarification mine).

A Muslim is to seek out and kill those who drove them out of their homes and land. This verse also says not to fight your enemy at the mosque/Ka'aba in Mecca and, by extension, any mosque, unless they attack you there. Muhammad Habib Shakir explains:

> *And kill them wherever you find them, and drive them out from whence [where] they drove you out, and persecution is severer than slaughter, and do not fight with them at the Sacred Mosque until [and unless] they fight with you in it, but if they do fight you, then slay them; such is the recompense [payment] of the unbelievers (bracketed clarifications mine).*

During the sixth century, before Muhammad and a religion called Islam and before the existence of a united Arabian Peninsula (i.e., Yemen,

Omar, Qatar, Bahrain, Kuwait, Saudi Arabia, and the United Arab Emirates), the Arabian Peninsula was a lawless place where intertribal wars were a common occurrence. There was no formal law or political organization, so each tribe conducted itself in an autonomous manner, owing loyalty only to the individual tribal chief. It was the local tribal leader who laid down the law for his people.[28] Of course, from a modern, enlightened view, it is always preferable not to go to war. However, to be fair, if a country commits to war—and this verse is in the context of having been attacked first—then they should totally commit to defending themselves with the only possible outcome being a victory.

(2:192) But if they desist [cease fighting], then indeed! Allah is Forgiving, Merciful (bracketed clarification mine).

This is self-explanatory. If they [the enemy] lay down their weapons and surrender, Allah forgives them; however, they are required to do more than just stop fighting as we read in the next verse.

(2:193) And fight them until persecution [fitna], is no more, and religion is for Allah. But if they desist, then let there be no hostility except against wrong-doers (bracketed clarification mine).

NOTE: The word for persecution/oppression in Arabic is *idtihad*, which is not the word used in this verse. *Fitna* is the Arabic word used here. Some scholars argue that the traditional meaning of *fitna*—as used here—is derived from an Arabic verb meaning "to tempt, lure, or seduce."[29] By using it in this context, Muhammad is made to appear as the persecuted victim, which explains away Islamic militancy to a gullible non-Muslim public. However, many scholars argue that historically, Muhammad was *not* being attacked at the time this verse was given to him. A more accurate translation of this verse would be, "And fight with them until there is no more disbelief and no more association of the worship of those wrongly associated with Allah" (i.e., the erroneous Muslim Trinity of Allah, Jesus and His mother Mary, Sûrah 5:116, paraphrased).

This verse has been mistakenly associated with a verse previously mentioned (verse 191), but in fact, it has nothing to do with it and would be better understood if it would state: *"Once they stop fighting/resisting, they must accept Islam as their religion. If they do not convert, they are wrongdoers and should be brought under Islamic submission" (paraphrase mine).* It is interesting to note that at the time of this revelation, Muhammad and his followers (approximately 120, give or take a dozen) had just been relocated to Yathrib (later renamed by Muhammad in his own honor as the "City of the Prophet" (i.e., *Madīnat an-Nabī* or Medina). When that revelation was given, Muhammad was not only respected in Yathrib; he was enjoying a peaceful existence without any hostilities from the Meccans.

(2:194) The forbidden month for the forbidden month, and forbidden things in retaliation. And one who attacks you, attack him in like manner as he attacked you. Observe your duty to Allah, and know that Allah is with those who ward off (evil).

A.J. Arberry translates this passage:
The holy month for the holy month; holy things demand retaliation. Whoso[ever] commits aggression against you, do you commit aggression against him as he has committed against you; and fear you God, and know that God is with the godfearing (bracketed clarification mine).

At this point, we should provide some historical background: Muhammad's men attacked a Meccan caravan and killed one of its people during the Pagan holy month of Rajab, which was forbidden.[30] Muhammad sought help from Allah, who some say bailed him out of trouble (his wife, Aisha, claimed Allah could deny him nothing[31]) by giving him this revelation. While the first part of this verse seems redundant or repetitive, it allows for a Muslim to retaliate in kind, especially during the holy months when warfare and killing are forbidden. Arabs had a tradition, supposedly dating from the time of Abraham, which allowed three months as holy months (*Dhu al-Qa'dah, Dhu al-Hijjah*, and *Muharram*). Those holy months were incorporated by Muslims as the time for the required pilgrimage (Hajj) to Mecca. The month of Rajab was also consecrated for the Hajj and is the seventh month on the Islamic lunar calendar, which precedes the month of Ramadan. As stated, during the holy months, hostilities were prohibited. That was also observed by Muslims unless a perceived affront was committed against them. It was referred to as *nasi'* (see Sûrah 2:217) and allowed for retaliation during the holy months. It gave Muslims an unfair advantage, and they used it to their benefit.

(2:195) Spend your wealth for the cause of Allah, and be not cast [down] by your own hands to ruin; and do good. Look! Allah loves the beneficent (bracketed clarification mine).

In context, Muslims are instructed to be charitable and generous toward those less fortunate. They have not destroyed themselves with lust, but are to strive for even higher goals by doing even more good. Allah loves those who do good.

(2:196) Perform the pilgrimage and the visit (to Mecca) for Allah. And if you are prevented, then send such gifts as can be obtained with ease, and shave not your heads until the gifts have reached their destination. And whoever among you is sick or has an ailment of the head must pay a ransom of fasting or almsgiving [charitable gifts for the poor] or offering. And if you are in safety, then whosoever contents himself with the visit for the Pilgrimage (shall give) such gifts as can be had with ease. And whosoever cannot find (such gifts), then a fast of three days while on the pilgrimage, and of seven when you have returned; that is, ten in all. That is for him whose folk are not present at the Inviolable [sacred] Place of Worship [the Ka'aba in Mecca]. Observe your duty to Allah, and know that Allah is severe in punishment. (Bracketed clarification mine.)

Before Muhammad conquered the Pagan city of Mecca, Arabs had made pilgrimages to the Ka'aba, which was the home to their 360 Pagan gods until Muhammad conquered it and converted the Ka'aba into a mosque for Allah.[32] Because of the resulting revenue for the city from the pilgrimages—when Muhammad conquered Mecca and converted the Ka'aba to a mosque—the city fathers pleaded with him to let them keep the annual Hajj (literally meaning "to attend the journey" or "pilgrimage"). Muhammad agreed and simply converted the Pagan ritual into an Islamic ceremony, which is still practiced today. (It seems that a little compromise kept the peace and made for good business. [33])

After Muhammad conquered Mecca and had gained followers from all over, he changed the required yearly Hajj to a lesser requirement of making at least one Hajj—for every able-bodied Muslim—in their lifetime (if they could afford it), preferably during the holy months, but allowed for a lesser Hajj during the year for those traveling from afar.

(2:197) The pilgrimage is (in) the well-known months, and whoever is minded to perform the pilgrimage therein (let him remember that) there is (to be) no lewdness nor abuse nor angry conversation on the pilgrimage. And whatsoever good you do Allah knows it. So make provision for yourselves (hereafter); for the best provision is to ward off evil. Therefore keep your duty unto Me, O men of understanding

Gabriel is setting the new ground rules for Muslims who make the Hajj to Mecca. The official pilgrimage occurs sometime around the 8th and 12th day of Dhu al-Hijjah, which is the last or twelfth month of the Islamic lunar calendar.

(2:198) It is no sin for you that you seek the bounty of your Lord (by trading). But, when you press on in the multitude from [the hill of] 'Arafât, remember Allah by the sacred monument. Remember Him as He has guided you, although before you were of those astray (bracketed clarification mine).

Arafât is both a special day of repentance (ninth day of the month of Dhūl Ḥijjah) as well as a place known as "Granite Hill" near Mecca, where Muslims spend the day during the holy days. It is also the place where Muhammad offered his last sermon. The sins of the pilgrims, up to that point in time, were forgiven if they fast that day.

In this verse, unlike the Pagan Arabs who would not work on or discuss their trade during the holy days, Allah is telling the faithful Muslims that work is honorable and not worldly. Therefore, it is good to maintain one's profession, even during the pilgrimage.

(2:199) Then hasten onward from the place whence the multitude hastens onward, and ask forgiveness of Allah. See! Allah is Forgiving, Merciful.

The faithful are told to move quickly, like the others, to seek Allah's forgiveness.

(2:200) And when you have completed your devotions then remember Allah as you remember your fathers or with a more lively remembrance. But of mankind is he who says: "Our Lord! Give unto us in the world," and he has no portion in the Hereafter.

This is a reflective verse commemorating the rituals just completed with the warning to do so with a sense of gratitude and respect and not be desirous of satisfying the lust of the flesh.

In footnote 223, where we read, *"...remember Allah as you remember your fathers,"* Yusuf Ali points out that it was the custom of the Pagan Arabs to praise their ancestors [forefathers] at the conclusion of the pilgrimage. Perhaps it was an endeavor by Muhammad to allow his Pagan converts to do the same in an attempt to offer something familiar like they had in their ritual.

(2:201) And of them (also) is he who saith: "Our Lord! Give unto us in the world that which is good and in the Hereafter that which is good, and guard us from the doom of Fire."

This is a set up for the next verse. Allah is acknowledging that many people with fleshly desires want to avoid going to Hell, so theypray for his help.

(2:202) For them there is in store a goodly portion out of that which they have earned. Allah is swift at reckoning.

Allah is not against material blessings, but it is the condition of a Muslim's attitude in life and how that life is conducted, which will influence where they go and how they will be blessed at their death. Allah is aware of their actions and words; he will be their judge.

(2:203) Remember Allah through the appointed days. Then whoso[ever] hastens (his departure) by two days, it is no sin for him, and whoso[ever] delays, it is no sin for him; that is for him who wards off (evil). Be careful of your duty to Allah, and know that unto Him you will be gathered (bracketed clarifications mine).

Muslims, who observe (celebrate) the holy days and fulfill the prescribed rituals, will find favor with Allah, but Allah also understands that they might, out of necessity, have to leave a couple of days before the allotted time is over. On the other hand, if they have to delay arriving by a few days, that is all right too—either way it should be for a good reason.

(2:204) And of mankind there is he whose conversation on the life of this world pleases you (Muhammad), and he calls Allah to witness as to that which is in his heart; yet he is the most rigid of opponents.

While Arberry and Shakir translate this obscure verse similarly, Yusuf Ali places a slightly different twist which clarifies this passage better:

> *There is the type of man whose speech about this world's life may dazzle you, and he calls Allah to witness about what is in his heart; yet is he the most contentious of enemies.*

This verse is warning Muhammad and the faithful that there are people who talk impressively about their concern for the world and its people, but falsely invoke the name of Allah as their witness! However, despite their claims, they are not moved by Muhammad's revelations and refuse to embrace Islam.

(2:205) And when he turns away (from you) his effort in the land is to make mischief therein and to destroy the crops and the cattle; and Allah loves not mischief.

This is a continuation of the last verse. It seems that when those hypocrites used Allah's name to appear godly, as soon as one's back was turned, those very same people looked for things they could harm, such as livestock and crops. In today's society, the equivalent might be graffiti on private property, stealing hubcaps, tires, etc., yet if they were caught, those very same hoodlums would appear innocent and claim, "As Allah is my witness, I am innocent!"

(2:206) And when it is said unto him: "Be careful of your duty to Allah," pride takes him to sin. Hell will settle his account, an evil resting-place.

Pride causes him to sin? Pride *is* a sin. We know the Bible teaches that pride precedes a fall (Proverbs 16:18), but not necessarily an additional sin; therefore, we are obligated to ask what sin is promoted here? Burning the planted fields and killing livestock (verse 2:205) would be a sin regardless of whether or not someone disagrees with the teachings of Muhammad, so we ask ourselves, "To what end would someone who disagrees with Muhammad benefit from such conduct?" This is not logical and makes no sense.

Perhaps this is one of those koranic passages that would be understood by indigenous Arabians because of their understanding of Middle Eastern culture and history. Many Islamic scholars explain this as the reason some of the passages in the Koran, unlike the Bible, are not always self-evident.

(2:207) And of mankind is he who would sell himself, seeking the pleasure of Allah; and Allah has compassion on (His) bondmen.

If one seeks to please another by dedicating his life to serving Allah, then Allah would be pleased; however, this could also be interpreted to be a jihadi verse—which promises, if one sells his life dying in a jihad—then heaven and Allah's pleasure are guaranteed.

(2:208) O you who believe! Come, all of you, into submission (unto Him); and follow not the footsteps of the devil. Look! He [Satan] is an open enemy for you (bracketed clarification mine).

We could say this verse is an understatement. I think most of us would agree it is always foolish to seek after Satan as opposed to being godly.

(2:209) And if you slide back after the clear proofs have come unto you, then know that Allah is Mighty, Wise.

If someone backslides after accepting Islam or rejects the teachings of Islam after hearing about it, they should be careful because—they are warned— *"... know that Allah is Mighty, Wise,"* Allah is all-powerful and knows what punishment you deserve.

(2:210) Wait they for naught [nothing] else than that Allah should come unto them in the shadows of the clouds with the angels? Then the case would be already judged. All cases go back to Allah (for judgment) (bracketed clarification mine).
A.J. Arberry translates this verse:

> *What do they look for, but that God shall come to them in the clouds-shadows, and the angels? The matter is determined and unto God all matters are returned.*

This implies that some wait in vain for miraculous signs and the revelation of Allah descending in the clouds with his angels to prove that the teachings of Muhammad are true. Yet consider, if they were to see Allah return this way, then it would already be Judgment Day, and their fate would be a foregone conclusion.

This seems to be borrowed from the Book of Acts, Chapter 1, when Jesus was through speaking to His disciples for the last time:

After He said this, He was taken up before their very eyes, and a cloud hid Him from their sight.

They were looking intently up into the sky as He was going, when suddenly two men dressed in white stood beside them. "Men of Galilee," they said, "why do you stand here looking into the sky? This same Jesus, who has been taken from you into Heaven, will come back in [the clouds] the same way you have seen Him go into Heaven" (Acts 1:9-11, NIV, bracketed clarification mine).

(2:211) Ask of the Children of Israel how many a clear revelation We gave them! He who alters the grace of Allah after it has come unto him (for him), look! Allah is severe in punishment.

By this time, the Christians and Jews had noticed that the Koran and the Bible were far different from each other; an explanation was needed to clarify the contradictions regarding Allah's "clear revelation," and Muhammad needed to explain the differences as being "altered." The two options Muhammad had were either (1) Allah got it wrong, or (2) the Jews and Christians rewrote the Bible.

OBSERVATION: We will add the caveat that in Islam, if someone writes a book, such as the one you are reading, which honestly looks at many of the Koran's and Hadith inconsistencies and questions Muhammad or Allah's accuracy regarding the Koran's, historical, scientific, or archaeological accuracy, that person is not to be debated; they must be eliminated (i.e., kill the messenger). Criticism—scholarly or innocent—which challenges Islam or the prophet—cannot be tolerated. In some countries, any type of critical observation regarding Islam or Muhammad is considered a "hate crime." The warning to those who critique the Koran is that they do so under the pain of death—something that is unique to Islam alone. This, although Christians and Jews are encouraged by Allah to compare the Bible with the Koran in order to see if there are any discrepancies (Sûrahs 2:23; 4:82, and 10:94). If they find them—they are to keep quiet.

As for the Bible—which Allah claims he gave to the Jews and Christians—it had become corrupted by them. Consider the following sûrah where Allah states:

We have, without doubt, sent down the Message and We will assuredly guard it (from corruption). (Sûrah 15:9, Yusuf Ali.)

If Allah is able to keep the Koran from becoming corrupted, then how did the Bible become corrupted? On the other hand, if Allah is not able to protect the Bible, which he claims he wrote, what guarantees that the Koran is not corrupted too?

(2:212) Beautified is the life of the world for those who disbelieve; they make a jest of the believers. But those who keep their duty to Allah will be above them on the Day of Resurrection. Allah gives without stint [limit] to whom He will (bracketed clarification mine).

This is a very biblical sounding verse since we can all agree that the world holds many wonderful and some not so wonderful attractions which tempt everyone; however, those who resist evil will do better on the Day of Judgment. The Bible teaches that only through Jesus *(Isa)* can we be saved on the Day of Judgment (Acts 15:1; Revelation 21:27). Notice that while it is inferred, there is no absolute guarantee of salvation here because *"Allah gives without stint [limit] to whom He will (bracketed clarification mine)."*

(2:213) Mankind were [was] one community, and Allah sent (unto them) prophets as bearers of good tidings and as warners, and revealed therewith the Scripture with the truth that it might judge between mankind concerning that wherein they differed. And only those unto whom (the Scripture) was given differed concerning it, after clear proofs had come unto them, through hatred one of another. And Allah by His Will guided those who believe unto the truth of that concerning which they differed [their differences]. Allah guides whom He will unto a straight path (bracketed clarification mine).

In the New Testament, the Greek term *ethnos* (ethnic) is rendered "nation." We are unable to determine what the word is in Arabic, but it might be more in line with the concept that humans are all one people or, as Pickthall translates it, *"one community."* God's revelation was not so much revealed throughout the various peoples of the human race, but—as Muslims would agree—it would be through the children of Abraham that the nations would eventually be blessed. The Bible teaches:

Now the LORD had said unto Abram, "Get you out of your country, and from your kindred [relatives], and from your father's house, unto a land that I will show you:

"And I will make of you a great nation, and I will bless you, and make your name great; and you shall be a blessing:

"And I will bless them that bless you, and curse him that curses you: and in you shall all families of the earth be blessed" (Genesis 12:1-3).

Sûrah 2:213 suggests that the scripture came to both Jews and Christians, and they hated each other: *"... after clear proofs had come unto them, through hatred one of another,"* yet the early church was Jewish, and the New Testament was a Jewish publication written by Jews about a Jew! Some Jews accepted Jesus as their Messiah, and others rejected Him, but they were still all Jews. This division among brethren is no different than what we see today in Islam between various schisms (i.e., Sunnis, Shiites, Kurds, Wahhabis, etc.). Like Christians and Jews—after Islam's founding and expansion—not all Muslims today are Arabs

As for this verse ending with the statement, *"And Allah by His Will guided those who believe unto the truth of that concerning which they differed. Allah guides whom He will unto a straight path ...,"* it appears that Allah is in control of who will be saved. The God of the Bible, however, is not desirous that *any* should perish (2 Peter 3:9).

(2:214) Or think you that you will enter Paradise while yet there has not come unto you the like of (that which came to) those who passed away before you? Affliction and adversity befell them, they were shaken as with earthquake, till the messenger (of Allah) and those who believed along with him said: When comes Allah's help? Now surely Allah's help is nigh [near] (bracketed clarification mine).

According to this verse, before Muhammad had his encounter with Gabriel and received Allah's new revelations, people were lost and in need of hope. Despite having the prophets of old, they were

170

tormented, suffering hardships, and their lives were shaken. Then Muhammad came
with his message of Islam (i.e., "submission") with the promise of help from Allah; yet Muslims still experience suffering and question their Islamic faith just as the people of the Bible did in biblical days, even though Allah's help was available to them then as it is now.

(2:215) They ask you, (O Muhammad), "what they shall spend." Say: "that which you spend for good (must go) to parents and near kindred [relatives] and orphans and the needy and the wayfarer [wanderer]. And whatsoever good you do, indeed! Allah is Aware of it" [bracketed clarifications mine].

This verse discusses being charitable toward one's parents, family, and those who are in need, such as orphans and transients because Allah sees the good you do. There is no doubt this is a biblical concept as we can see in the following Bible verses:

Honor your father and your mother, so that you may live long in the land the LORD your God is giving you (Exodus 20:12, NIV).

Religion that God our Father accepts as pure and faultless is this: to look after orphans and widows in their distress and to keep oneself from being polluted by the world (James 1:27, NIV).

(2:216) Warfare is ordained for you, though it is hateful unto you; but it may happen that you hate a thing which is good for you, and it may happen that you love a thing which is bad for you. Allah knows, you know not.

Many have read this verse and concluded that Islam is not a religion of peace. As Muhammad began expanding and acquiring new converts to Islam, it is obvious that not all of them wanted to fight—many were less revolutionary than his earlier recruits and preferred the more domestic and simple life of a herdsman or merchant. Because they refused to go with Muhammad when he went on his military excursions, it was necessary for Allah to come up with this more militant revelation.

This passage or any similar passage is not found anywhere in the Bible.

In defense of militant Muslims (the so-called "radical jihadists" who have allegedly hijacked the so-called "peaceful" religion of Islam), we offer the following observation: If Koran-believing Muslims embrace the guidelines enshrined in their holy book, which was given to them by their prophet, and they follow the warlord's (Muhammad) example, why would they be considered radical? First of all, the word "fundamental" comes from the word "foundation," and a foundation is a bedrock or belief structure upon which something is built. When one follows the fundamental teachings of his or her god, is that really radical? It is a generally accepted thought that those who pick and choose which parts of their religion they wish to accept or reject are the radicals and apostates. Remember, this is one of the last admonitions given to Muhammad, which replaces all the peaceful conciliatory passages given before it (including those conciliatory passages we read earlier in this sûrah that were given before this militant revelation).

On the other hand, the God of the Bible went out of His way to prevent warfare. He sent Jonah to Nineveh to warn them to repent so they would not be destroyed. He told Abraham that He would spare Sodom for the sake of ten good people. God also told Abraham that his descendants would have to wait four hundred years before they or their children would be able to inhabit the land of Canaan because the sin of the Amorites had not risen to the point where a just God would allow them to be destroyed.

As Jesus said, when speaking to His disciples:

> But I say unto you, "Love your enemies, bless them that curse you, do good to them that hate you, and pray for them which despitefully use you, and persecute you" (Matthew 5:44).

(2:217) They question you (O Muhammad) with regard to warfare in the sacred month. Say: "Warfare therein is a great (transgression), but to turn (men) from the way of Allah, and to disbelieve in Him and in the Inviolable [sacred] Place of Worship [the Ka'aba in Mecca], and to expel His people thence [accordingly], is a greater sin with Allah; for persecution is worse than killing. And they will not cease from fighting against you till they have made you renegades from your religion, if they can. And whoso[ever] becomes a renegade and dies in his disbelief: such are they whose works have fallen both in the world and the Hereafter. Such are rightful owners of the Fire: they will abide therein" (bracketed clarifications mine).

This is a revelation given to Muhammad when he sent out a small group of eight men, disguised as pilgrims with shaved heads on a reconnaissance mission. When a Meccan caravan was discovered, they attacked the caravan in order to take their merchandise and hostages. In the midst of the battle, a man was killed, and to make matters worse, it was during the Pagan Holy Month of Rajab.

Because of that mishap, Muhammad found himself in a difficult situation since it was forbidden to fight and especially forbidden to kill anyone during the Holy Month (Sûrah 2:194). What could Muhammad have done? He was responsible for sending those men out on their spy mission, yet he could not have afforded to lose face among his followers or the other tribes, so he appealed to Allah for absolution.

Once again, Muhammad was not disappointed because Allah came to his aid and offered the Prophet of Islam a way out by revealing this verse, which absolved him from any wrongdoing.

Still, because the people were aware of Muhammad's military adventures (and killing) during the "sacred months," they confronted him about his transgression. Muhammad confirmed that killing was forbidden during the Holy Month, with one exception provided by Allah.

Allah always bailed Muhammad out of sticky situations,[34] and this time was no exception. Because Muhammad's scouting party had shaved their heads to pretend they were pilgrims, he could explain the attacks on the caravan, and the death that ensued was not a violation of the longstanding tribal cessation of hostilities during the holy month. Allah proclaimed, in Muhammad's defense that:

An even "greater sin" is to turn Muslim pilgrims away from honoring Allah by preventing them from worshiping Allah or practicing their Muslim faith. Forbidding the worship of Allah was [and still is today] an even worse transgression than killing others in battle. If those disbelievers were to attack a Muslim [never mind in this case because it was the Muslims pretending to be pilgrims who attacked the Pagans], they were to slaughter all of them; if any Muslim turned from his faith and died with the disbelievers, that individual would go to Hell (paraphrase and bracketed clarifications mine)[35]

CONSIDER: When Muhammad's child bride, 'Aisha, reflected on how Allah allowed an exception for Muhammad to have as many wives as he wanted—while other men could only have four—she was probably thinking about those events (and other situations). It seemed when the Prophet of Islam encountered difficulties, Allah always came up with a *new* revelation, which bailed him out of trouble). When commenting on Sûrah 33:51, where Allah gave Muhammad permission to have any woman he wanted, 'Aisha stated, "*I feel that your Lord hastens in fulfilling your wishes and desires*" [i.e., "I feel your Lord can refuse you nothing"] (Hadith Sahih Bukhari, Vol. 6, Book 60 Hadith, Number 311, bracketed clarification mine.)

(2:218) Look! those who believe, and those who emigrate (to escape the persecution) and strive in the way of Allah, these have hope of Allah's mercy. Allah is Forgiving, Merciful.

For the Muslim refugees who are forced to migrate or fight in the cause of Allah and seek refuge because of their Muslim faith, Gabriel is assuring them they have the promise of hope, and Allah will show mercy toward them.

(2:219) They question you about strong drink and games of chance. Say: "In both is great sin, and (some) utility [benefit] for men; but the sin of them is greater than their usefulness." And they ask you what they ought to spend. Say: "that which is superfluous." Thus Allah makes plain to you (His) revelations, that haply [by chance] you may reflect [upon it] (bracketed clarifications mine).

Muhammad is now moving toward morally relevant Islamic doctrine. For Muslims, drinking alcohol and gambling is considered sinful, yet while Allah acknowledges that there could possibly be some benefit to having a small drink and gambling a little, the sinfulness far outweighs the benefits; therefore, Islam does not allow any drinking of alcohol or gambling in order for a Muslim to be assured of having a better life. If a Muslim has extra money, they are to spend it wisely.

(2:220) Upon the world and the Hereafter. And they question thee concerning orphans. Say: "To improve their lot is best. And if you mingle your affairs with theirs, then (they are) your brothers." Allah knows him who spoils from him who improves. Had Allah willed He could have overburdened you. Allah is Mighty, Wise.

It is a good work to take an orphan into your care and protect that child. (Muhammad was completely orphaned by the age of six, and if it was not for his Uncle Abu Talib, he might have wound up on the streets of Mecca as a beggar child or worse). Allah knows who is caring for the orphans and those who would use the poor orphan for their own gain. According to this verse, remember that you too could be in a bad way if Allah so chooses.

(2:221) Wed not idolatresses till they believe; for indeed! a believing bondwoman is better than an idolatress though she please you; and give not your daughters in marriage to idolaters till they believe, for indeed! a believing slave is better than an idolater though he please you. These invite unto the Fire, and Allah invites unto the Garden, and

unto forgiveness by His grace, and expounds His revelations to mankind that haply [by chance] they may remember.

During the time of Muhammad, the various tribes on the Arabian Peninsula believed in 360 Pagan gods (Allah, the moon god, was one) whose images they worshiped. Allah is telling Muhammad that marrying an unbelieving (idol-worshipping) woman is forbidden. He even goes so far as to say that intimacy with a Muslim slave is more preferred than being legally married to an unbeliever. It is also forbidden for a father to allow his daughter to marry an unbeliever. This verse goes on to say that to do any of these things will put the offender in Hell; however, if one follows Islamic law, he will receive the promise of blessed joy.

OBSERVATION: There are many explanations regarding the symbol of the crescent moon and star in Islam. The following is one of the more charming explanations. In the ancient, polytheist religions of the Arab peninsula, the moon god, Allah, had three daughters. They were Manat, al-Lat, and al-Uzza (Sûrah 53). One tradition is Al-Uzza (i.e., "the Mighty One") as the goddess of both the evening and morning star (Venus). We see her embraced by her father, Allah, in the crescent moon and star symbol of Islam (☪), which appears on the top of mosques, as well as on the flags of many Islamic countries. Nevertheless, whether or not Allah is the moon god has no bearing on the teachings of Islam and, therefore, is just interesting trivia.

NOTE: There has been a lot of revisionist history about Islam since 9/11 by Muslims who seek to justify the negative points about their religion. In researching Islam you will find all sorts of pseudo-historical justifications, along with the use of peaceful verses (that have been used to counter the more

(2:222) They question you (O Muhammad) concerning menstruation. Say: "It is an illness, so let women alone at such times and go not in unto them till they are cleansed. And when they have purified themselves, then go in unto them as Allah hath enjoined upon you."

176

Truly Allah loves those who turn unto Him, and loves those who have a care for cleanness.

Observers might question the koranic pronouncement of a woman's period as an illness because—medically—it is not. Menstruation is an incredible female bodily mechanism, which cycles a new ovum (egg) every month and cleanses the womb while preparing for the next ovum cycle and the possibility of conceiving a new life. This is, at the very least, an astounding synchronized design for procreation.

The concept of a microscopic human egg during the seventh century was unknown. The general thought was that when a man planted his seed in a woman, her womb acted similarly to fertile soil in which the seed would grow; consequently, it would be centuries before the process of conception to birth was fully understood.

Still, the Creator of the process is God, so it is a bit curious that Allah, if he is who he claims he is, should know a woman's cycle is created, as well as knowing that a pathogen, which is the cause of diseases, is not involved in the process. However, we can agree that most religions like Islam and Judeo-Christian theology teach that one should abstain from intimate relations during the menstrual flow.

(2:223) Your women are a tilth [fertile soil] for you (to cultivate) so go to your tilth as you will, and send (good deeds) before you for your souls, and fear Allah, and know that you will (one day) meet Him. Give glad tidings to believers, (O Muhammad) (bracketed clarification mine).

Gabriel is allowing for Muhammad and other Muslim men to enjoy their women. The Bible talks about the patriarchs and Israel's kings having more than one wife and concubines, but the Bible does not teach that God approved of—or encouraged—more than one wife per man:

Therefore shall a man leave his father and his mother, and shall cleave unto his wife: and they shall be one flesh (Genesis 2:24).

If any be blameless, the husband of one wife ... (Titus 1:6a).

Nevertheless, because of sexual immorality, let each man have his own wife, and let each woman have her own husband (1 Corinthians 7:2).

While it is true that the Kings of Israel had many wives, the God of the Bible never approved of it. He made it very clear that even the king should have only one wife:

Neither shall he [the king] multiply wives to himself, that his heart turns not away (Deuteronomy 17:17a, bracketed clarification mine).

It is important to repeat that the Bible does not hide the custom of multiple wives and the possession of slaves, but it never approves of such practices; rather it recognizes its reality and instructs those who practice those cultural traditions to humanely deal with them for the sake of their wives and slaves.

As we see in koranic verse 2:223, Allah approves of multiple wives and encourages men to have sexual relations with their wives whenever they want, but before they do, they are expected to do good deeds toward fellow believers and fear Allah, so Allah will bless them when they appear before him.

(2:224) And make not Allah, by your oaths, a hindrance to your being righteous and observing your duty unto Him and making peace among mankind. Allah is Hearer, Knower.

When swearing an oath in Allah's name, Muslims have to make sure it is for a righteous reason, not just a kneejerk reaction; otherwise, they will be held accountable for what they have sworn. Traditionally, Sharia Law supersedes any manmade law or constitution by which a Muslim must swear to an oath. In the same way, if a Muslim is bound by law to swear to an oath for the sake of ascending to a position of authority in a non-Muslim country, Allah will not hold that Muslim accountable for breaking that oath if it will aid in the establishment of Islam.

Muslims are to be righteous, peacemakers, and always do good deeds (notwithstanding the jihadist passages which abrogate the conciliatory passages). Allah is aware of what they do.

We would like to point out here, unlike what we just read in the Koran, the Bible teaches that Christians should not swear by anything in Heaven (which includes God) or on earth:

> But above all things, my brethren, swear not, neither by Heaven, neither by the earth, neither by any other oath: but let your yea be yea; and your nay, nay; lest you fall into condemnation (James 5:12).

(2:225) Allah will not take you to task for that which is unintentional in your oaths. But He will take you to task for that which your hearts have garnered. Allah is Forgiving, Clement [merciful] (bracketed clarification mine).

Pickthall is unclear with his translation, which says, "... *which your hearts have garnered.*" Out of the three translations we referenced, Yusuf Ali clarifies it best when he writes, "... *the intention in your hearts.*"

This is a continuation of the previous verse. Allah is forgiving and understands that sometimes people might invoke his name by accident, but a more important issue for Allah is what their hearts intended.

Once again, contrast this verse with one in the Bible, which says:

> You shall not take the name of the LORD your God in vain; for the LORD will not hold him guiltless that takes His name in vain (Exodus 20:7).

179

Again you have heard that it was said to the people long ago, "Do not break your oath, but fulfill to the Lord the vows you have made. But I tell you, do not swear an oath at all: either by Heaven, for it is God's throne; or by the earth, for it is his footstool; or by Jerusalem, for it is the city of the Great King. And do not swear by your head, for you cannot make even one hair white or black. All you need to say is simply 'Yes' or 'No;' anything beyond this comes from the evil one" (Matthew 5:33-37, NIV).

(2:226) Those who forswear [disown] their wives must wait [abstain from sex] four months; then, if they change their mind, indeed! Allah is Forgiving, Merciful (bracketed clarifications mine).

This verse begins the section of Surah 2, which deals with Sharia Laws governing husbands, wives, and divorce. While Islam is mainly geared toward men, there are some open-minded concepts regarding women, especially considering the period of time (seventh century) when the laws were given.

If a husband and wife want to abstain from sex for a while or have a trial divorce, they should do it for no longer than four months. However, if the husband cannot control himself and desires to have intimate relations with his wife before the allotted time of abstinence (or trial divorce) has been completed, Allah understands. He can return to her with no harm done.

(2:227) And if they decide upon divorce (let them remember that) Allah is Hearer, Knower.

> *If, however, they decide to divorce, then they should follow through and not play games with each other because Allah does not approve of such behavior and is keeping track of what they do (Sûrah 2:227, paraphrase mine).*

(2:228) Women who are divorced shall wait, keeping themselves apart, three (monthly) courses. And it is not lawful for them that they should conceal that which Allah has created in their wombs if they are believers in Allah and the Last Day. And their husbands would do

better to take them back in that case if they desire a reconciliation. And they (women) have rights similar to those (of men) over them in kindness, and men are a degree above them. Allah is Mighty, Wise.

This verse, which is a continuation of the preceding verses, is part of Islamic Sharia Law regarding divorce. It is a common-sense approach to safeguard a man's family if the woman unknowingly becomes pregnant by her husband before their separation. We have broken this verse into three sections.

1. After a separation occurs, Muslim women are required to abstain from having sex. It also warns a woman that if she discovers she is pregnant, she should not hide it just because she wants to get away from her husband.
2. If it is discovered, during the time of abstinence, that the woman is pregnant, she is advised by Allah that it would be preferable for them to resume their marriage, although it is not demanded.
3. While women have rights, *"men are a degree above them"* because they are at a better advantage (property, power, finances, etc.) than women.

(2:229) Divorce must be pronounced twice and then (a woman) must be retained in honour or released in kindness. And it is not lawful for you that you take from women aught [anything] of that which you have given them; except (in the case) when both fear that they may not be able to keep within the limits (imposed by) Allah. And if you fear that they may not be able to keep the limits of Allah, in that case it is no sin for either of them if the woman ransom herself. These are the limits (imposed by) Allah. Transgress them not. For whoso transgresses Allah's limits: such are wrong-doers (bracketed clarification mine).

Again, we have an unusually progressive attitude toward women in light of the overall worldview during the seventh century. Men are to treat a woman with respect, whether or not they reconcile, and men should not demand back the things they gave to their wives during their marriage, with few exceptions; one is if the woman is so unhappy with her husband that she is willing to buy herself back from him. Another exception is if the wife is unfaithful (not necessarily in a sexual manner) because she criticizes her husband in matters of finance, belittling her husband, etc. The Muslim couple is required to honor this law because Allah is the one who imposes it.

(2:230) And if he has divorced her (the third time), then she is not lawful unto him thereafter until she has wedded another husband. Then if he (the other husband) divorce[s] her it is no sin for both of them that they come together again if they consider that they are able to observe the limits of Allah. These are the limits of Allah. He manifests them for people who have knowledge (bracketed clarification mine).

After a Muslim man and woman are divorced, she is legally her own until she marries another man.

Within the proper time of separation previously mentioned (three months), she is free to marry someone else; however, if her second marriage ends in a divorce, she and her first husband are free to remarry if she is not put under duress to do so (see Sûrah 2:232 below).

(2:231) When you have divorced women, and they have reached their term, then retain them in kindness or release them in kindness. Retain them not to their hurt so that you transgress (the limits). He who does that has wronged his soul. Make not the revelations of Allah a laughing-stock (by your behaviour), but remember Allah's grace upon you and that which He has revealed unto you of the Scripture and of wisdom, whereby He does exhort you. Observe your duty to Allah and know that Allah is Aware of all things.

This is recapping the three months of probationary separation when a husband may either take his wife back or release her; however, if they stay married, he has to treat her with respect and not make her life miserable because it would reflect badly on Allah and the entire Muslim community. The husband is forewarned against this type of bad behavior. He cannot plead ignorance because Allah has enshrined his laws in both the Koran and through wisdom. It is every Muslim's sacred duty to be aware of what is written.

(2:232) And when you have divorced women and they reach their term, place not difficulties in the way of their marrying their husbands if it is agreed between them in kindness. This is an admonition for him among you who believes in Allah and the Last Day. That is more virtuous for you, and cleaner. Allah know; you know not.

This is the third mention of once the woman has observed the three months of separation period (making sure she is not pregnant), she is free to leave, and no one should prevent her from remarrying her husband or any other man; that includes her former husband if they mutually want to reconcile, and she is not forced into it.

(2:233) Mothers shall suckle their children for two whole years; (that is) for those who wish to complete the suckling. The duty of feeding and clothing nursing mothers in a seemly manner is upon the father of the child. No one should be charged beyond his capacity. A mother should not be made to suffer because of her child, nor should he to whom the child is born (be made to suffer) because of his child. And on the (father's) heir is incumbent the like of that (which was incumbent on the father). If they desire to wean the child by mutual consent and (after) consultation, it is no sin for them; and if you wish to give your children out to nurse, it is no sin for you, provide that you pay what is due from you in kindness. Observe your duty to Allah, and know that Allah is Seer of what you do.

Muslim children must be breast-fed until the age of two for parents who equally agree; however, for various reasons, with permission from the father, the mother can elect to hire a nursemaid (not unlike what Pharaoh's daughter did with Moses when she found him as a baby). If nursing the baby causes physical or other problems for the mother, the father cannot unreasonably force her to continue nursing. The father is also responsible for providing all the necessities for the well-being of his wife and children. When the children become adults, and their father might need care, the children are to look after the father.

(2:234) Such of you as die and leave behind them wives, they (the wives) shall wait, keeping themselves apart, four months and ten

days. And when they reach the term (prescribed for them) then there is no sin for you in aught [anything] that they may do with themselves in decency. Allah is informed of what you do.

If the wife is left a widow, she is obligated to be respectful of her late husband and herself and remain celibate for four months and ten days, at which time she is free to modestly enter into another honorable relationship. Allah is aware of what she does.

(2:235) There is no sin for you in that which you proclaim or hide in your minds concerning your troth with women. Allah knows that you will remember them. But plight not [do not create unnecessary burdens on] your troth [fiancé] with women except by uttering a recognised form of words. And do not consummate the marriage until (the term) prescribed is run. Know that Allah knows what is in your minds, so beware of Him; and know that Allah is Forgiving, Clement [merciful] (bracketed clarifications mine).

> *There is nothing wrong with falling in love. A man's desire for a woman is a natural thing; however, a man should not consummate his desire toward a woman outside of marriage because Allah sees everything he does, and he will be held accountable for his actions. A Muslim man is to be clear regarding his intent to marry and proclaim his love for a woman by abstaining and remaining chaste toward her until they can have a ceremony blessed by the community and Allah. Allah is especially aware of how men will tell a woman they want to marry them in order to have sex—"And do not consummate the marriage until (the term) prescribed is run" (paraphrase and bracketed clarification mine).*

(2:236) It is no sin for you if you divorce women while yet you have not touched them, nor appointed unto them a portion. Provide for them, the rich according to his means, and the straitened [for the financially poor] according to his means, a fair provision. (This is) a bounden duty for those who do good (bracketed clarification mine).

If a man has second thoughts after becoming engaged to a woman (although in all four of the translations we used, this passage says "women" and continues to refer to them in the plural) and has not had sex with her, it is all right for him to back out of the marriage commitment; however, the woman is entitled to just compensation, and it should be commensurate with the financial standing of the man. A wealthy man should be generous, but a poor man cannot bankrupt himself, should give as generously as he is able. In the eyes of their families and community, this parting gift is a just burden for the man who rejects the woman he once promised to marry.

In the Old Testament, we read that God hates divorce:

"For the LORD *God of Israel says That He hates divorce,* For it covers one's garment with violence," says the LORD of hosts [angelic armies]. "Therefore take heed to your spirit, That you do not deal treacherously" (Malachi 2:16, NKIV, emphasis added).

The issue of divorce is also addressed in the New Testament by Jesus *(Isa)*:

Some Pharisees came to Him to test Him. They asked, "Is it lawful for a man to divorce his wife for any and every reason?"

"Haven't you read," he replied, "that at the beginning the Creator made them 'male and female,' and said, 'For this reason, a man will leave his father and mother and be united to his wife, and the two will become one flesh' ? So they are no longer two, but one flesh. Therefore what God has joined together, let no one separate."

"Why then," they asked, "did Moses command that a man give his wife a certificate of divorce and send her away?"
Jesus replied, "Moses permitted you to divorce your wives because your hearts were hard. But it was not this way from the beginning. I tell you that anyone who divorces his wife, except for sexual immorality, and marries another woman commits adultery" (Matthew 19:3-9, NIV).

(2:237) If you divorce them before you have touched them and you have appointed unto them a portion, then (pay the) half of that which you appointed, unless they (the women) agree to forgo it, or he agrees to forgo it in whose hand is the marriage tie [the bridegroom]. To

forgo is nearer to piety. And forget not kindness among yourselves. Allah is Seer of what you do (bracketed clarification Pickthall's footnote).

If a man marries, he is required to provide his wife with a customary dowry; however, if he changes his mind regarding marriage and has not had an intimate relationship with her, it is his obligation to do the honorable thing, which is to pay her half of the dowry, unless she refuses to accept it, in which case he pays nothing.

(2:238) Be guardians of your prayers, and of the midmost prayer, and stand up with devotion to Allah.

Muslims have to follow prescribed hours and holy days of prayer as well as be diligent in studying the faith. As for the *"midmost prayer,"* that would be one of their five required daily prayers. No one has been able to say exactly which one of the prayers this verse references, but Muslim scholars have narrowed it down to the noon or afternoon prayer, with most of them agreeing it is probably the afternoon prayer.

(2:239) And if you go in fear, then (pray) standing or on horseback. And when you are again in safety, remember Allah, as He has taught you that which (heretofore) you knew not.

When Muslims are in warfare, whether they are standing guard or on horseback, they are still required to pray; however, when they are safe from a battle, they should pray in a manner prescribed (preparing for prayer with ritual cleansing, bowing with their forehead and nose touching the ground while facing toward Mecca).

(2:240) (In the case of) those of you who are about to die and leave behind them wives, they should bequeath unto their wives a provision for the year without turning them out, but if they go out (of their own accord) there is no sin for you in that which they do of themselves within their rights. Allah is Mighty, Wise.

While common consideration in the western world in today's society, this verse is one of the more enlightened Islamic passages concerning women living in the Mideast during the seventh century. It basically states that when a man knows he is going to die or is going off to war, he has to get all of his things in order. He must also be certain to provide a year's worth of supplies and money for his wives unless they want to find a safer place on their own (i.e., parent's home or other family members, etc.) and forego their provisions. If they relinquish the man's generosity, it will not be held against the man because his wives are free to do what they want.

(2:241) For divorced women a provision in kindness: a duty for those who ward off (evil).

This is another passage that is very enlightened for seventh-century women in the Middle East since it allows for a divorced woman to be compensated and taken care of based on how long she was married and how well she served her husband. This is offered to her out of respect and will assure that the husband will be able to keep evil at bay.

(2:242) Thus Allah expounded unto you His revelations so that you may understand.

A.J. Arberry translates this passage:

> *So God makes clear His signs for you; haply [by chance] you will understand (bracketed clarification mine).*

Allah has laid out his desire for the behavior of his followers so they can benefit from his wisdom.

(2:243) Bethink [Remember] you (O Muhammad) of those of old, who went forth from their habitations in their thousands, fearing death, and Allah said unto them: Die; and then He brought them back to life. See! Allah is a Lord of Kindness to mankind, but most of mankind give not thanks.

This passage encourages Muslims not to be afraid of dying; they should be courageous, not cowards. Some Islamic scholars suggest this is referring to the ancient Hebrews who left their homes in Egypt because they feared death from the plagues. This seems to be the case when we read three verses later in verse 246, the reference to the Jews in Egypt promising to fight but then fearing to do so.

As for the thousands Allah killed and then restored to life, that is simply a metaphor, possibly referring to the Hebrews who were punished by

God for not taking the Promised Land; they were condemned to wander in the desert for 40 years (Numbers 14:34) until all who were afraid to enter the Holy Land had died (Numbers 13; 14; 32:9-13; Joshua 5:6). Therefore, the thousands who died were those who rebelled against God. The thousands Allah brought back to life were those who had not rebelled against God, had any memory of Egypt, and would willingly go into Canaan and possess the land.

Consequently, as we see in the next verse, this passage might be intended as words of encouragement for Muslims who will become warriors of Islam, but are afraid of being killed in battle. Allah will protect those who serve and who are obedient to him, thus reassuring those who are now afraid to fight for the cause that dying in a jihad guarantees them life in paradise.

(2:244) Fight in the way of Allah, and know that Allah is Hearer, Knower.
War is a way of life for the fearless Muslim hordes. It is Allah's way, but Muslims should not fear because he is watching over them.

(2:245) Who is it that will lend unto Allah a goodly [generous] loan, so that He may give it increase manifold? Allah straitens [restricts] and enlarges [increases]. Unto Him you will return (bracketed clarifications mine).

Yusuf Ali states it this way:

> *Who is he that will loan to Allah a beautiful loan, which Allah will double unto his credit and multiply many times? It is Allah that gives (you) Want or plenty, and to Him shall be your return. Who is it that will lend unto Allah a goodly [generous] loan, so that He may give it increase manifold? Allah straitens [restricts] and enlarges. Unto Him, you will return (bracketed clarification mine).*

This goodly or beautiful loan to Allah is not meant as a direct loan of money to Allah, but a Sharia financing principle that says a loan should be made without interest among Muslims. By doing so, it is the same as if one was loaning money to Allah. Sharia banking has now been incorporated into most banking houses in the United States of America as a special accommodation for Muslims.[36]

This is reminiscent of the Gospel of Luke, where believers are encouraged to be financially generous because God will be generous to them, but unlike the Koran, the Bible is couched in verses of peace, not war. The Bible teaches that blessings are to be shared with others and not used to buy God's favor because He does not need our money or gifts.

 But love your enemies, do good to them, and lend to them without expecting to get anything back. Then your reward will be great, and you will be children of the Most High, because he is kind to the ungrateful and wicked.

Be merciful, just as your Father is merciful. Do not judge, and you will not be judged. Do not condemn, and you will not be condemned. Forgive, and you will be forgiven.

Give, and it will be given to you. A good measure, pressed down, shaken together and running over, will be poured into your lap. For with the measure you use, it will be measured to you (Luke 6:35-38, NIV).

(2:246) Bethink [Remember] you of the leaders of the Children of Israel after Moses, how they said unto a prophet whom they had: Set up for us a king and we will fight in Allah's way. He said: "Would you then refrain from fighting if fighting were prescribed for you?" They said: "Why should we not fight in Allah's way when we have been driven from our dwellings with our children?" Yet, when fighting was prescribed for them, they turned away, all save a few of them. Allah is aware of evil-doers (bracketed clarification mine).

This passage seems to be combining (which is not uncommon in the Koran) two unrelated Bible stories separated from each other by over a generation. King Saul is the king referred to first in this passage where we read, "...they said unto a prophet whom they had: 'Set up for us a king and we will fight in Allah's way' " The prophet here was Samuel and this incident actually came *after* the event referred to where we read, "*...when fighting was prescribed for them, they turned away, all save a few of them.*" The few Israelites being mentioned here preceded Saul becoming Israel's first king when Gideon's small band of 300 men defeated the Midianites. Let's take a closer look at the first part of this passage, which refers to 1 Samuel, Chapter 8, when the tribes of Israel asked the prophet, Samuel, to give them a King.

Israel did desire a king, but it was not for the purpose of fighting holy wars. It was because they wanted to be like all the other kingdoms who had leaders they could physically see. Prophets were fine, but an invisible God was another story. Even the Pagans had idols who could be seen and touched. In this case, the prophet was Samuel, and below is the biblical story presented in context:

When Samuel grew old, he appointed his sons as Israel's leaders. The name of his firstborn was Joel, and the name of his second was Abijah, and they served at Beersheba. But his sons did not follow his ways. They turned aside after dishonest gain and accepted bribes and perverted justice.

So all the elders of Israel gathered together and came to Samuel at Ramah. They said to him, "You are old, and your sons do not follow your ways; now appoint a king to lead us, such as all the other nations have."

But when they said, "Give us a king to lead us," this displeased Samuel; so he prayed to the LORD. And the LORD told him: "Listen to all that the people are saying to you; it is not you they have rejected, but they have rejected me as their king. As they have done from the day I brought them up out of Egypt until this day, forsaking me and serving other gods, so they are doing to you. Now listen to them; but warn them solemnly and let them know what the king who will reign over them will claim as his rights."

Samuel told all the words of the LORD to the people who were asking him for a king. He said, "This is what the king who will reign over you will claim as his rights: He will take your sons and make them serve with his chariots and horses, and they will run in front of his chariots. Some he will assign to be commanders of thousands and commanders of fifties, and others to plow his ground and reap his harvest, and still others to make weapons of war and equipment for his chariots.

"He will take your daughters to be perfumers and cooks and bakers. He will take the best of your fields and vineyards and olive groves and give them to his attendants. He will take a tenth of your grain and of your vintage and give it to his officials and attendants. Your male and female servants and the best of your cattle and donkeys he will take for his own use. He will take a tenth of your flocks, and you yourselves will become his slaves. When that day comes, you will cry out for relief from the king you have chosen, but the LORD will not answer you in that day."

But the people refused to listen to Samuel. "No!" they said. "We want a king over us. Then we will be like all the other nations, with a king to lead us and to go out before us and fight our battles" (1 Samuel 8:1-20, NIV).

The last part of Sûrah 2:246 states, *"...they turned away all save a few of them,"* which seems to be confusing the biblical story of Gideon, who won a war against the Midianites with a small band of 300 men. That historical account is found in Judges, Chapter 7, where Gideon was facing a large army of Midianites against his approximately 32,000 Israelis. Nevertheless, some of the men were afraid, so God had Gideon tell the men that those who were afraid could return home, leaving only 10,000 Israelites willing to fight (Judges 7:3).

During that time, or ever in the history of Israel, they did not have a human king; it had been a theocracy (ruled by God). Israel was ruled by God's authority through His prophets and leaders of the people; they were known as "judges." Because of the prideful boasting of the Israelites, God told Gideon, who was a judge of Israel at the time, to reduce the number of fighting men even more:

But the LORD said to Gideon, "The people *are* still *too* many; bring them down to the water, and I will test them for you there...."Everyone who laps from the

191

water with his tongue, as a dog laps, you shall set apart by himself... And the number of those who lapped, *putting* their hand to their mouth, was three hundred men; but all the rest of the people got down on their knees to drink water.... "By the three hundred men who lapped I will save you, and deliver the Midianites into your hand. Let all the *other* people go, every man to his place" (Judges 7:4-7, NKJV).

(2:247) Their Prophet said unto them: "Look! Allah has raised up Saul to be a king for you." They said: "How can he have kingdom over us when we are more deserving of the kingdom than he is, since he has not been given wealth enough?" He said: "Look! Allah has chosen him above you, and has increased him abundantly in wisdom and stature. Allah bestows His Sovereignty on whom He will. Allah is All-Embracing, All-Knowing."

Allah seems to have forgotten that the name of the prophet was Samuel. This is another Bible story with a distinctive koranic twist. The people never complained about the financial status of Saul, as the Koran states, because he was a simple man, and the time of great wealth would not start until after the monarchy began. As for the part of this verse, which states, "... *Allah has chosen him above you, and has increased him abundantly in wisdom and stature*," seems to be confusing Solomon, who was the third king of Israel, with King Saul, who was the first. Biblically, the Israelis were overjoyed to have a man of Saul's handsome and tall stature to reign over them.

The Bible states:

When Samuel had all Israel come forward by tribes, the tribe of Benjamin was taken by lot. Then he brought forward the tribe of Benjamin, clan by clan, and Matri's clan was taken. Finally Saul son of Kish was taken. But when they looked for him, he was not to be found. So they inquired further of the LORD, "Has the man come here yet?"

And the LORD said, "Yes, he has hidden himself among the supplies." They ran and brought him out, and as he stood among the people he was a head taller than any of the others. Samuel said to all the people, "Do you see the man the LORD has chosen? There is no one

192

like him among all the people." Then the people shouted, "Long live the king!" (1 Samuel 10:20 -24, NIV.)

As we stated above, the last part of this koranic passage where we read, *"Allah...has increased him abundantly in wisdom and stature,"* is more reminiscent of King David's son, Solomon, whose stature was filled with rich abundance from God, as well as receiving the gift of wisdom from God (1 Kings 3:5-13).

And God said to Solomon, Because this was in your heart, and you have not asked riches, wealth, or honor, nor the life of your enemies, neither yet has asked long life; but has asked wisdom and knowledge for yourself, that you may judge my people, over whom I have made you king: *Wisdom and knowledge* is granted unto you; and I will give you riches, and wealth and honor, such as none of the kings have had that have been before you, neither shall there any after you have the like (2 Chronicles 1:11-12, emphasis added).

(2:248) And their Prophet said unto them: Indeed! the token of his kingdom is that there shall come unto you the ark wherein is peace of reassurance from your Lord, and a remnant of that which the house of Moses and the house of Aaron left behind, the angels bearing it. See! herein shall be a token for you if (in truth) you are believers.

Once more, we have dialogue exclusive to the Koran. In the last part of this verse, we are told *"and a remnant of that which the house of Moses and the house of Aaron left behind, the angels bearing it."*

The Arc of the Covenant was always protected and maintained in good condition. The angels never carried, brought, or touched it at any time. It had an interior compartment that contained a golden pot (i.e., overlaid with gold (Hebrews 9:4); in the golden pot was mana (Exodus 16:31), along with the rod of Aaron, which blossomed (Numbers 17:5) and the original Ten Commandments (Exodus 25:16, 40:20; Hebrews 9:5).

The confusion about angels and the Ark of the Covenant might have been because it had two carved cherubim with outstretched wings facing each other on the top (Exodus 25:20). Even though the Levites never allowed the Ark of the Covenant to be out of their care, there were two exceptions. One time it fell into the hands of the Philistines (1 Samuel 5; 1 Samuel 6:1-10); another time was when the Ark sat upon a

cart pulled by oxen, and the oxen stumbled. To keep it from falling, an Israeli by the name of Uzzah reached out to steady it, but because Uzzah was not a Levite, he died the moment his hand touched the unstable Ark (1 Chronicles 13:9-12).

(2:249) And when Saul set out with the army, he said: "Indeed! Allah will try you by (the ordeal of) a river. Whosoever therefore drinks thereof he is not of me, and whosoever tastes it not he is of me, save him who takes (thereof) in the hollow of his hand." But they drank thereof, all save a few of them. And after he had crossed (the river), he and those who believed with him, they said: "We have no power this day against Goliath and his hosts." But those who knew that they would meet Allah [dying in a jihad is a guarantee of Islamic heaven] exclaimed: "How many a little company has overcome a mighty host by Allah's leave! Allah is with the steadfast [devoted]" (bracketed clarifications mine).

This is a continuation of verse 246 and the Koran's story of Gideon's battle with the Midianites being confused with Israel's encounter with the Philistines. The story being referred to here with the drinking of water test took place long before King Saul or the Philistine, Goliath, were even born! The method by which the men chose to drink the water (sip or gulp it) is not what is described in the Bible and had nothing to do with their loyalty to God because all the men were loyal to God.

When the battle spoken of here took place, the army that faced Israel was not the Philistines—as the Koran suggests—it was the Midianites. The story of the 300 men who sipped water from their hands rather than putting their faces to the pond drink as the others did, was centered on a man named Gideon, as we explained in the commentary

194

for verse 246. Gideon was a judge of Israel hundreds of years before the time of Israel's kings.

Because the Koran is repetitious, we must also be repetitious when addressing what is mistakenly taught here in light of the Bible. We have recapped the biblical story that the Koran wrongly incorporated:

> So Gideon took the men down to the water. There the LORD told him, "Separate those who lap the water with their tongues as a dog laps from those who kneel down to drink." Three hundred of them drank from cupped hands, lapping like dogs. All the rest got down on their knees to drink.

> The LORD said to Gideon, "With the three hundred men that lapped, I will save you and give the Midianites into your hands. Let all the others go home." So Gideon sent the rest of the Israelites home but kept the three hundred, who took over the provisions and trumpets of the others (Judges 7:5-8, NIV).

(2:250) And when they went into the field against Goliath and his hosts they said: "Our Lord! Bestow on us endurance, make our foothold sure, and give us help against the disbelieving folk."

The Koran is still confusing the two biblical stories of Gideon and Goliath. In the story where the Israeli army faced the Philistine army at a distance, they never took the field against Goliath because they were too afraid to face him and the Philistine army. We read in the Bible how Goliath taunted King Saul's "cowardly" Israeli army:

> Goliath stood and shouted to the ranks of Israel, "Why do you come out and line up for battle? Am I not a Philistine, and are you not the servants of Saul? Choose a man and have him come down to me. If he is able to fight and kill me, we will become your subjects; but if I overcome him and kill him, you will become our subjects and serve us." Then the Philistine said, "This day I defy the armies of Israel! Give me a man and let us fight each other." On hearing the

Philistine's words, Saul and all the Israelites were dismayed and terrified (1 Samuel 17:8-11, NIV).

(2:251) So they routed them by Allah's leave and David slew Goliath; and Allah gave him the kingdom and wisdom, and taught him of that which He willed. And if Allah had not repelled some men by others the earth would have been corrupted. But Allah is a Lord of Kindness to (His) creatures.

Gideon and his 300 troops routed the 135,000 Midianites army two and a half centuries earlier (Judges 7:20-22), but King Saul never engaged Goliath and the Philistine army head-on. Not only did King Saul not attack and "route" Goliath and the Philistine army, but the order of events of what actually happened is just the opposite in this revisionist, koranic version of the biblical story of David and Goliath.[37] The Bible teaches that the army of King Saul had nothing to do with the routing (retreat) of the Philistines. It was David—standing alone—who caused the Philistines to panic and take flight because he singlehandedly killed Goliath. The biblical story of David is as follows:

> Then he took his staff in his hand, chose five smooth stones from the stream, put them in the pouch of his shepherd's bag and, with his sling in his hand, approached the Philistine.

Meanwhile, the Philistine, with his shield-bearer in front of him, kept coming closer to David. He looked David over and saw that he was little more than a boy, glowing with health and handsome, and he despised him. He said to David, "Am I a dog that you come at me with sticks?" And the Philistine cursed David by his gods. "Come here," he said, "and I'll give your flesh to the birds and the wild animals!"

David said to the Philistine, "You come against me with sword and spear and javelin, but I come against you in the name of the LORD Almighty, the God of the armies of Israel, whom you have defied. This day the LORD will deliver you into my hands, and I'll strike you down and cut off your head. This very day I will give the carcasses of the Philistine army to the birds and the wild animals, and the whole world will know that there is a God in Israel. All those gathered here will know that it is not by sword or spear that the LORD saves; for the battle is the LORD's, and he will give all of you into our hands."As the Philistine moved closer to attack him, David ran quickly toward the battle line to meet him. Reaching into his bag and taking out a stone, he slung it and struck the Philistine on the forehead. The stone sank into his forehead, and he fell face down on the ground. So, David triumphed over the Philistine with a sling and a stone; without a sword in his hand, he struck down the Philistine and killed him (1 Samuel 17:40-50, NIV).

After David slew the giant Goliath, the Philistines turned and ran. Only then did the army of Saul pursue them:

When the Philistines saw that their hero was dead, they turned and ran. Then the men of Israel and Judah surged forward with a shout and pursued the Philistines to the entrance of Gath and to the gates of Ekron. Their dead were strewn along the Shaaraim road to Gath and Ekron (1 Samuel 17:51c-52, NIV).

(2:252) These are the portents [signs] of Allah which We recite unto you (Muhammad) with truth, and see! you are of the number of (Our) messengers.

Allah is claiming that he is speaking to Muhammad *"... with truth..., "* yet what we have been witnessing over the last several verses is nothing more than a blending of biblical stories and people, which in actuality, were separated by a century in time. Nevertheless, these verses are another perfect example of some of the anachronisms to be found in the Koran!

This verse concludes with Allah confirming that Muhammad is a part of the line of biblical prophets, probably for the benefit of the Jewish and Christian detractors.

(2:253) Of those messengers, some of whom We have caused to excel others, and of whom there are some unto whom Allah spoke, while some of them He exalted (above others) in degree; and We gave Jesus, son of Mary, clear proofs (of Allah's Sovereignty) and We supported

him with the Holy Spirit. And if Allah had so willed it, those who followed after them would not have fought one with another after the clear proofs had come unto them. But they differed, some of them believing and some disbelieving. And if Allah had so willed it, they would not have fought one with another; but Allah does what He will.

Two times Allah said he could have prevented the infighting with the "People of the Book" but chose not to stop them. One might wonder if the reason Allah did not intervene was that he either was not able or that he might have enjoyed the dissension between them. Once again, we have another attack on the Divinity of Jesus. This verse is suggesting that Allah sent out many prophets—some great—some not so great. One "prophet" who was elevated was Jesus, the "son of Mary." Muslims have trouble understanding the concept of the Trinity. They think that Christians believe what Mormons believe—that Mary was impregnated by God in the natural way (Brigham Young, Journal of Discourses, 8:115). To the Mormons and the Muslims, Mary was only a virgin in the carnal sense because she was not touched by a human, but was sexually impregnated by a spirit. According to the Koran, Muslims believe Christians teach that somehow God took Mary for a wife, and God and Mary's son, Jesus, became the third party "connected" to Allah (Sûrah 5:116; 28:62). This passage also inadvertently includes the third member of the Godhead, the Holy Spirit. (Remember, Islam denies the Trinity, even though the Koran shows ignorance of what Christians believe the Trinity to be. Muslims also vehemently and consistently deny any other associate connected to Allah).

Of course, this is not what Christians believe. While honoring Mary, they do not believe she became a goddess through a sexual liaison with God. Jesus took on the flesh of man (John 1:14), but He has existed since the beginning of time, eons before the Virgin Mary was born.

Before we explain how the Virgin Mary became pregnant, we must make a little detour to an event that shortly followed the Resurrection of Jesus.

His disciples gathered in an upper room, locking the door behind them. The room could only be accessed by stairs. One minute they were gathered all together in that locked room without Christ—and the next instant, from out of nowhere, Jesus appeared in their midst (John 20:19-23; Luke 24:36-37). If the door was still locked, how did that happen?

The Bible is not clear on the matter, but many of you might recall a television series called "Star Trek," where the spaceship's engineer, "Scotty," could transport members of the crew from the Starship Enterprise to a selected spot on a planet or transported across space into another starship. If Jesus could suddenly appear in the upper room as a solid, fully human being and not a ghost, His spirit could have just as easily been transported and fused into Mary's ovum while He was still in spiritual form as a member of the Godhead; thus, He would avail Himself of the egg in Mary's womb to provide Himself with the perfect catalyst necessary to be fully God and fully man, born of a virgin as prophesied hundreds of years before (Isaiah 7:14)

...Christ Jesus: Who, being in very nature God [the second co-equal person of the Godhead], did not consider equality with God something to be used to His own advantage [willing to give up His exalted position]; rather, He made Himself nothing [gave up His co-equal position in the Trinity] by taking the very nature of a servant [putting Himself in the lower role of a Son subjected to His Father], being made in human likeness [by taking up residency in Mary's ovum] (Philippians 2:5-7, NIV).

The last part of verse 253 states that while Christians and Jews argue over the Scriptures, *"And if Allah had so willed it, they would not have fought one with another."* Subsequently, we are told that Allah could have intervened and settled the split between Jews and Christians if he had wanted to, but he didn't because Allah always did what he wanted to do, not what others wanted him to do; therefore, one can conclude that Allah was unjust not to clarify an honest debate between people who truly loved and wished to please him.

(2:254) O you who believe! Spend of that wherewith We have provided you ere [before] a day come when there will be no trafficking [marketing], nor friendship, nor intercession. The disbelievers, they are the wrong-doers (bracketed clarifications mine).

Once again, we have a verse unique to the Koran. This verse is discussing the final day when people will stand before God. There will be no intercession, a direct conflict with the teachings of Scripture that clearly state, "For there is one God and one mediator between God and men, the man Christ Jesus" (1 Timothy 2:5).

As we see in this biblical passage, Jesus is referred to as "...the man Christ Jesus." The Bible teaches that Jesus is fully man (Matthew 9:6) because He had human flesh from his mother; the Bible also teaches that Jesus is fully God (1 John 5:20) and without sin.

Concerning mankind, the sinful nature (which is not acknowledged by Islam) was the purpose of Christ coming to earth as a sacrificial Lamb of God to pay for our sins and overcome death for us through His resurrection.

As the Apostle Paul explains:

So will it be with the resurrection of the dead. The body that is sown is perishable, it is raised imperishable; It is sown in dishonor, it is raised in glory; It is sown in weakness, it is raised in power; It is sown a natural body; it is raised a spiritual body.

If there is a natural body, there is also a spiritual body. So it is written: "The first man Adam became a living being;" the last Adam [Jesus], a life-giving spirit." The spiritual did not come first, but the natural, and after that the spiritual. The first man was of the dust of the earth; the second man [Jesus] is of Heaven (1 Corinthians 15: 42-47, NIV, bracketed clarification mine).

A baby has a human spirit. Jesus, being God, always existed as a Divine Spiritual being, but chose to empty Himself out of the Godhead into an egg prepared for Him in Mary's womb. This was arranged, in part, so we could relate to God on our own level and know that God can relate to us in the same way. This also allowed us to know that God understands what it is like to be a human and face the uncertainties of life:

> Who, being in the form of God, thought it not robbery to be equal with God: But made Himself of no reputation, and took upon Him the form of a servant, and was made in the likeness of men.
> (Philippians 2:6-7, NIV).

Because Jesus is the Logos (reasoning) of God, He never had a father (progenitor) who preceded Him in the biological human and animal sense. He had always existed as God's reasoning (*Logos*); however, in order to relate to His mentally inferior creatures (human beings), God used a concept people could easily understand, the family structure, which is an authoritarian relationship between a father, a mother, and his children. Consequently, when the Logos (i.e., Greek for the Word of God, a Word not spoken or written but used in divine reasoning) inhabited a human body, He formed a unique composition—which combined the material world (fully man) and spiritual world (fully God). For this reason, Jesus always referred to YHWA (Yahweh) as His Father. We see this in Matthew 16:13-17, where Jesus acknowledged that He is both the Son of Man and the Son of God (see commentary for Sûrah 18:5).

CONSIDER: When a man and woman come together, a human child is formed. It is believed by many theologians that the curse of original sin (i.e., our sin nature) is passed down through the father, who is a son of Adam. Because Jesus did not have a human father, He did not inherit original sin. This is not to say that He was never tempted because Satan tempted Jesus (Matthew 4:1-11, Luke 4:1-13)—but even so—He never yielded to those sinful temptations and has remained the only sinless human being.

(2:255) Allah! There is no deity save Him, the Alive, the Eternal. Neither slumber nor sleep overtakes Him. Unto Him belongs whatsoever is in the heavens and whatsoever is in the earth. Who is he that intercedes with Him save by His leave? He knows that which

is in front of them and that which is behind them, while they encompass nothing of His knowledge save what He will. His throne includes the heavens and the earth, and He is never weary of preserving them. He is the Sublime, the Tremendous.

A.J. Arberry translates this passage:

> *God there is no god but He, the living, the Everlasting. Slumber sizes Him not, neither sleep; to Him belongs all that is in the heavens and earth. Who is there that shall intercede with Him save by His lead? He knows what lies before them and what is after them, and they comprehend not anything of His knowledge save as He wills. His throne comprises the heavens and earth; the preserving of them oppresses Him not; He is the All-high, the All-glorious.*

The second sentence of this passage is reminiscent of the Old Testament passage, which reads, "Behold, He that keeps Israel shall neither slumber nor sleep" (Psalm 121:4). It asks Muslims, *Who is he that intercedes with Him save by His leave?*" or as Abdullah Yusuf Ali translates it, *"Who is there can intercede in His presence except as He permits?"* This suggests to Muslims that Muhammad is the one Allah allows to intercede on their behalf. As the Islamic sage, Mir Taqi Mir wrote about himself,[38] "Why do you worry, O Mir, thinking of your black book [a book containing the names of those condemned]? The person of the Seal of the Prophets [Muhammad] is a guarantee for your salvation!" This verse, of course, is a flagrant inconsistency with the biblical declarations which proclaim:

Salvation is found in no one else, for there is no other name [Jesus] under Heaven given to mankind by which we must be saved (Acts 4:12, NIV).

You, then, why do you judge your brother or sister? Or why do you treat them with contempt? For we will all stand before God's judgment seat (Romans 14:10).

Jesus says unto him, "I am the way, the truth, and the life: no man comes unto [God] the Father, but by me" (John 14:6, bracketed clarification mine).

Therefore, God exalted Him to the highest place and gave Him the name above every name, that at the name of Jesus every knee should bow, in Heaven and on earth and under the earth, and every tongue acknowledge that Jesus Christ is Lord, to the glory of God the Father (Philippians 2:9-11, NIV).

Looking for that blessed hope, and the glorious appearing of the great God and our Savior Jesus Christ (Titus 2:13).

(2:256) There is no compulsion in religion. The right direction is henceforth distinct from error. And he who rejects false deities [Ar. طاغوت, ṭāġūt] and believes in Allah has grasped a firm handhold which will never break. Allah is Hearer, Knower (bracketed clarification mine).

Most of the twentieth-century English translators render the Arabic word *taghut* as meaning "satanic adversaries" or "rebel forces of Satan." In Pickthall's version, it is translated it as *"false deities;"* others translate *taghut* as meaning "rejects evil" or "disbelieves in the Shaitan [Satan]," which is less accurate than what is found in Arabic texts:

> *There is no compulsion in religion. True guidance has been made clearly distinct from error. Therefore, whoever renounce 'Taghut' (forces of Shaitan) and believes in Allah has grasped the firm hand-hold that will never break. Allah, Whose hand-hold you have grasped, hears all and knows all (Sûrah 2:256, Malik Al-Qur'an, clarification his).*

The majority of Islamic scholars agree that there are 6,236 verses in the Koran, yet this is the one verse used the most to "prove" Islam is a "peaceful religion." We are told in this passage that Muslims believe, *"There is no compulsion in religion."*

This text was also used to make that point by the National Geographic Magazine's December, 2001 edition, which—because of the nature of magazine publications written several months in advance—must have been written right after September 11, 2001, in order to promote the idea given by then-President George W. Bush that Islam is a "religion of peace." The problem is that the koranic "Verse of the Sword" (Sûrah 9:5) is just one of several jihadist verses found in the Koran–which abrogate (replace) the pleasant, conciliatory verse found here in Sûrah 2. It is used by Muslims and non-Muslims alike to "prove" that Islam is a "religion of peace." In defense of Sûrah 9, it was not written in the order in which it was placed in the Koran, like some defenders of Sûrah 2:256 would have us believe, but at a later date, thus, replacing Sûrah 2.[39]

Essentially, Sûrah 2:256 was an earlier verse and the 87th revelation given to Muhammad. After this conciliatory verse in Sûrah 2 was given to Muhammad, the prophet received a later verse, which not only reversed this particular verse, but it also reversed the other passive verses given to him up to that point in time. It wasn't until 26 revelations later, with the 113th revelation (the next to the last revelation given to Muhammad) when he received what is codified as Sûrah 9 in the Koran containing verse 5 known as the infamous "Verse of the Sword" passage which clearly states:

Then, when the sacred months have passed, then slay the idolaters wherever you find them, and take them (captive), and besiege them, and prepare for them each ambush. But if they repent and establish worship and pay the poor-due, then leave their way free. See! Allah is Forgiving, Merciful (Sûrah 9:5).

This also applies to the Islamic-perceived polytheistic Christians, who Muslims believe worship Jesus and His mother Mary as gods alongside Allah (Sûrah 5:116)

As we can see in Table 3, Sûrah 2 and all of its verses were in an earlier chapter given to Muhammad when he was weak. Sûrah 9 was a later chapter given when Muhammad and Islam were stronger; therefore,

Sûrah 9, verse 5 abrogates/replaces Sûrah 2, verse 256 (refer to Sûrah's order in Table 1, pages 17-20).

Table 3. Comparison of How Sûrah 9 Abrogates/Replaces Sûrah 2:

Koran Order	Actual Order	Sûrah Name	Verse Number:	City Received
Sûrah 2	87 Given Last	The Heifer/al-Baqara	286	Medina
Sûrah 9	113 Given First	Repentance/ At-Taubah	129	Medina

Still, many supporters of Islam have used this proof text to show that Islam is tolerant, despite the 114 jihadist verses arguing either disingenuously or out of ignorance that the second sûrah supersedes or abrogates any conflicting passages in the ninth sûrah. (Refer to Table 1 in the Introduction of this book.)

For the sake of argument, let's take a closer look at Sûrah 2:256, which begins, *"There is no compulsion [forcing] in religion."* This is open to various interpretations. By saying "there is no compulsion in religion," is this passage speaking to believers of other faiths who cannot be forced to accept Islam, as many Muslims insist, or is it referring to internal struggles concerning those who practice Islam? If it is speaking to Muslims regarding the doctrine of their own faith, then it is telling them there is no need to struggle against that which has already been settled by Allah. This makes sense, especially in light of the next verse, Sûrah 2:257.

Once Allah has given the final say on his revelations to Muhammad and changed (abrogated) the problems with previous revelations for something better (Sûrah 2:106), it is now complete or as the Koran states, *"The right direction is henceforth distinct from error,"* so there is no reason to question or change it.

Our current verse continues, *"And he who rejects false deities ... [Jews who do not accept Allah as the author of the Torah, Christians who believe in the Trinity and Christ as God, and Pagan gods] and believes in Allah has grasped a firm handhold which will never break. Allah is Hearer, Knower."*

Another possible explanation for a verse meant to teach tolerance, which has seemingly been ignored by some followers of Islam, could be explained by inadvertently misplacing it at some point in the Koran, perhaps by Caliph Uthman, the third Caliph in succession after the death of Muhammad. He commanded for all versions of the Koran, which differed from his copy, to be gathered up and sent to him to be burned. The burning of the various Korans (including the original one held by Muhammad's wife, Hafsah, which became known as the "Hafsah Codex") was destroyed somewhere around 644-656 A.D., but most likely in 651 A.D.

Either argument regarding this passage, suggesting that it was misplaced or misinterpreted, seems impossible in light of Islam's historical context as witnessed by the actions of Muhammad and those who followed him. Muslims who read and follow the Koran by implementing the violent teachings of Sûrah 9:29 rather than follow the more peaceful instructions found in Sûrah 2:256, which would make no sense if it were intended as a conciliatory passage toward those of other faiths. This paradoxical conflict becomes apparent when we read Sûrah 9:29.

> *Fight those who believe not in Allah nor the Last Day, nor hold that forbidden which has been forbidden by Allah and His Messenger, nor acknowledge the religion of Truth, [even if they are] of the People of the Book, until they pay the Jizya [a tribute tax for non-Muslims] with willing submission [to Islam], and feel themselves subdued [humbled before Islam] (Sûrah 9:29, Abdullah Yusuf Ali, bracketed clarifications mine).*

To be balanced, we must point out that even in Sûrah 9:29 above, while Bible believers ("People of the Book") are fair game to be subdued if they do not accept the religion of Islam, they are allowed—at the discretion of the Muslim conqueror—to escape death by becoming second class citizens (*dhimmi*) and subjected to extortion in order to live. They must also submit themselves to Islamic rule and Sharia Law. The extortion is in the form of a tribute tax known as *jizya*.

We also see in the Hadith, contrary to Sûrah 2:256, the explanation of this process:

> ... If they refuse to accept Islam, demand from them the Jizya. If they agree to pay, accept it from them and hold off your hands. If they refuse to pay the tax, seek Allah's help and fight them ... (Muslim: Book 19: Number 4294, approximately in the middle portion of the Hadith).

Thus, while the Koran suggests that Muslims cannot force their religion on others, they can still make life very unpleasant if they don't!

Perhaps this controversial passage is revealing that Muhammad came to the realization, while he could force people to give lip service to Islam, he could not force them to accept something inwardly if they did not believe it. Still, it would be wonderful if all Muslims, from the early Caliphs and Imams throughout the Middle Ages, up to and including today, would have interpreted Sûrah 2:256 as a conciliatory passage without the condition of subjugation or dhimmitude and allowed that interpretation to have played a more central role in their religion. Sadly, actions speak louder than words. Unfortunately, as we pointed out near the beginning of this conciliatory passage, it was abrogated by Sûrah 9:5, which was a later (92nd) revelation given to Muhammad after the earlier (87th) Sûrah 2:256 was revealed to him. Remember, when there are conflicting verses in the Koran, the last revelation is the one that takes precedence.

NOTE: It is possible that the reason for all of today's continued violence by Islamists can be found in the Bible where God describes the nature of Ishmael and his descendants:

And he (Ishmael) will be a wild man; his hand will be against every man, and every man's hand against him; and he shall dwell in the presence of all his brethren [Israel] (Genesis 16:12, bracketed clarification mind).

Maybe this is the reason why modern-day Muslims, regardless of which branch of Islam they belong to, attacked Israel when it was reborn on May 14, 1948. This might also explain the invention of a pseudo-nation known as "Palestine" (Ishmael's descendants) in the midst of Israel

(Ishmael's brethren), along with the Muslims' refusal to acknowledge Jerusalem as the capital of biblical Israel. This might also serve to explain all the ongoing jihads, boycotts, and continued state of war existing against the tiny nation of Israel.

(2:257) Allah is the Protector of those who have faith: from the depths of darkness He will lead them forth into light. Of those who reject faith the [their] patrons [Jewish, Christian, and Pagan gods] are the evil ones [devils]: from light [knowing Allah] they will lead them forth into the depths of darkness. They will be companions of the fire, to dwell therein (For ever). (Bracketed clarifications mine.)

Although this could be referring to Trinitarians (leading people of faith out of darkness into light), it is much more likely that it is talking about the Pagan Arabs of the Arabian Peninsula and surrounding countries. In the previous verse we were told, "There is no compulsion [forcing] in religion," yet in this verse, as well as other verses, we are told Allah controls who is or is not saved:

"Allah is the Protector of those who have faith: from the depths of darkness He will lead them forth into light." However, while "there is no compulsion in religion" (Surah 2:256), *"...those who reject faith the [their] patrons [Pagan and Christian gods] are the evil ones [devils] from light [knowing Allah] they will lead them forth into the depths of darkness"* (bracketed clarifications mine), and—as we are told in the last part of this verse—where it says, *They will be companions of the fire [Hell].* This seems unjust.

(2:258) Bethink [Remember] you of him [Nimrod] who had an argument with Abraham about his Lord, because Allah had given him the kingdom; how, when Abraham said: "My Lord is He who gives life and causes death," he answered:" I give life and cause death". Abraham said: "Look! Allah causes the sun to rise in the East, so do you cause it to come up from the West." Thus was the disbeliever bashed [ashamed]. And Allah guides not the wrong-doing folk (bracketed clarifications mine).

Muhammad Habib Shakir's translation is a little clearer:

Have you not considered him (Namrud) [Nimrod] who disputed with Ibrahim [Abraham] about his Lord, because Allah had given him the kingdom? When Ibrahim said: "My Lord is He who gives life and causes to die," he [Nimrod] said: "I give life and cause death." Ibrahim said: "So surely Allah causes the sun to rise from the east, then [can you] make it rise from the west;" thus he who disbelieved was confounded; and Allah does not guide aright the unjust people (bracketed clarifications mine).

To begin with, exactly what *"kingdom"* Allah is supposed to have given Abraham is not clear. We know it is not Shinar because Abraham left that region soon after continuing on his way to the Promised Land. Nimrod[40] was the king of Shinar who built the Tower of Babel sometime before 2200 B.C. Abraham was born around 1996 B.C. and lived 175 years (Genesis 25:7); he most likely died around 1821 B.C. Keep in mind, the numbering of years before 1 A.D. is mirrored (i.e., counted backward, which can cause some confusion).

In the spirit of fairness, there are several Hebrew and Islamic legends surrounding Nimrod and Abraham's interaction with each other, but nothing reliable. However, some of those legends are found in the Talmud and Midrash. A compendium of the Hebrew Oral Torah (i.e., Oral Law) and traditions began in the second century B.C., along with the Talmud and Midrash rabbinical works of the Middle Ages. The Koran and its story of Abraham and Nimrod were not written until the seventh century A.D. It seems this conversation between Nimrod and Abraham is probably another koranic anachronism drawn from Hebrew, as well as Arab, traditions developed after the second century A.D.[41]

For the sake of argument, assume this koranic story happened, as stated, by allowing for the time of Nimrod and Abraham—although doubtful—to be overlapped. By agreeing that Nimrod and Abraham might have lived at the same time, it is important to note that a story involving such a meeting does not appear anywhere in the Bible or in other archaeological writings or inscriptions from that time period. Furthermore, if such a meeting were to have taken place, it would present some problems as revealed in the biblical story of Nimrod:

Now the whole world had one language and a common speech. As people moved eastward, they found a plain in Shinar and settled there.

They said to each other, "Come, let's make bricks and bake them thoroughly." They used brick instead of stone, and tar for mortar. Then they said, "Come, let us build ourselves a city, with a tower that reaches to the Heavens, so that we may make a name for ourselves; otherwise we will be scattered over the face of the whole earth."

But the LORD came down to see the city and the tower the people were building. The LORD said, "If as one people speaking the same language, they have begun to do this, then nothing they plan to do will be impossible for them. Come, let us go down and confuse their language so they will not understand each other."

So the LORD scattered them from there over all the earth, and they stopped building the city. That is why it was called Babel—[for the reason that the people sounded like illogical babbling] because there the LORD confused the language of the whole world. From there the LORD scattered them over the face of the whole earth (Genesis 11:1-9, NIV, bracketed clarification mine).

The king of Shinar, at the time the tower of Babel was constructed, was Nimrod, the great-grandson of Noah through the line of Noah's son, Ham, whose son was Cush.

Cush was the father of Nimrod, who became a mighty warrior on the earth. He was a mighty hunter before the LORD; that is why it is said, "Like Nimrod, a mighty hunter before the LORD." The first centers of his kingdom were Babylon, Uruk, Akkad and Kalneh, in Shinar (Genesis 10:8-10, NIV).

NOTE: The reason we are going into such detail is so you can separate the biblical account from the non-biblical Hebrew and Islamic folklore, which tells the myth of Abraham's meeting with King Nimrod; nevertheless, the events in the oral traditions could not have occurred until after the Tower of Babel was constructed sometime before 2200 B.C. (Dating of ancient events vary, allowing

As established, Nimrod was a descendant of Noah's son, Ham, while Abraham was a Semite. The Semites were descended from Noah's son, Shem, from whom the Semites got their name. The point is that everyone spoke one language until God scattered them by confusing their common language into many languages. The Tower of Babel was built sometime after the landing of Noah's ark, and because of that, it is reasonable to assume there was not a great number of people in Babylon. When God scattered those inhabitants, they were probably formed into small family groups (tribes). It is not unreasonable to conclude that the children of Ham and the children of Shem remained within their own separate family groups, yet spoke different languages. You can read more about it in Genesis 11:1-9.

We are unable to document from any reliable sources that Abram (Abraham) was ever in Babylon during the time of Nimrod or before God called him to leave his homeland (Genesis 12:1). While it is not clear, the Bible seems to indicate that Abram (Abraham) was born in Ur after the Tower of Babel event. This is based on biblical records, which say that Haran, the brother of Abraham, was born and died in Ur (Genesis 11:28). Because the Bible is silent on their father, Terah, having lived anyplace else before or at the time the brothers were born, it is reasonable to assume that Abram (Abraham) was also born in Ur.

We were unable to find any maps showing Abraham traveling southeast from Babylon to Ur, but many maps show the Patriarch's travels northwest from Ur through the Fertile Crescent, and then turning westward along the Mediterranean coast of Canaan.[42] Abraham is first mentioned in Genesis 11:8-9 when God had him leave his home in the land of the Chaldeans and travel northwest (possibly passing through Babylon).

Even if we could compress the time to accommodate Nimrod and Abraham living at the same time, Abraham would not have been able to understand the language spoken in Babylon. The Bible indicates that the language commonly spoken during the time of Nimrod was confused (Genesis 11:9) or, in other words, that was the time when different languages came into existence. (An example would be like the diversity of modern English, Hebrew, Chinese, German, etc.). Because of the newly formed languages, ethnic groups were unable to communicate with the other newly formed ethnic groups; they became segregated by their various new languages, which was the trigger that caused them to spread out in different directions from Babylon.

Even if Abraham had lived in Babylon during Nimrod's time, it would stand to reason that after God confused the languages, Abraham and his family would no longer be able to communicate with Nimrod and Nimrod's family. This lack of communication would have caused Abraham—like the others—to take his family and leave Babylon to migrate southeast to the land of Ur.

> OBSERVATION: If Abraham could have spoken the same language as Nimrod, there would have been no reason for Abraham's family to leave Babylon! For that reason, it makes no sense for the Koran to suggest that Abraham held an audience with Nimrod of Babylon. It makes for a good story, but it is highly improbable. Aside from the language barrier—for such an important event like that to take place—it certainly would have been recorded in the Bible.

(2:259) Or (bethink [remember] you of) the like of him who, passing by a township [43] [which had fallen into utter ruin, exclaimed: "How shall Allah give this township life after its death?" <u>And Allah made him die a hundred years,</u> then brought him back to life. He said: "How long have you tarried ?" (The man) said: "I have tarried a day or part of a day." (He) said: "Nay, but you have tarried for a hundred years. Just look at thy food and drink which have not rotted! Look at your ass! And, that We may make you a token unto mankind, look at the bones, how We adjust them and then cover them with flesh!" And

212

when (the matter) became clear unto him, he said: "I know now that Allah is Able to do all things." (Underlined emphasis added.)

Trying to determine how this verse fits with the dialogue of this sûrah is anybody's guess. This is not the only "Rip Van Winkle" story in the Koran. We will be addressing another story about the sleepers in Sûrah 18:12, where the sleepers are asked if they knew how long they had been asleep.

As for this passage, we do not know if Abraham is still speaking to Nimrod or not because once again, the verses are becoming disjointed. This appears to be more of an unrelated parable or commingling of stories other than an actual event. This parable's moral: Time is nothing to Allah, but because time is irrelevant, Allah can do whatever he pleases with time and events.

(2:260) And when Abraham said (unto his Lord): "My Lord! Show me how you give life to the dead," He said: "Do you not believe?" Abraham said: "Yes, but (I ask) in order that my heart may be at ease." (His Lord) said: "Take four of the birds and cause them to incline unto you, then place a part of them on each hill, then call them, they will come to you in haste, and know that Allah is Mighty, Wise."

Once again, we embark on an area that is unique to the Koran and the Apocrypha (books with a suspicious origin and rejected as Scripture).

The Koran now shifts focus to a story regarding Abraham, who allegedly asked Allah how he could bring the dead back to life. Allah told him to kill some birds in various ways (depending on the translation), and Allah would bring them back to life. The Bible has nothing like this casual and insensitive disregard for the life of God's creatures just to prove He can do something. The God of the Bible cares very much for the well-being of all of His creatures and is aware when even a sparrow falls to earth and dies (Matthew 10:29)!

OBSERVATION: There is no logic to this passage, unlike biblical passages, which are uniform in their translations. The conflicting koranic translations give credibility to the Muslims' claim that the Koran can only be understood in its original Arabic language, unlike the Bible, which uses three languages: Hebrew, Aramaic (the official language of the Babylonian Court) and the international language of Koine Greek. In addition to these published languages, Peter and the Apostles preached the gospel in many more languages, including Arabic, at the same time so everyone could hear the Gospel message in their own language during Pentecost (Acts 2:4-11).

(2:261) The likeness of those who spend their wealth in Allah's way is as the likeness of a grain which grows seven ears, in every ear a hundred grains. Allah giveth increase manifold to whom He will. Allah is All-Embracing, All-Knowing.

The Koran now shifts to the subject of tithing.

Unlike the Bible, the Koran is very disjointed, perhaps because so much of what Muhammad recited was written down by his scribes on whatever was at hand. That most likely resulted in a huge amount of Muhammad's revelations written on stones and bones lying around. That alone could have made it difficult to reassemble Muhammad's dictates in the proper order at some future date. Perhaps this could possibly explain many of the koranic inconsistencies we have observed. Either way, those various ideas were then assembled, and now exist in the Koran.

We should point out that this verse sounds very much like the tithing concept found in the Bible. Many churches today promote the idea of sowing seed (money) into God's kingdom. Who would argue that financially supporting the work of the one true God is a bad thing? Jesus cautions us with this parable regarding our tithes and the motivations behind them:

Two men went up to the temple to pray, one a Pharisee and the other a tax collector. The Pharisee stood by himself and prayed: "God, I thank you that I am not like other people-robbers, evildoers, Adulterers-or even like this tax collector. I fast twice a week and give a tenth of all I get."

But the tax collector stood at a distance. He would not even look up to heaven, but beat his breast and said, "God, have mercy on me, a sinner."

I tell you that this man, rather than the other, went home justified before God. For all those who exalt themselves will be humbled, and those who humble themselves will be exalted (Luke 18:10-14).

(2:262) Those who spend their wealth for the cause of Allah and afterward make not reproach and injury to follow that which they have spent; their reward is with their Lord, and there shall no fear come upon them, neither shall they grieve.
The grateful giver never complains that he gave up some things for Allah and remains content by his actions. According to this verse, Allah will provide blessings for that man.

(2:263) A kind word with forgiveness is better than almsgiving [charitable gifts for the poor] followed by injury. Allah is Absolute, Clement [merciful] (bracketed clarification mine).

Kindness by helping someone is better than charity, followed by doing harm afterward. Allah does not need charity and does not appreciate phonies.

(2:264) O you who believe! Render not vain [self-serving in] your almsgiving [charitable gifts for the poor] by reproach and injury, like him who spends his wealth only to be seen of men and believes not in Allah and the Last Day. His likeness is as the likeness of a rock whereon is dust of earth; a rainstorm smites [hits] it, leaving it smooth and bare. They have no control of aught [anything] of that which they have gained. Allah guides not the disbelieving folk (bracketed clarifications mine).

With the statement, *"by reproach and injury,"* Muslims are told not to be shamed by disbelievers who outwardly give generously, not for their love of Islam, but rather to receive the admiration of others, *"like him who spends his wealth only to be seen of men and believes not in Allah …."* This is similar to the biblical story of the widow's mite:

As Jesus looked up, He saw the rich putting their gifts into the Temple treasury. He also saw a poor widow put in two very small copper coins. "Truly I tell you," He said, "this poor widow has put in more than all the others. All these people gave their gifts out of their wealth; but she out of her poverty put in all she had to live on"(Luke 21:1-4, NIV).

Of course, the lesson to be learned from this Scripture in the Bible is that we should give out of love for God, not for self-glorification. Those who give to impress have already received their reward through the admiration of other people.

(2:265) And the likeness of those who spend their wealth in search of Allah's pleasure, and for the strengthening of their souls, is as the likeness of a garden on a height. The rainstorm smites [hits] it and it brings forth its fruit twofold. And if the rainstorm smite it not [does not hit it], then the shower. Allah is Seer of what you do (bracketed clarification mine.)

It seems that those who seek to please Allah by giving from their wealth to his cause have come a long way toward pleasing him and purifying themselves. According to this sûrah, they will benefit to a greater or lesser degree, depending on their offering.

However, as we just discussed in the commentary for verse 264, the God of the Bible is not impressed with large sums of money; He looks at the heart of the giver, not the amount given.

(2:266) Would any of you like to have a garden of palm-trees and vines, with rivers flowing underneath it, with all kinds of fruit for him therein; and old age has stricken him and he has feeble offspring; and a fiery whirlwind strikes it and it is (all) consumed by fire. Thus Allah makes plain His revelations unto you, in order that you may give thought.

Allah is asking the obvious question: Would anyone want to live in a paradise, a place where they could retire comfortably by the time they reach their old age? Yet if their children are not good stewards, it would all be for nothing because they would find their affairs ruined with nothing for old age. Their children would have ruined what they had worked so hard for, like a whirlwind catching it up and depositing it flames. This also applies to what a person is laying up in Islamic heaven. Would not it have been better if he had paid attention to the clear teachings of Islam and layed up his riches in the hereafter? Allah is telling Muslims they should think about that.

(2:267) O you who believe! Spend of the good things which you have earned, and of that which We bring forth from the earth for you, and seek not the bad (with intent) to spend thereof (in charity) when you would not take it for yourselves save with disdain; and know that Allah is Absolute, Owner of Praise.

As we have read before, this passage is suggesting that Muslims who have been blessed should be generous toward others less fortunate than themselves and not give something of lesser value while bragging about how generous they are. If the situation were reversed, they would not appreciate being given an inferior gift; therefore, Muslims are advised not to be a hypocrite.

(2:268) The devil promises you destitution and enjoins on you lewdness. But Allah promises you forgiveness from Himself with bounty. Allah is All-Embracing, All-Knowing.

Muslims are warned that the devil will try to make them miserable so they will abandon themselves into carnal lust in order to try and escape from their misery, but they should not be fooled. Allah promises that he will forgive them if they repent and heap on them wonderful blessings because he is so caring.

(2:269) He gives wisdom unto whom He will, and he unto whom wisdom is given, he truly has received abundant good. But none remember except men of understanding.

Allah bestows gifts of insight and wisdom to whomever he chooses. This verse reinforces the fact, in Islam, a person has no choice in the matter. The second part of this verse is because a man is given wisdom, he knows to avoid Satan, but only those with Allah's gift of wisdom understand it. Some Muslim scholars go a little further, suggesting that he will not only be wise enough to avoid Satan but will receive wealth, most of which will be given to the less fortunate.

(2:270) Whatever alms [charitable gifts for the poor] you spend or vow you vow, indeed! Allah knows it. Wrong-doers have no helpers

Muslims are to be careful about how they tithe or what promises they make. Allah knows their motivation and everything they do. Deceivers will not receive Allah's help.

(2:271) If you publish [make known] your almsgiving [charitable gifts for the poor], it is well, but if you hide it and give it to the poor, it will be better for you, and will atone for some of your ill-deeds. Allah is Informed of what you do (bracketed clarification mine).

This is beginning to seem like Déjà vu. It is not clear why Gabriel keeps harping on this subject. Again, we are told if Muslims brag about their charity, it would serve as an example for others to be generous in their giving. On the other hand, they should not concern themselves with revealing how much they gave, but if they do it in secret, Allah will bless them more abundantly; therefore, they will be able to pay off some of their sins. Allah is aware of what they do.

This also conflicts with the lesson just seven verses earlier in Sûrah 2:264 (please refer to the comments we shared in that verse) where the man—who gave for all to see—received his reward.

The Bible teaches us not to brag in order to receive the admiration of others, but to:

Be careful not to practice your righteousness in front of others to be seen by them. If you do, you will have no reward from your Father in Heaven (Matthew 6:1, NIV).

(2:272) The guiding of them is not your duty (O Muhammad), but Allah guides whom He will. And whatsoever good thing you spend, it is for yourselves, when you spend not save [except] in search of Allah's countenance [face]; and whatsoever good thing you spend, it will be repaid to you in full, and you will not be wronged (bracketed clarifications mine).

According to this verse, while Muhammad brings Allah's message to the people, it is not his responsibility if they refuse to accept it because Allah decides who will or will not be "enlightened." This verse might be intended to help Muhammad save face when the people of the Bible (mostly Jews), who were living in Medina, did not accept what Muhammad was telling them. Muslims are encouraged to do good deeds because that is a virtuous way to earn Allah's blessings as opposed to the God of the Bible who is not impressed with the works of men who
try to earn His blessings because He does not want any man to boast that he can impress God or buy Him (Ephesians 2:8-9).

Sûrah 2:272 also leads us to believe that people have no choice in accepting Islam when it tells us, "... *Allah guides whom He will.*"

CONSIDER: If this is so, then why does Allah choose not to let everyone accept Islam? If Allah denies some people the ability to believe—and then because they do not believe—is it justifiable to command them to: "Fight against such of those who have been given the Scripture as believe not in Allah nor the Last Day, and forbid not that which Allah hath forbidden by His Messenger, and follow not the religion of truth, until they pay the tribute readily., being brought low," (Sûrah 9:29, bracketed clarification mine).

(2:273) (Alms [charity] are) for the poor who are straitened [financially poor] for the cause of Allah, who cannot travel in the land (for trade). The unthinking man accounts them wealthy because of their restraint. You shall know them by their mark: They do not beg of

men with importunity. And whatsoever good thing you spend, indeed! Allah knows it. (bracketed clarifications mine.)

Muslims should be aware of the humble Muslims in their midst who might be in need. They should consider the reason why they do not walk around with their hand out. It is not because they are financially well off—just the opposite. They need their Muslim brothers' help but are too embarrassed to ask for it. Muslims who are financially comfortable should make sure that the poorer Muslims might, in fact, be less fortunate than themselves and should be helped to make the required hajj to Mecca. Allah knows who is helping them.

(2:274) Those who spend their wealth by night and day, by stealth and openly, verily [truly] their reward is with their Lord, and there shall no fear come upon them neither shall they grieve (bracketed clarification mine).

This is a continuation of the previous verse encouraging Muslims to take every opportunity to be charitable, whether out in the open where everyone can see or in private where no one is aware of their generosity. Either way, Allah observes their generosity, or he will bless and protect the generous ones.

(2:275) Those who swallow usury [overcharge or interest] cannot rise up [from the grave] save [like] as he arises (lifts up) whom the devil hath prostrated by (his) touch. That is because they say: "Trade is just like usury;" whereas Allah permits trading and forbids usury. He unto whom an admonition from his Lord comes, and (he) refrains (in obedience thereto), he shall keep (the profits of) that which is past, and his affair (henceforth) is with Allah. As for him who returns (to usury) - Such are rightful owners of the Fire. They will abide therein (bracketed clarifications mine).

Allah is telling his believers that engaging in trade is perfectly all right, but not to go about "padding the profits" or charging interest—like those who serve Satan—when they allow someone to make payments toward a purchase. If a Muslim has been involved in wrongful profits, they should stop and repent. Allah will forgive them, but he will not forgive those who continue to profit unfairly; those who continue to do will end up in Hell.

(2:276) Allah has blighted [eliminated] usury [overcharging or interest] and made almsgiving [charitable gifts for the poor] fruitful. Allah loves not the impious [wicked] and guilty (bracketed clarifications mine).

Allah forbids moneylending for a profit and will punish those who practice it; however, Allah encourages charitable actions and fairness; as a result, he will help charitable Muslims prosper. Allah disdains those who take unfair advantage of others
(2:277) Look! those who believe and do good works and establish worship and pay the poor-due, their reward is with their Lord and there shall no fear come upon them neither shall they grieve.

It is interesting how many times and different ways this theme has been repeated within just the past dozen or so verses. Again, we are told that Allah rewards those who do good works, takes care of the poor, and worships Allah. Muslims who do this have nothing to fear, nor will they grieve.

(2:278) O you who believe! Observe your duty to Allah, and give up what remains (due to you) from usury [overcharging or interest], if you are (in truth) believers (bracketed clarification mine).

Committed Muslims must forego unjust profits for Allah's sake, and if they overcharged or made interest, they should give it to Allah.

OBSERVATION: These repetitive verses are examples of how the Koran reinforces Sharia Law.

(2:279) And if you do not, then be warned of war (against you) from Allah and His messenger. And if you repent, then you have your principal (without interest). Wrong not, and you shall not be wronged.

This verse was revealed to Muhammad after he conquered Mecca. At that time, the Pagan Arab tribes, who were accustomed to charging interest, were told that if they continued that practice, Muhammad would declare war on them, which would have a devastating effect. Presumably, that was to protect Muslims from having to pay large amounts of money to the infidels, thus keeping it in their own pockets.

Today, this Sharia Law still applies; if Muslims are found conducting unfair commerce, Allah will use Muhamad to carry out a jihad against them, but if they repent and deal honestly with others (i.e., not charge interest on money loaned), no harm will come to them (Sûrah 2:279).

This is another fundamental difference between Islam and Judeo-Christian banking. Despite the warning in Leviticus 25:37 against charging interest, most Bible-believing people think it is fair to charge simple interest. However, a strong argument could be made against compounded interest as evil and unscrupulous, especially when it is front-loaded (the majority of the first payments are applied toward interest, and not the balance each time a payment is made. It is similar to a credit card or mortgage, which can take up to 10, 15, 30, or more years, where the lender figures the interest and puts it at the front end while continuing to add on interest to the existing interest as well as the original purchase price). The result of compounded financing is less money going toward the actual loan until most of the interest is recuperated, with the borrower winding up paying double or triple the cost of the actual value of the financed items. One of the reasons for such a high return for the lender is that compounded interest is really interest charged on interest.

(2:280) And if the debtor is in straitened [financially difficult] circumstances, then (let there be) postponement to (the time of) ease; and that [but if] you remit the debt as almsgiving [charitable gifts for the poor] would be better for you if you did but know (bracketed clarifications mine).

If a fellow Muslim owes money and is having difficulty making the payments because of financial reversals, then the Muslim lender should allow the less fortunate one to wait until he is once again able to make payments. An even better thing to do would be to forgive the debt and write it off as charity. In case the borrower is unaware of that, it would be a generous gesture to accommodate them.

(2:281) And guard yourselves against a day in which you will be brought back to Allah. Then every soul will be paid in full that which it has earned, and they will not be wronged.

A time will come when Muslims will no longer live on the earth. When that happens, they will stand before Allah and be judged according to how they lived their lives

(2:282) O you who believe! When you contract a debt for a fixed term, record [it] in writing. Let a scribe record it in writing between you in (terms of) equity [fairness]. No scribe should refuse to write [the contract] as Allah has taught him, so let him write, and let who incurred the debt dictate, and let him observe his duty to Allah and his Lord, and diminish naught [nothing] thereof. But if he [who] owes debt is of low understanding [limited knowledge, limited awareness, or senile], or weak or unable himself to dictate, then let the guardian of his interest dictate in (terms of) equity [fairness]. And call [bring] to [two] witness[es], from among your men, two witnesses. And if two men be not (at hand) [available] then a man and two women, of such you approve as witnesses, so that if the one [woman] errs (through forgetfulness) the other will remember. Be you not averse [against] to writing down (the contract) whether it be small or great, with (record of) the term thereof [specified]. That is more equitable [fair] in the sight of Allah and more sure [stronger] for testimony, and the best way of avoiding doubt between you; save [except] only in the case when it is actual merchandise which you transfer among yourselves from hand to hand [among yourselves]. In that case it is no sin for you if you write it not. And have witnesses when you sell one to another, and no harm be done to scribe or witness. If you do (harm to them) indeed! It is a sin to you. Observe your duty to Allah. Allah is teaching you. Allah is knower of all things (bracketed clarifications mine).

OBSERVATION: Notice how long this one verse is. In some of Muhammad's earlier sûrahs, it was not uncommon to have one short sentence broken into two or three verses, such as Sûrah 1, "The Opening," which is six verses composed from only two sentences.

Verse 282 is codified in Sharia Law regarding contracts. It advises that any agreement of consequence should be written down to avoid future misunderstandings and allows for the fact that some people (like Muhammad) are not able to read or write; therefore, a scribe (i.e., secretary, transcriber) should be the one to draw up the contract. If one of the parties is unable to grasp some of the more complicated details of the transaction, someone—preferably a guardian—should be there to help arrange the agreement on his behalf. Professional scribes should always make themselves available for such a transaction, as should any other witnesses.

It is a good practice to have a written agreement; it does not matter how simple or complex the contract is, with one exception: If Muslims are performing a simple transaction, such as a hand-to-hand exchange, then it is not considered a sin if both parties agree to forgo making a written contract. Tricking the other party is sinful and, therefore, forbidden. Allah is aware of everyone's actions.

Putting all this aside, there is something very revealing midway through this verse regarding the value of women. Observe that in the section stipulating that witnesses should be called to verify the contract:

> ...And call [bring] to [two] witnesses, from among your men, two witness[es]. And if two men be not (at hand) [available] then a man and two women, of such you approve as witnesses, so that if the one [woman] errs (through forgetfulness) the other will remember....

OBSERVATION: According to this section, Sharia Law places the value of a woman at half that of a man. It takes the testimony of two women to equal the value and respect of one man's witness.

(2:283) You be on a journey and cannot find a scribe, then a pledge in hand (shall suffice). And if one of you entrusts to another let him who is trusted deliver up that which is entrusted to him (according to the pact between them) and let him observe his duty to Allah. Hide not testimony. He who hides it, verily [truly] his heart is sinful. Allah is aware of what you do (bracketed clarification mine).

The Koran continues the subject of contracts with a particular situation where there is no scribe available. It suggests making a deal with the equivalent of a handshake and leaving something of value as a guarantee to bind the contract, especially if money or property is involved. Once again, the Koran warns that the people involved should not be disingenuous or try to put something over on the other person; that is considered sinful; Allah is watching.

(2:284) Unto Allah (belongs) whatsoever is in the heavens and whatsoever is in the earth; and whether you make known what is in your minds or hide it, Allah will bring you to account for it. He will forgive whom He will and He will punish whom He will. Allah is Able to do all things.

No matter what, Allah is aware of everything happening in the universe. He knows what everyone is thinking and doing; therefore, no one is unable to hide anything from him. Beware of wrongdoing because forgiveness or punishment will follow. Muslims are better off practicing goodness since Allah is able to do what he wants.

One troubling part of this verse, which we often see repeated, is at the end of the passage where it reaffirms that Allah is not bound by anything: *"He will forgive whom He will and He will punish whom He will."* Allah is under no constraints to routinely punish evildoers. He can ignore good or evil deeds if he chooses because, according to the Koran, *"... Allah is Able to do all things."*

(2:285) The messenger believes in that which has been revealed unto him from his Lord and (so do) believers. Each one believes in Allah and His angels and His scriptures and His messengers—We make no distinction between any of His messengers—and they say: "We hear,

and we obey. (Grant us) Your forgiveness, our Lord. Unto Thee is the journeying."

Muhammad is committed to what he is revealing. He teaches that you should have faith in Allah, his angels, and the Scriptures of the Old and New Testaments as well as the Koran. Allah makes no distinction between his prophets, which is another subtitle attack on the Divinity of Christ because in Islam, Jesus is no better or no worse than any other prophet with the exception of Muhammad who is the seal—and by extension—the greatest of the prophets (Sûrah 33:40). They would be wise to do as they have been taught. It ends basically asking for Allah to be forgiving toward them at the end of their life's journey.

(2:286) Allah tasks [burdens] not a soul beyond its scope. For it (is only) that which it has earned, and against it (only) that which it has deserved. Our Lord! Condemn us not if we forget, or miss the mark! Our Lord! Lay not on us such a burden as you did lay on those before us! Our Lord! Impose not on us that which we have not the strength to bear! Pardon us, absolve us and have mercy on us, Thou, our Protector, and give us victory over the disbelieving folk (bracketed clarification mine).

This passage is presented as a prayer and, in some respects, is similar to the LORD's prayer (Matthew 6:9-13). It echoes the biblical truth found in 1 Corinthians:

There has no temptation taken you but such as is common to man[kind]: but God is faithful, who will not suffer you to be tempted above that you are able [to endure]; but will with the temptation also make a way to escape, that you may be able to bear it (1 Corinthians 10:13 bracketed clarification mine).

NOTES:

1. Sahih al-Bukhari (Vol. 9, Book 84, No. 6922).

2. Muslim ibn al-Hajjaj, Sahih Muslim, trans. Abdul Hamid Siddiqui (Houston: Dar-us-Salam Publications, 2007), [Number 1676].

3. Allah is He Who created seven Firmaments *and of the earth a similar number*. Through the midst of them (all) descends His Command: that you may know that Allah has power over all things, and that Allah comprehends all things in (His) Knowledge" (Sûrah 65:12, Abdullah Yusuf Ali, emphasis added). Arguably, this is another Koranic revision without biblical or scientific endorsement.

4. A Cherub is one of the highest-ranking angels of God. The plural in Hebrew adds "*im*." In Hebrew grammar, the "*im*" *(yud mim)* is the English equivalent of using an "s" to pluralize a word. The translators of the 1610 A.D. King James Bible added an "s" to the Hebrew word "Cherubim"—making it "Cherubims"—which is redundant and makes it a double plural, which is not only grammatically incorrect but technically incorrect as well. This is also an example of how a passage of Scripture might theoretically become corrupted; however, it is important to note that it still does not affect the meaning or accuracy of the passage. (NOTE: Painters of the Renaissance developed the picture of Cherubs appearing as little babies with wings.)

5. Isaac married his second cousin, Rebekah, the grandniece of his father, Abraham's brother, Nahor (Genesis 24:1-67), and Jacob married his first cousin, Rachel, the daughter of his mother, Sarah's brother, Laban (Genesis 28:1-3; 29:21-28).

6. Joseph Jacob and Louis H. Gray, "JewishEncyclopedia.com," The Kopelman Foundation *SABEANS* - "The references to (the Sabaean) religion are for the most part names of deities... lack of description renders a reconstruction of the Semitic pantheon practically impossible. It is clear, however...that the religion of Sheba closely resembled the pre-Islamic Arabian cult and showed certain affinities with the Assyro Babylonian system as well."

7. Clarence L. Barnhart, ed., The American College Encyclopedic Dictionary, Vol. II (Chicago: Spencer Press, Inc., 1959). Sabaean from "Saba" (Biblical Sheba), an inhabitant of Saba, also Sabaean.

8. In addition to Sûrah 7:166, Sûrah 5 Gabriel adds swine with the apes: "Say (Muhammad): 'O People of the Book! Do you disapprove of us for no other reason than that we believe in Allah, and the revelation that had come to us and that which came before (us), and (perhaps) that most of you are rebellious and disobedient?' Say [Muhammad]: 'Shall I point out to you something much worse than this (as judged) by the treatment it received from Allah? those who incurred the curse of Allah and His wrath, those of whom some He transformed into *apes and swine,* those who worshipped evil;- these are (many times) worse in rank, and far more astray from the even path!' " (Sûrah 5:59-60, Abdullah Yusuf Ali, bracketed clarification mine, emphasis added).

9. Clarence L. Barnhart, ed., The American College Encyclopedic Dictionary, Vol. I (Chicago: Spencer Press, Inc., 1959). *The Dark Ages.* "(1) The time in history from about A.D. 476 to about A.D. 1000; and (2) (occasionally) the whole of the Middle Ages, from about A.D. 476 to the Renaissance." Note: "Muhammad began receiving his revelations around 610 A.D

10. Hanson, Erin, "Oral Traditions." *Indigenous Foundations*, University of British Columbia, 2009, N.p., n.d. Web. 18 June 2013. "Western discourse has come to prioritize the written word as the dominant form of record-keeping and until recently, Westerners have generally considered that oral societies record and document their histories in complex and sophisticated ways ... (but) many still depend on oral traditions and greatly value the oral transmission of knowledge as an intrinsic aspect of their cultures and societies."

11. "Purgatory, the condition, process, or place of purification or temporary punishment in which, according to medieval Christian and Roman Catholic belief, the souls of those who die in a state of grace are made ready for Heaven. Purgatory (Latin: purgatorium; from purgare; "to purge") has come to refer as well to a wide range of historical and modern conceptions of postmortem suffering short of everlasting damnation." "Purgatory | Roman Catholicism." Encyclopædia Britannica Online. n.d. Web. 13 Sept. 2013.

12. The Books of 1 and 2 Maccabees are Jewish historical publications of the second century B.C. (These books are not divinely inspired because there are contradictions between the two versions). In 2 Maccabees 12:38-46, because Judas Maccabee believed in the resurrection, he offered sacrifices and prayers for the slain Hebrew soldiers who died in battle wearing Pagan amulets (for protection). If this were possible, then the dead who are prayed for would still have to be purged of their sin. Martin Luther disagreed with praying for the dead in his "95 Theses" ("... it is appointed unto men once to die, but after this the judgment" [Hebrews 9:7]) so the Roman Church added the Books of the Maccabees to their Bible in answer to Luther's charge.

13. Timothy F. Lull and William R. Russell, Ed., *Martin Luther's Basic Theological* Writing, 2nd ed. (Minneapolis: Augsburg Fortress Press, 2005), 42 in ft. n. 8. Pope Severinus (638-40 and Pope Pascal I (817-24) "preferred to remain longer in purgatory that they might have greater glory."

14. Sûrah Al-Baqara 2:87-90, *Towards Understanding the Quran - Quran Translation Commentary - Tafheem Ul Quran.* Islamic Foundation UK, n.d. Web. 21 Sept. 2016.

15. Herbert J. Muller, *Arabia Before Islam*, 2013, "Economic Conditions: Economically, the Jews were the leaders of Arabia. They were the owners of the best arable lands in Hijaz, and the best farmers in the country. They were also the entrepreneurs of industries that existed in Arabia in those days, and enjoyed a monopoly of the armaments industry;" "Arabia before Islam." *Al-Islam.org.* N.p., n.d. Web. 20 July 2013.

16. Joseph W. Meri, ed., "Jinn," Medieval Islamic Civilization: An Encyclopedia, Vol. 1 (New York: Routledge, 2006), 420-421. "Genie," "jinn," "djinn" refer to Islamic spiritual beings found in the Koran, Hadith, and other Muslim writings. They are intelligent creatures who are separate from humans. Angelic beings are able to manifest themselves in physical form. The jinn consists of smokeless and scorching fire who, like humans, can act with benevolence or maliciousness (see Sûrah 72, "the jinn" or "al-Jinn").

17. The editors of Encyclopædia Britannica. "Harut and Marut." *Encyclopædia Britannica*. Encyclopædia Britannica, Inc., 20 July 1998. Web. 17 Feb. 2016.

18. Christy Wilson, *The Qur'an...the World's Religions* (Oxford: Lion Handbook, 2008), 315. Muslim tradition asserts that the Koran always existed in heaven from the beginning of time and was miraculously revealed by Gabriel to Muhammad, who memorized it verbatim. If this is so, why did Allah have to keep revising (abrogating) it?

19. Arthur Jeffery, *Islam: Muhammad and His Religion* (Indianapolis: Bobbs-Merrill Co. Inc., 1958), 66.

20. "What advantage then has the Jew, or what *is* the profit of circumcision? Much in every way! Chiefly because to them were committed the oracles of God" (Romans 3:1-2).

21. So far, the archaeological and historical, oral traditions of the people in the Arabian Peninsula, as well as historical writings during the pre-seventh century A.D., do not exist regarding either Abraham in the Arabian Desert or him offering Ishmael as a sacrifice to God. The son offered in the Koran is never named. Could it be, as the Bible records that (1) it was Isaac who was offered by Abraham on Mt. Moriah (where the Temple was later built), and (2) the koranic version, where Abraham offered Ishmael, is where the Ka'aba now stands?

Andrew Rippin. *The Qur'an: Formative Interpretation* (Aldershot: Ashgate, 1999), 92-95. Quoting Norman Calder. In *The Qur'an: Formative Interpretation*, we read, "Although most Muslims today believe it was Ishmael that was offered in Mecca, earlier traditions consisted of over 264 mythical oral traditions with 131 believing Isaac was the child offered while 133 believe it to be Ishmael." Norman Calder tells us, "Oral narrative is marked by instability of form and detail from version to version, and by an appropriate creative flexibility which makes of every rendering a unique work of art." "The alleged, attempted sacrifice of Ishmael" on Eid al-Adha (Feast of Sacrifice) is one of two *official* Islamic holidays (Eid Al-Fitr and Eid Al-Adha [Ramadan is a month set aside for fasting during daylight hours]); yet there is not any historical evidence, including the Bible and archaeology, which can support it. It is only supported by Muslim tradition.

22. Asad, Muhammad. *The Message of the Qur'an* (London: The Book Foundation, 2012). This Koran was first published in Spanish (Gibraltar) in 1980 and later in English on December 1, 2008. Currently, it is no longer available except as an e-publication through Kindle.Tor Andrae, *Muhammad: The Man and His Faith* (Mineola: Dover Publications, 2000), 136-137.

23. Richard J.A. Talbert, *Plutarch on Sparta* (London: Penguin Books, 1988). Sparta was a city in Greece, which rose to become the dominant Grecian military power around 650 B.C. They took "on the austere, military character which it has been associated with ever since" (p. 2). They were "free and self-sufficient" (p. 45). They led a hard life by our standards, rejecting luxury in order to remain tough and ready for battle.

24. Mamdouh N. Mohamed, *Hajj & Umrah from A to Z* (self-published, Jan. 1, 1996). Although Mamdouh is self-published, he is still considered a reliable source by many. (Al-Safa and Al-Marwah are also known as Safa and Marwah). "Safa and Marwah are two small mountains located in the Masjid al-Haram in Mecca, Saudi Arabia, where Muslims travel back and forth seven times during the ritual pilgrimages of Hajj and Umrah." There are no page numbers, but this information can be accessed under section "R, Making Sa'ee."

25. Noel Scott, Jafar Jafari, *Tourism in the Muslim World* (Bingley Emerald Group Publishing Ltd., 2010), 5. The Hajj (or Haj) is one of the largest, annually occurring pilgrimages in the world. In 2008, there were around 2.5 million pilgrims.

26. *Halal* means "permissible." "Halal foods are foods that Muslims are allowed to eat under Islamic Shari'ah Law." Halal. *Wikipedia*. Wikimedia Foundation, n.d. Web. 22 May 2013.

27. Muller, Herbert J. "Arabia before Islam." *Al-Islam.org*. N.p., n.d. Web. 27 Mar. 2017.

28. Hans Wehr, Cowan, J. Milton, ed. *A Dictionary of Modern Written Arabic* (3rd ed) (Urbana: Spoken Language Services, 1976), *fitna* , 696.

29. Saul S. Freedman *A History of the Middle East* (London: McFarland & Co., 1937), 112

30. Aisha, Muhammad's child bride, told Muhammad, "I feel your Lord can refuse you nothing" (Hadith Sahih Bukhari, Volume 6, Book 60, Hadith No: 311).

31. "When Allah's Apostle arrived in Mecca, he refused to enter the Ka'ba while there were idols in it, so he ordered them to be removed. The pictures of the (Prophets) Ibrahim and Ishmael, while holding arrows of divination in their hands, were carried out. The Prophet said, 'May Allah ruin them (the infidels) for they knew very well they (Ibrahim and Ishmael) never drew lots by these (divination arrows). Then the Prophet entered the Ka'ba and said, 'Allahu Akbar' in all its directions and came out and not offer any prayer therein ..."

32. "When Allah's Apostle arrived in Mecca, he refused to enter the Ka'ba while there were idols in it, so he ordered them to be removed. The pictures of the (prophets) Ibrahim and Ishmael, while holding arrows of divination in their hands, were carried out. The Prophet said, 'May Allah ruin them (the infidels) for they knew very well they (Ibrahim and Ishmael) never drew lots by these (divination arrows). Then the Prophet entered the Ka'ba and said, 'Allahu Akbar' in all its directions and came out and not offer any prayer therein ..." (Sahih Al-Bukhari, Book 59, Hadith 584) "Hajj." *ACADEMIC*, Enacacademic, enacademic.com/ dic.nsf/enwiki/46076.

33. See endnote 30.

34. *The Life of Muḥammad: A Translation of ibn Isḥāq's Sīrat Rasul Allāh* with introduction & notes by Alfred Guillaume, Oxford University Press, 1955, page 287-289

35. As we document in our book *What Every Bible Believer Needs to Know About Islam,* the names of many those banks include Bank of America, CitiBank, J.P. Morgan Chase, NASDAQ, Merrill Lynch, GE Capital, Goldman Sachs, etc.

36. Bible Hub, "Bible Timeline," n.d.; Web. 28 June 2013. Dates supplied by "Bible Timeline." Gideon fought the Midianites around 1169 B.C. in the Jezreel Valley, which is a large fertile plain in an inland valley south of the Lower Galilee region. It is also known as the "Megiddo Valley," the place of the future War of Armageddon spoken of in Revelation 16:16. David fought Goliath in 1024 B.C. in the Elah Valley, which runs from

the inland Judean foothills west to the Mediterranean Sea. There are around 149 years and 200 miles separating the two events

37. Norman L., Geisler and Abdul Saleeb. *Answering Islam: The Crescent in Light of the Cross*. (Grand Rapids, MI: Baker, 2002), 88.

38. "The Quran's Verses of Violence." *What Makes Islam so Different?* The Religion of Peace, n.d. Web. 06 Sept. 2016.

39. Robert J. Menner, "Nimrod and the Wolf in the Old English 'Solomon and Satyr,' " Journal of English and Germanic Philology 37 (1938), 332–384.

40. Abraham and Nimrod are never mentioned as contemporaries in the Bible; however, there are several myths which mention them interacting in the false or *pseudo-Philo* writings of the mid-second century A.D. (some less reliable sources place them as early as 25 A.D.) and also in the Midrash Rabba, "Rabbah" (רבה), meaning "great," Chapter 38:13. Circa sixth century A.D. Likewise, Islam picked up—and added—these myths to the Koran in the seventh century.

41. The Bible Study Site, Abraham's Journey Map. BibleStudy.org. Web. 2 July 2013.

42. Pickthall observes in his footnote 1: Most of the commentators agree that the reference here is to Jerusalem in ruins, while the following words tell of the vision of Ezekiel.

☪

SÛRAH 18

THE CAVE (KAHF)
(Revealed at Mecca)

In the name of Allah, the Beneficient, the Merciful.

(18:1) Praise be to Allah Who has revealed the Scripture unto His slave, and had not placed therein any crookedness,

Honor is to be given to Allah, who has given the Koran to his servant, Muhammad, and has not put anything dishonest in it.

(18:2) (But has made it) straight, to give warning of stern punishment from Him, and to bring unto the believers who do good works the news that theirs will be a fair reward,

As we often repeated in this book, Islam is a religion of works, although the only guarantee of attaining heaven is by dying in a jihad (struggle) against the infidel (Sûrah 2:216; 3:157). This verse continues the thought from the previous verse:

> *... but has given approved teachings in warning to those who will not believe in the teachings of Islam—a great punishment awaits them, but for Muslims, there will be a good reward (paraphrase mine).*

(18:3) Wherein they will abide for ever;

This is the Muslims' reward—to live eternally in their paradise.

(18:4) And to warn those who say: "Allah has chosen a son,"

This sûrah begins with an attack on the Divinity of Jesus, giving us yet another example of how obsessed and threatened Islam is regarding the Divinity of Jesus, the Son of God (John 10:36).

(18:5) (A thing) whereof they have no knowledge, nor (had) their fathers, Dreadful is the word that comes out of their mouths. They speak naught [nothing] but a lie.

In the ongoing koranic attack on the Divinity of Jesus, the assertion here is that Christians living today (and their fathers before them) do not have any legitimate reason to believe God has a Son. The Koran says to speak such a thing is evil because Christians tell a lie; yet, as we show in great detail in our commentary of Sûrah 2:254, Jesus *(Isa)* said in the gospels,[1] that He is both the Son of Man (His human body) as well as the Son of God (His eternal Divine essence). We will turn to the gospel once again for a recorded eye witness account of the Divinity of Jesus:

When Jesus came into the coasts of Caesarea Philippi, He asked His disciples, saying, "Whom do men say that I the Son of man am?"

And they said, "Some say that you are John the Baptist: some, Elias; and others, Jeremiah, or one of the prophets."

He said unto them, "But whom say you that I am?"

And Simon Peter answered and said, "You are the Christ, the Son of the living God."

And Jesus answered and said unto him, "Blessed are you, Simon Barjona [son of Jonah]: for flesh and blood has not revealed it unto you, but *my Father which is in Heaven*" (Matthew 16:13-17, bracketed clarification mine, emphasis added).

Remember, in Sûrah 4:82, Allah says to judge what is presented in the Koran by using the Bible as the standard by which to judge it. In light of the Bible, it becomes impossible to justify Allah's claim that the gospel was *taught to* Jesus but *not about* Jesus (Sûrah 48:29).

(18:6) Yet it may be, if they believe not in this statement, that you (Muhammad) will torment your soul with grief over their footsteps.

We have a better understanding of this verse by using Muhammad Habib Shakir's translation:

Then maybe you [Muhmmad] will kill yourself with grief, sorrowing after them [Christians], if they do not believe in this announcement [that God has no Son] (bracketed clarifications mine).

Gabriel appears to be concerned that Muhammad, who is a very committed and pious Muslim, might be so troubled by a Christian's refusal to denounce the deity of Christ that he could possibly become fretful and worry himself to the brink of death.

OBSERVATION: At this point, keep in mind that Sûrah 18 has four unrelated stories: (1) The story of young Christians who slept in a cave for over 300 years; (2) the story of the good Muslim farmer verses the bad Christian farmer; (3) the story of Moses and Al Khidr, who we call the "wise man from Allah." He traveled and taught Moses many surprising things. (Khidar is never mentioned by name, but most Islamic scholars believe he is Allah's servant mentioned in this story), and (4) the story of Dhû'l Qarneyn (Alexander the Great). These stories have drawn some controversy through the years. Several explanations have been put forth regarding the meanings of them, especially the section regarding Moses and the "wise man from Allah," which is also broken down into several stories. In our commentary regarding these various unrelated events, we have decided to focus on the explanations which are more relevant to readers who have a biblical point of view.

(18:7) Look! We have placed all that is in the earth as an ornament thereof that we may try them: which of them is best in conduct.

237

Each one of our four translators uses a different word for Pickthall's word, *"ornament,"* so we must define the term *"ornament"* in light of how the other words are also used here relate to this passage; it is awkward at best. The use of the word *"ornament "* does not suggest something like earrings or hanging ornaments on a tree, although it is similar. It means an "enhancement" or "enrichment."

Gabriel is consoling Muhammad by reminding him he decorated the earth with people, and through testing, Allah will know who is worthy.

(18:8) And lo! We shall make all that is thereon [the earth] a barren mound Verily (bracketed clarification mine).

A.J. Arberry translates barren mound as *"barren dust."* Yusuf Ali's translation reads, *"as dust and dry soil"* (without growth or herbage). Another way of putting it would be to say it is like a desert, desolate and void of life.

(18:9) Or deemest [presume] you that the People of the Cave and the Inscription are a wonder among Our portents [signs]? (Bracketed clarifications mine.)[2]

> *Or do you think that the Companions of the Cave and of the Inscription were wonders among Our Sign [miracle]? (Yusuf Ali, bracketed clarification mine).*

With this verse, we are introduced to the first unrelated story in this sûrah traditionally referred to as "People of the Cave" (اصحاب الكهف) told by Allah's wise servant, Al-Kahf (the Green Man)[3] from which this sûrah gets its name (al-Kahf, i.e., The Cave). In reality, what is presented is an earlier miraculous Christian folk tale known as "The Seven Sleepers" which is a story believed to have been taken from the Latin work of Gregory of Tours.[4]

This passage begins by describing a cave with sleepers and a vague inscription on it. We are informed that sleepers and the cave's inscription are somehow miraculous, although this is the only time, we will see a reference to the mysterious inscription.

238

Historically the reason this story and others appear here in Sûrah 18 is to deal with challenges brought to him by the pagans in Mecca who were trying to discredit him. Daniel C. Peterson explains how two of the seemingly unrelated stories contained in this sûrah (the Sleepers and *Dhû'l-Qarneyn*, i.e., Alexander the Great) were inspired not by Allah but by old legends suggested as a credibility test for Muhammad by the Jews of Yathrib:

> The leaders of the Quraysh sought also to discredit Muhammad by casting doubt on the validity of his claim to revelation. The early biographies tell of a delegation sent to Yathrib to consult the Jews residence there about Muhammad, as they were surely greater experts on prophets and how to deal with them than the pagans of Mecca. The Jews, say the accounts, supplied three diagnostic questions to put to Muhammad. If he could answer the questions, they said he was a genuine prophet of God. If he could not, he was a fraud.

> They were to ask him, first, about some young men who left their people in ancient times. He should be able to tell them about these young men and their wonderful story. Second, they were to ask Muhammad about a traveler who had reached the ends of the earth, both to the east and to the west. Third, they were to request that he tell them about the spirit, and exactly what it is.[5]

Thus, in order to find out if Muhammad was truly speaking for God, he should have known how many sleepers there were in the Syriac Christian legend. (The title alone would have one believe the answer is obvious, but apparently, Muhammad wasn't very familiar with the myth about the cave in Ephesus and its sleepers.)

(18:10) When the young men fled for refuge to the Cave and said: "Our Lord! Give us mercy from the presence, and shape for us right conduct in our plight."

In the original story of the "Seven Sleepers of Ephesus" (other cities are claimed as well, it was clear that the youth were Christians who lived in Ephesus. (One of the first Christian churches was in Ephesus, which was introduced to us in Acts 19:1). The youth were forced to flee because some Pagans—with the blessings of the Roman Emperor, Decius (249-251 A.D.), wanted to martyr them. Up to this point, the story is the same in the Koran's version; the youths were looking for a safe place to hide while fleeing from the Pagans. Finally, they came across a cave and pleaded with Allah for mercy and asked him what they should do.

(18:11) Then We sealed up their hearing in the Cave for a number of years.

Regarding this verse, historian, Rev. W. St. Clair Tisdall, writes:

> *Then Allah closed up their hearing in the cave for a period of years. As the tradition goes, they slept for three hundred nine years.*[6]

Al-Kahf-Malik also sheds light through his translation and clarification:

> *So We put upon their ears a cover (put them into a deep sleep) for a number of years in the cave,*

(18:12) And afterward We raised them up that We might know which of the two parties would best calculate the time that they had tarried.

In Sûrah 2:259, we saw a man, who Allah caused to die for a hundred years—for whatever reason—and was later awoken and asked if he knew how long he had been sleeping? In this verse, Allah awoke the sleepers and asked them the same question: Could any of them *"calculate the time that they had tarried [been asleep]"?* (Bracketed clarification mine.)

For some reason, it is apparently important to Allah to see who can make the best guess (both in this verse and in Sûrah 2:259). If *"two parties"* means two groups, then what separates them as groups—philosophies, skin color, or tribes? The next verse implies nothing separates them other than them divided into two teams so they can compete for the correct answer.

(18:13) We narrate unto you their story with truth. Lo! they were young men who believed in their Lord, and We increased them in guidance.

Gabriel is relaying this story, which makes Rip Van Winkle look minor-league and insists the story is true. We know that the sleepers were monotheistic because we are told *"... they were the young men who believed in their Lord,"* and Allah acknowledges that he *"... increased them in guidance."* These "young men" (who had aged 309 plus years) were allowed special protection from Allah because they believed in him, and, according to this verse, he blessed them with good.

(18:14) And We made firm their hearts when they stood forth and said: Our Lord is the Lord of the heavens and the earth. We cry unto no god beside Him, for then should we utter an enormity [horrible thing] (bracketed clarification mine.)

> And Allah gave them stout hearts because they knew that Allah was the Lord of Heaven and earth. They declared to Allah that there is no God beside him; to say so would be blasphemous (paraphrase mine).

(18:15) These, our people, have chosen (other) gods beside Him though they bring no clear warrant (vouchsafed) [revealed] to them. And who does greater wrong than he who invents a lie concerning Allah? (Bracketed clarification mine.)

When the Koran states, "These, our people, have chosen (other) gods," it is referring to the Pagan gods. The challenge here is that the Pagans are not able to prove that their gods exist. Gabriel then asks who could be more wrong than someone who would "... invent a falsehood against Allah?"

(18:16) And when you withdraw from them and that which they worship except Allah, then seek refuge in the Cave; your Lord will spread for you of His mercy and will prepare for you a pillow in your plight.

Gabriel says the lads were able to escape to the cave. They turned their backs on the Pagan world and held fast to their belief in one god—Allah—which establishes them as Muslims. Because of their unshakeable faith, Allah showed them his mercy and protection by allowing them to escape—through centuries of sleep—while hidden in the cave.

(18:17) And you might have seen the sun when it rose [then] move[ed] away from their cave to the right, and when it set go past them on the left, and they were in the cleft thereof. That was (one) of the portents of Allah. He whom Allah guides, he indeed is led aright, and he whom He sends astray, for him you wilt not find a guiding friend (bracketed clarifications mine).

Gabriel now embarks on a somewhat unusual illustration when he tells us:

> *"And you might have seen the sun when it rose and as it moved away from their (the sleepers) cave to the right—and when it kept moving toward the left and set while they (the sleepers) were still in the cave."*

This might suggest that as the sun rose and moved across the sky toward the west, no direct sunlight entered the cave, which would have exposed the sleepers to discovery by the Pagans, Christians, or hungry animals. Because the sunlight could not reach the sleepers in the cave, their bodies would not be sunburned or damaged in any way by the harshness of the sun. We are then told, *"whom Allah wills to be led in the right way (of Islam) will be led in the right way, and those whom Allah leads astray will be lost with no one to help him"* (paraphrase mine).

The Koran is clearly fascinated with the sun, as we will observe later in this sûrah when the Koran has the sun running a course counter to nature in verses 87 and 91. Days are counted by the rhythm of the "sunrise-sunset" events as a staple of counting time. Some students of the Koran have suggested that when the sun is at its zenith, it is closest to the throne of Allah.

NOTE: As we previously pointed out, Sûrah 18 is an apocalyptic chapter broken into four parts: (1) The sleepers (verses 9-26), which we are now reading; (2) the story of the good Muslim farmer verses the bad Christian farmer in verses 32-43; (3) Moses' and Allah's wise servant, verses 60-82, and (4) the adventure of Dhul-Qarnayn, which means the "Possessor of Two Horns." As we have previously expressed, it is believed by most Muslim scholars that Dhul-Qarnayn is Alexander the Great, whose last expedition ended with the discovery of where the sunsets, mentioned later in this sûrah (verses 85 and 86); so keep in mind the Koran's transitory fascination with the sun in this sûrah.

(18:18) And you would have deemed them waking though they were asleep, and We caused them to turn over to the right and the left, and their dog stretching out his paws on the threshold.

Speaking for Allah, Gabriel is basically explaining:

And if you would have accidentally come upon them, it would have appeared as though they were dead, but I caused them to start moving, even though their eyes were closed, making it look like the dead was waking up. I did the same with their dog—caused to him stretch—although he too appeared to be asleep. If you had seen this and looked closely at them with their eyes closed, without a doubt, you would have turned and runaway full of fear (paraphrase mine).

(18:19) If you had observed them closely you [would have] had assuredly turned away from them in flight, and had been filled with awe of them (bracketed clarification mine).

With this verse, we are presented with a Koran learning opportunity.

At this point, for whatever reason, Pickthall divides this passage into two verses instead of one verse like most translations do. By assigning the last half of this verse into a separate new passage, the rest of the verses in Sûrah 18 have now increased by one number higher than most of the other English translations. Therefore, the numbering would not always be the same if we were to compare Pickthall with Yusuf Ali, Muhammad Habib Shakir, and A.J. Arberry. To be fair, Arberry's numbering system has also been numerically out of sync several times. This is also a problem with Pickthall and Arberry's translations. However, the numbering in no way changes the integrity or order of the translations, it simply affects the way the verses are numbered and not their order (flow) of revelation. To compensate for these discrepancies, the newer translations are more uniform and have been revised (not necessarily accurately) to appeal to Western sensitivities.

In order to make the Koran more accessible in looking up passages like that of the Bible, the German Orientalist Gustav Flugel, during 1834, developed what is believed to be the first numbering system, which is the basis for most of the European as well as some other translations of the Koran. Later in 1925, King Fu'ad of Egypt created a numbering system for the Koran, somewhat different from that of Flugel's method. You may notice in this translation of Pickthall's that the opening verse, which reads, "In the name of Allah, the Beneficent, the Merciful," known as the Opening or al-Fatiha verse, is not counted as a verse; the exception being the Indo-Pakistani systems which usually does count it as a verse. While confusing, the actual passages remain faithful, despite their differences in numbering. This is good information to remember in the event you wish to compare the wording of the various translations.

(18:20) And in like manner We awakened them that they might question one another. A speaker from among them said: "How long have you tarried (remained)?" They said: "We have tarried a day or some part of a day." (Others) said: "Your Lord best knows what you have tarried." Now send one of you with this silver coin unto the city, and let him see what food is purest there and bring you a supply thereof. Let him be courteous and let no man know of you (bracketed clarification mine).

We are told that Allah awakened them but never assured them that they need not worry about their pursuers because they had been asleep for 309 years. (We see this number revealed six verses later.) Be that as it may, we can see why the sleepers might have been hungry and needed food. Believing they had only been asleep for a day and not told any differently. They would naturally assume that the people pursuing them might have gone into the city to find them and raise the alarm to watch out for them, so they had to be cautious.

(18:21) For they, if they should come to know [who] you [are], will stone you or turn you back to their religion; then you would never prosper (bracketed clarifications mine).

According to this verse, we also see that the sleepers, who had taken sanctuary in this cave, remembered there was a town nearby. But they were still afraid that the town was a pagan town whose occupants would try to convert the sleepers into paganism.

(18:22) And in like manner We disclosed them (to the people of the city) that they might know the promise of Allah is true, and that, as for the Hour, there is no doubt concerning it. When (the people of the city) disputed of their case among themselves [regarding the sleepers], they said: Build over them a building; their Lord knows best concerning them. Those who won their point said: "We verily [certainly]; shall build a place of worship over them" (bracketed clarification mine).

Now we quickly shift from the previous dialogue where the inhabitants of the city are told by Gabriel that Allah's promise is true (unless, of course, he decides to abrogate/repeal it as we are told he does in Sûrahs 2:106 and 16:101). It is confusing because what is the promise from Allah that is referenced here?

NOTE: There are several Muslim countries believed to have the cave of the "Seven Sleepers." One example can be found in the village of N'Gaous, located in the Aures mountain range, where there is a mosque known as the "Mosque of the Seven Sleepers." Because the cave was never a burial chamber, building a mosque over it is allowed under Sharia Law.

(18:23) (Some) will say: "They were three, their dog the fourth," and some will say: "Five, their dog the sixth," guessing at random: and (some) say: "Seven, and their dog the eighth." Say "(O Muhammad): My Lord is best aware of their number. None knows them save a few. So contend not concerning them except with an outward contending, and ask not any of them concerning them."

This answer on the actual number of sleepers in the cave seems to be all over the place.[7]

It seems that the Jews gave good counsel when they told the Meccans to ask Muhammad how many sleepers were in the cave. This story was known for centuries before Muhammad, so the Jews of Yathrib (Medina) knew the number when they had the Meccans ask Muhammad about this story in order to see how legitimate Muhammad was.

Perhaps Allah's vague answer will provide cover for Muhammad regarding the actual number of the "seven sleepers." Then again, because Gabriel is vague about the number of sleepers, the Meccans could conclude that Muhammad does not know the answer

Still, according to this verse, we are led to believe that Allah does know how many sleepers there were; whether or not he wants to reveal that number to Muhammad is his prerogative, and because he's god, people should respect his decision as final.

(18:24) And say not anything, indeed! I shall do that [provide an answer] tomorrow" (bracketed clarification mine),

> *Arguing with critics might be causing Muhammad some anxiety, so Muhammad reveals that Gabriel told him to "keep quiet about the number of sleepers because Allah will reveal that answer tomorrow" (paraphrase mine).*

To the casual observer, it might seem that Gabriel is conveniently allowing Muhammad to put off the answer to this problematic question until the next day, which will give him time to come up with something. Meanwhile, Muhammad now has an excuse to keep silent.

(18:25) Except if Allah will. And remember your Lord when you forget, and say: "It may be that my Lord guides me unto a nearer way of truth than this."

This is a continuation of the last verse to this verse which together reads:

> And say not anything, Indeed! I shall do that [provide an answer] tomorrow, Except if Allah will. And remember your Lord when you forget and say: "It may be that my Lord guides me unto a nearer way of truth than this" (bracketed clarification mine).

This is an "escape clause" for Muhammad, which allows him to tell the people that Allah does indeed know the answer, and if He chooses, He will reveal the number of sleepers tomorrow; nevertheless, it's such a trivial matter to Allah that he might not want to be bothered with revealing how many sleepers there are. Therefore, we shouldn't be obsessed with the number of sleepers either. By allowing Allah to put off the answer as to how many sleepers there were until tomorrow, hopefully, those testing Muhammad might forget all about it or not run into Muhammad the next day.

(18:26) And (it is said) they tarried [remained] in their Cave three hundred years and add nine.

This verse quickly redirects away from the problematic number of sleepers in the cave to the answerable number of years in the cave, which according to the revised Muslim version, is the mystical 300 plus 9 years are the years they slept, which could mean 300 solar years plus 9 solar years, which still puts the lunar calendar at 309 years, although the seasons would be off.

The Koran's "Miraculous" Number 309

The following is an extra-koranic event which is part of Muslim folklore, relating to the importance of the number "309." This mystical-Muslim number is the Koran's subtle way of associating the story of the "sleepers" with Alexander the Great and the birth of Jesus. According to the *Syriac Infancy Gospel*, the census taken during the time of Jesus' birth was done in the 309th year of the Alexandrian era. This reference point in numbering years began the year Alexander the Great's son, (Alexander IV, his only legitimate heir) died in 309 B.C. The year he died was considered to be the first year of the Alexandrian Era, which is also known today as the beginning of the Alexander (or Coptic) calendar.

NOTE: Alexander the Great claimed to be divine and the son of the god, Zeus,[8] but in light of the Koran's obsessive denial of the Divinity of Christ as the Son of God, it appears that Alexander's claim to Divinity was apparently unknown to Muhammad and the angel, Gabriel. On the other hand, if they did know about it, then perhaps claiming the famous conqueror of the known world as a Muslim prophet far outweighed Alexander's alleged Divinity and the fact that he was a well-known Pagan polytheist.

In the *Syriac Infancy Gospel,* Joseph accompanied Mary on their trip (and that is where the story departs from the biblical account). While on the trip, Mary went into labor, so they were forced to take refuge in a cave where Jesus was born in 309 of the Alexandrian calendar.[9]

However, in the Koran's version, Mary had birth pangs on her journey, but she did not travel with her betrothed husband, Joseph, nor did she give birth in a cave. In Sûrah 19 titled, "Mary," we read, "And the pains of childbirth drove her to the trunk of a palm-tree" (Sûrah 19:23).

In both stories of the sleepers and Nativity in the Koran, there is a period of 309 years centered around a cave. Some Islamic scholars suggest there is an intended mystical connection drawn since both are revolving around a 309-year period signifying how Allah was able to manipulate control over people and historical events. [10]

(18:27) Say: "Allah is best aware how long they tarried. His is the invisible of the heavens and the earth. How clear of sight is He and keen of hearing! They [the sleepers] have no protecting friend beside Him, and He makes none [Jesus] to share in His government" (bracketed clarifications mine).

248

Here, Gabriel tells Muhammad that Allah knows best how long the sleepers have been asleep in the cave. He is the invisible God of the Heavens and earth (or he knows the unseen things of the heavens and earth). He sees very clearly, and his hearing is perfect, but Allah never reveals the number of sleepers in the cave. While the Christians refer to them as the "Seven Sleepers of Ephesus," the Muslim version is known as the "People of the Cave."

Note: Near the beginning of this story, we are told Allah knew how long the sleepers were in the cave and was agreeable to providing the answer. On the other hand, when it actually came time to reveal the number of how many sleepers there were, Allah could not be bothered to provide the Meccans an answer to their test. That caused Muhammad to fail the test, just as the Jews of Yathrib warned the Meccans would happen. (Allah never did tell Muhammad how many sleepers there were.) Many of them rejected Muhammad and his new religion. (See commentary for Sûrah 18:22.)

Gabriel concludes the story of the sleepers by doing a quick sidestep, deflecting and redirecting the attention of Muhammad's audience to the recurring attack on the Divinity of Jesus; he told his audience the sleepers have no other protecting friend besides Allah, and they have none (not Jesus) with whom to share his ruling authority.

(18:28) And recite [repeat] that which has been revealed unto you of the Scripture of your Lord. There is none who can change His words, and you will find no refuge [Jesus] beside Him (bracketed clarifications mine).

Because the term "Scripture" can be applied to either the Bible or the Koran, it is not really clear as to which "Scripture" is being referred to here, especially because the subject matter is dealing with the third-century Christian legend of the Seven Sleepers of Ephesus. This legend precedes the Koran and may be mistaken by Muhammad as having come from a biblical source. Having said that, most Muslim scholars agree that the "Scripture" being referred to here is the Koran. Gabriel is telling Muhammad no one can change what Allah has revealed. This verse ends by restating the underlying theme of the Koran attacking the Divinity of Jesus with the reminder that Allah has no one other than himself. Thus, in closing, Muhammad deflects once again from the controversy regarding the number of sleepers and reinforces that it is only in Allah where anyone can find refuge.

(18:29) Restrain yourself along with those who cry unto their Lord at morn and evening, seeking His countenance; and let not your eyes overlook them, desiring the pomp of the Life; of the world; and obey not him whose heart We have made heedless of Our remembrance, who follows his own lust and whose case has been abandoned (bracketed clarification mine).

Gabriel continues to instruct Muhammad:

Control yourself so you will not wander into the desires of the world but continue like the Muslims who pray the required daily prayers and seek Allah's face. Watch over them as well, forgoing the glitter of the world, and do not pay attention to those who have rejected Allah. As for those who are worldly, *".... obey not him whose heart We have made heedless of Our remembrance..."* and whose case has been abandoned (paraphrase mine).

After hearing the preaching of Islam, then comparing the Koran with history and the Bible, it is not surprising why people rejected the teachings of Islam. That caused great concern to Muhammad until Allah came to his aid by revealing he is the one who caused the detractors to reject Islam; after doing so, Allah abandoned them.

(18:30) Say: "(It is) the truth from the Lord of you (all). Then whosoever will, let him believe, and whosoever will, let him disbelieve." Look! We have prepared for disbelievers Fire. Its tent encloses them. If they ask for showers, they will be showered with water like to molten lead which burns the faces. Calamitous [dreadful] [is] the drink and ill the resting-place! (Bracketed clarifications mine.)

Gabriel continues:

> *Warn them, Muhammad, that you are telling the truth as you have received it from Allah, the Lord of everyone. It is up to each person to either believe or not believe, but be aware that those who disbelieve will go to Hell. Allah predicts—when those who go to Hell ask for water to relieve them from the fire—he will shower them with water that is like molten lead, and their faces will be burned. Dreadful will be their drink—and their abode in Hell will be horribly hostile (paraphrase mine).*

OBSERVATION: As we saw in verse 29, we were told the reason people reject Allah is because he is the one who takes control of their hearts: "...whose heart We have made heedless [oblivious] of Our remembrance ...;" therefore, Allah is the one who prevents people from receiving the message of Islam.

(18:31) Lo! as to those who believe and do good works—Lo! We suffer [allow] not the reward of one whose work is goodly to be lost (bracketed clarification mine).

Once more, we see the works-based salvation message in the Koran as contrasted to the biblical verse found in Ephesians 2:89, where it says we are saved by grace, not by works.

(18:32) As for such, theirs will be Gardens of Eden, wherein rivers flow beneath them; therein they will be given armlets of gold and will wear green robes of finest silk and gold embroidery, reclining upon throne therein. Blest the reward, and fair the resting-place!

Gabriel says that those who do good works and are pleasing to Allah will enjoy paradise. They will be clothed with exquisite garments and wear golden jewelry while reclining on a throne as a king. In Islam, the promise of Paradise exploits man's base carnal lust.

We see another depiction of Islamic heaven in Sûrah 78:

Surely for the god-fearing awaits a place of security, gardens and vineyards and maidens with swelling breasts, like of age, and a cup overflowing (Sûrah 78:31-34, A.J. Arberry).

It appears that the of the Muslim translators seem to be embarrassed reguarding sûrah 78:33 causing them to edit the Arabic passage and leave half of the passage when they translate their English versions of the Koran thereby censoring the erotic promise of well-developed maddens. Some defenders of the Muslim faith even try to say what is really being described are raisins.[11]

OBSERVATION: In the Bible, there is no sex or need for harems in Heaven like the Koran has (Sûrah's 44:51-55; 52:17-20; 55:56-57; 78:31, etc.). In Heaven, believers in Christ will be like the angels (only without wings), neither giving in marriage nor being married (Matthew 22:30). Angels do not have sexual relations since they do not need to procreate in order to replace their numbers because they never die. People in Heaven will also be immortal and likewise, they have no need to replace themselves and, therefore, will not have carnal desires. This is another glaring discrepancy between the Koran and the Bible. Apparently, the Muslim's heaven caters to the lusts of the flesh, to say the least.

In the next verse, we move into the second story.

(18:33) Coin [create] for them a similitude [parable]: Two men, unto one of whom We had assigned two gardens of grapes, and We had surrounded both with date-palms and had put between them tillage [cultivation] (bracketed clarification mine).

Now without warning, Muhammad shifts to the second story about two men who Allah had given separate vineyards. Allah surrounded the vineyards with date palms and prepared the soil, which separated them.

(18:34) Each of those gardens gave its fruit and withheld naught [nothing] thereof. And We caused a river to gush forth therein (bracketed clarification mine).

As the story goes, the gardens were wonderful and provided an abundant amount of fruit. Allah also provided a river to flow from springs onto the various properties to nourish the plants.

(18:35) And he [the boastful of the two men] had fruit. And he said unto his comrade, when he spoke with him: "I am more than you in wealth, and stronger in respect of men" (bracketed clarification mine).

However, we are told that one of the men became proud and haughty. He bragged that his garden made him wealthier and better than the others, including the second man to whom Allah had also provided a garden.

(18:36) And he went into his garden, while he (thus) wronged himself. He said: "I think not that all this will ever perish."

It seemed to the haughty farmer that his bountiful garden was because of his exceptional talent, and while he held that attitude, this verse says referring to his haughty attitude, "... *he (thus) wronged himself.*" Because of his belief that it was all his doing, the haughty farmer assumed that his garden would always bear fruit and supply him with plenty of nourishment for him. It was heaven on earth.

(18:37) I think not that the Hour (of Judgment) will ever come, and if indeed I am brought back unto my Lord I surely shall find better than this as a resort (bracketed clarification mine).

Besides his unfounded pride in himself and the garden, this foolish man never thought the hour of judgment would come, but if it did, he believed God would prosper him there even more than he had here on earth!

(18:38) His comrade [the humble farmer], while he disputed with him, exclaimed: "Disbelieves you in Him [Allah] Who created you of dust, then of a drop (of seed), and then fashioned you a man?"

This is another koranic "combo-creation" version of Genesis 2:7, where Adam was made from the dust of the ground (which we all agree), but Adam's creation was not followed by a "drop." Both Yusuf Ali and A. J. Arberry translates this as "...*then out of a sperm-drop.*"

Perhaps this is poetic liberty and is referring to how Adam's descendants were created through sperm (which is half correct) since it was believed to contain the seed, and thus, how the farmer was created by his father long after Adam himself was originally created from dust. The problem with this verse is only the woman has the seed, which is the egg, and the man's "drop" is similar to how bees fertilize plants with its pollen (plant sperm), but the pollen itself is not the seed. Aside from that, this sentence is fairly simple to understand. The humble Muslim farmer is asking the haughty Christian farmer if his Lord is Allah.

(18:39) "But He is Allah, my Lord, and I ascribe unto my Lord no partner" [Jesus].

Again, the Koran cannot resist the opportunity to present its underlying theme of attacking the Divinity of Christ. We also discover that the likable and humble farmer is Muslim because he ascribes no partner to Allah, unlike the prideful Christian farmer does.

(18:40) If only, when you entered your garden, you had said: "That which Allah wills (will come to pass)! There is no strength save [except] in Allah!" though you see me as less than you in wealth and children (bracketed clarification mine).

The poor godly Muslim farmer is saying to the haughty farmer that he should have been humble because Allah allowed him to succeed, but instead, the wealthy farmer wrongly belittled the poor Muslim farmer because you "... see me as less than you in wealth and children."

(18:41) "Yet it may be that my Lord will give me better than your garden, and [that He] will send on it [the haughty farmer's garden] a [lightning] bolt from heaven, and some morning it will be a smooth hillside" (bracketed clarifications mine).

The humble farmer is telling the haughty farmer, who has been more blessed than himself, that maybe Allah will take pity on and also provide him with a fruitful farm. At the same time, maybe Allah will send a lightning bolt from heaven and render the haughty farmer's garden useless by destroying the various tiers on the hillside. (We read in Sûrah 18: 40, where Arberry, Pickthall, and Shakir translated the haughty farmer's garden as being located on a hillside.) "Should a thunderbolt *strike your terrace and cause a landslide, then the hillside would no* longer be terraced, thus unable to be planted" (paraphrase mine). A terraced hillside allows for a level planting area and a flat surface for both planting and retaining water; by not terracing the hillside, the water would drain properly.

(18:42) "Or the water of the garden will run off underground so that you will never be able to find it."

This verse continues from the previous verse as the humble Muslim farmer suggests that perhaps Allah will dry up the haughty man's springs that produce the rivers with which he waters his land.

(18:43) And his fruit was beset (with destruction). Then began he to wring his hands for all that he had spent upon it, when (now) it was all ruined on its trellises, and to say: "Would that I had ascribed no partner [Jesus]to my Lord!"

As this story comes to an end, we see another favorite koranic conclusion to a story that loves to attack the Divinity of Jesus. Thus, at the end of this verse, we discover that the haughty farmer is, in fact, a haughty "Christian" farmer. As we study the various translations of the Koran, it becomes obvious that the Muslim translators are faithful to the original Arabic style of an indirect approach, as opposed to direct opposition to denying the Trinity and Deity of Christ. It is a fair technique to use when subtly attacking an opponent's belief, while still trying to bring them around to your way of thinking; yet, when we read between the lines (or even see the obvious point being made), the poetic license fades as the overarching attack on Christianity, along with the recurring theme of the Koran attacking the deity of Christ is so obvious.

Bearing this in mind, we will continue our biblical interpretation of the Koran in light of the Bible and uncover the parts of it, which are subtly trying to undermine the Judeo-Christian doctrine, as well as reveal what is actually being promoted.

As we stated at the outset of this verse's commentary, it ends with the haughty farmer revealed as one of those Trinitarian believers who then became very distressed and repentant because he then realized he was one of the evil, misguided Christians. He acknowledged that he insulted Allah by wrongfully believing that Jesus is the Son of God and understands that his misguided faith in Jesus is the reason why his vineyard is withering on the vine.

(18:44) And he had no troop of men to help him as against Allah, nor could he save himself.

According to this verse, the repentant, haughty, Christian farmer realizes that he cannot help himself, nor can his Christ. There is no one to help him face Allah, nor can he do anything to gain Allah's help.

(18:45) In this case [there] is [only] protection [coming] from Allah, the True. He is best for reward, and best for consequence (bracketed clarifications mine).

We are told once again—concerning the haughty Christian farmer's failing crops and wealth—only Allah is able to protect him. Allah is the one who decides the consequences of what a person does. Allah is the true and greatest god for providing any kind of result in the matter, be it a reward or a consequence.

(18:46) And coin [make-up] for them the similitude [parable] of the life of the world as water which We send down from the sky, and the vegetation of the earth mingles with it and then becomes dry twigs that the winds scatter. Allah is able to do all things (bracketed clarification mine).

A.J. Arberry translates it this way:

And strike for them the similitude (likeness) of the present life: it is as water that We send down out of Heaven, and the plants of the earth mingle with it; and in the morning it is straw [and] in the winds scatter[ed]; and God is omnipotent (all-powerful) over everything (bracketed clarifications mine).

Gabriel is telling a parable of life. It is like the rain which waters the plants. The water strengthens and nourishes them, but with the passing of time, things change. There is no more vitality because the once young and promising plant grew old, shriveled up, died, and became dust in the wind. According to this verse, Allah is all-powerful. He is able to give life and take it away.

(18:47) Wealth and children are an ornament of the life of the world. But the good deeds which endure are better in the Lord's sight for reward, and better in respect of hope.

Gabriel is saying that life is appreciated by most when they are surrounded by wealth and children, but what is even better is doing good deeds that have lasting results with the anticipation Allah will bestow even more blessings.

(18:48) And (bethink [remember] you of) the [Judgment] Day when we remove the hills and you see the earth emerging, and We gather them together so as to leave not one of them behind (bracketed clarifications mine).

Arberry, Shakir, and Ali translate *"hills"* as *"mountains."* At first glance, we wonder what is actually being gathered? It is a little vague, but what is obvious is that the mountains were removed and are now gathered together for the people of the earth. In context, however, we see that it is not the mountains, but the people of the Last Day who are gathered.

And do you not think that on Judgment Day after we level all the mountains that we will not gather you also? We will gather everyone from all over the world and not overlook even one of you (paraphrase mine).

The mountains being flattened here might be echoing Revelation 16 where we read:

> Now the great city [Babylon] was divided into three parts, and the cities of the nations fell. And great Babylon was remembered before God, to give her the cup of the wine of the fierceness of His wrath. Then every island fled away, and the mountains were not found (Revelation 16:19-20, NKJV).

(18:49) And they are set before the Lord in ranks (and it is said unto them): Now verily [truly] have you come unto Us as We created you at the first. But you thought that We had set no tryst [appointed time] for you (bracketed clarifications mine).

This seems to be a Last Days prophecy when all will appear stripped naked before Allah just as they were created, despite some of the people's disbelief in a life after death or a judgment (doom's) day.

(18:50) And the Book is placed, and you see the guilty fearful of that which is therein, and they say: "What kind of a Book is this that leaves not a small thing nor a great thing but has counted it!" And they find all that they did confronting them, and the Lord wrongs no one.

This is referring to a book in which everything a person does in their life is written down—right to the minutest detail—both good deeds as well as bad. This is not unlike the Book of Life spoken about in the Bible eight times, which is also known as the "Lamb's (Jesus') Book of Life" (Exodus 32:32; Daniel 12:1; Philippians 4:3; Revelation 3:5, 13:8, 20:12, 15, 21:27).

(18:51) And (remember) when We said unto the angels: Fall prostrate before Adam, and they fell prostrate, all save [except] Iblîs [Satan]. He was of the jinn, so he rebelled against his Lord's command. Will you choose him [Adam] and his seed for your protecting friends instead of Me when they are an enemy unto you? Calamitous [a disaster] is the exchange of the evil-doers! (Bracketed clarifications mine.)

258

OBSERVATION: The word "jinn" sometimes (i.e., genie), is exclusive to Islamic mythology and alien to Judeo-Christian and Western thought.

This passage is unbiblical. Remember, Allah said we are supposed to judge the Koran by the Bible, which he claims he revealed to mankind [Sûrah 3:3; 4:82; 5:47).

Allah tells those who stand before him on Judgment Day that when he created Adam, he told the angels to bow down on their faces (a position of worship) before Adam. They all obeyed except Satan.

The devil in this passage is a jinn who is protesting against Allah, showing favoritism toward humans who are—as Satan claims here—Allah's enemy and evil-doers over the faithful angels.

Another problem with this passage is when Satan asks, *"Will you choose him [Adam] and his seed for your protecting friends instead of Me...."* Since when does God need a protector—a protector from what? Who or what can harm God? In light of Genesis 1:26 and 2:15, Adam was made a steward (proctor) over God's creation. Muhammad Habib Shakir drops the term "protectors" and simply translates it, *"What! would you then take him and his offspring for friends rather than Me?"* (Sûrah 18:50), which seems less confusing and makes more sense. The fall of Satan in the Bible was because sin was found in him (Ezekiel 28:14-15) before humans had succumbed to sin. It was Satan who influenced the sinless Adam and Eve into their fallen state by calling God's Word into question (Genesis 3:1).   Furthermore, the Bible teaches us that angels do not bow before men, and people do not bow before angels. We can see the true relationship between angels and people through an event which happened when God took the Apostle John up to Heaven, and he encountered an angel:

Then he said to me, "Write: 'Blessed *are* those who are called to the marriage supper of the Lamb!' " And he said to me, "These are the true sayings of God." And I fell at his feet to worship him. But he said to me,

259

"See *that you do* not *do that!* I am your fellow servant, and of your brethren who have the testimony of Jesus. Worship God! For the testimony of Jesus is the spirit of prophecy" (Revelation 19:9-10, NKJV, emphasis added).

(18:52) I made them not to witness the creation of the heavens and the earth, nor their own creation; nor choose I misleaders for (My) helpers

Gabriel is saying that Allah did not allow people to see how he created the Heavens and the earth or even how they came to be created by him. Combined with the last verse, Allah does not *"choose misleaders,"* as does Satan and people who ignore their prophets and turn others away from the truth. We see this in regard to those "misleaders" who come against Muhammad and the truth of Islam. In this case, they would be the Pagans, Jews, and Christians who mislead people away from Muhammad and his teachings of Islam.

(18:53) And (be mindful of) the Day when He will say: "Call those partners of Mine [Mary and Jesus, Sûrah 5:116] whom you pretended." Then they will cry unto them, but they will not hear their prayer, and We shall set a gulf of doom between them (bracketed clarifications mine).

Here we are, once again, treated to the ongoing and obsessive underlying theme of the Koran's attacks on the Trinity and the Divinity of Jesus. What Muhammad is really saying here is that the day will come when Allah will say to the foolish Christians on Judgment Day, *"Call those partners of Mine [Jesus and Mary]"* to see if they can help!" But Jesus and Mary will be deaf to their prayers because they are only human and can do nothing. In the end, Allah will send Christians to Hell.

(18:54) And the guilty behold the Fire and know that they are about to fall therein, and they find no way of escape thence [then].

Continuing the theme of the previous verse, Gabriel is saying that because the Christians worship Jesus as the Son of God, they are condemned to the fires of Hell, and since Allah has no associates, Jesus *(Isa)* cannot help them.

(18:55) And verily [truly] We have displayed for mankind in this Qur'ân all manner of similitudes, but man is more than anything contentious (bracketed clarification mine).

Another way of saying this is the following paraphrase based on other translations:

> *Truly, we have shown mankind all kinds of examples in the Koran that are similar to the Bible, but some people will not accept what Allah is saying; instead, they will be quarrelsome, holding fast to their old misconceived beliefs. They argue that they are right, and Allah is wrong (paraphrase mine).*

(18:56) And naught [nothing] hinder mankind from believing when the guidance comes unto them, and from asking forgiveness of their Lord, unless (it be that they wish) that the judgment of the men of old should come upon them or (that) they should be confronted with the Doom [judgment]. (Bracketed clarification mine.)

Perhaps a better way to say this would be:
> *Nothing can obstruct people from believing in what Allah claims is truth and seeking his forgiveness, yet these ungodly people will only believe that their faith is wrong if Allah were to send a great disaster upon them as he did to those infidel nations of the past. They reject the truth of Islam that Muhammad is teaching and argue that if they are wrong, then prove it by bringing on the Day of Judgment (paraphrase mine).*

(18:57) We send not the messengers save as bearers of good news and warners. Those who disbelieve contend with falsehood in order to refute the Truth thereby. And they take Our revelations and that wherewith they are threatened as a jest.

Allah sent the biblical prophets to encourage mankind, as well as advise and warn them, but they still insist on believing a lie. Those who will not accept the teachings of Allah either believe in false, or they will not accept what is taught to them by Muhammad, believing it is all foolishness.

(18:58) And who does greater wrong than he who has been reminded of the revelations of his Lord, yet turns away from them and forgets what his hands send forward (to the Judgment)? Look! on their hearts We have placed coverings so that they understand not, and in their ears a deafness. And though you call them to the guidance, in that case they can never be led aright.

Once again, Allah brings comfort to Muhammad regarding those Christians and Jews who reject his message of Islam.

To put it another way:

So who is it that does wrong other than the Jews or Christians who have been reminded of the teachings originally given through the Bible and still refuse to accept what Allah is now proclaiming? Christians and Jews will be judged for refusing your teachings, but don't feel bad, Muhammad, because Allah placed a covering on their hearts so they cannot understand nor hear the truth when you tell it to them because Allah has made it so they can never be saved (paraphrase mine).

(18:59) Your Lord is the Forgiver, Full of Mercy. If He took them to task (now) for what they earn, He would hasten on the doom for them; but theirs is an appointed term from which they will find no escape.

Allah is not in a rush to pronounce judgment; he will allow them to live out their predestined time before he acts against them. When that time comes, you can be assured that they will not be able to escape punishment. Again, we have conflicting statements; sometimes, we are told that Allah controls whether or not people accept Islam, and at other times, like here, we are told that Allah is giving the unbelievers time to repent. Which is it?

(18:60) And (all) those townships! We destroyed them when they did wrong, and We appointed a fixed time for their destruction.

And as for the evil cities we destroyed in the past, we decided when their appointed time of destruction would be (paraphrase mine).

(18:61) And when Moses said unto his servant: I will not give up until I reach the point where the two rivers meet, though I march on for ages.

Once again, we observe the Koran taking another disjointed turn with this incomplete thought as we shift into the third story of this sûrah. Some Muslim scholars argue that this story was inserted to impress disbelievers not to always look at the surface of what is told and the accuracy of Muhammad's revelations, but rather to consider the hidden universal truths that are revealed.

To that end, we now begin the story of Moses and Allah's wise servant, who is not to be confused with the servant Moses is speaking to here. We will also see similarities between this story and some themes found in the Bible regarding Israel's escape from Egypt on their way to Canaan.

This story begins by Moses telling his Hebrew servant he will not give up (apparently, they are traveling) until he reaches the headwaters of the two rivers, even if it takes him forever!

Pickthall and Shakir say where the two rivers meet, while A.J. Arberry agrees with Yusuf Ali by using the word *"seas."* Using the term *"seas"* seems to make more sense because, in the next verse, three of our four translations agree on the word *"sea,"* except Pickthall, who uses the word *"waters."* Nevertheless, the following story about Moses is not verified by archaeology or the Bible and is found only in the Koran.

(18:62) And when they reached the point where the two [rivers] met, they forgot their fish, and it [the fish] took its way into the waters, being free (bracketed clarifications mine).

In another disjointed verse, fish appear in the storyline, but there is no explanation as to how or why.

When Moses and his servant finally reached the headwaters, it appears they had caught fish, but some Islamic scholars like Imam Baqir (677-733 A.D.), the fifth Shia Imam and Imam Sadiq (700; 702-765 A.D.), the sixth Shia Imam, believe that Moses and his servant, brought salted fish with them on their trip. Although there is no mention of it in this passage, the Imams agree that while Moses' servant was rinsing the fish, they came alive in his hand and escaped into the sea; however, it seems more likely that Moses and his servant just set aside what was to be their meal and the fish—for whatever reason—slipped, unbeknown to them, into the water and washed out to sea. The only thing clear in this passage is that some fish, for whatever reason, made their way back into the river and flowed straight out to sea while Moses and his servant were distracted.

At this point the Koran does not make it clear if (1) the fish were salted and not alive; (2) they were accidentally knocked into the water, or (3) they were in a basket lowered into the water to keep them fresh, but they did escape from the basket.

(18:63) And when they had gone further, he said unto his servant: Bring us our breakfast. Verily [truly] we have found fatigue in this our journey (bracketed clarification mine).

Apparently, Moses and his servant continued on their journey and forgot about the fish until they had walked quite a distance, at which point they became tired and hungry, and made a decision to eat and rest:

> *After they had gone a little further, Moses asked his Hebrew servant to get their breakfast. It had been a long and exhausting trip, and they were in need of some nourishment (paraphrase mine).*

(18:64) He said: "Did you see, when we took refuge on the rock, and I forgot the fish—and none but Satan caused me to forget to mention it—it took its way into the waters by a marvel."

He replied: "Did you see (what happened) when we took ourselves to the rock? I did indeed forget (about) the fish: none but Satan made me forget to tell (you) about it: it took its course through the sea in a marvelous way!" (Paraphrase of Yusuf Ali's translation.)

(18:65) He said: This is that which we have been seeking. So they retraced their steps again.

Moses said the place they had just come from was the place they were looking for, so he told his Hebrew servant they should go back.

(18:66) Then found they one of Our slaves, unto whom We had given mercy from Us, and had taught him knowledge from Our presence

Yusuf Ali translates it this way:

So they found one of Our servants, on whom We had bestowed Mercy from Ourselves and whom We had taught knowledge from Our own Presence.

On their way, Moses and his Hebrew servant ran into *"…one of Our slaves,"* whom we will refer to as "Allah's wise servant.[10] That is very interesting because, according to the Koran, Moses was also supposed to be a Muslim prophet of Allah (Sûrah 19:51). That alone makes this encounter a bit peculiar with the wise servant from Allah teaching Moses instead of Allah, which he directly did with the other prophets and Muhammad. In the biblical account, God spoke directly to Moses many times (Exodus 2:23-24; Exodus, Chapters 13 through 20, and Chapter 32).

In this section, Moses appears to be ignorant about Islam, and if this is to parallel the Bible (which it does not), then at what point does Moses come to personally know God, and at what point does he become a prophet? Notice also that this is the last time we will hear from Moses' Hebrew companion and servant.

Could it be this passage—which introduces the wise servant of Allah— is designed to explain how Moses came to know Allah? Are we to assume this takes place just after he killed the Egyptian who was beating the Hebrew slave (Exodus 2:12) and before marrying the Priest of Midian's daughter (Exodus 2:21)? Like many passages in the Koran, we are left with more questions than answers.

(18:67) Moses said unto him: May I follow you, to the end that you may teach me right conduct of that which you have been taught?

Moses is asking Allah's wise servant if he can follow him to learn Allah's teachings.

(18:68) He said: See! you cannot bear with me (bracketed clarification mine).

The wise servant of Allah is saying, *"Look, you won't be able to have patience with me" (paraphrase mine),* yet Moses is supposed to learn patience through Allah's wise servant. It is at this point when Moses' Hebrew servant vanishes.

(18:69) How can you bear with that whereof you cannot compass any knowledge?

Muhammad Habib Shakir's translation:

> *And how can you have patience in that of which you have not got a comprehensive knowledge?*

Or to paraphrase it:

> *... and how can you be patient in learning something about which you have no background or understanding?*

(18:70) He said: "Allah willing, you shall find me patient and I shall not in aught [anything] gainsay [argue with] you" (bracketed clarifications mine).

Again, we have to deal with a modern translation written in Old English. Ali's translation makes a little more sense:

266

Moses said: "Thou will find me, if Allah so will[s], (truly) patient: nor shall I disobey you in aught [anything]" (bracketed clarification mine). (Sûrah 18: 69, Yusuf Ali, bracketed clarification mine).

Moses answers the wise servant of Allah and explains that he will be patient with Allah's help and not disobey him if the man will kindly teach him.

(18:71) He said: "Well, if you go with me, ask me not concerning aught [anything] till I myself make mention of it unto you."

Muhammad Habib Shakir's translation:

He [the wise servant of Allah] said: "If you would follow me, then do not question me about anything until I speak to you about it." (Bracketed clarification mine).

So, the wise servant of Allah agrees that he would instruct Moses if he would keep quiet and not interrupt him while he is teaching, and only speak when he is spoken to.

(18:72) So they twain [both] set out till, when they were in the ship, he [the wise servant of Allah] made a hole therein. (Moses) said: "Have you made a hole therein to drown the folk thereof? You verily [truly] have done a dreadful thing" (bracketed clarifications mine).

The story becomes more intriguing as Moses and the wise servant of Allah continued on their journey and eventually came to a boat, which they boarded. While sailing, the wise servant of Allah decided to sink the boat, which would have drowned the crew and other passengers (which is reminiscent of how God destroyed Pharaoh's army by drowning them in water after Moses and the children of Israel crossed the Red Sea):

And the Egyptians pursued, and went in after them to the midst of the sea, even all Pharaoh's horses, his chariots, and his horsemen.

267

And it came to pass, that in the morning watch the LORD looked unto the host of the Egyptians through the pillar of fire and of the cloud, and troubled the host of the Egyptians,

And took off their chariot wheels, that they drove them heavily: so that the Egyptians said, "Let us flee from the face of Israel; for the LORD fights for them against the Egyptians." And the LORD said unto Moses, "Stretch out your hand over the sea, that the waters may come again upon the Egyptians, upon their chariots, and upon their horsemen."

And Moses stretched forth his hand over the sea, and the sea returned to his strength when the morning appeared; and the Egyptians fled against it; and the LORD overthrew the Egyptians in the midst of the sea. And the waters returned, and covered the chariots, and the horsemen, and all the host of Pharaoh that came into the sea after them; there remained not so much as one of them (Exodus 14:23-28).

OBSERVATION: Both the Koran and the Bible record the Exodus account of the Israelites leaving Egypt and being pursued by Pharaoh and his army. Both accounts also record the drowning of the Egyptians in the Red Sea, so why is the Koran referring to this story here? Are we to accept it as true? If not, what is the purpose of Moses experiencing this déjà vu adventure? If we are to believe this story as factual, then we must ask why there are no historical or biblical accounts of Moses ever having taken a side trip with just a Hebrew servant and then being diverted to yet another excursion by a prophetic guide before or after he left Egypt.

(18:73) He said: "Did I not tell you that you could not bear with me?"

The wise servant of Allah is basically telling Moses, "See, I said you would not be able to be patient with me (paraphrase mine)."

(18:74) (Moses) said: Be not wroth [angry] with me that I forgot, and be not hard upon me for my fault (bracketed clarification mine).

Moses asks for forgiveness because, in the excitement of the moment when the ship was sinking, he forgot he would not question anything that happened and begs the wise servant of Allah to forgive him.

18:75 So they twain [both] journeyed on till, when they met a lad, he [the wise servant of Allah] slew him. (Moses) said: "What! Have you slain an innocent soul who has slain no man? Verily [truly] you have done a horrid thing" (bracketed clarifications mine).

The two continued on their mutual journey until they saw a young man when the wise servant of Allah killed the lad. It shocked Moses, so he asked the wise servant of Allah why he would do such a horrible act to an innocent boy.

This strange killing of the lad is very troubling; however, the Koran's message of why this young man had to be killed will be explained in verse 81 below.

(18:76) He said: "Did I not tell you that you could not bear with me?"

Again, the wise servant of Allah reminds Moses that he warned him it would be hard to travel and learn from him.

(18:77) (Moses) said: "If I ask you after this concerning aught, keep not company with me. You have received an excuse from me."

Yusuf Ali translates this passage:

> (Moses) said: "If ever I ask you about anything after this, [then] keep me not in your company: then would you have received (full) excuse from my side" (Sûrah 18:76, Yusuf Ali, bracketed clarification mine).

Moses promises once again that he will not ask him about anything he does, but without a doubt, the next time it happens, the wise servant of Allah will have a good excuse to part company with him.

(18:78) So they twain [both] journeyed on till, when they came unto the folk of a certain township, they asked its folk for food, but they

269

refused to make them guests. And they found therein a wall upon the point of falling into ruin, and he [the wise servant of Allah] repaired it. (Moses) said: "If you had wished, you could have taken payment for it" (bracketed clarifications mine).

They continued to a town and asked if they may have some food, but the town's people refused. As they walked through the community, the wise servant of Allah repaired a wall, which was about to collapse. (This is suggestive of the biblical story found in Joshua 6:20 where the walls of Jericho fell down. If this is an allegory, it seems a little out of sync for Moses because the walls of Jericho fell *after* Moses had died.) Nevertheless, in this koranic tale, Moses asked his companion why he had done such a good deed for people who would not feed them, especially when the wise servant of Allah could have received money for repairing the wall.

(18:79) He [the wise servant of Allah] said: "This is the parting between you and me! I will announce unto you the interpretation of that you could not bear with patience" (bracketed clarification mine).

Moses again questions the wise servant of Allah and is told again that now they will definitely part ways; however, before they do, the wise servant of Allah will explain to Moses the several events he had witnessed.

(18:80) As for the ship, it belonged to poor people working on the river, and I wished to mar [damage] it, for there was a king [coming from] behind them who is taking every ship by force (bracketed clarifications mine).

As we suggested earlier, this is reminiscent of a story in the Bible where Pharaoh came against Moses and the Israelites when it seemed he had them trapped because they had the sea at their backs. God used the sea to rescue the children of Israel, just like the wise servant of Allah used the sea to save the poor people's boat from the current evil king when he sank their ship. This scenario is almost like being in a parallel universe. We can understand sinking docked ships to prevent them from falling into the wrong hands, but how were the poor people saved when their only means of escape sank after it had set sail? We certainly hope they were good swimmers, especially after Moses asked the wise servant of Allah, "Have you scuttled it in order to drown those in it?" (Sûrah 18:71b.)

(18:81) And as for the lad, his parents were believers and We feared lest he should oppress them by rebellion and disbelief.

Verses 80 and 81 together are reminiscent of the Hebrews in the Sinai desert, whose fathers had been believers in God, but many turned to idolatry and worshipped the golden calf (Exodus 32:4-6). Likewise, the wise man from Allah explained that he killed the lad, not because his parents were godly and did not deserve such a son; but because the boy was not a follower of Allah. He knew he would be a rebellious teenager, ungrateful for all the blessings from his parents and Allah.

Again, Allah's wise servant is referring to one of the main subjects of the Exodus story when the Jews refused to go into the Promised Land because they feared giants, but how this relates to that story is still not clear. Is it because the miraculous events surrounding Moses, which are pursued by Pharaoh and his army in the desert (a sea of sand), had not yet happened, and that this is meant as an allegorical foreshadowing to establish some sort of prophetic credibility for the Koran?

(18:82) And We intended that their Lord [Allah] should [ex]change him for them for one better in purity and nearer to mercy (bracketed clarifications mine).

This is reminiscent of Allah's excuse when he promised something and then went back on his word:

> *Whatever communications We abrogate [resend/revoke] or cause to be forgotten, We bring one better than it or like it....* (Sûrah 2:106, Muhammad Habib Shakir, bracketed clarification mine).

Shakir translates this passage this way:

So we desired that their Lord might give them [the parents] in his place one better [son] than him in purity and nearer to having compassion. (Muhammad Habib Shakir, bracketed clarification mine).

This allegory parallels the Bible where Moses, after discovering the Golden Calf, gathers his brother, Aaron (the high priest) and all who love God, to kill the rebellious Hebrews who had turned to idolatry, leaving alive only the children of Israel who honored God (Exodus 32:26-29).

(18:83) And as for the wall, it belonged to two orphan boys in the city, and there was beneath it a treasure belonging to them, and their father had been righteous, and their Lord intended that they should come to their full strength and should bring forth their treasure as a mercy from their Lord; and I did it not upon my own command. Such is the interpretation of that wherewith you could not bear.

Again, Muhammad Habib Shakir gives us a clearer interpretation:

And as for the wall, it belonged to two orphan boys in the city, and there was beneath it a treasure belonging to them, and their father was a righteous man; so your Lord desired that they should attain their maturity and take out their treasure, a mercy from your Lord, and I did not do it of my own accord. This is the significance of that with which you could not have patience.

We are told that the wall belonged to two orphan boys. This is similar to the biblical story of the harlot, Rahab, whose home was built using part of the wall which surrounded Jericho. Rahab assisted God's people when they were sent into the city on a spying mission. She also helped to hide them when the soldiers went to her house looking for the Hebrew spies (Joshua 2:1-7). In this koranic story, like Rahab, their father was a righteous man, and Allah wanted the boys to benefit from their father's good works. In the biblical story, because Rahab risked her life helping the Hebrew spies and not her own people, the God of the Hebrews rewarded her by allowing her and her family to live after the walls of Jericho fell, and the Hebrew soldiers killed all the town's

272

inhabitants (Joshua 6:20-22). The wise servant from Allah made sure the wall was a blessing for the two orphan boys, just like the portion of the wall of Jericho was blessed for Rahab and her family's sake.

So now, Moses knows the last hidden truth taught to him by the wise servant of Allah.

(18:84) They will ask you [Muhammad] of Dhû'l-Qarneyn. Say: "I shall recite unto you a remembrance of him" (bracketed clarification mine).

We are now abruptly—almost like finding ourselves in a crazy dream—transported again to a fourth and completely different story regarding another Islamic prophet, the *Dhû'l-Qarneyn* (Dhû'l meaning "dual" or "two" + *Qarneyn* or *Qurnayn*; *Quarn* meaning "horn"). Shakir spells *Dhû'l-Qarneyn as* "Zulqarnain," making it one word. We prefer Arberry's spelling only because he spells it phonetically (so we know how to pronounce it) as "Dool Karn-**ain**." Together, they mean the "two-horned one," which is a crown of authority, also believed by most scholars to be Alexander the Great.[12]

In the Bible, we are able to understand plainly who is being discussed. The Bible's historical events are also confirmed by archaeology. Biblical Scripture is always clear, while the Koran is sometimes vague and unprovable.

One example of koranic vagueness is found in this passage regarding the personage of *Dhû'l-Qarneyn*, whose identity has caused many scholars to find themselves all over the historical map. For centuries, it was thought *Dhû'l-Qarneyn* was, in fact, Alexander the Great; however, when the Koran was put under scrutiny by various Islamic scholars, many events described in the Koran became a source of embarrassment and required modifications to what Gabriel was saying or describing. After discussions among some Islamic scholars, they chose to incorporate some Christian folklore (i.e., the Apocrypha). The Apocrypha (false writings which claim "hidden knowledge") is incorporated more times in the Bible than it is in the Koran. Remember, we concern ourselves with scholarly research, primarily using the Bible as directed by the Koran in Sûrah 4:82 and Sûrah 10:94, to name two. Whenever possible, we avoid any references to Christian myths or the Apocrypha unless we are forced to do so by the Koran itself, such as the previous story of the seven sleepers at the beginning of this sûrah (verses 9-26).

As we pointed out in the commentary inset note for verse 26, it was known that Alexander the Great was a Pagan who worshipped the Greek gods and goddesses and even claimed to be a son of god, stating his father was *Zeus*. Knowing this, why would Gabriel—speaking for Allah—include a Pagan as an Islamic prophet [13] or even another person claiming to be the son of God? Perhaps, this is why more recent Islamic scholars have concluded that Alexander the Great could never be the *Dhû'l-Qarneyn*, who is spoken about, citing Alexander's Pagan polytheism. As we read the following passages, one thing becomes clear; the event surrounding Gog and Magog could only apply to one historical figure—Alexander the Great.

We will visit this again in Volume III *of* our three-volume series, *Islam Exposed, Islam: Science—Bible—Archaeology and Myths.* For now, we will proceed by acknowledging that the weight of historical evidence points to the Alexandrian persona of the *Dhû'l-Qarneyn*.

(18:85) Look! We made him strong in the land and gave him unto every thing a road.

Muhammad Habib Shakir's translation sheds a little bit more light on this verse:

> *Surely We established him in the land and granted him means of access to everything.*

This makes it clear that we are talking about Allah handpicking a very important man. The power and strength Allah gave him leads us to believe Allah held him in high status. Because *"a road"* or *"access to everything"* is incorporated in this verse by various translations, it appears that Allah is sending this king out into the world on an important mission.

(18:86) And he followed a road.

The king is beginning a journey.

> OBSERVATION: As we previously mentioned in discussing the sleepers (Sûrah 18:23-31), there is a mystical fascination with the sun in the Koran. On this journey, we will see more than one road and more than one incident concerning the sun.

(18:87) Till, when he reached the setting-place of the sun, he found it sitting in a muddy spring, and found a people there-about. We said: "O Dhû'l-Qarneyn! Either punish or show them kindness."

Here we have another problematic verse. To begin with, most would agree that a seventh-century man, standing on our planet and looking at our sun, would judge it to appear around the same size or smaller than our moon when it is rising or setting. The size of the heavenly lights depends on the angle of the earth in regards to the sun or the angle of the moon (a harvest moon seems very big and bright in the night sky), although, in reality, the sun is always brighter than the moon. Without a doubt, our earth appears to be bigger than both of them; therefore, one can hardly fault a person from the seventh century to misjudge the moon and sun's relative proportions as seemingly very small compared to our world, which appears to be the case in this verse.

Regardless of who the king is in this story, we are treated to the cosmic knowledge that the sun is setting in a muddy spring. It would be illogical for Allah, who—according to the Koran—created everything to declare such a concept; yet we know: (1) The earth revolves around the sun, and even allows for a poetic license or relative perception; (2) we have the sun setting in a pool of muddy water on the planet earth, but how can this be when the actual size of the sun is so big? Scientists tell us that it would take over 1,000,000 earths to fill our sun,[14] and (3) even if it were possible for a smaller sun to set in a murky pool of water on our planet, one of two things would have to happen—either of which would only allow for this event to occur once; (a) the sun would boil away all the water, or (b) the water would extinguish the sun.

Consider: Why would Allah allow something like mythology to be incorporated into the Koran without explaining the reason for putting it there? Later, in verses 93 and 94, we are treated to a story, which is supposed to be based on a historical event—but the sun setting in a pool of muddy water—is the thing of which myths are made. The Bible contains fictitious stories (parables), and those stories are always explained. What makes this perplexing passage even more troubling—from a Muslim's viewpoint—is if one suspects that this verse is a myth, what is to stop someone from making the claim that other koranic passages might be myths as well?

Again, in the spirit of fairness, we must point out that today's Muslim scholars have tried to defend this embarrassing passage by suggesting that the translation is incorrect, yet we have four different translations of the Koran, each of which interprets it the same; nevertheless, some koranic apologists offer an alternative thought.

In today's world, many Muslim apologists (defenders of Islam) have rewritten the Koran to be more compatible with western-thought and science. One example can be found here in verse 86 regarding the phrase "...*the setting-place of the sun...sitting in a muddy spring*." The argument given by some Muslim apologists is that the Arabic phrase, *magh-ribash-sham-si,* should be translated like the Sahih International Western-friendly version: "*Until, when he reached the setting of the sun, he found it [as if] setting in a spring of dark mud.*" While on the surface, saying the English translations are bad might seem to be a plausible explanation; after all, God would know the sun does not set in a mud puddle! This Islamic revision is an example of "taqiyya," which allows a Muslim to lie if it furthers the cause of Islam. Despite this, Muslim modifications in the original four English translations, which state,"...*when he reached the setting-place of the sun, he found it setting in a muddy spring [Pickthall and Arberry], ("murky water," Ali, "into a black sea," Shakir)*" are accurate translations. How do we know this? We use Islamic documentation by one of Muhammad's own friends, Abu Dharr, who had a discussion with the Prophet about this very verse:

> Once I was with the Prophet (riding) a donkey on which there was a saddle or (piece of) velvet. That was at sunset. He said to me, 'O Abu Dharr, do you know where this (Sun) sets?" I said, 'Allah and His Messenger know better." He said, 'It sets in a spring of murky water, (then) it goes and prostrates before its Lord, the Exalted in Might and the Ever-Majestic, under the Throne. And when it is time to go out, Allah allows it to go out and thus it rises. But, when He wants to make it rise where it sets, He locks it up. The sun will then say, "O my Lord, I have a long distance to run." Allah will say, "Rise where you have set" that (will take place) when no (disbelieving) soul will get any good by believing them.[15]

OBSERVATION: For a moment, think about how it is possible that a spherical object could prostrate (bow) itself in any direction; it cannot. Yet to be fair to Muhammad, in the seventeenth century, no one could have known that the sun was shaped like a ball because it appears like a round plate and a plate could be laid prostrate, as is commonly done on a dining room table.

Another strange comment by Muhammad is that the sun is conversing

with Allah as if it were a living object, which it is not. If this were simply an allegorical discussion, what is the allegorical point? It appears that what the prophet is seriously sharing with his friend, Abu Dharr, is what he believes to be the truth.

Be that as it may, when Alexander arrives at the place where the sun sinks into the pool, we are introduced to a group of indigenous people. Allah tells Alexander, "O Dhû'l-Qarneyn! Either punish or show them kindness." Why is Allah giving an order to Alexander to punish or not punish these people? Either they did something wrong and deserved to be punished, or what they did was not really so bad that it allowed Alexander to be gracious and forgive them. We are never told the reason behind this curious passage.

Finally, assuming the Dhû'l-Qarneyn is Alexander the Great, he would not have traveled west toward the ends of the world, which is the direction the sun appears to set because, historically, when Alexander set out to establish his empire, he traveled with his army from Macedonia and Greece, eastward toward Persia. However, we do not want to mislead anyone because historical records tell us that after Alexander conquered Persia, he turned to the West in order to conquer Egypt.

(18:88) He [Alexander] said: "As for him who does wrong, we shall punish him, and then he will be brought back unto his Lord [Allah], Who will punish him with awful punishment!" (Bracketed clarifications mine.)

This verse is interesting since it is an instruction on discipline. Alexander says he will punish those who are wrongdoers and send them back to Allah. Presumably, the punishment is capital punishment. The wrongdoer will pay for his transgressions with his life and then receive a second punishment at the hands of Allah, which will be even worse. Still, it is not clear what wrongdoings were committed.

(18:89) But as for him who believes and does right, good will be his reward, and We shall speak unto him a mild command.

That's it? We know even less than when we were first introduced to these people. Alexander is acting as Allah's instrument of justice on earth, and Alexander will also be generous toward those who do right. The obedient individuals will receive a reward for good works because Alexander will be kind toward the do-gooder, but we are still left with the question as to what this story is about. Who did what and to whom? Was this story even necessary? I will leave that up to you to decide.

(18:90) Then followed he [Alexander] a (another) road (bracketed clarification mine).

Arberry says, *"Then he followed a way,"* and Shakir tells us, *"...he followed (another) course,"* while Yusuf Ali says, *"followed he another way."* So now we are introduced to "another road in this verse." The translations introduce us to "way" or *"(another) course,"* which appears to be a second path. Where will it lead?

(18:91) Till, when he [Alexander] reached the rising-place of the sun, he found it rising on a people for whom We [Allah] had appointed no shelter therefrom (bracketed clarifications mine).

Yusuf Ali translates it as follows:

> *Until, when he came to the rising of the sun, he found it rising on a people for whom We had provided no covering protection against the sun (Sûrah 18:90, Yusuf Ali).*

Apparently, Alexander does an about-face (eastward) as the road now leads Alexander to the place where the sun rises and another group of mysterious people.

Addressing the first part of this verse from our perspective, we understand it appears that the sun rises in the east and sets on the other side of the world in the west. However, allowing for the fact that the sun never moves, and it is the rotation of the earth, which causes the allusion of the sun's movement, there can never be a point on the planet where it can be said that this is the place where the sun starts rising or setting. It is all relevant, depending on where you are standing; it is like chasing a rainbow! Be that as it may, even from our limited perspective, the distances involved would appear to be quite far apart. It is important to realize that Alexander conquered lands from Macedonia (north) through Persia (southeast) and then eastward into the exotic lands of India, as well as westward through the Middle East and toward the farthest lands from Greece by foot, and then Egypt. From a seventh century perspective, who else but Dhû'l-Qarneyn (i.e., Alexander the Great) had conquered so much of the ancient world, and who would be able to have that kind of firsthand knowledge as to where the sun might have risen and set?

As for the second part of this verse, we are also told that the people who lived at that end of the planet were caused to suffer by Allah—for whatever reason, which again is not clear—but we do know they did not have any relief from the sun, which would indicate there were no trees, caves, stones, or buildings of any kind for shade.

(18:92) So (it was). And We knew all concerning him.

In another translation, Yusuf Ali states:

(He left them) as they were: We [Allah] completely understood what was before him (bracketed clarification mine).

Allah is still overseeing the quest Alexander is on, but what he is looking for is not found at the place of the rising sun either. Allah, on the other hand, knows Alexander's future, according to this verse.

(18:93) Then he followed a road

So much for this second group of suffering people; the reason for their introduction appears to be a mystery.

Moving on, we now have the third road (Ali, Shakir, and Arberry all indicate "another road") introduced, which Alexander must now travel on in his quest for something which is still not clear.

(18:94) Till, when he came between the two mountains, he found upon their hither [nearer] side a folk that scarce could understand a saying.

Muhammad Shakir translates it:

Until when he reached (a place) between the two mountains, he found on that side of them a people who could hardly understand a word.

Alexander arrives in a valley with people living on the hillsides who speak a language that is too difficult for him to understand, yet in the next verses, we see they are able to overcome the language barrier.

(18:95) They said: "O Dhû'l-Qarneyn! Look! Gog and Magog are spoiling the land. So may we pay you tribute on condition that you set a barrier between us and them?"

A.J. Arberry translates this passage:

> *They said, "O Dhool Karnain, behold. Gog and Magog are doing corruption in the earth; so shall we assign to you a tribute, against your setting up a barrier between us and between them?"*

The people are proposing that Alexander the Great protect them and their land from Gog and Magog. In exchange for his military expertise, they are willing to pay him a substantial price.[16]

(18:96) He [Alexander] said: "That wherein my Lord [Allah] has established me is better (than your tribute). Do but help me with strength (of men), I will set between you and them a bank (bracketed clarifications mine).

Again, Yusuf Ali has a clearer translation:

> *He said: "(The power) in which my Lord has established me is better (than [your] tribute): Help me therefore with strength (and labor):[and] I will erect a strong barrier between you and them:" (Bracketed clarifications mine.)*

Alexander is declaring that Allah made him a prophet something greater than any of their honor or wealth could make him; however, if the people of the land would supply him with an army to fight against their enemies, he will help them in return by providing a fortified barrier between them and Gog and Magog. In the first century, Josephus informs us that Gog and Magog were known as the Scythians.[17]

(18:97) Give me pieces of iron - till, when he had levelled [leveled] up (the gap) between the cliffs, he said: "Blow!" - till, when he had made it a fire, he said: "Bring me molten copper to pour thereon."

So Alexander made a fence from iron to span the gap in the valley which lay between the two mountains.[18]

(18:98) And (Gog and Magog) were not able to surmount [climb] it, nor could they pierce [make a hole in or under] (it).
The fortification created at the direction of Alexander stopped Gog and Magog because, as this verse tells us, they were unable to scale the wall or dig under it.[19]

(18:99) He [Alexander] said: "This is a mercy from my Lord; but when the promise of my Lord comes to pass, He will lay it low, for the promise of my Lord is true" (bracketed clarification mine).

We must return to Muhammad Habib Shakir's verse 47 (Pickthall's verse 48) to see how Muhammad is revisiting this apocalyptic reference:

> And the day [Judgment Day] on which We will cause the mountains to pass away and you will see the earth a leveled plain and We will gather them and leave not any one of them behind (Sûrah 18:47, Muhammad Habib Shakir, bracketed clarification mine).

Alexander is telling the people that Allah is the one showing mercy to them. He explains that whatever Allah promises will come to pass. Just as the people had to deal with the mountains, the day will come when there will be no mountains. The events Gabriel is using here and those shown previously in verse 47 are reminiscent of the biblical prophet, Ezekiel's words:

"And it shall come to pass at the same time when Gog shall come against the land of Israel," says the Lord GOD, "that my fury shall come up in my face.

"For in my jealousy [to protect Israel] and in the fire of my wrath have I spoken, Surely in that day there shall be a great shaking in the land of Israel;

"So that the fishes of the sea, and the fowls of the Heaven, and the beasts of the field, and all creeping things that creep upon the

282

earth, and all the men that are upon the face of the earth, shall shake at my presence, *and the mountains shall be thrown down, and the steep places shall fall*, and *every wall shall fall to the ground*" (Ezekiel 38:18-20, bracketed clarification mine, emphasis added).

OBSERVATION: These passages from the Koran also appear to have been lifted from the Bible concerning the nation of Israel.

(18:100) And on that day we shall let some of them surge against others, and the Trumpet will be blown. Then We shall gather them together in one gathering.

In keeping with the Koran's disjointed sûrahs, here we see that as abruptly as Alexander the Great appeared, he is just as equally and abruptly dismissed.

Gabriel, speaking for Allah, now concludes this sûrah with an apocalyptic message, loosely incorporating verses reminiscent of the Bible. We are reading about events that will happen in the Last Day when Allah will allow some countries to war against others (which is reminiscent of the Bible when it tells us that the whole world will come against Jerusalem). We are also told seven times in the Hadith that the *Last Hour* won't come until Muslims declare war against the Jews:

The Day of Judgement will not come about until Muslims fight the Jews, when the Jew will hide behind stones and trees. The stones and trees will say "O Muslims, O Abdullah (or Abd Allah meaning Servant of Allah), there is a Jew behind me, come and kill him." However, the Gharkad tree (also known as the "Boxthorn tree") would not do that because it is one of the trees that belongs to the Jews (Sahih Muslim 41 6985, bracketed clarification mine; ref. also Sahih Muslim 41, 6981; Sahih Muslim; 41:6982; Sahih Muslim 41:6983 Sahih Muslim 41:6984; Sahih al-Bukhari 4:52:177; Sahih al-Bukhari 4:56:791).

283

In this verse, we are told that Allah will decide when to sound the trumpet, which will bring all the nations together. However, Allah seems to forget why he is bringing the nations together. We will explain the reason why, according to the Bible:

"Listen, I tell you a mystery: We will not all sleep, but we will all be changed—in a flash, in the twinkling of an eye, *at the last trumpet.* For the trumpet will sound, the dead will be raised imperishable, and we will be changed" (1 Corinthians 15:51-52, NIV, emphasis added).

A prophecy: The word of the LORD concerning Israel. "The LORD, who stretches out the Heavens, who lays the foundation of the earth, and who forms the human spirit within a person, declares: 'I am going to make Jerusalem a cup that sends all the surrounding peoples reeling. Judah will be besieged as well as Jerusalem. On that day, when all the nations of the earth are gathered against her, I will make Jerusalem an immovable rock for all the nations. All who try to move it will injure themselves' (Zechariah 12:1-3, NIV).

In those days and at that time, when I restore the fortunes of Judah and Jerusalem, *I will gather all nations* and bring them down to the Valley of Jehoshaphat. There I will put them on trial for what they did to my inheritance, my people Israel, because they scattered my people among the nations and divided up my land. (Joel 3:1-2, NIV, emphasis added).

(18:101) On that day We shall present hell to the disbelievers, plain [for all] to view (bracketed clarification mine).

Gabriel is telling Muhammad that during the final events leading up to the Last Day, it will be like Hell, and all those who reject Allah will be witnesses to what is coming on the earth. We see a similar event in the Book of Revelation, Chapter 14, where a metaphor regarding the grapes of wrath produces a carnage of blood that will flow 184 miles long and as deep as the bridle on a horse. That description covers almost the entire length of modern-day Israel, which is approximately 260 miles long:

> Still another angel, who had charge of the fire, came from the altar and called in a loud voice to him who had the sharp sickle, "Take your sharp sickle and gather the clusters of grapes from the earth's vine, because its grapes are ripe." The angel swung his sickle on the earth, gathered its grapes, and threw them into the great winepress of God's wrath. They were trampled in the winepress outside the city, and blood flowed out of the press, rising as high as the horses' bridles for a distance of 1600 stadia [a method of measuring; here it equals about 184 miles] (Revelation 14:18-20, NIV, bracketed clarification mine.)

(18:102) Those whose eyes were hoodwinked from My reminder, and who could not bear to hear.

A.J. Arberry's translation:

> *...the unbelievers whose eyes were covered against My remembrance, and they were not able to hear.*

In the previous verse, we were told about the Hell unbelievers will see. We were also told that their eyes were unable to see the truth revealed by Allah. In this verse (verses 101-102, should be one verse, not two), we are told why this occurred; it was because they refused to listen to Allah's warnings.

(18:103) Do the disbelievers [Christians] reckon that they can choose My bondmen [slaves, Mary, and Jesus, Sûrah 5:116] as protecting friends beside Me? Behold! We have prepared hell as a welcome for the disbelievers (bracketed clarifications mine).

> *Do the Christians believe they can turn to Jesus (Isa) and His mother—who are my servants for deliverance from Hell? (Paraphrase mine.)*

285

(18:104) Say: "[Muhammad] Shall We inform you who will be the greatest losers by their works?" (Bracketed clarification mine.)

> *Say to them, Muhammad, "Do you want to know whose actions are going to cause them to suffer even more [in Hell] because of what they have done?" (Paraphrase mine.)*

(18:105) Those whose effort go astray in the life of the world, and yet they reckon that they do good work.

This verse is a continuation from the previous verse, and when combined, both verses inform us that the ones who will find themselves in Hell are the naive people who think that the god(s) will be content if they do good. Another view is for the agnostics, who strive for the comforts of this world and do charitable work. They never give Heaven or Hell any thought. To them, if there happens to be an afterlife, they should be alright because they have done good works.

(18:106) Those are they who disbelieve in the revelations of their Lord and in the meeting with Him. Therefore their works are vain, and on the Day of Resurrection We assign no weight to them.

> *Those people are the ones who disregarded the warnings and did not take Allah's revelations to Muhammad seriously, but they still do good works. Their lost souls reason if there is a hereafter and they stand before Allah, their charitable works will bail them out. How foolish because the good works they have done will gain them nothing (paraphrase mine).*

(18:107) That is their reward: hell, because they disbelieved, and made a jest of Our revelations and Our messengers.

Gabriel continues:

> *Because they did not listen to what we revealed through Muhammad and the biblical prophets and rejected Allah's prophets, they will go to Hell, regardless of the good they might have done (paraphrase mine).*

This is a clever way to include Muhammad as being in the same biblical class with the biblical prophets who, through their time-tested prophecies, have proven to be legitimate prophets!

(18:108) Lo! those who believe and do good works, theirs are the Gardens of Paradise for welcome,

My paraphrase of Gabriel's proclamation:

> *Those who become Muslims and perform good deeds will be rewarded with the beautiful flowing Gardens of Paradise (paraphrase mine).*

(18:109) Wherein they will abide [live], with no desire to be removed from thence [there] (bracketed clarifications mine).

> *Their eternal home will be so wonderful; it will be a place they will never want to leave! (Paraphrase mine.)*

(18:110) Say: [Muhammad] "Though the sea became ink for the Words of my Lord, verily [truly] the sea would be used up before the words of my Lord were exhausted, even though We brought the like thereof to help" (bracketed clarifications mine).

Gabriel continues to instruct Muhammad:

> *Tell them, Muhammad, "If the ocean were to turn into ink to write down all that I am telling you, the sea would dry up before all the words of Allah could be told, even though we would fill up another ocean with more ink to help" (paraphrase mine).*

This sounds like it was borrowed from the biblical passage written about Christ, which reads:

And there are also many other things that Jesus did, which, if they should be written one by one, I suppose that even the world itself could not contain the books that would be written. Amen (John 21:25).

287

(18:111) Say: [Muhammad] "I am only a mortal like you. My Lord inspired in me that your Allah is only One God [not a Trinity]. And whoever hopes for the meeting with his Lord, let him do righteous work, and make none sharer [with another] of the worship due unto his Lord" (bracketed clarifications mine).

A.J. Arberry's translation of this passage:

> *Say: "I am only a mortal the like of you; it is revealed to me that your God is One God. So let him, who hopes for the encounter with his Lord, work righteousness, and not associate with his Lord's service anyone".*

Basically, Gabriel is saying:

> *Tell the people, Muhammad, "You too are only human, but that I revealed to you I am one god. Let them know that if they ever hope to come to me, they must do good works and remember, Christians need not apply; I am sending all of them to Hell" (paraphrase mine).*

We finally arrive at the conclusion of Sûrah 18, ending it on the same note as we started, bemoaning the Divinity of Jesus.

NOTES:

1. Jesus also acknowledges that He is the Son of God in the following gospel passages: Matthew 26:63-64, 28:19; Mark 14:61-62; John 10:36, 14:9.
2. "Seven Sleepers," *Wikipedia*, Wikimedia Foundation. "According to Muslim scholars, God [Allah] revealed these verses because the people of Mecca challenged Muhammad with questions that were passed on to them from the Jews of Medina in an effort to test his authenticity" (bracketed clarification mine).
3. Rev. W^m St. Clair Tisdall, *The Source of Islam* (Edinburgh Privately Published, 1901; reprint. Nashville: Center for the

Study of Political Islam, 2011), 48. Gregory of Tours Latin work is cited as the earliest source of the "Seven Sleepers" legendary myth.

4. Daniel C. Peterson, Foreward by Khaleel Mohammed. *Muhammad, Prophet of God* (Grand Rapids: Wm. B. Eerdmans Publ. Co., 2007), 75.

5. Tisdall, *The Source of Islam*, 48.

6. It has been suggested by some, that during that period of time, there were several versions of the sleeper story circulating, causing many to dispute the correct number of sleepers. They argue, If Muhammad was a true prophet, surely he would be able to give them an inspired answer as to the correct number. Whether or not this explanation is true—why would Allah give any credibility to a mythical story in the first place? Since Allah is divine, should he have not known better?

7. "Alexander the Great," *Encyclopædia Britannica Online*. Encyclopædia Britannica, n.d. Web. 14 Sept. 2016. In Egypt, "the priest gave him the traditional salutation of a pharaoh, as son of Amon; Alexander consulted the god on the success of his expedition but revealed the reply to no one. Later the incident was to contribute to the story that he was the son of Zeus and, thus, to his 'deification.' "

8. *The Arabic Gospel of the Infancy of the Saviour.* Ante-Nicene Fathers. Ed. Alexander Roberts and James Donaldson. 4th ed. Vol. 8 (Peabody: Hendrickson, 2004), 405. "Mary told Joseph that the time of the birth was at hand and that she could not go into the city; but, said she, *let us go into this cave*. This took place at sunset" (2b, emphasis added). 405, paragraph 2.

9. S. Baring-Gould, trans. *Myths of the Seven Sleepers of Ephesus.* Whitefish: Kessinger, LLC, Publ., 2010. Muhammad changed the original 360 years that the youths slept to 309 years to coincide with the Alexandrian underlying theme showing how Allah is in control of history and how he coordinates the years to fit his purposes. In the original story, instead of 309 years, we read, "Three hundred and sixty years passed, and in the thirtieth year of the reign of Theodosius, there broke forth a heresy denying the resurrection of the dead .... 'Now, it happened that an Ephesian was building a stable on the side of

Mount Celion, and finding a pile of stones handy, he took them for his edifice, and thus opened the mouth of the cave. Then the seven sleepers awoke, and it was to them as if they had slept but a single night.' "

10. Kevin Van Bladel, *The Alexander Legend in the Qur'ân* (New York: Rutledge, 2007), 181.

William Montgomery Watt: *al-Iskandar, Encyclopaedia of Islam*, 2nd ed., Vol. IV, 1997, 127. Dhû'l-Qarneyn was, in fact, Alexander the Great. He is considered not only a Muslim but also a prophet of Islam.

Andrew Runni Anderson. "Alexander's Horns." *Transactions and Proceedings of the American Philological Association*, vol. 58, 1927, p. 100., doi: 10.2307/282906. "The horns of Alexander ... have had a varied symbolism. They represent him as a god, as a son of a god, as a prophet and propagandist of the Most High, as something approaching the role of a messiah, and also **as the champion of Allah"** (bolded emphasis added).

11. "Muslim Mastectomy or 'he Miracle of Disappearing Breasts Surah An-Naba' (78:33)." *Surah An-Naba' 78:33*, www.answering-islam.org /Quran/Versions/078.033.html. Accessed 15 June. 2013.

12. Why is this observation relevant? Muslim love to attack the Bible as a "pornographic book", because "such language is not fitting for the word of God", e.g. regarding the story of Lot, or God's condemnation of Israel in Ezekiel 23. It is however, the Qur'an that paints a thoroughly carnal paradise

13. "Alexander the Great." *Oxford Islamic Studies Online*, OXFORD UNIVERSITY PRESS, Arabic al-Iskandar. Conqueror of Egypt and the Persian Achaemenid Empire and founder of cities. Often identified with Dhu al-Qarnayn, "the two-horned" of the *Quran* (18:83–94), who figures prominently in Muslim eschatology by serving the cause of the righteous. *Considered a Muslim believer and a prophet by some.*

14. Jonathan Keohane and Jim Lochner. *National Aeronautics and Space Administration Goddard Space Flight Center*. "Imagine the Universe: How many times the earth would fit inside the sun?" *NASA, 1997,* Web. 16 July 2013.

15. Found in *Sunan Abu Dawud, Hadith Vol. 4, Book 32, No. 3991 and also* Musnad Ahmad, Hadith 21459 al-Risala, ed. In light of modern-day science, much of the Hadith has been dismissed as unreliable and not to be taken too seriously; nevertheless, before scientists discovered the sun's size and that the earth was a sphere revolving around the sun, the Hadith— Concerning subjects such as this—was considered accurate. Did Muhammad, in fact, actually say this to his friend, Abu Dharr, as the Hadith tell us, or was this erroneously added at some later date? Hadith aside, this story is found in Sûrah 18:86 of the Koran, which is supposed to be infallible. In light of the Koran's many anachronisms, we will leave that up to you to decide for yourself.

16. Peter G. Bietenholz, *Historia and Fabula: Myths and Legends in Historical Thought from Antiquity to the Modern Age* (New York: E.J. Brill, 1994), 122. The first-century Jewish historian and scholar, This would account for the koranic inclusion and confirmation that Alexander the Great had this actual historical encounter with what was believed to be Gog and Magog, as recorded in the first century A.D.

17. Ibid. The first-century Jewish historian and scholar, "Josephus Flavius, shows that in the first century B.C., the Scyths were in Jewish circles commonly associated with Gog and Magog." This would account for the koranic inclusion and confirmation that Alexander the Great had this actual historical encounter with what was believed to be Gog and Magog, as recorded in the first century A.D. "Magog, a son of Japheth, was the founding father of the Magogia [Mongolians], better known as the Scyths [Scythes]. Living in the region of the Tanais and Maotic marches, the Scyths [Scythes]—that much is historical fact … On one occasion, they defeated one of the generals of Alexander the Great" (bracketed clarification mine, emphasis added).

18. Ibid. "To prevent further intrusions, Alexander locked them up in their homeland by *barring their passage through the Caucasus Mountains with iron gates*."

19. R. M Dawkins, & Andrew Runni Anderson. *Alexander's Gate, Gog and Magog, and the Enclosed Nations: By Andrew Runni*

Anderson (Cambridge: Medival Academy of America, 1932), 28-29. "He [Dhul-Qarnayn/Alexander] dammed up the valley between the two mountains, and said: 'Ply your bellows.' And when the iron blocks (ingots) were red with heat, he said: 'Bring me molten brass to pour on them: Gog and Magog *could not scale it or dig their way through it'* " (bracketed clarification mine, emphasis added).

☪

SÛRAH 19

MARY (Miriam)
(Revealed at Mecca)

Because of the centrality of Christ to the New Testament and the importance of His relationship to His mother, the Virgin Mary, and His relationship to God the Father, we must study with care Sûrah 19 titled, "Mary." It is important to see the Islamic perspective regarding Mary and how it compares with both the historical and biblical concepts presented in the Bible. By comparing the Bible and the Koran, you will be better able to judge for yourself if the author of the Bible and the Koran are the same—as the Koran claims—one should do (Sûrah 5:47).

Sûrah 19 titled, "Mary," or in Hebrew,"Miriam" (מִרְיָם), or in Arabic, "Maryam" (مريم) is fasanating as it presents what we are to believe is a biblical rendering of the birth of Jesus (remember Allah leads us to believe he also wrote the Bible sûrah 4:82) Yet surprisingly in this nativity sûrah, we are also forced to address the birth of Buddha, since the koranic version of the birth of Christ is more in line with the birth of the Buddha!

(19:1) Kâf. Hâ. Yâ. A'în. Şad.

The meaning of this verse is unintelligible. Most Muslim scholars simply say they don't know the meaning of those letters, but it does not matter because Allah does!

Dr. Muhammad Taqi-ud-Din states, "These letters are one of the miracles of the Qur'an, and none but Allah (Alone) knows their meanings."[1]

OBSERVATION: Dr. Muhammad Taqi-ud-Din's comment concerning Sûrah 19:1 is a good example of associating the Koran with miracles where there are none. Another so-called miracle claimed by Muslims is the Koran itself. The Koran contains no miracles other than self-fulfilling ones apart from the claim that Muhammad split the moon in two (Sûrah 54:1-3) for which no astronomical records of that time are found anywhere in the world that confirm such an event. Imagine should the moon split in two what havoc it would cause the tidal system of the earth much less the disruption of the gravitational pull of the moon now weakened into two smaller bodies being drawn down to the earth resulting in the complete obliteration of the planet! Contrast this with the Bible, which is over 25% prophecy consisting of numerous, actual signs, and miracles, many of which have been fulfilled some as recent as the 20th century (Ezekiel 36, 37) with some in the process of being fulfilled today (Zechariah 12:3) and some to be completed in the future.

19:2) A mention of the mercy of Your Lord unto His Servant Zachariah.

This sûrah opens with Allah about to give a blessing to Zachariah, a first-century Temple priest.

(19:3) When he cried unto his Lord a cry in secret,

The reason why Allah is about to show grace toward the priest, Zachariah, is because he is privately appealing to Allah about an important matter that is troubling him.

Zachariah makes his plea:

(19:4) Saying: "My Lord! Behold! the bones of me wax feeble and my head is shining with grey hair, and I have never been unblest in prayer to You, my Lord."

Zachariah is explaining to Allah how he has grown old and tired; his hair is turning gray, and because Allah has always answered his prayers, this is the most humble and desperate prayer he has ever presented for Allah's blessing.

(19:5) "Lo! I fear [what] my kinsfolk [will do] after me [I die], since my wife is barren. Oh, give me from Your presence a successor (bracketed clarifications mine),

Zachariah is expressing his fear to Allah that he is the last male in his family line because his wife has not been blessed with a child. When a man dies without leaving an heir, it is a Jewish tradition for his wife to marry his brother. The first son of that marriage becomes the deceased husband's namesake and heir. Sadly, at the ages of Zachariah and his wife, such an arrangement was not possible. (Zachariah seems to be implying that since he is the last in his line, his brothers must be dead.)

The translation by Yusuf Ali is more revealing:

> "Now I fear (what) my relatives (and colleagues) (will do) after me: but my wife is barren: so give me an heir as from Yourself, —

In his footnote #2459, Yusuf Ali suggests that when Zachariah states, "*Oh, give me from Your presence a successor,*" he might be possibly referring to an adopted son, which is compatible with the other two translations we use. This also makes sense when we read the continuation of this passage in the following verse:

(19:6) Who shall inherit of me and inherit (also) of the house of Jacob. And make him, my Lord, acceptable (unto You)" successor (bracketed clarification mine)

This is really the second part of the preceding verse and probably should have remained with it.

Like all Hebrews, Zacharias was descended from Jacob (Israel); there is not a single "Jacobob" tribe as such. Since Zacharias was descended from Jacob's son Levi, which made him a Levite, he hoped that any adopted son of Hebrew descent would be permissible.

We must point out here that this may be another glaring biblical conflict, as the Bible never suggests that Zacharias asked God to allow him to adopt a son:

> And there appeared unto him [Zacharias] an angel of the Lord standing on the right side of the altar of incense. And when Zacharias saw him, he was troubled, and fear fell upon him. But the angel said unto him, Fear not, Zacharias: for your prayer is heard; and your wife Elisabeth shall bear you a son, and you shall call his name John (Luke 1:12–17, bracketed clarification mine).

(19:7) (It was said unto him): "O Zachariah! Lo! We bring thee tidings of a son whose name is John; we have given the same name to none before (him)."

Regarding the first use of the name John here, it appears that the angel, Gabriel, is showing inconsistencies between what he says in the Koran and what he previously stated in the Bible. Gabriel makes the sweeping statement that the name John (*Yahya* in the original Arabic and translated as *lōabbēs ee-o-an'-nace* in Greek) was created exclusively for Zachariah's son, John the Baptist, inferring that before John was born, the name was nonexistent.

A careful study of the origins of the name John shows this is not historically accurate. John is an English equivalent of the Hebrew name *Yochanan*. There is no "J" in the Hebrew Aleph-Bet. In the English translations of the Old Testament Bible, John appears as, *Johanan* or *Jehohanan,* which was a popular name in ancient Israel and appears numerous times in the Hebrew Old Testament (2 Kings 25:23; 1 Chronicles 3:15, 3:24; 6:9-10; 12:4, 12:12; 2 Chronicles 28:12; Ezra 8:12, 10:6; Nehemiah 6:18, 12:22-23; Jeremiah 40:13, 15-16; 41:13-16; 42:1, 8; 43:2). So once more, we have another Koran inaccuracy, which results in the rewriting of history by getting the facts incorrect.

296

OBSERVATION: The God of the Bible never made such a mistake.

Background: In the biblical version, Zacharias was chosen as the priest to offer incense to God in the Temple, which was done by the priest drawing lots. The winner was selected to serve God in the Temple that day, where specific prayers had to be said. We can only imagine that Zacharias—being the godly man he was—faithfully recited those prescribed prayers. While Zacharias was shocked by the appearance of the angel, Gabriel, he would not be surprised that God would acknowledge the Levitical prayers offered in the Temple for His people:

> And there appeared unto him an angel of the Lord standing on the right side of the altar of incense. And when Zacharias saw him, he was troubled, and fear fell upon him (Luke 1:11).

But what happened next was totally unexpected:

> ... the angel said unto him, "Fear not, Zacharias: for your prayer is heard; and your wife Elisabeth shall bear you a son, and you shall call his name John" (Luke 1:13).

The prayers of the Temple priest were usually for Israel, but perhaps God chose this time to acknowledge that He was aware of the deep longing in Zacharias' heart for a son. Zacharias could not have known that the birth of his son was an event God had predestined from the very foundation of the world—an event that would be tied to the long-awaited coming of the Messiah.

Let's look at the prophetic Bible verse that foretold of the birth of John, Zacharias' son, in the Old Testament:

> Behold, I will send my messenger, and he shall prepare the way before me: and the LORD, whom you seek, shall suddenly come to his temple, even the messenger of the covenant, whom you delight in: behold, he shall come, says the LORD of hosts [angelic armies] (Malachi 3:1).

We also see a foreshadowing in the Bible about John the Baptist in the Book of Isaiah:

> The voice of him that cries in the wilderness, "Prepare you the way of the LORD, make straight in the desert a highway for our God" (Isaiah 40:3).

Again, in the Gospel of Luke, we read about the confirmation regarding the birth of John the Baptist, who would announce the coming of the Lord Jesus *(Isa)* the Messiah:

> As it is written in the book of the words of Esaias [Isaiah] the prophet, saying, "The voice of one crying in the wilderness, 'Prepare you the way of the Lord, make his paths straight' " (Luke 3:4, bracketed clarification mine).

(19:8) He said: "My Lord! How can I have a son when my wife is barren and I have reached infirm old age?"

Similar to this verse in the Bible, this wonderful news was not something Zacharias was expecting to hear while he was offering Temple prayers. Zacharias and his wife had grown old and frail, so it was unlikely he would still be praying for a son. The Bible makes it clear he and his wife had given up hope a long time ago; therefore, Zacharias did not believe Gabriel as we read in the following paragraphs:

In the Bible, the angel, Gabriel (the same angel who is allegedly relating this koranic story), surprises Zacharias and tells him about the impending birth of a son he and his wife will be having. The Bible explains the revelation of Zacharias' impending fatherhood this way:

> And Zacharias said unto the angel, "Whereby shall I know this? for I am an old man, and my wife well stricken in years."
>
> And the angel answering said unto him, "I am Gabriel, that stands in the presence of God; and have been sent to speak unto you, and to show you these glad tidings" (Luke 1:18-19).

298

Note that the Bible spells Zacharias with an "s" at the end of his name, as we can see in the verse above, while Pickthall spells Zachariah with an "h."

(19:9) He said: "So (it will be)". Your Lord said: "It is easy for Me, even as I created you before, when you was [were] naught [nothing]." (Bracketed clarifications mine.)

A.J. Arberry translates it:

> Said He, "So it shall be; your Lord says, 'Easy is that for Me, seeing that I created you in a former time, when you were nothing' "

In other words, Allah tells Zachariah he created him and planned for his birth even before Zachariah existed. So, it is no challenge for Allah to create a son for Zachariah any more than it was for Allah to create him.

(19:10) He [Zachariah] said: "My Lord! Appoint for me some token." He [Allah] said: "Your token is that you, with no bodily defect, shall not speak unto mankind three nights" (bracketed clarification mine).

Muhammad Habib Shakir's translation is more accurate:

> He said: "My Lord! give me a sign." He said: "your sign is that you will not be able to speak to the people three nights while in sound health."

This passage is attempting to incorporate the biblical fact that Zacharias was made dumb (could not speak) for a period of time. Perhaps the Koran is confusing the three days when Jesus spoke of the time He would be "... three days and three nights in the heart of the earth" (Matthew 12:40) or the three months His mother, Mary, spent with her cousin Elisabeth—Zacharias' wife—during her pregnancy (Luke 1:56). What is true, however, is that Zacharias was dumb until the birth of his son (probably for nine months), but not as a *sign* the Koran wants us to believe; it was meant to be a punishment in the Bible's version as we read in the Gospel of Luke:

And, behold, you shall be dumb, and not able to speak, until the day that these things shall be performed, because you believe not my words, which shall be fulfilled in their season (Luke 1:20).

And Mary [mother of Jesus] abode with her about three months, and returned to her own house.

Now Elisabeth's full time came that she should be delivered; and she brought forth a son.

And her neighbors and her cousins heard how the Lord had showed great mercy upon her; and they rejoiced with her.

And it came to pass, that on the eighth day they came to circumcise the child; and they called him Zacharias, after the name of his father.

And his mother answered and said, "Not so; but he shall be called John." And they said unto her, "There is none of your kindred that is called by this name."

And they made signs to his father, how he would have him called.

And he asked for a writing table and wrote, saying, "His name is John." And they marveled all.

And his mouth was opened immediately, and his tongue loosed, and he spoke, and praised God (Luke 1:56-64, bracketed clarification mine).

(19:11) Then he came forth unto his people from the sanctuary, and signified to them: "Glorify your Lord at break of day and fall of night."

Zacharias left the Temple after he had finished his service before God and concluded his discussion with the angel Gabriel. Because Zacharias was no longer able to speak, he signaled to the others (how we are not sure). This is biblically accurate as we can see in our revisit of the passage from Luke 1:10 in context:

And, behold, you will be dumb, and not able to speak, until the day that these things shall be performed, because you believed not my words, which shall be fulfilled in their season.

And the people waited for Zacharias and marveled that he tarried [remained] so long in the Temple.

And when he came out, he could not speak to them: and they perceived that he had seen a vision in the temple: for he beckoned unto them, and remained speechless (Luke 1:20-22, bracketed clarification mine).

However, the Koran has added dialogue the Bible does not have. The Koran has Zacharias telling the people—even though he could not speak—they should "glorify God in the morning and at the beginning of the night."

(19:12) (And it was said unto his son): O John! Hold fast the Scripture. And we gave him wisdom when a child,

A.J. Arberry agrees with using the English name "John" while Shakir and Ali use the Arab name "Yahya."

In another disjointed verse, the Koran makes a giant leap to a young John the Baptist and shows Allah giving the young man a specific instruction to, *"Hold fast the Scripture."* This, of course, was referring to the Tanakh (Hebrew Bible) since the Koran would not appear for over half a millennium in the future.

(19:13) And compassion from Our presence, and purity; and he was devout,

This is a continuation of the previous verse, which is also a broken sentence for whatever reason, but it is completed in the following verse:

(19:14) And dutiful toward his parents. And he was not arrogant, rebellious.

It is curious to consider why it took three verses to present one simple sentence, or why they began breaking the dialogue into verses where they did (see Introduction).

If we combine verses 12-14, they give us the completed train of thought:

> *(And it was said unto his son): O John! Hold fast the Scripture. And we gave him wisdom when a child, And compassion from Our presence, and purity; and he was devout, And dutiful toward his parents. And he was not arrogant, rebellious (Sûrah 19:12-14).*

Basically, we have Allah's overall description of the blessings bestowed on John the Baptist and how he was an obedient child who was even-tempered and reverent.

(19:15) *Peace on him the day he [John] was born, and the day he dies and the day he shall be raised alive! (Bracketed clarification mine.)*

This verse ends with a reference to the Last Day and the resurrection:

While this has a pleasant and melodic flow to it, John the Baptist's death was anything but peaceful. He was held bound in a dingy prison cell, and then had his head chopped off!

For Herod himself had given orders to have John arrested, and he had him bound and put in prison. He did this because of Herodias, his brother Philip's wife, whom he had married. For John had been saying to Herod, "It is not lawful for you to have your brother's wife." So Herodias nursed a grudge against John and wanted to kill him. But she was not able to because Herod feared John and protected him, knowing him to be a righteous and holy man. When Herod heard John, he was greatly puzzled; yet he liked to listen to him

Finally, the opportune time came. On his birthday, Herod gave a banquet for his high officials and military commanders and the leading men of Galilee. When the daughter of Herodias came in and danced, she pleased Herod and his dinner guests.

The king said to the girl, "Ask me for anything you want, and I'll give it to you." He promised her with an oath, "Whatever you ask, I will give you, up to half my kingdom."

She went out and said to her mother, "What shall I ask for?"

"The head of John the Baptist," she answered.
At once, the girl hurried in to the king with the request: "I want you to give me right now the head of John the Baptist on a platter."

The king was greatly distressed, but because of his oaths and his dinner guests, he did not want to refuse her. So he immediately sent an executioner with orders to bring John's head. The man went, beheaded John in the prison, and brought back his head on a platter. He presented it to the girl, and she gave it to her mother (Mark 6:17-28, NIV).

(19:16) *And make mention of Mary in the Scripture, when she had withdrawn from her people to a chamber looking East,*

Gabriel instructs Muhammad to refocus on the biblical story of the Nativity, but it is anything but biblical. Notice how the story begins with Mary leaving her family and retiring to a room facing "East" with a capital "E." We know Mary lived in Nazareth, a small mountain basin of the lower Galilee north of Megiddo, located north of Jerusalem of Judea. To the east of Nazareth is the Jordan River, which flows into the Dead Sea. Perhaps the Koran has Mary facing "East" to infer she would be facing Mecca, which would be to the east of the Dead Sea. If that's the reason, it suggests that Mecca is holier than Jerusalem, but Mecca of the first century A.D. was a Pagan city. There is no parallel passage for this to be found in the Bible. It would make no sense for a Jewish girl to pay homage toward the direction of a first-century Pagan Arabia. Most certainly, if Mary were going to choose a particular direction to face, she would have chosen to face southward toward Jerusalem and the Temple of God.

(19:17) And had chosen seclusion from them. Then We sent unto her Our Spirit and it assumed for her the likeness of a perfect man.

Once again, we have yet another disjointed passage. In this verse, Pickthall says *"....had chosen seclusion from them,"* while Arberry says, *"...she took a veil apart from them...;"* Shakir says, *"...she took a veil (to screen herself) from them...;* "Yusuf Ali says, *"She placed a screen (to screen herself) from them...."*

Why would she think it necessary to do such a thing if she had already left her family to take up residence far away from them in the east? Do they have telescopic eyes? Next, we read in another disjointed sentence, *"Then we sent unto her Our Spirit and it assumed for her the likeness of a perfect man."* Arberry says, *"We sent unto her Our Spirit that presented himself to her a man without fault."* Shakir says, *"then We sent to her Our Spirit, and there appeared to her a well-made man."*

> OBSERVATION: In context, we know Mary was not pregnant at that time, so once again we ask why would she want to remove herself away from prying eyes and either hide behind or wear a veil? Perhaps what the Koran wants us to believe is that Mary wanted to remove herself from her people to seek Allah's help in becoming pregnant; yet if Mary was desirous of having a child, would it not make more sense for Mary to ask Allah for a husband and avoid being shamed? We do not read anywhere in the Koran about Mary having a husband.

It is good to pause here and explain that in the biblical version, Mary never left her home before her divinely appointed conception. Girls who observed the Torah never left their father's house until they were married, although she was engaged to Joseph at the time. After she had become miraculously pregnant, Mary stayed three months with her cousin, Elisabeth, the wife of the Levitical priest, Zacharias:

And Mary arose in those days, and went into the hill country with haste, into a city of Judah; And entered into the house of Zacharias, and saluted [greeted] Elisabeth. And it came to pass, that, when Elisabeth

304

heard the salutation of Mary, the babe leaped in her womb; and Elisabeth was filled with the Holy Ghost (Luke 1:39-41, bracketed clarification mine).

(19:18) She said: "Look! I seek refuge in the Beneficent One from you, if you are Allah-fearing."

In combination with Sûrah 19:17, Mary sees a spirit that looks like a man and explains to him that she is seeking safety in Allah. She then questions him to see if he is Allah-fearing. Maybe this is one of those verses in the Koran which cannot be correctly translated. Why would Mary seek Allah's help from a person who, like herself, also serves Allah? Why not directly pray to Allah instead of asking a stranger if he is a believer who could intercede on her behalf? All the translations we have read are just as confusing.

A.J. Arberry translates this verse:

> She [Mary] said, "Take refuge in the All-merciful from you [Allah]! If you fear God [Allah]." (Bracketed clarification mine.)

(19:19) He said: "I am only a messenger of your Lord, that I may bestow on you a faultless son."

In reply to Mary's concern, the spirit—who was in the form of a man—says he will give her a holy male child. We are told in the Bible that the angel who appeared to Mary and Joseph was Gabriel. The angel, Gabriel, of the Koran, gives Muhammad this story, but he does not claim to be the angel speaking to Mary. It is also interesting to note that Mary's betrothed, Joseph, the carpenter—with whom the biblical Gabriel spoke—is never mentioned in the Koran. Why would Mary want a son if she were not betrothed/married? Such a pregnancy could result in her being stoned to death!

(19:20) She said: "How can I have a son when no mortal has touched me, neither have I been unchaste?"

This echoes the biblical passage, which reads:

"How will this be," Mary asked the angel, "since I am a virgin?" (Luke 1:34, NIV.)

However, in Sûrah 3, the Koran contradicts itself. Apparently, Gabriel forgot, according to the Bible, he was the only angel who appeared to Mary (Luke 1:26-27) because in Sûrah 3, Gabriel tells us in all four of the translations we referenced, there were several angels (but not him) who appeared to Mary.

The Koran's version:

And when the angels said: "O Mary! See! Allah has chosen you and made you pure, and has preferred you above (all) the women of creation" (Sûrah 3:42, emphasis added).

Three verses later in Sûrah 3 verse 45, we read:

(And remember) when the angels said: "O Mary! See! Allah gives you glad tidings of a word from Him, whose name is the Messiah, Jesus, son of Mary, illustrious in the world and the Hereafter, and one of those brought near (unto Allah)." (Sûrah 3:45, emphasis added.)

Notice the Koran's ongoing attack regarding the Divinity of Jesus when Gabriel tells Mary her son's name is "the Messiah, Jesus, son of Mary," which is more of a title than a name.

We see, in various excerpts from the Koran, where Gabriel says there were between one and several angels visiting Mary. Again, in the spirit of fairness, the Bible does speak of several angels, but they appear to the shepherds and only after the birth of Jesus:

For there is born to you this day in the city of David a Savior, who is Christ the Lord. And this *will be* the sign to you: You will find a Babe wrapped in swaddling cloths, lying in a manger. And suddenly there was with the angel a multitude of the heavenly host praising God and saying: "Glory to God in the highest, And on earth peace, goodwill toward men [mankind]!"

So it was, when the angels had gone away from them into heaven, that the shepherds said to one another, "Let us now go to Bethlehem and see this thing that has come to pass, which the Lord has made known to us" (Luke 2:11-15, NKJV, bracketed clarification mine).

(19:21) He said: "So (it will be)." The Lord said: "It is easy for Me. And (it will be) that We may make of him a revelation [prophet] for mankind and a mercy from Us, and it is a thing ordained."

The spirit-man from Allah tells Mary it will happen because Allah said it would. It is easy for Allah to do, and the child will be a Prophet of Islam who will be filled with revelations for mankind from Allah, which will be a blessing for everyone concerned!

OBSERVATION: Although Jesus is mentioned or referred to more than any other person in the Koran, there is never any mention about Jesus' (*Isa's*) ministry or what those revelations from Allah were other than he *gave* Jesus the gospel (Sûrah 5:46). Of course, this is impossible because (1) there are four gospels not "a" gospel, and (2) the gospels teach about Jesus, not something *taught to Jesus* by Allah. The Greek word gospel means "Good News" in English. To make it possible for humans to relate to God, the Good News is that God became a man (God incarnate), and by doing so, Jesus became the perfect, sinless sacrifice for humanity and—as the Yom Kippur goat was sacrificed for all of Israel's sins—Jesus was also sacrificed for all of our sins when He was crucified on the cross.[2] Nevertheless, we must receive His gift or forego salvation. "But now Christ is risen from the dead, and has become the firstfruits of those who have fallen asleep" (1 Corinthians 15:20), all of which the Koran vehemently denies.

(19:22) And she conceived him [Jesus], and withdrew with him [Jesus] to a far place.

Arberry and Shakir also use the word *"withdrew,"* while Yusuf Ali uses the word *"retired."* Now we begin to see some events that are extreme departures from the biblical account of the birth of Christ. As we previously pointed out, Mary's (betrothed) husband, Joseph, is nowhere to be seen or heard from in the Koran, but we are told Mary does leave with the baby Jesus to an unnamed place far away. Contrary to the Koran's version of the nativity, the Bible tells us that after Mary conceived, she went by herself to stay awhile with her cousin, Elisabeth, and did so without any companion male or angel:

> At that time Mary got ready and hurried to a town in the hill country of Judea, where she entered Zechariah's home and greeted Elizabeth. When Elizabeth heard Mary's greeting, the baby leaped in her womb, and Elizabeth was filled with the Holy Spirit. In a loud voice she exclaimed: "Blessed are you among women, and blessed is the child you will bear!" "But why am I so favored, that the mother of my Lord should come to me?" "As soon as the sound of your greeting reached my ears, the baby in my womb leaped for joy. Blessed is she who has believed that the Lord would fulfill his promises to her!" (Luke 1:39-44, NIV.)

As we previously mentioned, Mary stayed with Elizabeth for about three months and then returned home (Luke 1:56, NIV); yet in the Koran's version of the nativity, Mary conceives and then departs to a secluded place.

(19:23) And the pangs of childbirth drove her unto the trunk of the palm-tree. She said: "Oh, would that I had died ere[instead of] this and had become a thing of naught [nothing], forgotten!" (Bracketed clarifications mine.)

Yusuf Ali makes this verse a little clearer:

And the pains of childbirth drove her to the trunk of a palm-tree: She cried (in her anguish): "Ah! would that I had died before this! would that I had been a thing forgotten and out of sight!"

308

(19:24) Then (one) cried unto her from below her, saying: "Grieve not! The Lord has placed a rivulet beneath thee,"

It is understandable that if someone should have happened to be there at the time, they might have wondered whose voice it was coming from under (below) Mary. We are told who it was in the translation offered by Muhammad Habib Shakir:

Then (the child) called out to her from beneath her: "Grieve not, surely your Lord has made a stream to flow beneath you."

Astonishingly, this child is the newly born Jesus *(Isa)* speaking to His mother at birth! Even though we believe that Jesus is God incarnate (in the flesh) (Isaiah 9:6; 2 John 1:17; Colossians 1:15), the Bible never suggested that Jesus spoke at

Fig. 2. This is the Virgin Mary having just given birth to Jesus under a Palm tree. Jesus is seen on the opposite right, wrapped in a blanket crowned with flames (Islamic art uses flames instead of a halo), speaking encouragement to His mother.
(16th century Turkish drawing)

birth so one could not be faulted for wondering where this idea of baby Jesus speaking at birth came from. Perhaps Gabrael is confusing the nativity of Jesus with the nativity of another person.

We are able to see what is being described in verses 23 and 24 above in the 16th century Muslim rendering of Mary having just given birth to Jesus (lying on the ground to the tight of Mary and the palm tree). This of course presents historical problems that force us to question the Koran's trustworthiness when dealing with the birth of Christ.

The Bible and the Koran both agree that Jesus was born of a virgin. That is where the Nativity's similarity ends. There is no mention of Mary's husband, Joseph, in the Koran. Unlike the Bible, Mary in the Koran had to bear her child, Jesus alone.

Perhaps this confusion between the unbiblical passage in the Koran, which reads, *"And the birth pangs surprised her [Mary] by the trunk of the palm-tree,"* can be explained by looking at another birth, the birth of Buddha.

Fig. 3. This is Queen Maya having just given birth to birth to Buddha under the Bo Tree. Buddha is seen speaking after taking his 7th step under the Bo Tree.

(Laotian temple painting)

"It was the custom in those days for a woman to return to her parent's home in order to give birth. And so, when the time had almost come for the baby to be born, Queen Maya (another form of the name Mary[1]) and many of her friends and attendants left the palace of the king and began the journey to her childhood home. They had not traveled far when the Queen asked that they stop and rest. She knew the baby would be born very soon. They had reached the beautiful gardens of Lumbini, and the queen went into this garden looking for a comfortable place in which she could give birth.... A large tree bent down one of its branches, and the Queen took hold of it with her right hand. Supporting herself in this way, she gave birth to a son."[3]

Part of the Buddha nativity is when the Buddha was born he was born under a Bo tree, and as he dropped to the ground Buddha took seven steps and—as we just read in this verse of the Koran's version of the birth of Jesus—he also spoke out loud.

Combining verses 22,23 and 24, we are told when Mary "... withdrew with him [baby Jesus] to a far place" (verse 22), "the pangs of childbirth drove her unto the trunk of the palm-tree" (verse23) where she gave birth to Jesus (verse 24). To summarize, Mary is on a trip without her espoused husband, Joseph and gives birth under a tree before she arrives at the "far place" to where she was traveling.

In the biblical version, we see Mary traveling from Nazareth to Bethlehem of Judea accompanied by her espoused husband, Joseph.

And it came to pass in those days, that there went out a decree from Caesar Augustus that all the world should be taxed. (And this taxing was first made when Cyrenius was governor of Syria.)

And all went to be taxed, every one into his own city.

And Joseph also went up from Galilee, out of the city of Nazareth, into Judea, unto the city of David, which is called Bethlehem (because he was of the house and lineage of David):

To be taxed with Mary his espoused wife, being great with child.

And so it was, that, while they were there, the days were accomplished that she should be delivered (Luke 2:1-6).

Notice that there are three things different in the original biblical version: (1) Mary is with Joseph; (2) they made it to their destination, which was Bethlehem, before giving birth, and (3) there is no mention of trees in the birthing process.

(19:25) "And shake the trunk of the palm-tree toward you, you will cause ripe dates to fall upon you."

Jesus, thinking His mother needed something to eat immediately after His birth, tells her to shake the date tree under which she has just given birth. according to the Koran, as we see here, Jesus can speak as soon as He is born.

311

OBSERVATION: The Koran claims that before Jesus was born, He was an acknowledged prophet of Islam and never died, because Allah raptured (i.e., caught up) Jesus to himself (Sûrah 4:158). Conversely, Muhammad was not born under any unusual circumstances and was orphaned by the age of six. He was 40 years old when he received revelations from Gabriel and enlightenment from Allah. We are told that Muhammad was the last and greatest Prophet of Islam (arguably the *only* prophet of a religion called Islam). The curious thing is that the Koran never explains or gives an example of why Muhammad was the greatest other than he could not read or write (Sûrah 1:158; 29:48), but he was good at retention (memorizing) and as a warlord. While Muhammad might have excelled at killing people, Jesus *(Isa)* could bring people back to life after they died (Mark 5:18-26; Luke 7:11-17; John 11:41-44). Which is the greater feat?

(19:26) So eat and drink and be consoled. And if you meet any mortal, say: "Look! I have vowed a fast unto the Beneficent and may not speak this day to any mortal."

The newly born Jesus continues to encourage His mother to take pleasure in food and drink. Then, in a complete about-face, Mary is told to inform anyone who might approach her that she is not eating but fasting for Allah. In other words, she is told to lie (Satan is the father of lies, John 8:44). Jesus also tells her that she cannot speak to any mortal—although she must break her silence to tell them she cannot speak or eat! This is indeed curious since Jesus *(Isa)*, according to the Koran, is supposed to be a prophet of Islam, and shortly after He is born, he is telling his mother not only to eat and drink but also to lie about it! Muslim prophets cannot lie or deceive (Surah 3:161).

On the next page, we have placed a chart to enable you to compare the three major religions' nativity stories. Notice how the biblical version compares with the other two and how the other two compare with each other.

Table 4. The Nativity Stories of Three Major Religions

NATIVITY OF THE BIBLICAL JESUS	NATIVITY OF THE KORAN'S JESUS (ISA)	NATIVITY OF THE BUDDHA
1. Mary traveled with her espoused husband, Joseph.	1. Mary traveled without her husband.	1. Maya (or Mary) traveled without her husband.
2. Mary and Joseph left their home, not out of desire, but because of a Roman edict that forced them to go.	2. Mary willingly left home because she desired to travel to another place to give birth.	2 Maya willingly left home because she desired to travel to another place to give birth.
3. Mary completed her journey while still pregnant.	3. On the way, Mary was unexpectedly overtaken by birth pangs.	3. On the way, Maya was unexpectedly overtaken by birth pangs.
4. Mary did not give birth until she and Joseph arrived in Bethlehem.	4. Mary stopped at a spot where there were trees.	4. Maya stopped at a spot where there were trees.
5. Mary gave birth to Jesus in a stable.	5. Mary gave birth at the foot of a tree.	5. Maya gave birth at the foot of a tree.
6. Mary's newborn baby never spoke when He was born.	6. Mary's newborn baby began to speak moments after He was born.	6. Maya's newborn baby began to speak moments after he was born.

Joseph   Jesus   Mary
16th Century Roman Nativity
by Baldassare Peruzzi

Mary/Jesus birthed under palm
16th Century Turkish Drawing

Queen Maya/Buddha birthed under bo tree
Ancient Temple Wall Painting Date Lost

313

(19:27) Then she brought him to her own folk, carrying him. They said: "O Mary! You have come with an amazing thing."

Mary now turns away from her journey to a "far place" and returns home. Her return home with a new baby shocks her family.
(19:28) "O sister of Aaron! Your father was not a wicked man nor was your mother a harlot."

Sister of Aaron, Moses' brother? We will address that shortly, but first, we must address Mary's family, who are bewildered about the newborn baby because she is from a good family. No one would ever think that Mary would sin by having a baby out of wedlock. (Joseph is mysteriously missing in the Koran.)

We certainly can understand Mary's family being stunned that she had a newborn. Still, it makes no sense the Koran would say that Mary was the sister of Aaron, who was a Levite, because Mary was from the House of David, from the tribe of Judah, something the angel, Gabriel, was apparently unaware of or had forgotten!

This is the genealogy of Jesus the Messiah, the son of David, the son of Abraham: Abraham was the father of Isaac, Isaac the father of Jacob, Jacob the father of Judah and his brothers (Matthew 1:1-2).

For He [Jesus] of whom these things are said belonged to a different tribe, and no one from that tribe has ever served at the altar [only those from the tribe of Levi].

For it is clear that our Lord descended from Judah, and in regard to that tribe [Judea], Moses said nothing about [them serving as] priests. And what we have said is even more clear: if another priest like Melchizedek appears, one who has become a priest not on the basis of a regulation as to his ancestry but on the basis of the power of an indestructible life (Hebrews 7:13-16, NIV, bracketed clarifications mine).

314

The Bible and the Koran both agree that Mary was a virgin when she conceived (Luke 1:34 and Sûrah 19:20). According to the Bible, Mary had to be from the tribe of Judah and a descendant of King David so her Holy Child could be descended through a bloodline from Israel's great king, David, as the Bible clearly states:

> He will be great and will be called the Son of the Most High. The Lord God will give Him the throne of his father David (Luke 1:32, NIV).

> The LORD swore an oath to David, a sure oath He will not revoke: "One of your own descendants I will place on your throne" (Psalm 132:11, NIV).

Now here is where the Koran might have become confused. Mary had a cousin named Elisabeth, who happened to be married to a Levitical priest, but her only relationship to the tribe of Levi was through her brother-in-law, Zacharias. It seems that Gabriel is confusing Mary, the mother of Jesus, with Aaron and his sister, whose name is also Mary (Miriam). Again, we have another Koranic anachronism separated by approximately 1,500 years with the two Mary's born on two separate continents (Africa and Asia Minor).

The story begins in Exodus 1, where Pharaoh ordered all newly born Hebrew sons to be killed ("... cast into the river," verse 22). In Exodus 2, we read how a Hebrew woman from the house of Levi gave birth to a male child (Moses), but saved him by putting him in a basket and setting him adrift in the Nile River while his sister watched from afar:

> His [Moses] sister [Miriam] stood at a distance to see what would happen to him.

> Then Pharaoh's daughter went down to the Nile to bathe, while her attendants were walking along the riverbank. She saw the basket among the reeds and sent her female slave to get it. When she opened it, she saw the baby. He was crying, and she felt sorry for him. "This is one of the Hebrew babies," she said.

Then his sister asked Pharaoh's daughter, "Shall I go and get one of the Hebrew women to nurse the baby for you?"

"Yes, go," she answered. So the girl got the baby's mother. Pharaoh's daughter said to her, "Take this baby and nurse him for me, and I will pay you." So the woman took the baby and nursed him. When the child grew older, she took him to Pharaoh's daughter and he became her son. She named him Moses, saying, "I drew him out of the water" (Exodus 2:4-10, NIV, bracketed clarifications mine).

Moses and his two siblings were from the tribe of Levi. He had a sister, Miriam, and a brother, Aaron.

The name of Amram's wife *was* Jochebed the daughter of Levi, who was born to Levi in Egypt; and to Amram she bore Aaron and Moses and their sister Miriam.

Therefore, the sister of Aaron, who was spoken about in the Bible, was Miriam (Mary), the same name as Jesus' mother; however, Jesus' mother, unlike her cousin who married a Levite, married a descendent from the House of David (Joseph) who—like herself—was from the tribe of Judah.

OBSERVATION: Yet again, we have a koranic anachronism—confusing two different people who had the same name, Miriam/Mary. (1) They belonged to two different tribes of Israel; (2) were born on two separate continents (Egypt in Africa vs. Judea in Asia Minor), and (3) separated by a time span of over 1,400 years. Since the Koran states that Allah is "all wise" (Sûrah 9:15), you would think that Allah would have recognized those discrepancies.

(19:29) Then she pointed to him. They said: "How can we talk to one who is in the cradle, a young boy?"

It is not clear why Mary is pointing to the baby without saying anything. Remember that in verse 26, Mary took a vow not to speak to any mortal *that* day; however, this event did not happen on her "day of silence" because she had to travel back to her home. Therefore, Mary could not have possibly arrived at her home that same day. Consider too that she had just given birth, an event that would have taken her a few days to recuperate, as well as the time and distance required for her to return home from the palm grove. Still, the Koran does not explain Mary's silence. It might be because it is confusing her with the husband of her cousin, Elizabeth (wife of Zechariah), who could not speak until their son, John, was born (Luke 1:19-20). Mary stayed with them for three months during her own pregnancy (Luke 1:56). What is even stranger in this verse is her family's response, stating the obvious when they said, *"How can we talk to one who is in the cradle, a young boy?"*

(19:30) He [Jesus] spoke: "Look! I am the slave of Allah. He has given me the Scripture and has appointed me a Prophet (bracketed clarification mine).

Once again, we get into the realm of the Pagan nativity stories by having the newborn baby Jesus speaking like an adult. He is saying that he spoke from the crib, proclaiming that Allah made Him a prophet and a slave.

This is another contradiction, as well as a seemingly desperate attempt to have Jesus endorse Islam for the benefit of Muhammad's Christian audience despite the Koran's continuing attack on His Divinity. In the Bible, Jesus claimed to be the Son of God, who likewise claimed Jesus to be His Son:

 And Jesus, when He was baptized, went up straightway out of the water: and, behold, the Heavens were opened unto Him, and He saw the Spirit of God descending like a dove, and lighting upon Him: And behold a voice from Heaven, saying, "This is my beloved Son, in whom I am well pleased" (Matthew 3:16-17).

(19:31) And hath made me blessed wheresoever I may be, and hath enjoined upon me prayer and alms-giving so long as I remain alive,

The newborn Jesus proclaims that Allah has generously blessed Him with prayer and charitable giving.

While Jesus did teach the principle of charity and the importance of taking care of the poor, He put His words into action by healing the sick, casting out demons, and raising the dead (see Luke 6:20-21; 4:16-19; 11:39-42; 12:16-21; 14:12-14; 16:19-25; Matthew 25:34-36; Mark 10:21-22; 12:41-44):

And Jesus went about all Galilee, teaching in their synagogues, and preaching the Gospel of the kingdom, and healing all manner of sickness and all manner of disease among the people. And His fame went throughout all Syria: and they brought unto Him all sick people that were taken with divers diseases and torments, and those which were possessed with devils, and those which were lunatic, and those that had the palsy; and He healed them (Matthew 4:23-24).

When the even[ing] was come, they brought unto Him many that were possessed with devils: and He cast out the spirits with His word, and healed all that were sick (Matthew 8:16, bracketed clarification mine).

Jesus said to her, "Did I not say to you that if you would believe you would see the glory of God?"

Then they took away the stone *from the place* where the dead man was lying. And Jesus lifted up *His* eyes and said, "Father, I thank You that You have heard Me And I know that You always hear Me, but because of the people who are standing by I said *this,* that they may believe that You sent Me."

318

Now when He had said these things, He cried with a loud voice, "Lazarus, come forth!"

And he who had died came out bound hand and foot with graveclothes, and his face was wrapped with a cloth. Jesus said to them, "Loose him, and let him go."

Then many of the Jews who had come to Mary, and had seen the things Jesus did, believed in Him (John 11:40-45, NKJV).

(19:32) "And (has made me [Jesus]) dutiful toward her [Mary] who bore me, and has not made me arrogant, unblest [without favor]" (only bracketed clarifications mine).

Continuing from the previous verse, the newborn baby Jesus is claiming that Allah created Him to be a good son to Mary, and yet again, His stepfather, Joseph is not mentioned and is nowhere to be found in the Koran.

(19:33) "Peace on me the day I was born, and the day I die, and the day I shall be raised alive!"

According to the Koran, Jesus (like John the Baptist in verse 15) proclaimed that he had a peaceful birth and would have a peaceful death, but (like John) the Bible tells it differently. In the Old Testament, we read the prophecy about Jesus' unpleasant death:

Who has believed our report? and to whom is the arm of the LORD revealed?

For He shall grow up before Him as a tender plant, and as a root out of a dry ground: He has no form nor comeliness; and when we shall see Him, there is no beauty that we should desire Him [He was not attractive].

He is despised and rejected of men; a man of sorrows, and acquainted with grief: and we hid as it were our faces from Him; He was despised, and we esteemed Him not.

Surely He has borne our griefs, and carried our sorrows: yet we did esteem Him stricken, smitten of God, and afflicted.

But He was wounded for our transgressions, He was bruised for our iniquities: the chastisement of our peace was upon Him; and with His stripes we are healed.

All we like sheep have gone astray; we have turned everyone to his own way; and the LORD has laid upon Him the iniquity of us all.
He was oppressed, and He was afflicted, yet He opened not His mouth: He is brought as a lamb to the slaughter, and as a sheep before her shearers is dumb, so He opened not His mouth.

He was taken from prison and fom judgment: and who shall declare His generation? for He was cut off out of the land of the living: for the transgression of my people was He stricken.

And He made His grave with the wicked, and with the rich in His death; because He had done no violence, neither was any deceit in His mouth (Isaiah 53:1-9, bracketed clarification mine).

(19:34) Such was Jesus, son of Mary: (this is) a statement of the truth concerning which they [Christians] doubt (only bracketed clarification mine).

In this verse, we continue with the Koran's predisposed paranoia of attacking the Divinity of Christ by referring to Jesus *(Isa)* only as the "son of Mary" and reaffirms, once again, in the very next verse that Allah has no son. It then acknowledges that Christians do not believe it.

We acknowledge once again that the gospel (i.e., Good News) is when God sent his only (unique, monogenés) Son, Jesus, in order to become the perfect, sinless sacrifice for humanity by dying for our sins on the cross. Through His resurrection, He conquered death as the resurrected Christ, all of which the Koran vehemently denies. To preach another gospel is blasphemy:

But though we, or an angel from heaven, preach any other gospel unto you than that which we have preached unto you, let him be accursed.

As we said before, so say I now again, "if any man preaches any other gospel unto you than that you have received, let him be accursed" (Galatians 1:8-9).

(19:35) It befits not (the Majesty of) Allah that He should take unto Himself a son. Glory be to Him! When He decrees a thing, He says unto it only: "Be!" and it is.

Gabriel is saying it does not benefit *"Allah that He should take unto Himself a son."* Yusuf Ali says, *"It is not befitting to the majesty of God that He should beget a son."* The reason for Muhammad and other cults who believe that Jesus was "begotten" *("beget")* is because a created being comes from a bad translation in *biblical* Scripture regarding the Greek word *monogenés* as "begot." To say that Jesus was "begotten" not only makes it sound like Mary conceived Jesus in the normal way, but that is exactly what "begotten" means: to procreate, to generate offspring, only instead of being impregnated by a man, she was impregnated by Allah. Yet in the original biblical version, as we have addressed before, the Greek word *monogenés*, which is translated as "begotten," really means "unique" or "one of a kind." Nevertheless, this seemingly confused angel, Gabriel, who tells us that Allah has no son, told Jesus' stepfather, Joseph, that Jesus is indeed the Son of God:

But while he thought on these things, behold, the angel of the LORD appeared unto him in a dream, saying, "Joseph, you son of David, fear not to take unto you Mary your wife: for that which is conceived in her is of the Holy Ghost.

"And she shall bring forth a son, and you shall call His name JESUS [GOD SAVES]: for He shall save His people from their sins" [only God can save us from sin].[2]

Now all this was done, that it might be fulfilled which was spoken of the Lord by the prophet, saying,

"Behold, a virgin shall be with child, and shall bring forth a son, and they shall call His name Emmanuel, which being interpreted is, 'God with us' " (Matthew 1:20-23, Isaiah 7:14; bracketed clarifications mine).

(19:36) "And look!" [Jesus tells his mother] "Allah is my Lord and your Lord: So serve Him. That is the right path" (bracketed clarification mine).

This is the ongoing dialogue of the newly born baby Jesus speaking to His mother, Mary. While the four translations we used are basically the same, the A.B. Al-Mehri translation[3] is also basically the same, but with one clarification; it has an insertion at the beginning of this verse, which in context, indicates baby Jesus is still talking to His mother, Mary:

> *(Jesus said), "And indeed, Allah is my Lord and your Lord [mother], so worship him. That is a straight path" (A. B Al-Mehri, Sûrah 19:36, bracketed clarification mine).*

Here is another subtle koranic attack on the Divinity of Jesus, which consistently puts words into His mouth, this time allegedly having Jesus admit He is not the son of Allah but is just his lowly servant!

(19:37) The sects among them differ: but woe unto the disbelievers from the meeting of an awful Day.

We can understand better what is said through Abdullah Yusuf Ali's translation:

> *But the sects [the Greek and Roman Catholic Churches and the Jews] differ among themselves: and woe to the unbelievers because of the (coming) Judgment of a Momentous Day (bracketed clarifications mine).*

It appears Gabriel is warning us that the "People of the Book" are more focused on their differences when they should be listening to Muhammad—but they will find out when it is too late, come Judgment Day.

(19:38) See and hear them on the Day they come unto Us! Yet the evil-doers are to-day in error manifest.

Gabriel is telling Muhammad to wait—the day is coming when Christians and Jews will stand before Allah and how they will be crying in repentance, but as for now, they refuse to see how evil and wrong they are.

(19:39) And warn them of the Day of anguish when the case has been decided. Now they are in a state of carelessness, and they believe not. Muhammad is advised to warn those Christians and Jews who will not accept Islam that it will be bad for disbelievers on the day they stand before Allah. Even today, they are in a state of recklessness in their disbelief.

(19:40) Lo! We, only We, inherit the earth and all who are thereon, and unto Us they are returned.

This verse makes it clear that after the Last Days come, only Allah will inherit and have complete control over the earth and everything on it. Those who died before will also be returned to Allah, who will give them their just rewards.

(19:41) And make mention (O Muhammad) in the Scripture of Abraham. Lo! he was a saint, a Prophet.

Abraham did not write any books of the Bible, nor were there any Scriptures named after him, but his story was written in the Scriptures, thanks to Moses. However, it is more likely that the "scripture" discussed in this passage refers to the Genesis account regarding Abraham, who is also the father of the Arabs. For that reason, Allah may be reminding Muhammad to include it in the Koran. Now we once again take an unexpected turn toward a new subject.

(19:42) When he [Abraham] said unto his father: "O my father! Why worships you that which hears not nor sees, nor can in aught [anything] avail [be useful]?"

This passage is exclusive to the Koran and not found in the Bible. It implies that Abraham's father was an idolater, but it seems presented more as a challenge aimed at his own relatives and tribe.

We will briefly look at the background regarding Abram's (Abraham's) family, as recorded in the Bible. We see in the Bible Abram's father, Terah, left Ur and took Abram and the family with him:

> Terah took his son, Abram, his grandson, Lot, son of Haran, and his daughter-in-law [also his daughter Genesis 20:12], Sarai, the wife of his son Abram, and together they set out from Ur of the Chaldeans to go to Canaan. But when they came to Harran, they settled there (Genesis 11:31, NIV).

It was after Abram's father died when God told him to leave Harran and continue on the journey to Canaan.

> Now the LORD had said unto Abram, "Get you out of your country, and from your kindred [relatives], and from your father's house, unto a land that I will show you" (Genesis 12:1, bracketed clarification mine).

OBSERVATION: There is not a conversation in the Bible—as Sûrah 19:42 suggests—where Abram lectured his father to repent from serving Pagan gods.

(19:43) "O my father! Look! there has come unto me of knowledge that which came not unto thee. So follow me, and I will lead you on a right path."

As we showed in the commentary for the last verse, biblically, it was Terah, Abram's father, not Abram, who was the initiator of moving the family (Genesis 11:31).

(19:44) "O my father! Serve not the devil. Look! The devil is a rebel unto the Beneficent."

The Bible does not give any indication Terah ever served the devil.

(19:45) "O my father! Look! I fear lest a punishment from the Beneficent overtake you so that you become a comrade of the devil."

This is sheer conjecture without any substantial biblical evidence, to be fair, there are some unbiblical myths and Jewish folklore that do exist, which suggest that Terah was an idolater. We have seen how the Koran frequently borrows more from the Apocrypha (unreliable sources) than from the actual Bible; therefore, we should not be too surprised to find those myths in this koranic account.

NOTE: As previously discussed, we are instructed by Allah to judge the Koran by the Bible (Sûrah 4:82; 5:47). Accordingly, we will continue to limit our critique basically to what is revealed by God in the Scriptures.

(19:46) He said: "Rejects you my gods, O Abraham? If you cease not, I shall surely stone you. Depart from me a long while!"

In relaying this unbiblical story, we now have a very angry Terah threatening his son, Abraham. Terah threatens to stone Abraham (Abram) to death in this verse if he does not stop preaching that there is only one God!

OBSERVATION: The problem with this koranic story is at that particular time in biblical history, his name was not Abraham, but Abram, so we see another chronological error in the Koran. God did not change Abram's name to Abraham during his father's lifetime; He changed it when Abraham, himself was very old (Genesis 17:5). Most scholars believe that Abram was 99 years old when God changed his name to Abraham. Allah, claiming to be God, should have remembered that.

(19:47) He said: "Peace be unto you! I shall ask forgiveness of my Lord for you. Look! He was ever gracious unto me."

We are now shown how the koranic Abraham (still Abram at this point in the Bible) is taking a godly attitude of showing compassion toward his alleged Pagan, idol-worshipping father, and telling him he will seek Allah's forgiveness for his father's errant ways.

(19:48) "I shall withdraw from you and that unto which you pray beside Allah, and I shall pray unto my Lord. It may be that, in prayer unto my Lord, I shall not be unblest.
So the koranic Abraham takes leave from his father and those Pagan idols to whom he prays, repeating for the third time he will be praying to Allah for his father and trusting Allah will forgive and help him.

(19:49) So, when he had withdrawn from them and that which they were worshipping beside Allah, We gave him Isaac and Jacob. Each of them We made a prophet.

This suggests that because the koranic Abraham left his father and all his father's Pagan gods, Allah rewarded Abraham by giving him his son, Isaac, and grandson, Jacob, both of whom Allah also made prophets. An even more accurate description of Isaac and Jacob would be the title of "Patriarchs."

OBSERVATION: Out of the first three Hebrew patriarchs, Isaac is the only one who did not have his name changed. (Abram became Abraham, and Jacob became Israel and had 12 sons who were the patriarchs of the 12 tribes of the nation of Israel.)

(19:50) And we gave them of Our mercy, and assigned to them a high and true renown.

The Koran is now referring to Isaac and Jacob and how Allah made them famous.

(19:51) And make mention in the Scripture of Moses. Behold! he was chosen, and he was a messenger (of Allah), a prophet.

Gabriel is instructing Muhammad to include stories about Moses in the Koran because Allah claims him as one of his Islamic prophets. We know how much the Jews revere Abraham and Moses, so this would surely be instrumental in trying to lure the Jews into Islam.

(19:52) We called him from the right slope of the Mount, and brought him nigh in communion.

This is an interesting geographical puzzle. Without going into too great of detail, we will address the problem of exactly what "Mount" is referred to here and the part of the mountain Gabriel is describing.

Some background: After the younger prince, Moses, killed an Egyptian soldier and escaped to Midian, he married Zipporah, the daughter of Jethro, a Midian Priest. About 40 years later, he saw a burning bush in the region near Mount Sinai, where God told him to take his brother Aaron (mentioned in the next koranic verse) and return to Egypt.

Here's the reader's problem when coming across this type of geographical description in the Koran. Without a compass reference supplied to those not familiar with how Arabs understood geographical references during that period of time, it is very confusing as to where the right slope of the mountain was and where the person looking at the mountain was actually standing.

The riddle is if one were standing on the north side of a mountain and facing that mountain, the right slope of the mountain would be facing west. On the other hand, if a person were on the south side of that same mountain, from the onlooker's point of view, the mountain's right slope would be facing toward the east. We would have different results if we were to continue this exercise regarding the person facing the mountain on the east and west sides as well, but we would never really know if the right slope of that mountain was north, south, east, or west. Although Muslim scholars offer varying explanations, it is generally accepted that in the Middle East during that time, if an Arab knew where one departed from (point A) and where the journey would end (point B), the Arab reading this story would have a clear idea of what was happening. Therefore, if one were leaving Midian (point A) on his way to Egypt (point B), the route taken would be known, as well as the landmarks. Knowing that, it would make perfect sense for someone living then to understand what side of the known trade route that particular mountain was located on in relation to where Moses stood. However, not knowing where the trade routes were 4,000 years ago when Moses was alive, we in the West would be hard-pressed to know exactly where the right slope of the mountain is today. Interestingly, this is the same mountain where Moses would later receive the Ten Commandments.

(19:53) And We bestowed upon him of Our mercy his brother Aaron, a prophet (likewise).

This verse once again brings up Aaron supposedly Jeus' uncle (verse 28) and Moses' brother, upon whom Allah also bestowed a special office.

(19:54) And make mention in the Scripture of Ishmael. Indeed! he was a keeper of his promise, and he was a messenger (of Allah), a prophet.

This passage is an attempt to give credibility to Muhammad as the last and greatest prophet. We are informed that Ishmael, the ancestor of Muhammad, was also appointed by the God of the Bible as a prophet, which makes the probability of Muhammad's anointing as a prophet possible—contrary to the teachings of the Bible (Genesis 17:21).

As we read in the Bible, Ishmael was loved by Abraham, who asked God to bless him (Genesis 17:18), and God promised to make Ishmael the father of twelve princes (Genesis 17:20). We also know God's covenant will only be honored through Isaac (Genesis 17:19, 21) and, therefore—as the Bible also states—Scripture can only be transmitted through the descendants of Isaac (Genesis 17:19), not through Ishmael and his descendants (Romans 3:1-2).

(19:55) He [Ishmael] enjoined [instructed] upon his people worship and almsgiving [charitable gifts for the poor], and was acceptable in the sight of his Lord. (Bracketed clarifications mine).

Since [Ishmael's] Lord found worship and charity as good things to engage in, he encouraged his family to worship and be charitable toward the poor.

(19:56) And make mention in the Scripture of Idris. Look! he was a saint, a prophet;

A.J. Arberry similarly relates this passage:

And mention in the Book Idris; he was a true man [not a spirit], a Prophet. We raised him up to a high place (bracketed clarification mine).

Idris (Arabic, إدريس) is referring to a prophet who was a charitable and godly man.[5] There is debate among some Muslim scholars as to who the prophet, Idris, was. Some think God took him to heaven before he died; therefore, many Islamic scholars believe he was the pre-flood, biblical figure known as Enoch.[6]

(19:57) And We raised him to high station.

If we are talking about Enoch, this becomes an understatement because God literally took him bodily while still alive to be with Him in Heaven (Genesis 5:24).

(19:58) These are they unto whom Allah showed favour from among the Prophets, of the seed of Adam and of those whom We carried (in the ship) with Noah, and of the seed of Abraham and Israel, and from among those whom We guided and chose. When the revelations of the Beneficent were recited unto them, they fell down, adoring the weeping.

The Koran is making a broad sweeping statement in this verse. This verse claims that all prophets from Adam onward "*fell down adoring the weeping*" each time they encountered God. We must allow Pickthall's interpretation, as well as the other three translations we have referenced, to mean that every one of the prophets of Islam, including Jesus *(Isa)*, literally fell prostrate on the ground "weeping tears of joy" every time God appeared to them. While the Bible does show prophets sometimes falling before God, it does not usually depict the prophets as falling and weeping in a universal manner; therefore, in the spirit of fair-mindedness, we will suggest that the Koran is possibly using poetic license to contrast the way Muslim's pray, compared to the way Jews and Christians pray.

(19:59) Now there had succeeded them a later generation whom have ruined worship and have followed lusts. But they will meet deception. Where we read in this passage, "...*whom have ruined worship*" is translated by Arberry as *"waisted the prayer."* Ali translates it as *"missed the prayers,"* and finally, by Shakir as *"who neglected prayers."* This would indicate that the forerunner of religious neglect in favor of sinful desires, which we call "sin," was the slacking off of prayers. In the Arabian Peninsula in Muhammad's day, all the Arabian tribes worshipped one or more of the 360 various Pagan gods. Allah is the god of Muhammad's Quraysh tribe,[7] yet most of the Koran is directed toward Jews and Christians with an underlying-theme, running the length of the Koran, attacking the Deity of Jesus *(Isa).*

It also suggests that the descendants of the prophets previously described (who were all Hebrews with the possible exceptions of the pre-flood prophets, Adam, Enoch, and Noah) strayed into Paganism and idolatry from time-to-time, which allowed their lust to have free reign.

(19:60) Save him who shall repent and believe and do right. Such will enter the Garden, and they will not be wronged in aught—

The continuation of the last verse implies that some "People of the Book" have repented and embraced Islam. As a result, they will benefit when Judgment Day arrives.

(19:61) Gardens of Eden, which the Beneficent has promised to His slaves in the Unseen. Lo! His promise is ever sure of fulfilment—

This is part of another ongoing theme regarding the paradise and the Last Day awaiting those who accept Islam.

(19:62) They hear therein no idle talk, but only Peace; and therein they have food for morn and evening.

Now we are seeing a thinly veiled appeal to the lust of the flesh in the sense most people love a peaceful and relaxing environment with offerings of delicacies. In Heaven, there is no need for nourishment, although it appears there will be food (Matthew 8:11-12; Revelation 19:9).

(19:63) Such is the Garden which We cause the devout among Our bondmen to inherit.

These heavenly offerings are exclusive to those who follow Allah.

(19:64) We (angels) come not down save by commandment of your Lord. Unto Him belongs all that is before us and all that is behind us and all that is between those two, and your Lord was never forgetful—

As we've seen throughout this book, the angel, Gabriel is the emissary between Allah and Muhammad. He is now reinforcing his credibility and authority to challenge the "People of the Book" by citing his credentials. Note, in his translation, Pickthall (as well as Arberry) translates it as *"all that is between those two,"* instead of translating this passage as Yusuf Ali did. Ali writes, *"…what is before us and what is behind us and what is between…,"* Pickthall and Arberry's translation could be referring to Adam and Eve because of the reference to the Garden of Eden (vs. 61), but it could also refer to those who accept Islam or not.

Nevertheless, Muhammad Habib Shakir's translation is similar to Yusuf Ali and translates this verse *"whatever is before us and whatever is behind us and whatever is between these,"* which might mean "what has gone on before (up until now)." However, this verse is more likely regarding judgment between the believers and disbelievers, which becomes more apparent in verse 73.

(19:65) Lord of the heavens and the earth and all that is between them! Therefor, worship you Him and be you steadfast [devoted] in

His service. Know you [will be] one that can be named along with Him? (bracketed clarifications mine).

This verse is still a continuation of the preceding verse. It is a proclamation that Allah is the *"Lord of the heavens (in Islam, there are seven Heavens, Sûrah 2:29) and earth,"* followed by a rhetorical question rejecting Jesus and/or the Trinity. To paraphrase it, we are asked: *Do you know of any other name equally worthy to Allah?*

As we continue to use the Bible to judge the Koran—as the Koran instructs us to do (Sûrahs 4:82; 5:47; 10:94)—we will offer biblical verses in answer to the koranic challenge in this verse (65) which challenges us: *"Know you [will be] one that can be named along with Him?"* The Bible itself offers the one and only name above all names, both in Heaven and on earth:

Wherefore God also has highly exalted Him, and given Him a name which is above every name:

That at the name of Jesus every knee should bow, of things in Heaven, and things in earth, and things under the earth;

And that every tongue should confess that Jesus Christ is Lord, to the glory of God the Father (Philippians 2:9-11).

Neither is there salvation in any other [but Jesus]: for there is none other name under Heaven given among men, whereby we must be saved (Acts 4:12, bracketed clarification mine).

(19:66) And [a] man says: "When I am dead, shall I forsooth [in fact] be brought forth alive?" (Bracketed clarifications mine.)

In context, Gabriel is apparently ridiculing the scoffers who do not believe in the resurrection, but they will find out the truth when Allah sends them to be among those who will join the devils in Hell.

In answer to the rhetorical question asked in this verse, *"When I am dead, shall I forsooth [in fact] be brought forth alive?"* Jesus gave the answer to this taunting question when He was confronted at the tomb of Lazarus by his sister, Martha, who complained that if Jesus had only come earlier and healed her brother of his mortal sickness, Lazarus would still be alive:

> Now Martha, as soon as she heard that Jesus was coming, went and met Him, but Mary was sitting in the house. Now Martha said to Jesus, "Lord, if You had been here, my brother would not have died. But even now I know that whatever You ask of God, God will give You."

Jesus said to her, "Your brother will rise again."
Martha said to Him, "I know that he will rise again in the resurrection at the last day."

Jesus said to her, "*I am the resurrection and the life*. He who believes in Me, though he may die, he shall live" (John 11:20-25, NKJV, emphasis added).

> And Jesus lifted up *His* eyes and said, "Father, I thank You that You have heard Me. And I know that You always hear Me, but because of the people who are standing by I said *this,* that they may believe that You sent Me." Now when He had said these things, He cried with a loud voice, "Lazarus, come forth!" And he who had died came out bound hand and foot with grave clothes, and his face was wrapped with a cloth. Jesus said to them, "Loose him, and let him go" (John 11:41b-43, NKJV, emphases added).

(19:67) Does not man remember that We created him before, when he was naught [nothing]? (Bracketed clarification mine.)

We are in the midst of debating mankind's existence. How far can the knowledge of our self-existence go? What are we aware of before we were born, during life, and what comes after we die? This verse makes a point of Allah's all-encompassing knowledge and control of every aspect of a person's existence. We are told that even before we were born, Allah knew us. This very similar to a particular scripture found in the Bible:

"Before I formed you in the womb I knew you, and before you were born I consecrated you..." (Jeremiah 1:5a).

(19:68) And, by your Lord, verily [truly] We shall assemble them and the devils, then We shall bring them, crouching, around hell (bracketed clarification mine).

Allah is now warning that he will surely gather all the humans who have rejected him, along with all the devils and bring them weak and cowering to the brink of Hell.

(19:69) Then We shall pluck out from every sect [denominations] whichever of them was most stubborn in rebellion to the Beneficent (bracketed clarification mine).

The Koran must be referring to the "People of the Book" here because "every sect" is a deviation from a specific religion. In this case, it makes sense the Koran is referring to the Jews and the Christians who have ignored Muhammad's invitation to accept Islam. It would not make sense to assume this passage is referring to the Pagan Arab tribes because each one of their 360 Pagan gods would be heading up their separate religion or cult.

(19:70) And surely We are best aware of those most worthy to be burned therein.

In context, we are dealing with the life and death of those Allah will send to Hell.

OBSERVATION: The Koran offers no explanation regarding why there is death in the world. The reason the Bible gives for people dying is that death entered the world because of sin—and the wages of sin is death (Gen 2:17; 3:1-6; Romans 5:12; 6: 23).

(19:71) There is not one of you but shall approach it. That is a fixed ordinance of your Lord.

Muslims are not to fear Hell because Allah has pre-ordained for them not to be sent there. Yet Muhammad said that the majority of those in hell are women (Sahih al-Bukhari Vol. 1, Book 2 No. 29) and even he wasn't sure if he would go to heaven Sûrah 46:9..

(19:72) Then We shall rescue those who kept from evil, and leave the evil-doers crouching there.

The Koran repeats the assurance for Muslims that Allah will save them from Hell, but not the evil infidels, as the Koran explains in the next passage.

(19:73) And when Our clear revelations are recited unto them, those who disbelieve say unto those who believe: Which of the two parties (yours or ours) is better in position, and more imposing as an army?

It appears this is an ongoing dialogue about those who have heard the message given by Muhammad but reject it. To make matters worse, those who have rejected Islam are taunting the Muslims.

The unbelievers are asking the Muslims another rhetorical question, "Who has the better position?" There were more Pagans, Christians, and Jews at the time of this dialog, but we know that the Jews and Christians found many discrepancies between what the Koran passed off as biblical and actual Scripture; so perhaps this passage is addressing the vocal "People of the Book." Subsequently, from the Koran's point of view, all those who question Muhammad's revelations are mistakenly assuming they are right solely because they outnumber the Muslims.

(19:74) How many a generation have We destroyed before them, who were more imposing in respect of gear and outward seeming!

How many past generations of people, who were even more powerful and richer than those disbelievers, has Allah destroyed? The answer is understood to be many!

(19:75) Say: "As for him who is in error, the Beneficent will verily [truly] prolong his span of life until, when they behold that which they were promised, whether it be punishment (in the world), or the Hour (of doom) [i.e., the Hour of Judgment], they will know who is worse in

position and who is weaker as an army" (only bracketed clarifications mine).

It seems that Allah will give time to the people who belong to the select group of wealthy and powerful people who arrogantly think they have gained their power and positions without Allah's help. They expect to live a long time on the earth with riches, luxurious comfort, and many servants and soldiers to protect them; however, sooner or later, either on earth or at the hour of the resurrection, they will be judged and come to know they are in a worse position with weaker soldiers—Allah's servants are the ones who represent the greater army.

(19:76) Allah increases in right guidance those who walk aright, and the good deeds which endure are better in your Lord's sight for reward, and better for resort [choice]. (Bracketed clarification mine.)

We are told that those who seek Allah's guidance will receive it. Those who do good works are highly esteemed in Allah's eyes; consequently, they will assuredly profit.

(19:77) Have you seen him who disbelieves in Our revelations and says: "Assuredly I shall be given wealth and children?"

> *Have you noticed that there are some people who brag that they are doing just fine without accepting Islam? They brag they will do alright without Allah and still gain money and offspring (paraphrase mine).*

(19:78) Has he perused the Unseen, or has he made a pact with the Beneficent [Allah]? (Bracketed clarification mine.)

This verse is a partial set-up for the next verse (79), where we see a wealthy person who has ignored his spiritual obligations because he thinks he has it all and does not need "religion," and by thinking this way, he rejects Allah.

(19:79) Nay, but We shall record that which he says and prolong for him a span of torment.

Now we are presented with the answer:

336

No, but Allah will remember what he says and does by piling on him more and more punishment (paraphrase mine).

(19:80) And We shall inherit from him that whereof he spake [spoke], and he will come unto Us, alone (without his wealth and children). (only bracketed clarifications mine).

Speaking for Allah, Gabriel is saying, "And we will receive all of his boastings, but the time will come when he will still have to stand before me stripped of his children and wealth and all alone without anyone to help him."

(19:81) And they have chosen (other) gods beside Allah that they may be a power for them.

While the reference to "(other) gods" could mean Pagans, this could be a subtle attack on Christianity, as well, because of what we will read seven verses from this point in verse 88, which states, *"And they say: 'The Beneficent has taken unto Himself a son.' "* The Koran is still more concerned with the threat of Jesus' Divinity than it is with all the 360 Pagan gods in the Arabian Peninsula

(19:82) Nay, but they will deny their worship of them, and become opponents unto them.

It seems this passage refers to Mary and Jesus, who the Koran mistakenly teaches make up part of the Christian Trinity (Sûrah 5:116). On the Day of Judgement, when Christians call upon Mary and Jesus for help, they will be told, "You Trinitarians should never have worshiped us. We reject you because you associated us with Allah!"

(19:83) See you not [don't you see] that We have set the devils on the disbelievers to confound them with confusion? (Bracketed clarification mine.)

Now, the Koran attempts to explain why Pagans believe what they do and why Christians believe in Jesus as the Son of God while rejecting Allah and his claim that Jesus is not his son. According to this verse, the reason for the Christians' disbelief is because Allah sent devils to muddle the minds of Pagans and Christians, thus confusing them regarding the truth of Allah. In light of this, one wonders why

Muhammad keeps trying to convince the Jews and Christians that they should embrace Islam.

(19:84) So make no haste against them (O Muhammad). We do but number unto them a sum (of days).

Muhammad is instructed not to be in a hurry to convert the Christians because Allah has given them a limited number of days to repent before they die. Surely Allah remembers what he just said in the last verse—that he sent demons to trick unbelievers into not accepting Islam. This is confusing at best, and at worst, it is unfair. The God of the Bible tells us that He is not desirous that *anyone* should perish (2 Peter 3:9).

(19:85) On the Day when We shall gather the righteous unto the Beneficent [Allah], a goodly company (bracketed clarification mine).

This verse is part one of a three-part pronouncement, which suggests that Allah will reward those who accept him, and the following verse continues with warnings of judgment.

(19:86) And drive the guilty unto hell, a weary herd,

Now we have confirmation that the Christians who have not accepted belief in Allah will go to Hell.

(19:87) They will have no power of intercession, save him who has made a covenant with his Lord.

Part three of this dialogue (verses 85-87) implies that when Christians are sentenced to Hell, they will not have Mary or her son, Jesus (the Koran's ill-conceived idea of who makes up the Trinity, Sûrah 5:116), to help them. The thought finally concludes with the next verse.

(19:88) And they say: "The Beneficent has taken unto Himself a son."

And the Christians say that Allah has taken a son (paraphrase mine).

(19:89) Assuredly you utter a disastrous thing,

Without a doubt, you Christians are saying a terrible thing (paraphrase mine).

(19:90) Whereby almost the heavens are torn, and the earth is split asunder and the mountains fall in ruins,

Gabriel is telling us that because of this assault on Allah—claiming that Jesus *(Isa)* is his son (vs. 88)—the skies are on the verge of being ripped apart, the earth is on the verge of being broken in half, and all the mountain ranges are collapsing!

(19:91) That you [Christians] ascribe unto the Beneficent a son (bracketed clarification mine),

Notice the heavens and earth are not in jeopardy of being split apart because of the 360 gods of the Arabian pantheon, but only because Christians dare to believe that Jesus is the Son of God. If Jesus' claim was not true, why would it be a threat to Islam? We must ask ourselves why the Koran keeps fixating on denying the Divinity of Jesus over and over and over again.

The Koran insists that Jesus never claimed to be the Son of God (Sûrah 5:116), but the Bible tells us differently. Some background: In the Bible, we read of a trial where Jesus *(Isa)* was charged with all manner of things, yet Jesus remained silent.

Then the high priest stood up and said to Jesus, "Are you not going to answer? What is this testimony that these men are bringing against you?" But Jesus remained silent.

The high priest said to him, "I charge you under oath by the living God: Tell us if you are the Messiah, the Son of God."

"You have said so," Jesus replied. "But I say to all of you: From now on you will see the Son of Man [God made flesh, John 1:14] sitting at the right hand of the Mighty One and coming on the clouds of Heaven" (Matthew 26:62-64, NIV, bracketed clarification mine).

(19:92) When it is not meet [worthy] for (the Majesty of) the Beneficent that He should choose [adopt] a son (only bracketed clarification mine).

Once again, we are instructed, *ad infinitum,* that it was never possible for the glorious and merciful Allah to have a son. The Bible states that Jesus *(Isa)* was always a part of the Godhead—the very "reasoning" (logos) of God. Furthermore, the Bible confirms that nothing was made without Jesus. Because God had to *reason* how to create everything, having the ability to reason must have always been a vital part of God's makeup (John 1:1-4; Philippians 2:5-8).

(19:93) There is none in the heavens and the earth but comes unto the Beneficent as a slave.

This verse is a little awkward, but basically, it states that everyone who is in one of the heavens or earth—will have to come before Allah.

(19:94) Verily [truly] He knows them and numbers them with (right) numbering (only bracketed clarification mine).

> *It is true that Allah knows everyone, both righteous and lost, and keeps track of them all (paraphrase mine).*

(19:95) And each one of them will come unto Him on the Day of Resurrection, alone.

> *Everyone who has ever lived on earth will one day stand before Allah alone, without any help from Jesus (paraphrase mine).*

(19:96) Behold! Those who believe and do good works, the Beneficent [Allah] will appoint for them love (bracketed clarification mine).

Again, the works-based Islamic religion rewards those who do good works. This is the opposite of biblical doctrine, which teaches:

For by grace you have been saved through faith, and that not of yourselves; it is the gift of God, not of works, lest anyone should boast (Ephesians 2:8-9, NKJV).

(19:97) And We make (this Scripture) [i.e., Koran] easy in the [Arabian] tongue, (O Muhammad) only that you may bear good tidings therewith unto those who ward off (evil), and warn therewith the forward [hostile] folk (only bracketed clarifications mine).

Muhammad is informed that Allah is making his revelations simple for Arabs to understand because Muhammad can preach to them in Arabic, thus allowing the Arabs to ward off evil. This passage is also used against critics or " hostile folk," who point out problems in the Koran, which allows Muslim defenders to argue that it is the fault of the translation because the Koran can only be truly understood in the "holy language" of Arabic.[8] In fact the Arabs did hear the Good News or Gospel in their own Language while visiting Jerusalem on the Day of Pentecost, Acts 2:11.

(19:98) And how many a generation before them have We destroyed! Can't you (Muhammad) see a single man of them, or hear from them the slightest sound?

As for those generations of Jews and Christians who refused to acknowledge Allah, they are all destroyed. Muhammad is told to appreciate this truth because he will never see or hear from them, not even the slightest whisper (paraphrase mine).

NOTES:

1. Dr. Muhammad Taqi-ud-Din and Dr. Muhammad Muhsin Khan Trans., *Interpretation of the Meanings of the Nobel Qur'an in the English Language* (Riyadh: Saudi Arabia, Darussalam Publ. 1999), Sûrah 19.

341

2. "... you shall call his name JESUS: for He shall save His people from their sins" (Matthew 1:21). Only God can save you from your sins as we see in the following gospel passage from Mark, which shows that is exactly who Jesus presents Himself as: "When Jesus saw their faith, He said unto the sick of the palsy, 'Son, your sins be forgiven you.' But there was certain of the scribes sitting there, and reasoning in their hearts, 'Why does this man thus speak blasphemies? who can forgive sins but God only?' And immediately when Jesus perceived in His spirit that they so reasoned within themselves, He said unto them, 'Why reason you these things in your hearts? Whether is it easier to say to the sick of the palsy, 'Your sins be forgiven you;' or to say, 'Arise, and take up your bed, and walk?' But that you may know that the Son of man has power on earth to forgive sins (He says to the sick [man] of [with] the palsy), I say unto you, Arise, and take up your bed, and go your way into your house' " (Mark 2:5-11, bracketed clarifications mine). Compare with Matthew 9:2-13 and Luke 5:17-32.

3. Elizabeth Lyons, Heather Peters, *Buddhism:*
   The History and Diversity of a Great Tradition (Philadelphia, University of Pennsylvania Museum of Archaeology and Anthropology, 1985), 5. "The story of the historical Buddha's life tells us that *he was born* a prince of a noble Indian family....He stood upright at birth, took seven strides, and *spoke*: 'This is my last birth—henceforth there is no more birth for me.' "

4. A.B. Al-Mehri, *The Qur'ān: with Sūrah Introductions and Appendices: Saheeh International Translation* (Birmingham, UK: The Qur'ān Project, 2010), 251.

5. Juan Eduardo Campo and J. Gordon Milton, ed., Encyclopedia of Islam. *Idris* (New York: Infobase Publishing, 2009), 344. *Idris*: "probably originated as a term in ancient Hebrew for an interpreter."

6. Ibid., 559.

7. *And We caused Jesus, son of Mary, to follow in their footsteps, confirming that which was (revealed) before him in the Torah, and We bestowed on him the Gospel wherein is guidance and a light, confirming that which was (revealed) before it in the*

Torah - a guidance and an admonition unto those who ward off (evil). (Sûrah 5:46, Pickthall)

8. Dr. Zahid Aziz. "Shakir Identified." The Lahore Ahmadiyya Islamic Movement, n.d. Web. 25 Mar. 2015. In an article written by Dr. Aziz, we can see how many Islamic scholars believe that the Koran can only be understood in its original language of Arabic. He shows this by questioning the validity of a translation of the Koran attributed to Muhammad Habib Shakir: "In the second half of the article I attempted to discover further about the identity of 'Shakir'... I was able to show that: 'It is abundantly clear that the Egyptian Shakir to whom this translation is attributed could not possibly have translated the Quran as he was opposed on religious principle to translating the Quran into any language).' " Author's note: It would appear that this is not a new opinion based on Sûrah 19:97, which states Allah revealed the Koran to Muhammad in the Arabic language.

☪

THE KORAN VOLUME II

Volume II of the Koran begins with Sûrah 21 and ends with 114; however, we begin with Sûrah 28, which is near the beginning of Volume II, followed by an additional 18 short sûrahs, the shortest and less controversial chapters. They range from a few paragraphs to just a sentence or two, broken into several verses at the end of the Koran's second volume (i.e., verses 97-114). These sûrahs should also be of interest to our Jewish friends.

As we explained in Volume I, Chapter 1 of our three-volume series, *Exposing Islam: A Simple Crash Course on Islam,* the Koran is divided into two volumes like the Bible's Old and New Testaments; however, unlike the Bible, the Koran contains no prophetic words or fulfillment of prophecies (self-fulfilling prophecy excepted). We also explained that the Koran's chapters (sûrahs) and verses are not chronological but arranged more according to length. As also previously stated, Allah claims to be the author of both the Bible and the Koran, yet they are composed entirely differently. Had Allah composed the Koran like he allegedly claims to have written the Bible, then much of the Koran's second volume would have been placed first since it generally contains the earliest (e.g., Genesis) and shortest revelations that were given to Muhammad; however, because some of the newer pronouncements abrogate or replace earlier commandments, it makes sense that the Koran is arranged in the manner it is. See Table 1 at the beginning of this volume, which allows us to know the times when Allah changed his mind and for us to distinguish which conflicting verses take precedence. Later in this section, we will familiarize ourselves with some of those first sûrahs and verses where Allah is more agreeable.

Presumably, unlike the prophets of the Bible, Muhammad needed to begin by receiving short revelations (sûrahs), until he was able to handle the larger and longer revelations (sûrahs).

SÛRAH 28

THE STORY (Qasas)
(Revealed at Mecca)

In the name of Allah, the Beneficent, the Merciful.

In addition to the Muslims, many people (including some Christians) like to show their casual familiarity with the Koran. They think they can prove that both God and Allah are the same gods by pointing out that the Koran actually contains a lot of the Bible. We saw some examples of this in the preceding sûrahs. Still, Sûrah 28 is an excellent example of many instances where the Koran retells some interesting, if not controversial, and distorted, biblical stories. In this sûrah, we will once again look at those contrasts between the Bible and the Koran's version of the same events. You can judge for yourself—in light of all the historical and biblical anomalies—if the God of the Bible and the author of the Koran are the same people.

(28:1) Tâ. Sîn. Mîm.

These are the names of letters. Some researchers have trouble with the meaning of this opening verse. All of the four English translations of the Koran we referenced for this work, as well as other versions we have read all avoid translating this into English, so we researched each letter's name as Arabic to English words. *Tâ* (ت) is not listed as a standing word; neither are *Sîn* (ش) nor *Mîm* (م), but all are names of Arabic and Hebrew letters. These are the corresponding Hebrew letters: Tav (ת), Sin (ש), Mim (מ). We found that these letters are from what is known as the Semitic writing system, which only uses consonants. Dr. Abdalqadir as-Sufi (also known as "Ian Dallas") was born in Scotland during the 1930s and converted to Islam in 1967. He suggests that *"Tâ. Sîn. Mîm"* stand for: "These are the signs of the Clear Book," but that would be redundant since the following verse has been translated into English without any problem, and it basically says the same thing.

To be inclusive, we should share the fact that Allâmah Nooeuddin (1840 — ?),[1] makes the observation that this opening is also the beginning of the last two verses and he believes that the letters stand for attributes of Allah: (1) i.e., 'al-Latîf (الطيف) the benign; (2) al-Samî (السميع) the Hearing, and (3) al-Majîd or Al-'Alîm (العليم) the All-Knowing. How he derives this out of *Tâ. Sîn. Mîm.* is not clear, but we thought it should be included anyway.

(28:2) These are revelations of the Scripture that make plain.

Both Abdullah Yusuf Ali and Muhammad Habib Shakir translate this verse basically the same:

These are Verses of the Book that makes (things) plane/clear.

Arberry translates *"Book"* as *"Manifest Book,"* while Pickthall, as we can see here, uses the term *"Scripture."* Whichever translation you use, it is an account from the Bible that is about to be presented.

(28:3) We narrate unto you (somewhat) of the story of Moses and Pharaoh with truth, for folk who believe.

Gabriel is stating that he is now going to relate the true story of Moses and Pharaoh to the believers of Islam.

It is interesting to notice that Pickthall inserted the clarification "somewhat" into the verse, which seems to imply that even he realized this Koran's version of the Exodus is a bit unorthodox in context. It's important to know that the time frame surrounding these events revolves around 1446 B.C., as we will see in verse six.

(28:4) Behold! Pharaoh exalted himself in the earth and made its people castes. A tribe among them he oppressed, killing their sons and sparing their women. Indeed! he was of those who work corruption.

Verse 4 discusses the Pharaoh, who came into power after the Hyksos (the people who ruled Egypt during Joseph's time) were defeated. It was the Hyksos Pharaoh who invited Joseph's father and his family to relocate to Egypt.

> Now there arose a new king over Egypt, who did not know Joseph (Exodus 1:8, NKJV).

Verse 4 is compatible with Exodus 1, where we read about the Hebrew children:

> And Pharaoh charged all his people, saying, "Every son that is born you shall cast into the river, and every daughter you shall save alive" (Exodus 1:22).

(28:5) And We desired to show favour unto those who were oppressed in the earth, and to make them examples and to make them the inheritors,

Gabriel is explaining how Allah is aware of the plight of the Hebrews and helped them to rise above their oppressors and provide an inheritance.

(28:6) And to establish them in the earth, and to show Pharaoh and Haman and their hosts that which they feared from them.

At the very outset of this sûrah, we only had to go as far as this verse in order to find a disturbing problem, which is the inclusion of an Amalekite living in Medo-Persian by the name of Haman as Prime Minister of Egypt under Pharaoh. It appears this verse is commingling the biblical book of Esther with the biblical book of Exodus. The Bible teaches that when Esther became queen in 478 B.C., Haman was the Prime Minister under Xerxes I (King Ahasuerus), the king of the Medo-Persians:

After these events, King Xerxes honored Haman, son of Hammedatha, the Agagite [Amalekite], elevating him and giving him a seat of honor higher than that of all the other nobles. All the royal officials at the king's gate knelt down and paid honor to Haman, for the king had commanded this concerning him (Esther 3:1-2).

OBSERVATION: The appearance of Haman as Pharaoh's Prime Minister is unique to the Koran and is not reflected in archaeological or any other historical accounts. In the Bible's Exodus account regarding Moses fleeing Egypt with the children of Israel, Haman is nowhere to be found. In Sûrah 28, "The Story," we find one of the best known examples of historical mistakes found in the Koran and as an aside, it is ironic to realize that both Pharaoh and Haman were historically two of the most treacherous adversaries of the Jewish people, although they lived a thousand years and two continents apart.

(28:7) And we inspired the mother of Moses, saying: "Suckle him and, when you fear for him, then cast him into the river and fear not nor grieve. Surely! We shall bring him back unto you and shall make him (one) of Our messengers."

The problem with this passage is that Moses' mother knew if Pharaoh's soldiers would find her baby boy, no doubt they would kill him. In the Bible, God did not instruct Moses' mother one way or the other, nor did He predict who or what he would become. We do not even know if his mother was religious. She simply took the chance of placing her son in a basket among the river reeds.

Now a man [Amram] of the tribe of Levi married a Levite woman [Jochebed], and she became pregnant and gave birth to a son. When she saw that he was a fine child, she hid him for three months. But when she could hide him no longer, she got a papyrus basket for him and coated it with tar and pitch. Then she placed the child in it and put it among the reeds along the bank of the Nile. His sister stood at a distance to see what would happen to him (Exodus2:1-4, NIV, bracketed clarification mine).

(28:8) And the family of Pharaoh took him up, that he might become for them an enemy and a sorrow, Surely! Pharaoh and Haman and their hosts were ever sinning

One of the problems with this verse is when we read "...*Pharaoh and Haman and their hosts...*" because Haman is borrowed from the story of "Esther." This is another koranic anachronism we will address later. Another problem with this verse is when Pharaoh found the baby Moses, he knew that Moses was a Hebrew. By Pharaoh's own proclamation, the baby should have been killed, not nurtured. The twist given here by Muhammad is that *"Pharaoh and Haman and their hosts were ever sinning."* Knowing that Moses was a Hebrew child, Pharaoh, and Haman reasoned how ironic it would be if they raised him to destroy his fellow Hebrews.

Historically, it was not Pharaoh or his people who found Moses; it was his daughter (Exodus 2).

(28:9) And the wife of Pharaoh said: "(He will be) a consolation for me and for you. Kill him not. Peradventure [perhaps] he may be of use to us, or we may choose him for a son." And they perceived not (bracketed clarification mine).

Again, this is an unbiblical passage since it was not Pharaoh's wife who found the child, nor was it Pharaoh who adopted Moses. Pharaoh's daughter (Exodus 2) adopted Moses, making Pharaoh his grandfather. Would not an omniscient god know that?

Then Pharaoh's daughter went down to the Nile to bathe, and her attendants were walking along the riverbank. She saw the basket among the reeds and sent her female slave to get it. She opened it and saw the baby. He was crying, and she felt sorry for him. "This is one of the Hebrew babies," she said (Exodus 2:5-6, NIV).

(28:10) And the heart of the mother of Moses became void, and she would have betrayed him if We had not fortified her heart, that she might be of the believers.

This unbiblical passage suggests Moses' mother knew where her baby was.(Moses' sister, Miriam, told her mother what had occurred). Because she missed him so much, she almost confessed to the Egyptians that Moses was her child, an event not mentioned in the Bible, but Allah intervened, and because she was a good Muslim, Allah caused her to be patient. Of course, the Koran would consider her a Muslim because Moses is regarded as a prophet of Islam (Sûrah 19:51-53).

(28:11) And she said unto his sister: "Trace him. So she observed him from afar, and they perceived not."

Compare this passage with verse 7 (just five verses earlier) with the Bible's version below and notice that Moses' mother, Jochebed, never told her daughter, Miriam, to spy on where Moses was after she placed the baby in the Nile; however, her daughter had been watching him from the time he was placed in the river:

> ... Then she [Moses' mother] placed the child in it [the papyrus basket] and put it among the reeds along the bank of the Nile. His sister stood at a distance to see what would happen to him (Exodus 2:3b-4, NIV, bracketed clarifications mine).

(28:12) And We had before forbidden foster-mothers for him, so she said: "Shall I show you a household who will rear him for you and take care of him?"

Muhammad Habib Shakir clarifies this passage for us:

And We ordained that he refused to suck any foster mother before, so she said: "Shall I point out to you the people of a house who will take care of him for you, and they will be benevolent to him?"

This would make sense if baby Moses had been discovered by a married woman such as Pharaoh's wife, who may have had other children of her own that she was nursing. Nevertheless, as we pointed out, Pharaoh's daughter found Moses, and she could not nurse a baby because she had not yet had a child of her own. Yet, the other mothers who could nurse were unable to encourage the baby to nurse with them, so that presented a predicament. Under the Koran's scenario, Moses' mother would not be needed unless, for whatever reason, the baby refused to suckle, as this passage suggests.

The Koran also attempts to explain the confusion of how baby Moses was reunited with his mother, but why would the Queen of Egypt feel the need to take on another baby and one who did not have royal blood? He could challenge and be a threat to her other children when he became an adult.

This scenario is a problem because, in the biblical account, it was Pharaoh's young unmarried daughter, who found Moses and was unable to nurse a baby; thus, a nursemaid was needed:

> Then his [Moses'] sister asked Pharaoh's daughter, "Shall I go and get one of the Hebrew women to nurse the baby for you?" "Yes, go," she answered. So the girl went to get the baby's mother (Exodus 2:7-8, NIV, bracketed clarification mine).

As we read in the Bible, because Pharaoh's daughter was not married, Moses' sister immediately seized the opportunity to approach Pharaoh's daughter and suggested that she knew of a nursing woman who could breastfeed baby Moses.

(28:13) So We restored him to his mother that she might be comforted and not grieve, and that she might know that the promise of Allah is true. But most of them know not.

This is reminiscent of Exodus 2 in the Bible:

> Pharaoh's daughter said to her, "Take this baby and nurse him for me, and I will pay you." So the woman took the baby and nursed him.

When the child grew older, she took him to Pharaoh's daughter and he became her son. She named him Moses [an Egyptian name[2]], saying, "I drew him out of the water" (Exodus 2:9-10, bracketed clarification mine).

(28:14) And when he reached his full strength and was ripe, We gave him wisdom and knowledge. Thus do We reward the good.

This appears to be a transitional verse into manhood for Moses under Allah's benevolent protection.

(28:15) And he entered the city at a time of carelessness of its folk, and he found therein two men fighting, one of his own caste, and the other of his enemies; and he who was of his caste asked him for help against him who was of his enemies. So Moses struck him with his fist and killed him. He said: "This is of the devil's doing. Look! he is an enemy, a mere misleader."

In this verse, we read, *"and he found therein two men fighting, one of his own caste (a Hebrew), and the other of his enemies; and he who was of his caste asked him for help against him who was of his enemies."* One of his enemies? This does not make sense because Moses was a prince of Egypt and was treated with honor and respect because of his rank. Moses had no reason to think of the Egyptians as his enemies.

This verse is implying that a fight took place between an Egyptian citizen and a Hebrew. The Hebrew asked Moses for help because he knew Moses was a fellow Hebrew. He taunted him to help fight the Egyptian because it was understood he was their mutual enemy. This also makes very little sense because Moses was dressed like the Egyptian Prince he was, and the Hebrew slave, who is mentioned here, would hardly have considered himself to be an equal to Egyptian royalty, just as the Egyptian fighting the Hebrew would not have considered Prince Moses to be a threat.

Let's consider the last part of this verse, which reads, *"So Moses struck him with his fist and killed him. He said, "This is of the devil's doing. Look! he is an enemy, a mere misleader."* Moses had no intention of killing the man he struck who, by all accounts, appeared to be a strong person and should not have died when he hit him; therefore, when the man died, Moses, according to the Koran's interpretation, felt some remorse. In the last part of this verse, the Koran has Moses saying that Satan was his real enemy (not the man he had just killed), and it was

Satan who was the one responsible for the man's death. Moses believed the reason Satan caused this to happen was to bring the Egyptian's condemnation on him for taking sides with a Hebrew slave over the Egyptians.

The biblical account is entirely different. The two men were not fighting, and the Hebrew slave did not ask for help:

> One day, after Moses had grown up, he went out to where his own people were and watched them at their hard labor. He saw an Egyptian beating a Hebrew, one of his own people. Looking this way and that and seeing no one, he killed the Egyptian and hid him (Exodus 2:11-12, NIV).

It is generally accepted that the Egyptian was one of the soldiers in charge of the Hebrew slaves. For whatever reason, he was beating that particular slave who was helpless to defend himself. Moses was so enraged that he killed the Egyptian soldier after making sure that no one was watching.

(28:16) He [Moses] said: My Lord! Indeed! I have wronged my soul, so forgive me. Then He [Allah] forgave him. Behold! He is the Forgiving, the Merciful (bracketed clarifications mine).

Moses knew killing an Egyptian would not bode well for him since the Hebrew was a mere slave; however, there is no biblical indication Moses felt any remorse that he had done anything wrong by saving the slave from receiving a beating and might have even saved the Hebrew slave's life.

Some Muslim scholars suggest that by then, Moses had seen enough. Finally realizing that Pharaoh's government was corrupt and repressive, he pleads for Allah's forgiveness for having been a part of it.

(28:17) He said:" My Lord! Forasmuch as You have favoured me, I will nevermore be a supporter of the guilty."

Continuing from our commentary for the last verse, it might be that Moses was going to leave Pharaoh's court.

A. J. Arberry translates this passage in a manner that helps clarify it:

> He said, "My Lord, forasmuch as you have blessed me, I will never be a partisan [friend] of the sinners" (bracketed clarification mine).

While this dialogue would not be surprising for a biblical man of God to say, it is not in the Bible. The Bible does, however, have several Scriptures advising the Jews and Christians against keeping bad company (Proverbs 1:10; 13:20; 22:24-25; 1 Corinthians 15:33, etc.).

This passage would also work with the last part of our commentary in the previous verse if Moses had repented for being a part of Pharaoh's court and was preparing to leave his government. Of course, repenting of his life at Pharaoh's court would make perfect sense and another reason why Moses would be asking for Allah's forgiveness.

(28:18) And morning found him in the city, fearing, vigilant, when behold! he who had appealed to him the day before cried out to him for help. Moses said unto him: "Surely! you are indeed a mere hothead."

This is another historical problem since there is no indication anywhere in the Bible where Moses ever ran into the slave again, the one he had saved the day before. We must point out that the man Moses helped was not in a fight; rather, he was severely beaten by an Egyptian overseer.

(28:19) And when he would have fallen upon the man who was an enemy unto them both, he said: "O Moses! Would you kill me as you did kill a person yesterday. You would be nothing but a tyrant in the land, you would not be of the reformers."

In this revised version, the following day, Moses came across the same slave fighting yet another Egyptian—and the Egyptian who he was allegedly fighting shocked Moses when he asked him, "O Moses! Would you kill me as you did kill a person yesterday?" Of course, when compared to the Bible, as Allah challenged us to do, this appears to be pure fantasy.

The following is the original biblical version:

> The next day he went out and saw two Hebrews fighting. He asked the one in the wrong, "Why are you hitting your fellow Hebrew?" The man said, "Who made you ruler and judge over us? Are you thinking of killing me as you killed the Egyptian?" Then Moses was afraid and thought, "What I did must have become known" (Exodus 2:13-14, NIV).

It is interesting that this Hebrew slave would think that Moses was destined to be a deliverer of the Hebrew slaves when Moses looked nothing like a Hebrew; instead, he appeared as a Prince of Egypt! Was this slave also a prophet? At this point in time, Moses had no idea what his destiny would be. This is another koranic embellishment that is not found in the Bible.

(28:20) And a man came from the uttermost part of the city, running. He said: "O Moses! Look! the chiefs take counsel against thee to slay you; therefor escape. Look! I am of those who give you good advice.

This dialog is also extra-biblical since there are no indications in the Bible where Moses had another person warn him he was in trouble by a group of Egyptians taking counsel against him. On the contrary, the Bible indicates Moses realized he was in trouble when he encountered two Hebrews who were fighting:

> And when he [Moses] went out the second day, behold, two Hebrew men were fighting, and he said to the one who did the wrong, "Why are you striking your companion?"

357

Then he [one of the two Hebrew men] said, "Who made you a prince and a judge over us? Do you intend to kill me as you killed the Egyptian?" (Exodus 2:113-4, NKJV, bracketed clarification mine.)

The Bible then explains that at that point, Moses realized he had to flee Egypt: "Now when Pharaoh heard this thing, he sought to slay Moses. But Moses fled from the face of Pharaoh" (Exodus 2:15a, NKJV).

(28:21) So he escaped from thence [there], fearing, vigilant [watching carefully]. He said: "My Lord! Deliver me from the wrongdoing folk" (bracketed clarification mine).

Moses is asking God to save him from wrongdoers when it was he who killed the Egyptian.

See commentary regarding the next verse.

(28:22) And when he turned his face toward Midian, he said: Peradventure my Lord will guide me in the right road.

Verse 22 is similar to the biblical account where Moses fled Egypt, except in the Bible, Moses did not seek help from God. He hastily left Egypt of his own accord (Exodus 2:15).

CONSIDER: Moses was raised in the Palace of Pharaoh who was a Pagan and Moses may have appeared to be a Pagan at the time or an agnostic. We do know as a baby Moses' sister Miriam arranged for his real mother to nurse him (Exodus 2:7-10) so he may have gained some knowledge of YAWA from them although he was very young at the time. He might also have had his faith reinforced when he later married the daughter of Jethro (sometimes referred to as Reuel), a priest, (most likely of YAWA). However, the Bible is never clear on that or at what point in his life Moses came to know God.

(28:23) And when he came unto the water of Midian he found there a whole tribe of men, watering. And he found apart from them two women keeping back (their flocks). He said: "What aileth thee?" The two said: "We cannot give (our flocks) to drink till the shepherds return from the water; and our father is a very old man."

Actually, when Moses escaped to Midian, he found a well with a whole clan of *women*, not men:

> Now when Pharaoh heard this thing, he sought to slay Moses. But Moses fled from the face of Pharaoh, and dwelt in the land of Midian: and he sat down by a well.
>
> Now the priest of Midian had seven daughters: and they came and drew water, and filled the troughs to water their father's flock (Exodus 2:15-16).

(28:24) So he watered (their flock) for them. Then he turned aside into the shade, and said: "My Lord! I am needy of whatever good You send down for me."

Moses watered the animals, and according to this verse, he rested in the shade and called Allah to help him by sending whatever good things Allah would supply.

On the other hand, in the biblical account, Moses was not involved in any heavenly dialogue asking God for help, but he did witness some women who were calmly watering their animals until some rowdy, male shepherds came along and forced the women away from the well. It was at that point when Moses intervened and helped the women water their flock:

> And the shepherds came and drove them [the women] away: but Moses stood up and helped them, and watered their flock (Exodus 2:17, bracketed clarification mine).

(28:25) Then there came unto him one of the two women, walking shyly. She said: "Look! my father biddeth you, that he may reward you with a payment for that you did water (the flock) for us." Then, when he [Moses] came unto him [Jethro] and told him the (whole) story, he [Jethro] said: "Fear not! You have escaped from the wrongdoing folk."

As we saw in verse 23, the Bible recorded Moses' encounter with seven women, not two. It was those seven daughters, not Moses, who explained to their father what had happened at the well:

Now the priest of Midian had seven daughters: and they came and drew water, and filled the troughs to water their father's flock (Exodus 2:16).

When the seven daughters returned to their father sooner than he expected them to, they explained the events of that afternoon:

When they came to Reuel [Jethro] their father, he said, "How *is it that* you are come so soon today?"

And they said, "An Egyptian delivered us from the hand of the shepherds, and he also drew enough water for us and watered the flock."

So he said to his daughters, "And where *is* he? Why *is* it *that* you have left the man? Call him, that he may eat bread."

Then Moses was content to live with the man, and he gave Zipporah his daughter to Moses. And she bore *him* a son. He called his name Gershom, for he said, "I have been a stranger in a foreign land" (Exodus 2:18-21, NKJV, bracketed clarification added).

(28:26) One of the two women said: "O my father! Hire him! For the best (man) that you can hire is the strong, the trustworthy."

A.J. Arberry translates it as follows:

360

Said one of the two women, "Father hire him; surely the best man you can hire is the one strong and trusty."

(28:27) He said: "Indeed! I fain [would be pleased that I] would marry you to one of these two daughters of mine on condition that you hire yourself to me for (the term of) eight pilgrimages. Then if you complete ten it will be of your own accord, for I would not make it hard for you. Allah willing, you will find me of the righteous" (bracketed clarification mine).

This is another koranic anachronism—confusing people and events—not only separated by hundreds of miles, but also by over a half a millennium.

As we read in the biblical account of this story, Reuel (Jethro)[3] *gave* Moses one of his seven daughters, Zipporah (Exodus 2:21). The koranic account given here, with Moses as the key figure, is actually a retelling of the biblical story of Jacob and *his* uncle, Laban, but even that story is told inaccurately.

It was Jacob—not Moses—who had a contract for seven years—not eight—to earn Rachel from his Uncle Laban. The story goes that Laban was the man who had two eligible daughters. Jacob loved Laban's youngest daughter, Rachel, but before Rachel could become Jacob's wife, Laban told Jacob he had to work for him for seven years; however, unknown to Jacob, Laban switched daughters on him. Jacob was deceived into marrying Leah, believing she was her sister, Rachel, because Laban believed the oldest daughter had to be married first. When Jacob finds out what Laban has done, he pleads for Rachel, so Laban gives her to him with the understanding that he must work an additional seven years to earn her. This story of Jacob, Abraham's grandson, happened some 500 years before the Moses saga (Genesis 29:15-28) and in the Mesopotamian city of Nahor, hundreds of miles away from Midian (Genesis 24:10). There are many suggestions where Haran is located—from being in the Northern Galilee to the Arabian peninsula.[4] We believe it to be in Mesopotamia (Persia), where the lands of Ur and Haran are also located and have biblical significance to Abraham.

OBSERVATION: Notice the use of the term "eight pilgrimages" as a way of counting time in this verse. Where did that come from? We suggest it is referring to the religious pilgrimage (*Hajj*) to Mecca that is required of every Muslim at least once in their lifetime during the last month of the Islamic year. It is an annual event in Mecca known as "Dhul-Hajj" (or Dhul Hijjah) meaning the "Month of the Hajj." (The Pagans also had the same ritual before the time of Muhammad.) The time span of eight annual Hajj's (i.e., pilgrimages) could translate into eight years. Even so, when Moses was alive, neither he nor his father-in-law, Reule (Jethro), would have had any interest in the then, Pagan Hajj; if—for that matter—it was even performed at that time in history, which is doubtful. It would be thousands of years in the future when Muhammad's new religion would reinvent and incorporate the Hajj into the Five Pillars of Islam. As an interesting side note, Muslims began counting the year one on their calendar starting with Muhammad's escape or Hajj to Medina; thus, the use of counting pilgrimages (although not to Medina but Mecca) as a reckoning of time.

(28:28) He said: "That (is settled) between you and me. Whichever of the two terms I fulfil, there will be no injustice to me, and Allah is Surety [guarantee] over what we say."

As with the preceding verse, the story appears to have also been borrowed from the biblical story found in Genesis of Jacob, Laban, Leah, and Rachel. Of course, Moses never called on the name of Allah, nor did anyone else in the Bible.

(28:29) Then, when Moses had fulfilled the term, and was travelling with his housefolk, he saw in the distance a fire and said unto his housefolk: Bide [dwell] you (here). Look! I see in the distance a fire; peradventure [perhaps] I shall bring you tidings thence [from there], or a brand from the fire that you may warm yourselves.

Yusuf Ali has a better translation:

> *Now when Moses had fulfilled the term, and was travelling with his family, he perceived a fire in the direction of Mount Tur. He said to his family: "Tarry ye; I perceive a fire; I hope to bring you from there some information, or a burning firebrand, that you may warm yourselves."*

Of the four English translations of this verse, Yusuf Ali is the only one to name the mountain; however, most Islamic scholars believe that Mount Tur is Mount Sinai.

This verse is more aligned with Genesis, Chapter 29's account of Jacob (when Jacob finished working for Laban at the end of his two, seven-year terms) and the biblical account of Moses and the burning bush. Putting that aside, in the Bible's version, when Moses arrived at the burning bush, he was not traveling with his family. He was alone with his father-in-law's flock, and "*warming*" his "*housefolk*" from the cold weather was never an issue in the biblical account found in Exodus 3:

Now Moses kept the flock of Jethro his father in law, the priest of Midian: and he led the flock to the backside of the desert, and came to the mountain of God, even to Horeb [Mount Sinai].

And the angel of the LORD appeared unto him in a flame of fire out of the midst of a bush: and he looked, and, behold, the bush burned with fire, and the bush was not consumed.

And Moses said, "I will now turn aside, and see this great sight, why the bush is not burnt" (Exodus 3:1-3, bracketed clarification mine).

(28:30) And when he reached it, he was called from the right side of the valley in the blessed field, from the tree: "O Moses! Look! I, even I, am Allah, the Lord of the Worlds;"

"... *right side of the valley*"? Again, we have another koranic geographic description (see commentary on Sûrah 19:52). Because we know from

Sûrah 19:52 that Moses was facing north toward the southern slope of Mount Sinai, he would have to be on the southeastern side of the valley. This description of the location of the voice calling Moses is relative at best. The biblical version is as follows:

> And when the LORD saw that he turned aside to see, God called unto him out of the midst of the bush, and said, "Moses, Moses" And he said, "Here am I."

> And He said, "Draw not nigh hither [don't come close]: put off your shoes from off your feet, for the place whereon you stand is holy ground."

> Moreover He said, "I am the God of your father, the God of Abraham, the God of Isaac, and the God of Jacob. And Moses hid his face; for he was afraid to look upon God" (Exodus 3:4-6, bracketed clarification mine).

In the Bible, God never volunteered His name to Moses. When Moses asked God what His name was, the Lord answered, "I AM" (the eternal present) (Exodus 3:13-14). Many English-speaking people think God's name is Jehovah (German adaption of the Hebrew Tetragrammaton (יהוה YHWH or Yahweh ("J" does not exist in the Hebrew aleph-bet) meaning "to be;" however, God never refers to Himself—or is referred to—as Allah in the Bible.

(28:31) "Throw down your staff". And when he saw it writhing as it had been a demon, he turned to flee headlong, (and it was said unto him): "O Moses! Draw nigh and fear not. Look! you art of those who are secure [protected]." (Bracketed clarification mine.)

This part of the Koran's burning bush story is found in Exodus 4 of the Bible:

> And Moses answered and said, "But, behold, they will not believe me, nor hearken unto my voice: for they will say, 'The LORD has not appeared unto you.'"

And the Lord said unto him, "What is that in your hand?" And he said, "A rod."
And He said, "Cast it on the ground." And he cast it on the ground, and it became a serpent; and Moses fled from before it.

And the Lord said unto Moses, "Put forth your hand, and take it by the tail." And he put forth his hand, and caught it, and it became a rod in his hand:

That they may believe that the Lord God of their fathers, the God of Abraham, the God of Isaac, and the God of Jacob, has appeared unto you (Exodus 4:1-5).

(28:32) "Thrust your hand into the bosom of your robe, it will come forth white without hurt. And guard your heart from fear. Then these shall be two proofs from your Lord unto Pharaoh and his chiefs. Lo! they are evil-living folk."

This verse follows the biblical order but not what God actually told Moses. The Bible gives more detailed signs than the koranic version:

And the Lord said furthermore unto him, "Put now your hand into your bosom." And he put his hand into his bosom: and when he took it out, behold, his hand was leprous as snow.

And He said, "Put your hand into your bosom again." And he put his hand into his bosom again; and plucked it out of his bosom, and, behold, it was turned again as his other flesh.

And it shall come to pass, if they will not believe you, neither hearken to the voice of the first sign, that they will believe the voice of the latter sign.

And it shall come to pass, if they will not believe also these two signs, neither hearken unto your voice, that you shall take of the water of the river, and pour it upon the dry land: and the water which you take out of the river shall become blood upon the dry land (Exodus 4:6-9).

365

(28:33) He said: "My Lord! Look! I killed a man among them and I fear that they will kill me."

While this verse seems like something Moses might have been concerned with, this is another conversation *not* recorded in the Bible. (The event in this koranic verse happened when Moses was 40 years old, and it would be doubtful that anyone would remember it, much less recognize him when he was 80.)

(28:34) "My brother Aaron is more eloquent than me in speech. Therefor send him with me as a helper to confirm me. Look! I fear that they will give the lie to me."

Muhammad Habib Shakir translates this verse with a little more clarity:

> *"And my brother, Haroun [Aaron], he is more eloquent of tongue than I, therefore send him with me as an aider, verifying me: surely I fear that they would reject me" (bracketed clarification mine).*

Moses had a stutter, so he could not speak well (Exodus 4:10), but he was not the one who suggested to God that his brother, Aaron, speak for him. It was just the opposite. The Bible tells us it was God who suggested the idea to Moses (Exodus 4:14)—not the other way around as the Koran wants us to believe.

This is what God actually said in the Bible in response to Moses, complaining that he was not able to speak clearly:

But Moses said, "Pardon your servant, Lord. Please send someone else." Then the Lord's anger burned against Moses and He said, "What about your brother, Aaron the Levite? I know he can speak well. He is already on his way to meet you, and he will be glad to see you. You shall speak to him and put words in his mouth; I will help both of you speak and will teach you what to do. He will speak to the people for you, and it will be as if he were your mouth and as if you were God to him. But take this staff in your hand so you can perform the signs with it" (Exodus 4:13-17, NIV).

(28:35) He [Allah] said: "We will strengthen your arm with your brother, and We will give unto you both power so that they cannot reach you for Our portents. you twain, and those who follow you, will be the winners" (bracketed clarification mine).

Thus, Allah encouraged Moses not to be afraid; with Allah's help, he would triumph.

(28:36) But when Moses came unto them with Our clear tokens, they said: "This is naught [nothing] but invented magic. We never heard of this among our fathers of old."

Where this verse states, "This is naught [nothing] but invented magic. We never heard of this among our fathers of old," we have a problem because, *as* Joshua J. Mark tells us in an article for *ANCIENT HISTORY ENCYCLOPEDIA,* "To the Egyptians, a world without magic was inconceivable."[5] The Koran assumes we take it for granted that both Moses and Aaron performed the miracle of Aaron's staff, which was turned into a Serpent by God (see verse 31). None of the miracles are mentioned in this koranic verse, but for clarification, we will include the biblical version here:

> And Moses and Aaron went in unto Pharaoh, and they did so as the LORD had commanded: and Aaron cast down his rod before Pharaoh, and before his servants, and it became a Serpent.
>
> Then Pharaoh also called the wise men and the sorcerers: now the magicians of Egypt, they also did in like manner with their enchantments.
>
> For they cast down every man his rod, and they became Serpents: but Aaron's rod swallowed up their rods (Exodus 7:10-12).

On the following page, we have a chart that shows the Ten Plagues of Egypt that Sûrah 28 fails to mention.

Chart 3: The Ten Plagues of Egypt That Are Not Mentioned In Sûrah 28.

1	Exodus 7:10	Egypt's natural waterways turned into blood
2	Exodus 8:2	A plague of frogs infested all of Egypt
3	Exodus 8:16	A plague of lice from the dust of the land
4	Exodus 8:21	A horde of flies attacking everything
5	Exodus 9:3	A plague causing a terrible illness on all domestic animals.
6	Exodus 9:8	People and animals devastated with body boils
7	Exodus 9:18-25	A terrible hail of fire and ice destroying everything
8	Exodus 10:4-5	A plague of locust eating what was not destroyed by the hail
9	Exodus 10:21	Great darkness so thick it could be felt
10	Exodus 11:4-5	Death of the firstborn (cattle, people and Pharaoh's son)

Although it is curious why the Koran would leave out such important parts of the saga concerning Moses' miraculous encounters with Pharaoh while struggling to set his people free, we acknowledge that the Koran does refer to some plagues in Sûrahs 7 and 17; yet the plagues mentioned in Sûrah 7 are only half of the actual plagues we read about in the Bible:

> So We sent (plagues) on them: (1) Wholesale death [might be referring to the 10th plague of the death of the firstborn]; (2) Locusts; (3) Lice; (4) Frogs, and (5) Blood: Signs openly self-explained; but they were steeped in arrogance a people given to sin (Abdullah Yusuf Ali, Sûrah 7:133, numbering and punctuation added, bracketed clarification mine).

Arberry translates it:

So we let loose upon them (1) flood and the (2) locusts, the (3) lice and the (4) frogs, the (5) blood, distinct signs; but they waxed [grew] proud and were a sinful people (A. J. Arberry, Sûrah 7:133, numbering added and bracketed clarification mine).

The first plague recorded in the Bible was turning the Nile River to blood, referred to in the Koran as the "plague of blood; the second one was the "plague of frogs;" the third was the "plague of lice;" the eighth was the "plague of locusts," and the tenth was the "plague of death," only hinted at, not expounded on, in some translations of the Koran.

The Koran is also surprisingly silent about how the Jews were able to avoid the "plague of death," which took the lives of all the firstborn people and animals in Egypt. On the other hand, the Israelites' firstborns were spared because they followed God's instruction to paint the blood of an unblemished lamb on their doorposts and lintels of their homes so the plague of death would pass over them. The many Muslims—who insist that the Passover is in the Koran—are mistaken since they are confusing the general theme of Exodus with the more specific segment regarding the Passover.

There is a parallel to this unusual story. Consider that the lamb's blood was put on the doorposts and lintels of the Hebrew homes, not unlike the marks left on Jesus' bloody cross (on the left side where His left hand was nailed, on the right side where His right hand was nailed, at the top of the cross where His head—bloodied by the crown of thorns—left its mark, and on the floor's threshold where the blood dripped from the lintel, representing the bloodstains from Jesus' nailed feet).

For that reason, the commonality of the symbolism found in the Passover event, as recorded in Exodus and the crucifixion event of Christ recorded in the gospels, makes the story of the Passover very important for Christians. The Passover Seder is also a dramatic foreshadowing of the Last Supper, which preceded the Crucifixion of Christ—(something the Koran denies). In the Bible, God told the children of Israel, "Your lamb shall be without blemish, a male of the first year: you shall take it out from the sheep, or from the goats" (Exodus 12:5). He continued giving directions for the Passover Feast and instructed all Hebrews, "And this day shall be unto you for a memorial; and you shall keep it a feast to the Lord throughout your generations; you shall keep it a feast by an ordinance forever" (Exodus 12:14).

In the New Testament, Jesus is God's Passover Lamb as John the Baptist testifies: "... John sees Jesus coming unto him, and says, 'Behold the Lamb of God, which takes away the sin of the world' " (John 1:29b). "And looking upon Jesus as he walked, he says, 'Behold the Lamb of God' " (John 1:36).[6]

Muhammad knew this story as we see in the Koran with his persistent campaign that Jesus was not crucified. Maybe that is why the "Passover" was not included in the Koran—in order not to draw attention to its biblical validity.

To be fair, some Muslims have claimed that the story of the Passover was later included in the Hadith; however, for the first one hundred years after Muhammad's death, the Hadith (sayings) was an oral tradition before they began writing them down over the next few hundred years. That allowed for considerable editing, which resulted in revisionist history, as some Muslims have suggested.

In addition to the five plagues mentioned in this verse, the Koran also came up with four more plagues in Sûrah 17; however, the Koran is still shy one plague:

> To Moses We did give Nine Clear Signs: As the Children of Israel: when he came to them, Pharaoh said to him: "O Moses! I consider you, indeed, to have been worked upon by sorcery!" (Sûrah 17:101, bracketed clarification mine, emphasis added.)

While mentioning some plagues in the other sûrahs, we are confronted with more questions than answers: (1) Why did the Koran leave out some of the plagues, while including others in its various versions of the stories? (2) Since Muhammad was trying to win over the Jews to Islam, why did Allah not include one of the most important holidays (Passover), which is in the entire Bible—found in both the Old and New Testaments?

Did those exclusions just slip Allah's mind? (Of course, this would not make sense because Allah is supposed to know all things), or was it done on purpose? We must consider why the tenth and—most important plague of all—was lightly touched on in Sûrah 7:133, which is the very reason Pharaoh, finally let Moses take his people and leave Egypt:

Now the LORD spoke to Moses and Aaron in the land of Egypt, saying, "This month *shall be* your beginning of months; it *shall be* the first month of the year to you. Speak to all the congregation of Israel, saying: 'On the tenth of this month every man shall take for himself a lamb, according to the house of *his* father, a lamb for a household. And if the household is too small for the lamb, let him and his neighbor next to his house take *it* according to the number of the persons; according to each man's need you shall make your count for the lamb. Your lamb shall be without blemish, a male of the first year. You may take *it* from the sheep or from the goats. Now you shall keep it until the fourteenth day of the same month. Then the whole assembly of the congregation of Israel shall kill it at twilight. And they shall take *some* of the blood and put *it* on the two doorposts and on the lintel of the houses where they eat it. Then they shall eat the flesh on that night; roasted in fire, with unleavened bread *and* with bitter *herbs* they shall eat it. Do not eat it raw, nor boiled at all with water, but roasted in fire—its head with its legs and its entrails. You shall let none of it remain until morning, and what remains of it until morning you shall burn with fire. And thus you shall eat it: *with* a belt on your waist, your sandals on your feet, and your staff in your hand. So you shall eat it in haste. It *is* the LORD's Passover.

'For I will pass through the land of Egypt on that night, and will strike all the firstborn in the land of Egypt, both man and beast; and against all the gods of Egypt I will execute judgment: I *am* the LORD' " (Exodus 12:1-12, NKJV).

With the death of Pharaoh's son and because of all the deaths of the firstborn of the Egyptians, which included not only their children but livestock as well (Exodus 11:5), Pharaoh finally relented and let Moses and his people go!

Again, to be fair, in Sûrah 7:133, *"wholesale death"* is mentioned in passing, but more likely it was an afterthought with no details of its importance to the Egyptians or the Hebrews; nor are we told what effect it had on Pharaoh's decision to let the Hebrews go.

(28:37) And Moses said: "My Lord is Best Aware of him who brings guidance from His presence, and whose will be the sequel of the Home (of bliss). Lo! wrong-doers will not be successful."

Arberry's translation helps clarify this passage:

> *But Moses said, "My Lord knows very well who comes with the guidance from Him, and shall possess the Ultimate Abode [Heaven]; surely the evildoers will not prosper" (bracketed clarification mine).*

(28:38) And Pharaoh said: "O chiefs [Nobles in my court]! I know not that you have a god other than me, so kindle for me (a fire), O Haman, to bake the mud; and set up for me a lofty tower in order that I may survey the god of Moses; and lo! I deem him of the liars (bracketed clarifications mine).

Now, we undergo a complete shift or revision in the storyline away from the historical biblical order when, after Moses brought signs and wonders against Pharaoh and Egypt, he and the children of Israel were allowed to leave Egypt. Instead, the Koran now introduces us to another storyline entirely at odds—as well as being out of time and place (merging three different stories)—with the Exodus story and Bible history.

At the beginning of this verse, we read that Pharaoh is telling his court, *"O chiefs [Nobles in my court]! I know not that you have a god other than me...."* Pharaoh, like many other rulers, was considered a god, and Egypt had many gods besides Pharaoh, so we have another koranic historical error.

Next, we read in this koranic verse, *"...so kindle for me (a fire), O Haman, to bake the mud...."* The Egyptians did not use kiln-dried bricks for building;[7] rather, they used mud and straw to make bricks and the sun to bake them since there were very few wood resources in the desert. Because palm trees burn very quickly, they produce a small amount of heat. Using kilns to bake bricks in major building projects would have required firing hundreds of thousands of bricks at a time, which would have been impossible with the lack of resources. People who lived in areas like Egypt used the sun to bake their bricks, mainly to build their homes and warehouses. Surely Allah would have known that. The purpose given for Pharaoh being so strict was because he feared the Hebrew slaves would join Egypt's enemies and rebel against them:

Now there arose a new king over Egypt, who did not know Joseph. And he said to his people, "Look, the people of the children of Israel *are* more and mightier than we; come, let us deal shrewdly with them, lest they multiply, and it happen, in the event of war, that they also join our enemies and fight against us, and *so* go up out of the land" (Exodus 1:8-10, NKJV).

Regarding the reason the Hebrew slaves were making the sun-dried mud bricks, the Bible tells us that the Hebrews used the bricks to build two cities for Pharaoh, not pyramids: "Therefore they set taskmasters over them to afflict them with their burdens. And they built for Pharaoh supply cities, Pithom and Raamses" (Exodus 1:11, NKJV)

One of the reasons the pyramids have lasted for many thousands of years was because the Egyptians covered the sun-baked mud bricks with quarried stone. The Bible never mentions the Hebrew slaves, or anyone else for that matter, working with stone. The Bible does agree with the Koran, insofar as the Bible stating that the Hebrew slaves were making sun-baked bricks from mud and straw, as we discussed in the previous paragraph. It is also important to be aware the Bible never suggests the Hebrew slaves were building a tower to reach their God. Pharaoh was understandably upset that the Hebrew slaves wanted to stop their work for three days to go into the desert and worship their

God (Exodus 5:3). He reasoned that if he made the Hebrew slaves gather their own straw, it would be an even harder burden on them (Exodus 5:7), and they would stop making such ridiculous demands:

> Then the king of Egypt said to them, "Moses and Aaron, why do you take the people from their work? Get *back* to your labor." And Pharaoh said, "Look, the people of the land *are* many now, and you make them rest from their labor."

So the same day Pharaoh commanded the taskmasters of the people and their officers, saying, "You shall no longer give the people straw to make brick as before. Let them go and gather straw for themselves. And you shall lay on them the quota of bricks which they made before. You shall not reduce it. For they are idle; therefore, they cry out, saying, 'Let us go *and* sacrifice to our God.' Let more work be laid on the men, that they may labor in it, and let them not regard false words" (Exodus 5:4-9, NKJV, emphases added).

In this narrative alone, we begin to see three unrelated biblical stories combined. (1) The story of the Exodus (Africa), along with a character named Haman, which as we previously observed in Sûrah 28, is out of place and time with (2) the biblical story of Esther where Haman serves in the court of Xerxes (King Ahasuerus) That story that did not occur until some 1,000 years after the Exodus event and on the continent of Asia, and (3) the story of the Tower of Babble (Genesis 11:1–9) which also accrued thousands of years before the Exodus event, also on the continent of Asia.

OBSERVATIONS: Haman was descended from the Amalekites on the continent of Asia. The Bible tells us Haman's father's name was Hammedatha, the Agagite (Esther 3:1). "The name Hammedatha appears to be Persian and probably refers to an immediate ancestor.... The title 'Agagite' could refer to another immediate ancestor...; however, it is far more likely it refers to Agag, King of Amalek (1 Samuel 15:20)," from which Haman's family on his father's side might have descended.[8]

The third out-of-sequence event incorporated into this story is about a lofty tower built to reach God, which is none other than the biblical story of the Tower of Babel, an event that took place over a thousand years before on another continent (Genesis 11:3-9). In the biblical Exodus account, Pharaoh did not build a tower. Perhaps Muhammad confused the Babylonian ziggurat (Tower of Babel), with the similarly constructed Pyramid of Djoser with its six levels of steps.

Fig. 4. The Pyramid at Djoser

The Pyramid of Djoser (pronounced **Joe**-sir) was built under the supervision of Imhotep during the Old Kingdom period around 2700 B.C. It is a crude, tower-like building, as opposed to the latter, more streamlined, tri-angular pyramids; nevertheless, the purpose of the Egyptian step pyramid was to be used solely as a burial chamber for Pharaoh Djoser. It was never an archaic structure designed to be used as an observatory or stairway to Heaven. Egypt had many gods[9] during the time of Moses. Pharaoh was considered a god, so he would not find it particularly unusual for someone to have other gods in that polytheistic society.

To be objective, we have included a public domain source of a Muslim's argument regarding the inclusion of Haman appearing in Egypt during the time of Moses. Amro, a Muslim apologist, wrote the following discourse in 2013. We have reproduced it here because of its importance as a historical debate regarding the Koran confusing Pharaoh's court with the court of King Xerxes of Persia. This discourse is also an example of the aggressive nature of the Koran vs. the Bible, a debate that has become very prevalent in our society after the events in New York City on September 11, 2001.

The Muslim apologist, Amro, argues:

> Those who claim that the Prophet Muhammad wrote the Qur'an in light of the Torah and the Gospel also put forth the sophistry [fraudulent claim] that he [Muhammad] copied some of the subjects in the Qur'an wrongly

> The ridiculousness of this claim became obvious 200 years ago [1799 A.D.] when the Egyptian hieroglyphs were deciphered, and the name "Haman" was discovered.... However, with the spread of Christianity and its cultural influences during the second and third centuries A.D., the ancient Egyptians forgot their religion as well as the language, and the use of hieroglyphs came to a gradual stop. The year 394 A.D. is the last known time when a hieroglyph was used.... The name "Haman" was in fact mentioned in old Egyptian tablets. It was mentioned on a monument which now stands in the Hof Museum in Vienna, and in which the closeness of Haman to the Pharaoh was emphasized (Walter Wreszinski, Ägyptische Inschriften aus dem K.K. Hof Museum in Wien, 1906, J. C. Hinrichs' sche Buchhandlung).

> The dictionary, "The People in the New Kingdom," refers to Haman as "the head of the quarry workers" (Hermanne Ranke, Die Ägyptischen Personennamen, Verzeichnis der Namen, Verlag Von J J Augustin in Glückstadt, Band I, 1935. Band II, 1952) ... the Qur'anic verse that conveys how the Pharaoh requested Haman to build a tower is in perfect unison with this archaeological finding:

> Pharaoh said, "Council, I do not know of any other god for you apart from me. Haman, kindle a fire for me over the clay and build me a lofty tower so that perhaps I may be able to climb up to Moses' god! I consider him a blatant liar" (Sûrat al-Qasas: 38).[10] (Bracketed clarifications mine.)

Amro's statement is another anachronism. The "tower" should not be confused with the pyramids, which were used as burial chambers for the Pharaohs and were constructed during the time of the Old Kingdom (2500 B.C.). The time of Moses was around 1500-1200 B.C. during

Egypt's Middle Kingdom, some one thousand years after the building of the Pyramids, which were constructed out of both mud bricks as well as quarried stone. The tower referred to by Amro—which was supposedly built by Haman for Pharaoh to reach Moses' God—is a revision and incorporation of the Genesis story about the construction of the Tower of Babel. The tower that is discussed in the Bible was erected in Babylon shortly after the Noaic flood (Genesis 11:4) on the continent of Asia—not the continent of Africa where Egypt is located. Haman had nothing to do with the Genesis account since he did not exist for another fifteen hundred years after the Tower of Babel and a thousand years after the time of Moses. Just on these facts alone— never mind placing Haman in the story—the Islamic account we read here fails, as we have seen on several different archaeological and chronological accounts.

Amro continues:

> In conclusion, the discovery of the name Haman on ancient Egyptian tablets discredited another claim made by those who strive to find inconsistencies in the Qur'anic verses. Furthermore, the undeniable truth that the Qur'an is revealed by God is again proven without any doubt as the Qur'an miraculously conveyed historical information that could not have been found and deciphered in the Prophet's time.

This document is signed "*Amro.*"[11]

At the end of Amro's thesis, we have an independent opinion, other than our own, through the rebuttal of a Wikipedia editor who shares with us his educated critique at the end of Amro's thesis.

In the following, we have included the Wikipedia Talk editor's observations regarding the attempt by Amro to do a seemingly scholarly rejection of those who find problems with Islamic claims that the Persian/Semitic name Haman is also a shared Egyptian name. Amro cites the 1799 archaeological discovery in which it was alleged, "The name Haman was, in fact, mentioned in old Egyptian tablets." (We will address this further in Volume III of our three-volume series, *Islam Exposed, Islam: Science—Bible—Archaeology and Myths,* in Chapter 5, under the heading, "The Haman Hoax").

The Wikipedia editor's response follows:

Looking at the Egyptological references, I am slightly worried that they are largely [refering] to old texts. It is scarcely credible that Maspero can be cited as an authority on Egyptian architectural methods. Likewise, Ranke's dictionary is rather old (it is now superseded) and any information it might present on phonology is of dubious veracity (might as well quote Budge!) given that our knowledge in this area has moved on a little since then.

Egyptology has moved on a long way since the 1930s, and so the whole discussion of historicity needs either to be based on modern, recognized, authoritative Egyptological texts (so David Rohl does not count) or to acknowledge that the argument is tendentious [belligerent] and poorly founded in sound scholarship.

I find it worrying that the sole authority claimed is Maurice Bucaille, whom a quick Google search reveals to be a not entirely credible source, in that he clearly has an agenda as a proponent of the Islamic equivalent of sola scriptura (e.g., this piece which states that he argued for the accuracy of the Qur'an as a scientific text). In view of all this, I wonder if this piece requires a POV [point of view] tag, as it is far from clear to me that it is, in fact, neutral (bracketed clarification mine).

To allow for some of the confusion, we also learn Egyptologists have acknowledged that in ancient Egypt there were similar sounding names, specifically (aka Hemionu) which some have transliterated as Hemon, Hemiunu (aka Hemionu), a vizar serving under King Khnum-Khufu. He is also credited as the [high-ranking political minister or adviser and] architect of Khnum-Khufu's Great Pyramid at Giza (c. 2700-2190 B.C.). (One can see a statue of Hemiunu (aka Hemon) at the Hildesheim Museum in Hildesheim, Germany.) In the discussion, it was also pointed out, "Although the name Hemiunu /Hemon is quite similar to Haman, they are written differently and perhaps also pronounced differently[12] (bracketed clarifications mine).

In review, this is simply another sûrah in the Koran containing anachronisms due to the errors presented in its geographical, chronological, and historical information. The court at Susa, where we were introduced to Haman in the biblical account, was located in Persia or modern-day Iran. The additional problem with the koranic version is that the actual time of Haman (460 B.C.) and the actual time of Pharaoh and Moses (1,486 B.C.) are separated by some 1,026 years. The real story of Haman and Esther took place in the land of Persia in its capital city of Susa, which is approximately 1,000 miles east of Egypt on the neighboring continent of Asia; therefore, as we discussed in the commentary for verse 37, we have yet another Koranic anachronism of incorporating three different biblical events separated by over a thousand miles and a thousand years on two different continents!

(28:39) And he and his hosts were haughty [proud] in the land without right, and deemed that they would never be brought back to Us (bracketed clarification mine).

Pharaoh was king of the greatest empire on the earth at that time. His people were proud—and of course, Pharaoh was proud—he had every reason to be haughty; he was the greatest and most powerful man in the world! This verse leaves us wondering what Gabriel was thinking and what point he was trying to make.

(28:40) Therefor We seized him and his hosts, and abandoned them unto the sea. Behold the nature of the consequence for evil-doers!

This passage is debatable. In the biblical account, we are not explicitly told that Pharaoh drowned, only that his army was drowned.[13]

OBSERVATION: In this verse, the Koran once again jumps forward in the Exodus story to the confrontation between Pharaoh and Moses where the children of Israel are trapped with their backs to the Red Sea. By leapfrogging forward, the Koran avoids addressing the ten miraculous plagues brought against Egypt by the God of Abraham, Isaac, and Jacob as discussed in verse 36, and they are definitely not considered minor historical events.

(28:41) And We made them patterns that invite unto the Fire, and on the Day of Resurrection they will not be helped.

Arberry and Ali use *"leaders"* in place of *"patterns,"* while Shakir calls them *"Imams."*

This verse appears to be an afterthought of the previous verse, confirming that Pharaoh's army is destined for Hell and that they will not find any solace on Judgment Day. Like the Bible, the Koran tells us Pharaoh's army was destroyed; still, Pharaoh's soldiers were only following their king's orders. Why would Allah use the excuse to condemn rank and file soldiers to Hell solely on the basis they were following their king's orders when they pursued a group of people into what was to become—for Pharaoh's soldiers—a watery grave?

(28:42) And We made a curse to follow them in this world, and on the Day of Resurrection they will be among the hateful.

This passage is not only unclear but unbiblical as well. All four of our English translations of the Koran agree with the pronouncement, *"We made a curse to follow them* (Pharaoh and his army) *in this world"* (throughout their lives). That was a short curse because in verse 40, Allah "...*abandoned them unto the sea,*" where their lives ended almost immediately!

CONSIDER: If Pharaoh's entire army drowned in the sea, what would have been the need for *a curse to follow them in this world*? They were all dead! In the spirit of fairness, the confusion might be due to its inaccurate chronological order and translation into English.

(28:43) And We verily [in truth] gave the Scripture unto Moses after We had destroyed the generations of old: clear testimonies for mankind, and a guidance and a mercy, that haply [by chance] they might reflect (bracketed clarification mine).

God gave Moses the Pentateuch (the first five books of the Bible), but he did not receive the other 61 books of Scripture. This koranic verse has been used by some Muslims to claim that other parts of biblical Scripture, which might conflict with the Koran, are not really Scripture. Moses received the Scripture (Pentateuch or the first five books of the Bible) after "...[Allah] had destroyed the generations of old...," referring to Noah's Flood.

(28:44) And you (Muhammad) was [were] not on the western side (of the Mount) when We expounded unto Moses the commandment, and you was [were] not among those present (bracketed clarifications mine).

Speaking for Allah, Gabriel is pointing out the fact that Muhammad was not there when Allah was alleged to have given Moses the commandments, so he could not have known the facts that are now revealed to him by the angel Gabriel.

(28:45) But We brought forth generations, and their lives dragged on for them. And you was [were] not a dweller in Midian, reciting unto them Our revelations, but We kept sending (messengers to men). (Bracketed clarification mine.)

Because Muhammad was not alive during the time of Moses, the only way he could have conceivably reported what happened way back in history is because Allah is revealing the order of events to him. According to the Koran, this proves Muhammad heard from Allah because Muhammad could not read or write and, therefore, he could not have read about the events written in the Bible.

(28:46) And you was [were] not beside the Mount when We did call; but (the knowledge of it is) a mercy from your Lord that you may warn a folk [Arabs] unto whom no warner came before you, that haply [by chance] they may give heed (bracketed clarifications mine).

Gabriel continues to support the miracle of Muhammad receiving the Koran because the Exodus events took place thousands of years before Muhammad was born. Yet, Allah chose Muhammad as his last and greatest prophet and taught him the truths that were–revealed to Moses on Mount Sinai.

According to this passage, because the Arabs, up until then, had not been exposed to the wondrous biblical events, Muhammad was authorized to teach them the truth revealed to him by Allah so they— like the "People of the Book"—may also have that knowledge.

The verse ends with Allah telling Muhammad why he finally decided to do this. "...*you may warn a folk [Arabs] unto whom no warner came before you...*" The only problem we have with this revelation is in Sûrah 4:63, where we are informed that both Abraham and Ishmael were prophets of Islam and built the Holy Ka'aba in Mecca. Presumably, these two important prophets, while living in Mecca, would have taught the resident tribes, as well as Ishmael's descendants, all about Abraham, Sarah, Hagar, Isaac, Ishmael, and their god, Allah, because that is what prophets do.

We must take into account the hundreds of years that Christians and Jews (as well as the Arabs who converted to Christianity) living on the Arabian Peninsula. They would have shared their faith with the Pagan Arabs, yet we read here that Muhammad was the only one to bring the biblical stories about prophets and the God of the Bible to Mecca and the Arabian Peninsula.

(28:47) Otherwise, if disaster should afflict them because of that which their own hands have sent before (them), they might say: "Our Lord! Why send you no messenger unto us, that we might have followed Your revelations and been of the believers?"

Repeating what was argued by the Quraysh tribe (Yusuf Ali identifies *"them"* as the "Quraish" in his translation of this verse), Gabriel explains to Muhammad their frustration was because the "People of the Book" received revelations, but they did not. The Quraysh are asking Allah why he did not send them a prophet too, because if he had, they would have followed Allah's Signs and been among those who believed; they were cheated out of knowing the "true" religion. Up until now, as we previously stated, the Koran has told us that Abraham and Ishmael

382

were prophets to the Arabs, and they built the Ka'aba (Sûrah 2:127); and presumably taught them about the one "true" god. As for being taught about the Bible in Arabic, the Arabs actually *did* receive the gospel message in their own language, as we see in the following two Scriptures:

When the Day of Pentecost had fully come, they [Disciples of Jesus] were all with one accord in one place [the upper room]. And suddenly there came a sound from heaven, as of a rushing mighty wind, and it filled the whole house where they were sitting. Then there appeared to them divided tongues, as of fire, and *one* sat upon each of them. And they were all filled with the Holy Spirit and began to speak with other tongues, as the Spirit gave them utterance (Acts 2:1-4, NKJV, bracketed clarifications mine).

In the above Scripture, we read that the disciples of Jesus were sharing the gospel with a crowd when the Holy Spirit suddenly enabled them to speak in different tongues (languages). Therefore, the disciples shared the Word of God in the crowd's native languages.

In the following Scripture, we read they went out into the streets, and the people who had come to Jerusalem from all over the world heard them prophesying in their native languages:

Then they were all amazed and marveled, saying to one another, "Look, are not all these who speak Galileans? And how *is it that* we hear, each in our own language in which we were born?... Cretans *and Arabs*—we hear them speaking in our own tongues the wonderful works of God" (Acts 2:7-11, NKJV, emphasis added).

(28:48) But when there came unto them the Truth from Our presence, they said: "Why is he [Muhammad] not given the like of what was given unto Moses?" [Allah answers] "Did they not disbelieve in that which was given unto Moses of old?" They say: "Two magics [the Torah and Koran, that support each other"; and they say: "Indeed! in both we are disbelievers" (bracketed clarifications mine).

In this verse, Gabriel observes how the Meccans (home of the Quraysh tribe) taunt Muhammad by comparing him to Moses. They are debating, if God gave the Torah (Law) to the children of Israel written by His own finger in stone, why did not Allah do the same for Muhammad if—as he claims to be—a prophet of Allah?

Gabriel gives Muhammad the answer, which is now enshrined in the Koran, when he explains that the Meccans, like the Israelites, rejected the miraculous event on Mount Sinai, just like the Meccans were rejecting the oral witness of the Koran given to Muhammad by Allah. This, in and of itself, is a marvelous sign since Muhammad could not have known the revelations written in the Torah because he was unable to read or write, thus making this a miracle equal with that of Moses; nonetheless, like Moses, the people are rejecting Muhammad too. This straw man argument is easier to come up with, as opposed to Allah, allowing Muhammad the ability to perform miraculous signs and wonders.

(28:49) Say (unto them, O Muhammad): "Then bring a scripture from the presence of Allah that gives clearer guidance than these two [Torah and Koran] (that) I may follow it, if you are truthful" (bracketed clarification mine).

Muhammad Habib Shakir interprets this passage:

> Say: "Then bring some (other) book from Allah which is a better guide than both of them, (that) I may follow it, if you are truthful."

Regarding those questioning Muhammad about the validity of the revelations he has been receiving, Allah challenges them to produce a book for comparison, other than the Koran or the Torah, which Allah has already given.

Of course, at the time Allah gave that challenge to Muhammad, the Hadith or sayings of Muhammad would not be compiled for another one hundred years by Muhammad al-Bukhari, who completed it around 846 AD.

For the sake of clarification, this passage is referring to the authorship of the Bible and not that of the Hadith. We offer the following verse from the Koran (one of several), which verifies Allah's claim that he is the author behind the creation of the Bible:

> Look! We inspire you as We inspired Noah and the prophets after him, as We inspired Abraham and Ishmael and Isaac and Jacob and the tribes, and Jesus and Job and Jonah and Aaron and Solomon, and as We imparted unto David the Psalms (Sûrah 4:163, bracketed clarification mine).

Before we proceed, we must point out that David only wrote 73 of the Psalms, and while that is impressive, he still composed less than half of the 150 Psalms.

We are informed that it is perfectly proper for us not to seek another book but simply to compare, side-by-side, the two books Allah claims to have authored, which of course, is what we are doing with this book. This alone shows how inconsistent the Koran is when telling and retelling those biblical stories for which Allah claims he provided us. Performing miracles, as did the biblical prophets, would have definitely given Muhammad more creditability, but for whatever reason, Allah would not (or could not) allow Muhammad to have the ability to perform miracles.

(28:50) And if they answer you not, then know that what they follow is their lusts. And who goes farther astray than he who follows his lust without guidance from Allah. Surely! Allah guides not wrongdoing folk.

We look again to Muhammad Habib Shakir for clarity:

> But if they do not answer you, then know that they only follow their low desires; and who is more erring than he who follows his low desires without any guidance from Allah? Surely Allah does not guide the unjust people.

This verse claims that Christians and Jews are not really who they say they are; they only give lip service to their faith. Because they are more interested in making money and living the good life, they never take it on themselves to verify the teachings of Muhammad. The fact is, according to this verse, they never study the Bible either and, therefore, are among those *"who follow[s] his lust without guidance from Allah ...."* They are among the *"wrongdoing folk."*

(28:51) And now verily [in truth] We have caused the Word to reach them, that haply [by chance] they may give heed (bracketed clarifications mine).

In most translations of the Koran, *"Word"* is capitalized as it is here in the Pickthall translation; nevertheless, the Koran rejects God's Word (Logos), Jesus as being Divine (John 1:1-3, 3:16) vs. (Sûrahs: 2:136, 2:253; 3:45, 3:55, 3:59, 3:84; 4:171; 5:46, 5:110, 5:112, 5:114, 5:116; 33:7; 38; 43:57; 57:27; 61:6, 61:14).

(28:52) Those unto whom We gave the Scripture before it, they believe in it [Koran],

Gabriel is now suggesting that the true Bible-believing Jews and Christians believe and accept the message Muhammad brings from Allah. Perhaps this is to shame and marginalize the Meccans by showing how the Christians and Jews believe the truth, while the Meccans only reject it and even dare to question and challenge Muhammad's legitimacy as a biblical prophet.

(28:53) And when it is recited unto them, they say: "We believe in it. Indeed! it is the Truth from our Lord. Lo! even before it we were of those who surrender (unto Him)."

A.J. Arberry renders verses 51-53 this way:

Now we have brought them the Word; haply [by chance] they may remember. Those to whom We gave the Book before this believe in it and, when it is recited to them, they say, "We believe in it; surely it is the truth from the Lord. Indeed, even before it we had surrender[ed]" (bracketed clarifications mine).

The Koran even contains Bible stories, according to this verse; therefore, it is very much in harmony with the Bible. Supposedly, as a result, the Jews and Christians were happy to validate and embrace the message brought by Muhammad.

We are also informed that the people of the Bible enthusiastically agreed they knew Islam was true even before they had a chance to embrace it, yet the evidence of such a hearty endorsement by so many Christians and Jewish communities, at least from the historical perspective as suggested by verses 52 and 53, is strangely silent. This is not to say that some Christians and Jews did not willingly convert, but not on the scale these verses would have us believe. Perhaps this story was to encourage illiterate Christians and Jews to convert. It was only through the sword that the wholesale conversion to Islam took place.[14]

> *But when the forbidden months are past, then fight and slay the Pagans wherever you find them, and seize them, beleaguer them, and lie in wait for them in every stratagem (of war); but if they repent, and establish regular prayers and practice regular charity, then open the way for them: for Allah is Oft-Forgiving [often forgiving], Most Merciful (Sûrah 9:5, bracketed clarification mine).*

The Hadith also teaches:

The Prophet said, *"Paradise lies under the shades of the sword"* (Sahih Bukhari, Volume 4, Book 52, Number 73, emphasis added).

On the other hand, Jesus said:

"... "Put your sword in its place, for all who take the sword will perish by the sword" (Matthew 26:52, NKJV).

(28:54) These will be given their reward twice over, because they are steadfast [devoted] and repel evil with good, and spend of that wherewith [from what] We have provided them [bracketed clarifications mine].

Continuing from the previous verse, Muhammad is encouraging those Bible-believers to consider they will be blessed two times over if they accept Muhammad's teachings. If they do, they will be rejecting evil. He also advises them to be charitable and share what Allah has blessed them with.

(28:55) And when they hear vanity [vain talk] they withdraw from it and say: "Unto us our works and unto you your works. Peace be unto you! We desire not the ignorant" [bracketed clarification mine].

> *When smart people hear foolish talk, they should ignore it. Muslims have their good works, and the others have their useless works. "Peace be unto you who accept Islam. We will keep their smart achievements and leave the others who reject Islam to their stupidity" (paraphrase mine.)*

(28:56) Look! you (O Muhammad) guide not whom you love, but Allah guides whom He will. And He is Best Aware of those who walk aright.

Muhammad is told that just because he cares for someone does not necessarily mean he is able to convince them to accept Islam. On the other hand, as previously discussed, Allah can simply will a person to accept Islam because he knows who will be receptive. Presumably, Allah chooses who he wants and simply disregards the others. In contrast, the God of the Bible is not desirous that any should perish (2 Peter 3:9).

(28:57) And they say: "If we were to follow the Guidance with you we should be torn out of our land." Have We not established for them a sure sanctuary [Mecca], whereunto the produce of all things is brought (in trade), a provision from Our presence? But most of them know not (bracketed clarification mine).

Gabriel is suggesting that some people do not accept Islam because they fear the enemies of Muhammad will attack them, destroy their homes, and possibly be enslaved and carried off to a foreign country. Gabriel then reacts in a surprised manner by questioning their fear. Why do they not recognize the blessings they now have if it was not for Allah?

(28:58) And how many a community have We destroyed that was thankless for its means of livelihood! And yonder [over there] are their dwellings, which have not been inhabited after them save a little. And We, even We, were the inheritors (bracketed clarification mine).

This is a continuing rebuke of people who refuse Islam because they believe they have already been blessed and protected by their God or gods they have been worshipping. Gabriel warns them, if they do not accept Islam, they will not have to worry about Muhammad's enemies attacking them (verse 57) because Allah himself will come against them—just as he destroyed other thankless tribes who feared other people more than they feared Allah. Gabriel points out that if they do not believe his warning, they should look at the empty towns where they once lived safely. Everything belongs to Allah!

(28:59) And never did your Lord destroy the townships, till He had raised up in their mother(-town) a messenger reciting unto them Our revelations. And never did We destroy the townships unless the folk thereof were evil-doers.

Regarding the people who had been living in the towns and communities that had been destroyed, Muhammad argues they had always been given a chance because Allah had warned them to repent or be destroyed. Muhammad is cautioning them to accept Islam or pay the consequences—which is either death, enslavement, or pay the *jizya* (a tax paid to Muslims by non-believers).[15]

(28:60) And whatsoever you have been given is a comfort of the life of the world and an ornament thereof; and that which Allah has is better and more lasting. Have you then no sense?

Gabriel is telling disbelievers they are foolish not to convert because the comforts of life are short and temporary, while Allah's offerings are "*better and more lasting.*"

(28:61) Is he whom We have promised a fair promise which he will find (true) like him whom We suffer [allow] to enjoy awhile the comfort of the life of the world, then on the Day of Resurrection he will be of those arraigned [doomed]? (Bracketed clarification mine.)

Yusuf Ali has a better translation:

> Are (these two) alike? —One to whom We have made a goodly promise, and who is going to reach its (fulfilment), and one to whom We have given the good things of this life, but who, on the Day of Judgement, is to be among those brought up (for punishment)?

It seems that Allah is telling us about *"One to whom We have made a goodly promise, and who is going to reach its (fulfilment),"* through accepting Islam, while the Christians, as we will see in the next verse, have been allowed to enjoy a good life on earth because they refused to accept Muhammad and his Islamic teachings are doomed in the afterlife.

(28:62) On the day when He [Allah] will call unto them [Christians] and say: "Where are My partners whom you imagined?" (Bracketed clarification mine.)

Gabriel is saying that when Allah calls on Christians on Judgment Day, he will ask them where their imaginary Mary and Jesus are.

NOTE: This is an important verse regarding the authorship of the Bible and the Koran. As we have seen, the Koran's attack on the Trinity is a recurring theme, which exposes its ignorance of who actually makes up the Godhead and the biblical relationship of the Father, the Son, and the Holy Spirit, as revealed in the Bible (Matthew 28:19). Remember, Allah claims to have written the Bible, and wants us to compare it to the Koran, while at the same time saying Christians believe the Trinity consists of Allah, Mary (mother of Christ), and Jesus (Sûrah 5:116). From a biblical point of view, this brings up strong concerns as to who actually authored the Koran.

We can see how Muhammad seeks to correct this erroneous concept of Mary as Allah's wife and their begotten (via sexual intercourse) son, Jesus *(Isa)*. When speaking for Allah, he opines:

O Jesus son of Mary, "did you say unto men: "Take me and my mother as gods, apart from God?" (Sûrah 5:116, emphasis added.)

The answer has to be "no" because Jesus never said His mother was a god, but did Jesus claim Himself to be God? The answer is "yes" (John 8:58; 10:36).

Jesus heard that they had cast him out; and when He had found him, He said unto him, "Do you believe on the Son of God?" He answered and said, "Who is He, Lord, that I might believe on Him?" And Jesus said unto him, "You have both seen Him, and it is He that talks with you" (John 9:35-37).

Jesus said unto them, "Verily [Truly], I say unto you, Before Abraham was, I am (YAWA)." (John 8:58, bracketed clarification mine.)

Say you of Him, whom the Father has sanctified, and sent into the world, "You blaspheme; because I said, 'I am the Son of God?' '" (John 10:36.)

In the Book of Genesis, the crafty Serpent questions God's Word with Adam and Eve when he asks them the rhetorical question, "Did God really say, 'You must not eat from any tree in the garden?' " The answer is "no." On closer inspection, we see what God actually did say to Adam and Eve: "Of every tree of the garden you may freely eat; but of the tree of the knowledge of good and evil you shall not eat" (Genesis 2:16-17a, NKJV). Because the rhetorical question must be answered in the negative, the door is open for the Serpent to compromise Adam and Eve into sampling the forbidden fruit.

This is similar to the proverbial question put to an innocent husband in a court of law by the prosecuting attorney when he or she tells the husband on trial to answer only "yes" or "no" to the question, "Do you still beat your wife?" In this case, the husband cannot say "yes" because he never beat her. He cannot say "no" because that would imply he had been a wife-beater at least one time in his life. The poor husband cannot answer "yes," and he can't answer "no," nor can he "remain silent" because that would make it seem like not only did he beat his wife, but he is still beating her and does not want to admit it. It is a lose-lose situation for the husband!

Here is another question: "What was the original sin?" The answer is that Adam and Eve stopped and listened to the Serpent when he cleverly asked, "Did God really say ...?" which led to a "no" answer; yet did God say they could not eat from all the trees? Of course not. Did God say they could eat from the trees in the garden? Of course! However, God also told them they could not eat of one *specific* tree in the garden; that part of the inquiry Satan conveniently left out.

This is exactly the same thing we are dealing with here in this verse with its rhetorical question which asks, "On the day when He will call unto them [Christians] and say: 'Where are My partners whom you imagined?' " It is again referring to Sûrah 5:116 as we just read; however, let's take a closer look. This half-truth, a rhetorical question, is presented as a replay of an event from the past when Allah supposedly asked Jesus an important question regarding the Trinity and his relationship to him. Jesus responded: "O Jesus son of Mary, did you say unto men: 'Take me and my mother as gods, apart from God?' " (Sûrah 5:116.) As we previously stated, the answer must be "no" because Jesus never claimed His mother, Mary, was a god. The Koran is again is setting the stage to put words into Jesus' mouth.

So, did Jesus claim that His mother was married to Allah? The answer is "no." Did Jesus claim to be God's Son? The answer is, "Absolutely! That is why He was crucified." The earliest record of Jesus claiming to be God's Son was when He was only 12 years old (Luke 2:49). As for the crucifixion, the Bible records it numerous times, and historical records tell us the reason Jesus was crucified was that He claimed to be the Son of God. John 5:18 and Mark 14:61-63 are two of those records, along with extra-biblical documentation from the first and second centuries.[16]

Notice how the following biblical passages regarding Jesus' eternal existence as the Son of God, contrasts with the Koran's repetitive assertions that Allah has taken to himself no partners, no associates, and no son. As you read what the Bible says in contrast to the koranic claims, consider if it seems like the same author wrote them:

> Come you near unto me, hear you this; I have not spoken in secret from the beginning; from the time that it was, there am I [Jesus]: and now the LORD God [the Father] and His [Holy] Spirit, has sent me Isaiah 48:16, bracketed clarifications mine).

> Who has ascended up into Heaven, or descended? Who has gathered the wind in his fists? Who has bound the waters in a garment? Who has established all the ends of the earth? What is His name, and what is His Son's name, if you can tell? (Proverbs 30:4.)

From Heaven, God acknowledged Jesus as His Son while the Holy Spirit (the third person of the Trinity), taking the form of a dove, descended upon Jesus.

And Jesus, when He was baptized, went up straightway out of the water: and, behold, the Heavens were opened unto Him, and He saw the Spirit of God descending like a dove, and lighting upon Him And lo a voice from Heaven, saying, "This is My beloves Son, in whom I am well pleased" (Matthew 3:16-17, bracketed clarification mine).

Yet again, Allah claims to have no son.

If Jesus is a prophet of Islam—and Islamic prophets do not lie—why did He commission His disciples to do the following?

Go you therefore, and teach all nations, baptizing them in the name of the Father [God], and of the Son [speaking of Himself], and of the Holy Ghost (Matthew 28:19, bracketed clarification mine).

However, in case we forget the premise of this passage in the Koran, it basically calls God's Word into question as Satan did in Genesis 3:1 with a half-truth.

CONSIDER: When the Serpent questioned God's Word, Adam and Eve went along with his devious scheme. As a result, mankind fell from God's grace, and our sinful nature was passed down from generation to generation (Psalm 51:5)—a concept rejected by Muslims! Now the question becomes, "How will you relate to the question contained here in verse 62?"

(28:63) Those concerning whom the Word will have come true will say: "Our Lord! These are they whom we led astray. We led them astray even as we ourselves were astray. We declare our innocence before You: [yet] us [Allah] they never worshipped" (bracketed clarifications mine).

394

This verse is about Christians who were deceived by the devils (jinns) and led astray into believing that Allah had a son and a wife. They will beg Allah to forgive them because the only reason they lead others astray with tales of the Trinity was that they were led astray.

(28:64) And it will be said: "Cry unto your (so-called) partners (of Allah)." And they will cry unto them [Jesus and Mary], and they will give no answer unto them, and they will see the Doom. Ah, if they had but been guided! (Bracketed clarification mine.)

Muhammad Habib Shakir translates this passage:

> And it will be said: "Call your associate-gods." So they will call upon them, but they will not answer them, and they shall see the punishment; would that they had followed the right way!

We now know why Jesus is referred to and mentioned more than anyone else in the Koran, even more than Muhammad. It is because of the Koran's obsession with attacking the Divinity of Christ and the concept of the Trinity. As we have had to point out so many times, the Koran's concept of the Trinity is based on the false premise that the members of the Trinity are two humans (Mary and Jesus) who became attached/partnered to Allah (Sûrah 5:116).

Of course, not only is that wrong, but the Trinity is One God in three persons like a Cherub is one angel displaying four beings having the "face of a man, and the face of a lion, on the right side: and they four had the face of an ox on the left side; they four also had the face of an eagle" (Ezekiel 1:10). Consider also an equilateral triangle is one triangle manifested with three equal sides. Remove any side, and there is no longer a triangle but a crude trapezoid. Likewise, remove any member of the Trinitarian Godhead, and there is no longer the God Christians worship.

Furthermore, while the Koran claims that Allah is the author of the Bible, it foregoes its most fundamental teachings. Historically, many of those who have called on the name of the Lord have been delivered, but the name of the LORD in the Old Testament is the Hebrew

Tetragrammaton, which is spelled (in Hebrew), י (yud) ה (hey) ו (vuv) ה (hāy) only reversing the placement of the Hebrew letters, reading it right to left יהוה. We would write it and read it in English from left to right הוהי (YHWH). It is the distinctive personal name of the God of Israel, not Allah (Joel 2:32; 1 Kings 18:24, 37; Psalm 116:4; Romans 10:9; John 10:30, 17:11, 21).

This verse also foretells, *"... and they will see the doom."* "Doom" is a Middle English word for "judgment."

The verse continues, *"Ah, if they had but been guided!"* Think for a moment that Allah claims to have written the Bible; then he should know better than anyone that it is a valid guide for people. The Koran endorses the Bible and acknowledges Jesus as a prophet of Islam, and it is this so-called prophet of Islam who declared to the young man, "... I am the way, the truth, and the life: no man came unto the Father but by Me" (John 14:6). Could it be that an Islamic prophet is a liar? Jesus claimed to be the Son of God (Matthew 27:40; John 9:35, 10:36) as well as identified as such by others (John 20:28; Acts 7:59; Luke 1:35; John 1:18, 34, 49; 3:18; 5:18, 11:4, 27; 20:31; Acts 8:37; 1 John 3:8; 4:15; 5:5, 9, 20 and most importantly, God Himself (Matthew 3:17; 17:5; Mark 9:7; Luke 9:7, 35; 2 Peter 1:17).

(28:65) And on the Day when He will call unto them and say: "What answer gave you to the messengers?"

The Bible answers this question:

He that believes on Him [Jesus] is not condemned: but he that believes not [in Jesus] is condemned already because he has not believed in the name of the only begotten [GK: μονογενής, *i.e., monogenés* unique, one of a kind] Son of God (John 3:18, bracketed clarifications mine).
(28:66) On that day (all) tidings will be dimmed for them, nor will they ask one of another,

According to this verse, when the Christians stand before Allah on Judgment Day, they will have forgotten all they were taught about the Trinity and will not ask for Jesus.

(28:67) But as for him who shall repent and believe and do right, he haply [by chance] may be one of the successful (bracketed clarification mine).

Muhammad Habib Shakir puts it this way:

> *But as to him who repents and believes and does good, maybe he will be among the successful.*

Because the god of Islam denies Jesus' sacrifice for mankind on the cross,[17] Muhammad offers an alternative means of gaining salvation, based partially on works, when Gabriel states that forgiveness is achieved when one...*who shall repent and believe and do right....*" However, even with good works, the only guarantee in this verse is ...*he haply [by chance] may be one of the successful (bracketed clarification mine).* In Islam, there is no guarantee of heaven, nor is there is a guarantee of salvation unless you die in a jihad (Sûrah 4:74).

(28:68) Your Lord brings to pass what He wills and chooses. They have never any choice. Glorified be Allah and Exalted above all that they associate (with Him)!

Again, we are told, regarding salvation, Allah is the one who "... *brings to pass what He wills and chooses. They have never any choice.*" So why are people told that if they don't convert, they will go to Hell if they have no choice in the matter? Again, we must ask, "Which is it?"

As previously explained in the commentary for verse 62, the triune concept held by Muslims is that Christians attach Mary and Jesus to Allah as fellow gods, which Muslims—as they should—reject. Perhaps, it was because of the Catholic practice of venerating and praying to Mary that gave Muhammad the impression the Trinity was in the minds of Christians—God the Father, Mary—a woman who was made a goddess by her divine impregnation by having sex with Allah—and the Son they conceived and named "Jesus" *(Isa)* (Sûrah 5:116). This, of course, is a concept not found in the Bible.[18]

For this reason, we see the Koran's persistent attacks against the concept of the Trinity, followed by the claim that Allah chooses who he will save. As we see, here again, the Koran says Allah—not Muhammad or his followers—is who moves men's hearts to accept Islam because people have no say in their salvation.

On the contrary, the God of the Bible does not want any human being to perish. In fact, He deliberately puts off condemning the sinner in order to give everyone every opportunity to repent and come to Him of his or her own free will (2 Peter 3:9)!

By now, hopefully, it is very clear to our readers that the author of the Koran and the author of the Bible are not the same.

(28:69) And your Lord knows what their breasts conceal, and what they publish.

Yusuf Ali's translation is clearer:

> And your Lord knows all that their hearts conceal and all that they reveal.

Gabriel is confirming that Allah is aware of what people think since he knows what is in their hearts and what they promote.

(28:70) And He is Allah; there is no God save Him. His is all praise in the former and the latter (state), and His is the command, and unto Him you will be brought back.

Let's look at Shakir's version, which helps to clarify this passage:

> And He is Allah, there is no God but He! All praise is due to Him in this (life) and the hereafter, and His is the judgment, and to Him you shall be brought back.

The problem with this passage is how can the Good News (i.e., gospel) of the Bible, which teaches us that Jesus is our salvation, be so totally opposite to the teachings found in the Koran, especially when Allah claims authorship of the Bible?

To you We sent the Scripture in truth, confirming the Scripture that came before it, and guarding it in safety: so judge between them by what God has revealed, and follow not their vain desires, diverging from the Truth that has come to you (Sûrah 5:48a).

And in their [the biblical prophets] footsteps We sent Jesus the son of Mary, confirming the Law that had come before him: <u>We sent him the Gospel</u>: therein was guidance and light, and confirmation of the Law that had come before him: A guidance and an admonition to those who fear God. (Sûrah 5:46, emphasis and bracketed clarification added)

On the one hand, Allah is validating the Christ of the gospels, while on the other hand, he denies the truth it teaches. To claim something as true in one book, while denying its truth in another, not only creates a conflict between the Bible and the Koran, but it is an oxymoron as well!

> CONSIDER: Can the God of Heaven be double-minded? Not according to the Bible, which states, "A double-minded man is unstable in all his ways" (James 1:8). Biblically speaking, this is another example of conflicts with the Islamic claim of the Bible and Koran's single authorship.

(28:71) Say: "Have you thought, if Allah made night everlasting for you till the Day of Resurrection, who is a God beside Allah who could bring you light? Will you not then hear?"

This is more of the continuing saga of attacking the Divinity of Christ. Basically, Gabriel is asking why people have not wised up and accepted Allah because, after all, he could have made the night eternal, and people would have had to exist forever in darkness until the time of the resurrection. Allah brought us (day) light, so we don't have to live in eternal darkness. To make the point again that Allah has no associates, he asks, "... *who is a god beside Allah who could bring you light?*" The answer to that question is found in the Bible and disavows this passage by providing us with this response given seven hundred years before the Koran was revealed:

Then Jesus spoke to them again, saying, "I am the light of the world. He who follows Me shall not walk in darkness, but have the light of life" (John 8:12, NKJV).

(28:72) Say: "Have you thought, if Allah made day everlasting for you till the Day of Resurrection, who is a God beside Allah [Jesus, Mary] who could bring you night wherein you rest? Will you not then see?" (Bracketed clarification mine.)

Continuing with the koranic allegory:

If you had to live in an endless day of the bright sun until the time of the resurrection, how could you sleep? Who else but Allah could make the peaceful night for you to find rest—Mary? Jesus? Of course not—not according to the Koran! (Paraphrase mine.)

This verse suggests, "*who could bring you night wherein you rest— Mary? Jesus?*" The answer can also be found in the Bible, where Jesus personally answers several questions regarding Himself in that manner:

"I and my Father [God] are one" (John 10:30, bracketed clarification mine).

"... he that has seen Me has seen the Father [God]." (John 14:9b, bracketed clarification mine.)

"... you believe in God; believe in Me also" (John 14:1, NKJV).

CONSIDER: If—as the Koran claims—Jesus is a Muslim prophet, where did Jesus make that claim in the Bible?

(28:73) Of His mercy has He appointed for you night and day, that therein you may rest, and that you may seek His bounty, and that haply [by chance] you may be thankful.

> *People, aren't you glad that Allah made the world the way he did so you have time to work and play and time to rest and sleep? (Paraphrase mine.)*

(28:74) And on the Day when He shall call unto them and say: "Where are My partners whom you pretended?"

Once more, Muhammad is attacking Allah's only real threat, Jesus, the Son of God on his seemingly endless diatribe. It appears that Allah is very concerned that some might think he has taken Mary for a wife and Jesus as his son, which would make Mary a goddess and Jesus a God. Allah forbid!

(28:75) And We shall take out from every nation a witness and We shall say: "Bring your proof [because they can't]." Then they will know that Allah [alone] has the Truth [without Mary and Jesus], and all that they invented will have failed them (bracketed clarifications mine).

The answer to verses 74 and 75 is easily found in the Bible. Isaiah 9:6, 48:16; Proverbs 30:4; Luke 1:26-33; Matthew 3:17, 28:19, and Mark 1:11, is a partial list of the Scriptures which would provide the koranic request for proof, showing many of its claims to be less than accurate regarding the true nature of Jesus.

CONSIDER: Who do politicians and Muhammad try to discredit and marginalize over and over again? The answer is (1) people they are afraid of; (2) people who threaten their agendas, and (3) people who they have no good factual argument against who can defeat them! We see this all the time, both in politics and as we have seen repeatedly in the Koran.

(28:76) Now Korah was of Moses' folk, but he oppressed them; and We gave him so much treasure that the stores thereof would verily [truly] have been a burden for a troop of mighty men. When his own folk said unto him: Exult not; Behold! Allah loves not the exultant (bracketed clarification mine).

With this verse, the Koran makes another disjointed shift in subjects. After getting another dig in on the Trinity (verse 75), it now shifts to verse 76 and focuses on the biblical story regarding "Korah's Rebellion." Depicting Korah as a wealthy man who oppressed his fellow Hebrew slaves, we must ask, "How did he oppress them? He was a slave himself with no authority." This bears no resemblance to the Bible story itself, but it accurately points out that Korah was related to both Moses and Aaron.

Due to the confusion of some families found in the Bible and the Koran, we will now explain how Korah, Moses, and Aaron are related. Unlike the Koran, the Bible contains many and varied genealogies down through thousands of years, which is another way it establishes its authenticity and allows us to validate relationships.

Levi was the great-grandfather of Korah, Moses, and Aaron. Levi's son, Kohath, was the grandfather of Korah, Moses, and Aaron. Two of Kohath's sons were Amram and Izhar. Izhar's sons were Korah, Nepheg, and Zichri. Amram was the father of Moses, Aaron, and their sister, Miriam, which made Korah, Moses, Aaron, and Miriam first cousins. [19]

Fig. 5.   Hebrew Families as Depicted in Historical Art

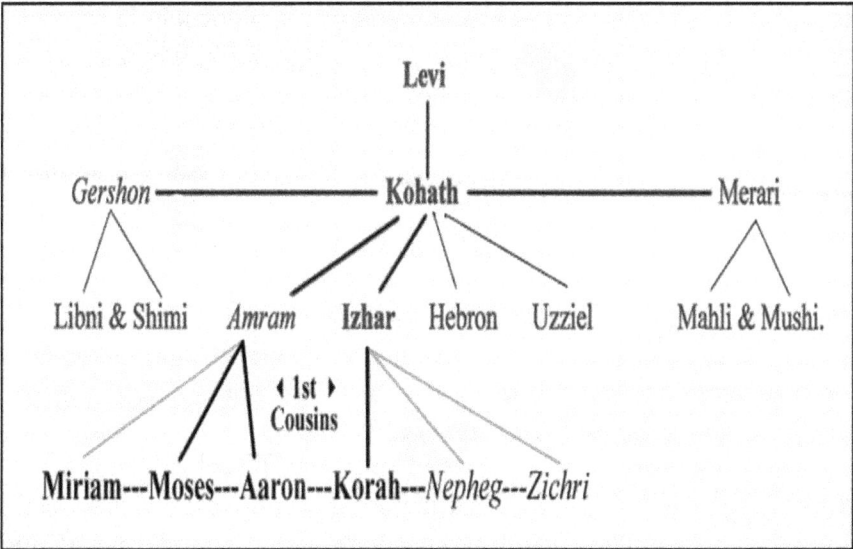

The Koran assigns abundant wealth to Korah when it states, "We gave him so much treasure that the stores thereof would truly have been a burden for a troop of mighty men."

Think about this: Korah's Rebellion took place on the heels of when Moses and the children of Israel hastily departed from Egypt. Shortly after they escaped from Pharaoh, Korah and his group confronted Moses' authority, as well as the establishment of Aaron and his sons as God's priestly cast. The reason it makes no sense that Korah would be incredibly wealthy (as the Koran states) is because he, like all the others, were lowly slaves. Despite Allah's claim that he gave Korah much wealth, the Bible says it was the Egyptians who gave some of their wealth to the Hebrews before they left Egypt.[20] It is reasonable to assume that because the Hebrew slaves had to leave Egypt in a hurry, they would not be able to take more than what they could individually carry.

The children of Israel endured forty years of wandering in the desert. If Korah were so wealthy like this passage in the Koran suggests, that he would need a troop of mighty men solely dedicated to the immense burden of transporting and protecting his vast wealth, where would he find them? As we stated, each family had their own plunder (treasure) taken from the Egyptians to protect after they left Egypt. They also had their hands full taking care of their own tents and household supplies, much less neglecting their personal property and welfare to take on the burden of someone else! It appears that the Koran failed to take into account the problem of pedigrees (the Jews were all slaves and not wealthy) and logistics; therefore, it is reasonable to deduce that Korah was not any better off, or received any more parting gifts than any of the other Hebrew slaves from the Egyptians.[21]

(28:77) But seek the abode of the Hereafter in that which Allah has given you and neglect not your portion of the world, and be you kind even as Allah has been kind to you, and seek not corruption in the earth; surely! Allah loves not corrupters,

Korah needs to realize that his acquired wealth came from Allah; therefore, he should be careful to use it for good. Gabriel says no one lives forever, and it would be best for Korah to share his blessings with an eye toward eternity, accomplished by being charitable, doing good works, and causing no harm to anyone. Allah loves those who are good.

(28:78) He [Korah] said: "I have been given it only on account of knowledge I possess." Knew he not that Allah had destroyed already of the generations before him men who were mightier than him in strength and greater in respect of following? The guilty are not questioned of their sins (bracketed clarification mine).

This verse recounts Korah's defense before Allah. *"I have been given it only on account of knowledge I possess."* Many Muslim scholars argue that Korah and his family were bankers/money lenders, which is how Korah and his family managed to gain so much wealth, yet the Hebrew slaves had no money to lend, much less lend to other slaves who were unable to pay it back. During those times, the Egyptians used a barter system. Their wealth was in the form of jewelry, property, animals, etc. Money, in the form of coins (first gold, followed by silver and other metals), was not introduced to ancient Egypt until the Greco-Roman period, which was over a thousand years later.[22] It is worth remembering that neither Korah nor any of the other Hebrew slaves had any wealth up until the time they escaped from Egypt.

Allah observes that Korah was foolish because he did not realize, in days gone by, there were whole groups of people far superior to Korah in wealth and strength. Allah dealt with their haughtiness accordingly.

(28:79) Then went he [Korah] forth before his people in his pomp. Those who were desirous of the life of the world said: "Ah, would that unto us had been given the like of what has been given unto Korah! Look! he is lord of rare good fortune" (bracketed clarification mine).

Korah went before his people with great splendor and wealth. We can only speculate who *"his people"* are. The Bible version does not mention any pomp or splendor, but it does tell us about those with whom Korah associated:

> Now Korah the son of Izhar, ... took *men;* and they rose up before Moses with some of the children of Israel, two hundred and fifty leaders of the congregation, representatives of the congregation, men of renown (Numbers 16:1-2, NKJV).

The implication in this koranic verse (28:79) suggests that Korah associated with *"Those who were desirous of the life of the world ...."* The reason they wanted to follow Korah was that they were impressed by his wealth. The Bible, on the other hand, says their rebellion was out of jealously and envy for power and priestly prestige, not money:

> They [Korah and company] gathered together against Moses and Aaron, and said to them, "*You take* too much upon yourselves, for all the congregation *is* holy, every one of them, and the LORD *is* among them. Why then do you exalt yourselves above the assembly of the LORD?" (Numbers 16:3, NKJV, bracketed clarification mine.)

(28:80) But those who had been given knowledge said: "Woe unto you! The reward of Allah [in the life hereafter] for him who believes and does right is better, and only the steadfast [devoted] will obtain it" (bracketed clarification mine).

The koranic version is a discussion between Korah and his followers, as well as a group of unnamed people. Allah tells them that he bestows privileges on those who believe in Allah, have the knowledge of Islam, and perform good deeds.

The actual biblical confrontation was regarding who should hold the priestly assignment, which was bestowed on Moses' brother and his clan (the Levites). Aaron and his sons were assigned this exalted position because Aaron spoke for God on Moses' behalf, not only before Pharaoh but also throughout their ordeals. We can see how God commissioned Aaron and his sons in the following passages:

And you shall command the children of Israel, that they bring you pure oil olive beaten for the light [Menorah], to cause the lamp to burn always.

[When you are] In the tabernacle of the congregation without the veil, which is before the testimony, Aaron and his sons shall order it from evening to morning before the LORD: it shall be a statute for ever unto their generations on behalf of the children of Israel (Exodus 27:20-21, bracketed clarification mine).

God personally bestows the priestly order on Aaron and his sons:

And take you unto you Aaron your brother, and his sons with him, from among the children of Israel, that he may minister unto me in the priest's office, even Aaron, Nadab and Abihu, Eleazar and Ithamar, Aaron's sons (Exodus 28:1).

As for the response to Korah's demands, the Bible says that Moses gave the reply when he heard their accusations. Korah claims that they were just as holy as the Levites, and they should have been able to attain the exalted position of priests. In the Bible, Moses addresses the congregation:

and he said to Korah and his company saying, "Tomorrow morning the LORD will show who *is* His and *who is* holy, and will cause *him* to come near to Him. That one whom He chooses He will cause to come near to Him ..." (Numbers 16:5, NKJV).

(28:81) So We caused the earth to swallow him and his dwelling-place. Then he had no host to help him against Allah, nor was he of those who can save themselves.

For some reason, the Koran is silent about the reason why God destroyed Korah and his group, but the Bible explains how Moses—acting on God's behalf—made a challenge before the entire congregation to put to rest, once and for all, any questions regarding Aaron and the *Levitical priestly commission* established by God:

And Moses said to Korah, "Tomorrow, you and all your company be present before the LORD—you and they, as well as Aaron. Let each take his censer and put incense in it, and each of you bring his censer before the LORD, two hundred and fifty censers; both you and Aaron, each *with* his censer." So every man took his censer, put fire in it, laid incense on it, and stood at the door of the tabernacle of meeting with Moses and Aaron. And Korah gathered all the congregation against them at the door of the tabernacle of meeting. Then the glory of the LORD appeared to all the congregation.

And the LORD spoke to Moses and Aaron, saying, "Separate yourselves from among this congregation, that I may consume them in a moment."

Then they fell on their faces, and said, "O God, the God of the spirits of all flesh, shall one man sin, and You be angry with all the congregation?"

So the LORD spoke to Moses, saying, "Speak to the congregation, saying, 'Get away from the tents of Korah, Dathan, and Abiram' "(Numbers 16:16-24, NKJV).

407

A few verses later, we see Moses speaking again to the children of Israel while Korah's 250 men were offering the incense to God in place of the divinely appointed Levites, thus accepting the challenge Moses had set before them:

> And Moses said: "By this you shall know that the LORD has sent me to do all these works, for *I have* not *done them* of my own will. If these men die naturally like all men, or if they are visited by the common fate of all men, *then* the LORD has not sent me. But if the LORD creates a new thing, and the earth opens its mouth and swallows them up with all that belongs to them, and they go down alive into the pit, then you will understand that these men have rejected the LORD."
> Now it came to pass, as he finished speaking all these words, that the ground split apart under them, and the earth opened its mouth and swallowed them up, with their households and all the men with Korah, with all *their* goods. So they and all those with them went down alive into the pit; the earth closed over them, and they perished from among the assembly. Then all Israel who *were* around them fled at their cry, for they said, "Lest the earth swallow us up *also!*"
>
> And a fire came out from the LORD and consumed the two hundred and fifty men who were offering incense (Numbers 16:28-35, NKJV).

(28:82) And morning found those who had coveted his place but yesterday crying: "Ah, welladay [woe! Alas!] Allah enlarges the provision for whom He will of His slaves and straitens [restricts] it (for whom He will). If Allah had not been gracious unto us He would have caused it [the earth] to swallow us (also). Ah, welladay! the disbelievers never prosper" (bracketed clarifications mine)

This verse discusses the moral aspects of the demise of Korah and drives home the point that before Allah brought judgment on him, his associates were very impressed by Korah's auspicious standing in the community; however, all that had changed just one day later.

Allah bestows status on people, and if he can make someone important, he can also break someone. Just like Allah had the ground swallow Korah, he could have done the same thing to anyone, but he did not. The moral of this story is Allah wants everyone to know—if they reject him, they will be sorry.

(28:83) As for that Abode of the Hereafter We assign it unto those who seek not oppression in the earth, nor yet corruption. The sequel is for those who ward off (evil).

Instilling the Islamic concept of works-based religion, the Muslim is told he might have a place in Heaven when he dies if he resists evil and does not oppress fellow Muslims. Allah looks favorably on those who reject doing harm and resist sinful temptations.

Regarding a works-based religion, the Bible says:

For it is by grace you have been saved, through faith— and this is not from yourselves, it is the gift of God— not by works, so that no one can boast (Ephesians 2:8-9).

(28:84) Whoso brings a good deed, he will have better than the same; while as for him who brings an ill-deed, those who do ill-deeds will be requited [held accountable for] only what they did (bracketed clarification mine).

Again, the Koran is reinforcing works as a means of obtaining salvation. Muslims are cautioned here to remember that good works result in good outcomes, while those who do evil will be held accountable.

(28:85) Indeed! He Who has given you the Qur'an for a law will surely bring you home again. Say: "My Lord is Best Aware of him who brings guidance and him who is in error manifest."

Shakar translates this passage:

Most surely He Who has made the Quran binding on you will bring you back to the destination. Say: "My Lord knows best him who has brought the guidance and him who is in manifest error" (Sûrah 28:85, Muhammad Habib Shakir).

While this verse could still apply to the story just presented about Korah, it could also be that this is again diverting into another reinforcement of Islamic Sharia Law. This verse reiterates the fact Allah is the originator of the Koran, and he revealed the Koran to Muhammad as the means by which to live their lives. Those who accept it will always return to its teachings. Allah is confident that those who read the Koran will accept its doctrine, yet many will reject the wisdom of it at their own expense. This passage is similar to a Bible teaching, which says:

BIBLE
Train up a child in the way he should go: and when he is old, he will not depart from it (Proverbs 22:6).

28:86) You [Muhammad] had no hope that the Scripture would be inspired in you; but it is a mercy from your Lord, so never be a helper to the disbelievers [Pagans, Jews, and Christians] (bracketed clarifications mine).

You (Muhammad) had no idea that once you heard the scripture (words of the Koran) that you would be so moved; however, the reason you accepted the teachings of the Koran is that Allah enabled you to accept it [and] caused you to believe it. Therefore, do not help or lend assistance to those who reject Allah and his teachings like the Pagans, Jews, and Christians (paraphrase and bracketed clarifications mine).

The part of this passage that says, "...never be a helper to the disbelievers" is, of course, referring to those Pagans, Jews, and Christians who don't buy into Islam. This verse is reminiscent of another passage that is more narrowly aimed at Jews and Christians:

O you who believe! Take not the Jews and the Christians for friends [because they reject Islam]. They are friends one to another. He among you who takes them for friends is (one) of them. See! Allah guides not wrongdoing folk (Sûrah 5:51, Muhammad Habib Shakir, bracketed clarification mine).

(28:87) And let them not divert you [Muhammad] from the revelations of Allah after they have been sent down unto you; but call (mankind) unto your Lord, and be not of those who ascribe partners (unto Him).

Abdullah Yusuf Ali simplifies this for us in his translation:

> *And let nothing keep you back from the Signs of Allah after they have been revealed to you: and invite (men) to your Lord, and be not of the company of those who join gods with God.*

By now, we have become accustomed to reading the Koran's constant attacks on the Divinity of Christ.

NOTE: Remember, Allah claims to have written the Bible and the Gospels, while still continuing to attack the very heart of the gospel or the Good News itself. What is this Good News? Jesus *(Isa)* explains it to us when He said: "For God so loved the [entire] world that He gave His only begotten Son" [as we previously explained begotten or monogenés, in Greek means one of a kind, or unique, but it does *not* mean it is a one of a kind, having been produced through a physical or spiritual sexual act, but rather by a miraculous infusion of Christ's spirit into the ovum of Mary. Think of it this way; the Spirit of Jesus was poured into the prepared human egg like you would pour tea into a cup[23] "..that whoever believes in Him should not perish but have everlasting life" (John 3:16, NKJV, bracketed clarifications mine).

(28:88) And cry not unto any other god along with Allah. There is no God save Him. Everything will perish save His countenance. His is the command, and unto Him you will be brought back.

We end this sûrah in the same way we ended Sûrah 18 with the Koran's underlying theme of attacking the Divinity of Jesus; the revelator of the Koran just can't help himself. We know of no other religion, other than Islam, that makes it a point to continually attack another religion in their "sacred writings!" If Jesus was not such a threat to the entity behind the Koran, it would have dismissed Jesus' claim of Divinity only once or twice and then moved on. Apparently, Jesus is such a threat to the spirit behind the Koran that it feels compelled to keep attacking who Jesus is. We don't see this done with the hundreds of Arabian gods, thousands of Hindu gods, or even the Buddha. Only the Divinity of Jesus is a threat to this entity—and for a good reason. If Jesus were just a Muslim prophet, he would not lie by saying he is the Son of God. Yet Jesus *does claim to be* the Son of God (John 10:36) as we see throughout the Bible and even receives worship (John 20:28). The reason the High Priest had Jesus crucified (Luke 22:70-71) was because He *did* claim to be Divine.

Consider: (1) If Jesus claims to be God when He is not, then He is either a liar (and who trusts or wants to follow a liar?); or (2) Jesus is crazy (and who would follow a crazy man?), or (3) Jesus is whom He claims to be, in which case He is a definite threat to the religion of Islam!

As we just observed, this concluding verse is a continuation of the Koran's ongoing attacks on the Trinity and Divinity of Christ. Allah is reinforcing his repetitive proclamations that if anyone is in need of help, do not try to come to him through any other god because there is no Triune Godhead as far as Allah is concerned. To look for help from anyone other than Allah is hopeless; look only toward the face of Allah since you can only be brought back to him and no one else.

Yet the Bible reveals a different message. The Koran claims that Jesus is a prophet of Islam, and Islamic prophets should not lie or deceive. In the Bible's Gospel of John (Allah claims to have authored the "Torah and the Gospel," Sûrah 3:3) Jesus confirms that He is the Son of God:

Say you of Him, whom the Father has sanctified, and sent into the world, you blaspheme; because *I said, "I am the Son of God:"* (John 10:36, emphasis added).

Jesus says unto him, "I am the way, the truth, and the life: no man comes unto the Father, but by me" (John 14:6)

And Jesus, when He was baptized, went up straightway out of the water: and, lo, the Heavens were opened unto Him, and He saw the Spirit of God descending like a dove, and lighting upon Him: And lo a voice from Heaven, saying, "This is my beloved Son, in whom I am well pleased" (Matthew 3:16-17, bracketed clarification mine).

This is He who came by water and blood—Jesus Christ; not only by water, but by water and blood. And it is the Spirit who bears witness, because the Spirit is truth. For there are three that bear witness in heaven: the Father, the Word, and the Holy Spirit; and these three are one. And there are three that bear witness on earth: the Spirit, the water, and the blood; and these three agree as one (1 John 5:6-8, NKJV).

Finally, the Bible records this testimony from the Apostle Peter, one of the twelve disciples and an eye witness to the ministry of Jesus, to whom Jesus gave the keys to the kingdom.[24] He said:

"For we have not followed cunningly devised fables, when we made known unto you the power and coming of our Lord Jesus Christ, but were eyewitnesses of His majesty. For He received from God the Father honor and glory, when there came such a voice to Him from the excellent glory, *'This is my beloved Son,* in whom I am well pleased.' "

And this voice which came from Heaven we heard, when we were with Him in the holy mount (2 Peter 1:16-18, emphasis added).

We have a direct conflict between the claims of the Koran and the testimony contained in the Bible. (Remember, Allah also claims he wrote the Bible Sûrah 3:79; 57:25) regarding Jesus' own claim about

413

Himself. In addition, Peter, a disciple of Jesus, also gave an eyewitness account, which is recorded in biblical records.[25]

NOTES:

1. Allâmah Nooeuddin. *Exegesis of the Holy Qur'ân: Commentary and Reflections*. Translated by Amatul Rahmân Omar and Abdul Mammân Omar, Noor Foundation International Inc, 2015. p. 788.

2. *New World Dictionary-Concordance* to the *New American Bible* (New York: World, 1970), 461. "She called his name Moses *(*Hebrew, משה): and she said, 'Because I drew him *(*Hebrew, משיתהו) out of the water.' " The name Moses is also associated with the Egyptian root word "*msy*" meaning child of, which can be seen in the ancient Egyptian names of Tuthmose and Ramesses, meaning "born" or "child."

3. John Gill (1697-1771). Firstly, for the sake of reference, we will look once again at the Bible passage, which states, "And Moses said unto Hobab, the son of Raguel the Midianite, Moses' father in law..." (Numbers 10:29a) versus "Now Moses kept the flock of Jethro, his father in law, the priest of Midian: and he led the flock to the backside of the desert, and came to the mountain of God, even to Horeb" (Exodus 3:1). Secondly, we have John Gills' explanation from BibleHub.com's commentaries regarding Moses's father-in-law: "Some think this Hobab was the same with (was the same person as) Jethro, whose father's name was Raguel or Reuel; so Jarchi and Ben Gersom; but rather (could be) Raguel or Reuel, and Jethro (all), seem to be the same and was Moses's father-in-law, and this Hobab was the son of him (or was his son), and brother of Zipporah, Moses's wife; and the same relation is designed whether the word is rendered his 'father-in-law' or his 'wife's brother,' so Aben Ezra; as it may be either; if the former, then it may be joined to Raguel, if the latter, then to Hobab: Jethro or Raguel, Moses's father-in-law, came to see him as soon as he came to Horeb" (archaic Eng. clarification mine); web. 24 September

2013). We also have some biblical scholars' explanations, through the use of oral traditions, the name "Reuel" was used in the Yahwist tradition while "Jethro" was used in the Elohist oral tradition.

4. William G. Dever, *Who Were the Early Israelites and Where Did They Come From?* (Grand Rapids: William B. Eerdmans Pub., 2006), 34.

5. Joshua J. Mark, "Magic in Ancient Egypt." *Ancient History Encyclopedia*, Ancient History Encyclopedia, 24 Feb. 2017.

6. For other biblical references regarding Jesus, the Lamb of God, see Revelation 5:6; 7:17; 14:10; 15:3; 19:9; 21:22; 21:23; 22:1; 22:3.

7. Gaston Maspero, *Manual of Egyptian Archaeology and Guide to the Study of Antiquities in Egypt: For the Use of Students and Travellers (1914)*. Reprinted ed. (Ithaca: Cornell U Library, 2009) .... In the Introduction on page 3, we read, "Burnt bricks were not often used before the Roman period (note 4), nor tiles, either flat or curved."

8. "Maya." *Oh Baby! Names*, 22 Oct. 2014, ohbabynames.com/all-baby-names/maya/. Queen Māyā is also the name of the mother of Buddha. As a Latinate form of "May", Maya may also be considered a nickname for Mary or Margaret, meaning "beloved" and "pearl,"

9. Kenneth Barker, ed., *The NIV Study Bible* (Grand Rapids: Zondervan, 1985). Footnote: Esther 3:1.

10. *Encyclopædia* Britannica, 1946 ed., s.v. "Pharaoh."

11. "Talk: Haman (Islam)." *Wikipedia*. Wikimedia Foundation, Web. 12 May 2013. 26 Mar. 2017.

12. Ibid.

Also note the controversial Egyptologist, David Rohl, as mentioned by the Wikipedia editor, is not mentioned in the Amro copy cited; however, one can access the Wikipedia site and discover that it has been sabotaged many times by scrolling down toward the end of the page to "POV vandalism" where we are informed many POVs are added and deleted on a regular basis (POV means "point of view" and, therefore, is not necessarily documentable). Understandably, many Islamic defenders tend to be very protective of their Koran and zealous in editing or attacking secular publications, which critique the Koran solely on historical and scientific data that might not be favorable to its content.

13. Ibid.

14. The Bible states that Pharaoh's army was drowned (Exodus 14:23-28; Psalm 106:9-11; Nehemiah 9:10-11); however, in Psalm 136:15, we are told that Pharaoh and his army were overthrown into the Red Sea. Many have cited this passage as a proof-text that Pharaoh was drowned along with his army; nevertheless, we have four verses from three books of the Bible that indicate Pharaoh's army drowned, and only one of the three could be taken to mean that Pharaoh might have drowned with his army by the use of the term "overthrown" (na'ar, Strong's word #5287); however, overthrowing someone does not necessarily mean to kill them; rather it means "power revoked," "shaken," "tossed aside" or "removed from office." If Pharaoh's army was destroyed, he would have been powerless against the great host of the Hebrews, and his power to destroy them would have definitely been overthrown by God. The death of Pharaoh—the most powerful man in the world at that time—would specifically have been highlighted in Scripture because of the sheer magnitude of his stature; therefore, because of the preponderance of the various Scriptures, it is probably safe to conclude (especially in lieu of no historical record of a Pharaoh of Egypt ever having lost his throne through drowning) that Pharaoh did not drown with his army. (NOTE: There is no clear evidence as to which Pharaoh the Bible is referring.)

15. Ergun Mehmet Caner and Emir Fethi Caner. *Unveiling Islam: An Insider's Look at Muslim Life and Beliefs* (Grand Rapid: Kregel Publications, 2002), 181. Muhamad said, "I have been sent with a sword between my hands to ensure that no one but Allah is worshiped, Allah who put my livelihood under the shadow of my spear and who inflicts humiliation and scorn on those who disobey my orders." (NOTE: This was taken from the Hadith Narrated by Ahmad, 4869; and classed as Saheeh (also spelled Sahih), meaning verified truthful by al-Albaani in *Saheeh al-Jaami'*, 2831).

16. Sahih Muslim 19:4294, "... If they refuse to accept Islam, demand from them the jizya [infidel tax]. If they agree to pay, accept it from them and hold off your hands. If they refuse to pay the tax, seek Allah's help and fight them ..." (bracketed clarification mine).

17. Habermas, 49-50. Non-Christian sources writing about Jesus' crucifixion: Josephus (37-100 A.D.), Tacitus (56-120 A.D.), Lucian of Samostan (125-180 A.D), and Mara Bar-Serapion (70-200 A.D.). There are no dates for birth and death of Mara, but he wrote a letter to his son mentioning Jesus and His death), Pliny the Younger (61-113 A.D.), and the Talmud (70—500 A.D.) probably entered around 200 A.D.

18. "For the preaching of the cross is to them that perish foolishness; but unto us which are saved it is the power of God" (I Corinthians 1:18).

19. "And when Allah said: 'O Jesus, son of Mary! Did you say unto mankind:' 'Take me [Jesus] and my mother [Mary] for two gods beside Allah?' " (Sûrah 5:116, bracketed clarification mine).

20. "These are the names of the sons of Levi according to their generations: Gershon, Kohath, and Merari .... The sons of Gershon were Libni and Shimei, according to their families. And the sons of Kohath were Amram, Izhar, Hebron, and Uzziel.... The sons of Merari were Mahli and Mushi. These are the families of Levi according to their generations. Now Amram took for himself Jochebed, his father's sister, as his wife, and she bore him *Aaron and Moses*.... The sons of Izhar were *Korah*, Nepheg, and Zichri" (Exodus 6:16-21, emphasis added).

21. The Bible relates that the children of Israel despoiled the Egyptians of their wealth before they began their exodus to the Promised Land, as God promised: "And I will make the Egyptians favorably disposed toward this people so that when you leave, you will not go empty-handed" (Exodus 3:21).

22. "The Lord had made the Egyptians favorably disposed towards the people [no one specifically], they gave them what they asked for; so they [all the children of Israel] plundered [acquired great wealth from] the Egyptians" (Exodus 12:36, NIV bracketed clarification mine). As we can see here, the Bible

infers that Korah or Kórach (Hebrew: קֹרַח), and others shared equally in this wealth.

23. The Earliest Known Gold Pharaonic Coin Author(s): BOLSHAKOV, A.O. Journal: Revue d'Égyptologie, Volume: 43 Date: 1992 Pages: 3-9.

24. In Philippians 2:7, we read, "But made Himself of no reputation, and took upon Him the form of a servant, and was made in the likeness of men." The Greek word used for the phrase, "made Himself of no reputation," which was in the original Greek, meant "self-emptying" or "poured out." We refer to this passage as the Kenosis passage.

25. "And I will give unto you the keys of the kingdom of heaven: and whatsoever you shall bind on earth shall be bound in heaven: and whatsoever you shall loose on earth shall be loosed in heaven" (Matthew 16:19).

26. "Inasmuch as many have taken in hand to set in order a narrative of those things which have been fulfilled among us, just as those who from the beginning were eyewitnesses and ministers of the word delivered them to us, it seemed good to me also, having had perfect understanding of all things from the very first, to write to you an orderly account..." (Luke 1:1-3, NKJV).

"For we did not follow cunningly devised fables [as the Koran insists] when we made known to you the power and coming of our Lord Jesus Christ, but were eyewitnesses of His majesty" (2 Peter 1:16, NKJV, bracketed observation mine).

☪

SÛRAH 97

POWER (Qadr)
(Revealed at Mecca)

In the name of Allah, the Beneficent, the Merciful.

(97:1) Look! We revealed it [the Message to Muhammad] on the Night of Power (bracketed clarification mine).

Some Muslim scholars suggest that this sûrah is reminiscent of the Nativity of Jesus, as we will see when we compare it to the Bible.[1]

Qadr or Al-Qadr, the name of this Sûrah, translates in English to mean "power/fate or predestination through divine destiny" and is one of Islam's Six Articles of Faith, [2] not to be confused with the "Five Pillars of Faith" (in the Sunni tradition) and the "Seven Pillars of Faith" (in the Shia tradition). It concerns itself, along with several other concepts, with angels and Islam's day of resurrection.

"Predestination" is also a New Testament concept:

> And those He predestined, He also called; those He called, He also justified; those He justified, He also glorified (Romans 8:30).

It is interesting that Muhammad uses this biblical concept, especially when compared side-by-side with the Bible:

> For those God foreknew He also predestined to be conformed to the image of His Son, that He might be the firstborn among many brothers and sisters (Romans 8:29).

Apparently, the concept of predestination through a person—known as the Son of God—does not fit the overarching theme of the Koran, which is, Allah has not taken to him a son (Sûrah 39:4; 6:101).

A.J. Arberry translates this verse as follows:

> Behold, We sent it [the Koran] down on the Night of Power (bracketed clarification mine).

Since the Koran was given to Muhammad in the evening, it established the "Night of Power," in which Allah began to reveal to Muhammad his powerful teachings.

(97:2) Ah, what will convey unto you what the Night of Power is!

Some translations use the word "destiny" instead of "power." Many Islamic scholars believe that this sûrah was the 25th one given to Muhammad in Mecca; however, others, like Abu Hayyan al-Ghamati, claim most scholars believe that it was given in Medina.[3] Because it is one of the earlier and shorter ones, we will go with Mecca; either way, it refers to a night of powerful revelations given to Muhammad.

(97:3) The Night of Power is better than a thousand months.

Muslims believe this night to be the very first time the angel, Gabriel, began revealing the Koran to Muhammad. It is also important to them because it occurs during their holy month of Ramadan. (Coincidently, Ramadan falls at the same time as the Pagan holiday that preceded it!)

Because of its divine nature, the whole night was infected with "Power"—a rare event in the cosmos which made it so special that those one thousand months (83.3 years which is longer than most people lived back then) could not be as wonderful as that one night was.

(97:4) The angels and the Spirit descend therein, by the permission of their Lord, with all decrees.

"The angels and the Spirit" are allowed to descend to earth and assist in bringing Allah's declarations and judgments as he directs. As we know, one of the angels is Gabriel (the angel allegedly giving

Muhammad this verse), but it remains unclear who the "Spirit" is. Could Allah be the Spirit addressed here? *"The angels and the Spirit descend therein..."*? No, because the verse continues with, *"... by the permission of their Lord [Allah]."*

We now have a koranic enigma because the Koran denies the Trinity, ascribing Mary in place of the Holy Spirit—the third person of the Godhead, and there is no indication anywhere in the Koran or Hadith where Islam allows for a godly duality of Allah and the Holy Spirit. Therefore, we are at a loss as to whom the *"Spirit"* is in this passage. On the other hand, some Muslim scholars suggest that the "Spirit" (with a capital "S") referred to here is the one giving Muhammad this revelation. The problem with this explanation is, as Gabriel points out, both *"The angels and the Spirit* (singular) *descend...,"* thus separating angels from the Spirit. Notice that Gabriel is an angel, and although angels are in the spirit realm, they are never referred to as angelic spirits using a capital "S." But, as we have come to find out, Islam is very flexible; unlike the Bible, Allah is allowed to fix problems that pop up in the Koran from time to time by changing what he had previously decreed (Sûrah 2:106). In a footnote by Pickthall, we are informed that this is "Gabriel or, as some commentators think, a general term for angels of the highest rank." If that is correct, then this passage would be redundant."

We can agree these koranic revelations descended upon Muhammad by the direct authorization of Allah; however, the Bible also mentions a time when the angels of Heaven came to earth prophesying with great joy:

And there were in the same country shepherds abiding in the field, keeping watch over their flock by night. And, lo, the angel of the Lord came upon them, and the glory of the Lord shone round about them: and they were sore afraid. And the angel said unto them, "Fear not: for, behold, I bring you good tidings of great joy, which shall be to all people. For unto you is born this day in the city of David a Savior, which is Christ the Lord. And this shall be a sign unto you; You shall find the babe wrapped in swaddling clothes, lying in a manger." And suddenly there was with the angel a multitude of the Heavenly host praising God, and saying, "Glory to God in the highest, and on earth peace, good will toward men." And it came to pass, as the angels were gone away from them into Heaven, the shepherds said one to another, "Let us now go even unto Bethlehem, and see this thing which is come to pass, which the Lord has made known unto us" (Luke 2:8-15).

(97:5) (That night is) Peace until the rising of the dawn.

This night is to be savored until the sun's first morning rays.

Because this concluding passage is just a continuation of the previous verse, we will allow that this passage still fits with the preceding biblical verse where we also have the angels praising God:

"Glory to God in the highest, and on earth peace, good will toward men" (Luke 2:8-15).

NOTES:

1. Karl-Heinz Ohlig, Gerd-R Puin, *Die dunklen Anfänge: neue Forschungen zur Entsttehung und frühen Geschichte des Islam.* [Translation: The Dark Beginnings: New Research on the Origin and Early History Islam] (Berlin: N.H. Schiller, 2006), 164.
2. J. Milton Cowan (ed.), *The Hans Wehr Dictionary of Modern Written Arabic* (Ithaca: Spoken Language Services, Inc., 1976).
3. Abdulmajeed Falah, "Grammatical Opinions of Abu Hayyan Andalusi between Theory and Practice." Arab Journal for the Humanities. Academic Publication Council, Kuwait University: Vol. 29, Issue 116. 2011.

☪

SÛRAH 98

(THE CLEAR EVIDENCE)
THE CLEAR PROOF (Baiyina)
(Revealed at Mecca)

In the name of Allah, the Beneficient, the Merciful.

(98:1) Those who disbelieve among the People of the Scripture and the idolaters could not have left off (erring) till the clear proof came unto them,

This is when Muhammad first began to receive teachings for the Koran from the angel, Gabriel. Allah included Christians and Jews, along with the Pagan Arab tribes, something not as prevalent in his later revelations; nevertheless, Muhammad believed the Jews and Christians should jump at the chance to embrace the message from Allah because of the biblical stories it includes. The problem, as we have seen, is that the same biblical stories have some very troubling inconsistencies when repeated in the Koran. It is those discrepancies that contributed greatly toward the Christians and Jews' rejection of Muhammad's religion.

(98:2) A messenger from Allah, reading purified pages

A.J. Arberry translates this verse:

> *A messenger from God, reciting pages purified. Therein true Books [Old and New Testaments] (bracketed clarification mine).*

Gabriel is explaining that he comes directly from Allah, and the messages he brings are as pure and holy as the Bible.

(98:3) Containing correct scriptures.

Gabriel is suggesting that these messages are accurate and on the same level as the Bible, as well as claiming that the Koran is also scripture.

(98:4) Nor were the People of the Scripture divided until after the clear proof came unto them.

The Koran continues its ongoing claim that Allah gave Christians and Jews the Bible with clear proofs that are in harmony with the Koran; however, because of the alleged false interpretations and corruption of the Scriptures (Old Testament vs. New Testament) created by the Jews and Christians, it caused a split between them. If they had not (allegedly) perverted the Bible, they would be able to see that the Koran is the last and final revelation from Allah. This is another *clear proof,* just like the first one (the Bible).

With all due respect, this flies in the face of historical and archaeological evidence that proves the Bible has been faithfully transmitted down through thousands of years. It has remained virtually intact with only minor deviations that do not negate the contextual meaning of the verse.[1]

We also have evidence that the Gospel of Mark was written within two decades of the death, burial, and resurrection of Jesus. Mark also revealed the prophecy of Jesus when He foretold of the destruction of the completed Temple building decades before the event actually happened in 70 A.D., an event only God could have known about and predicted![2]

The reason for the split between the Jews and the Christians was not due to the rewriting of Scripture but because of Jesus Himself. Jesus claimed He is God revealed in human form (John 9:35-37; 10:30, 36; Matthew 16:16-17, etc.), which was the cause for the division. Like Islam, some Jews rejected Jesus as the Messiah, while thousands of other Jews accepted Him as their Lord.

(98:5) And they [Christians and Jews] are ordered naught [nothing] else than to serve Allah, keeping religion pure for Him, as men by

nature upright, and to establish worship and to pay the poor-due. That is true religion (bracketed clarifications mine)

n the first part of this verse, *Christians and Jews "are ordered naught [nothing] else than to serve Allah."* Noticeably missing from this passage is the warning to keep the Ten Commandments or how the gospel, which Allah claims he gave Jesus, can only receive salvation through none other than Jesus the Christ in the New Testament (John 14:6; Acts 4:12).

Let's look at the last part of Sûrah 98:5, which states, *"... and to establish worship and to pay the poor-due. That is true religion."*

While we can agree that Jews and Christians seek only to serve God, they are also encouraged to help the poor and needy. In the Bible, *"pay the poor their due"* is not elevated above the many other unselfish, charitable acts prescribed. It is biblically understood to: "love the Lord your God with all your heart and with all your soul and with all your mind," which is the first and greatest commandment, and the second is very similar to it: "Love your neighbor as yourself" (Matthew 22:37-39). All other charitable works will then follow.

(98:6) See! those who disbelieve, among the People of the Scripture and the idolaters, will abide in fire of hell. They are the worst of created beings.

This is presented in an effort to intimidate the "People of the Scripture" (i.e., Christians and Jews who fail to embrace Allah as the same God of the Bible and the Christians who believe Jesus is the Son of God).

(98:7) (And) look! those who believe and do good works are the best of created beings.

Again, the Koran's focus is that one must also do good works to be "saved," despite the biblical teaching Christians are not saved by works, but through the unearned gift (grace) from God (Ephesians 2:89; Titus 3:3-8). Nevertheless, the fundamentals of most religions revolve around the concept that people should strive to be good and helpful (charitable) whenever possible. As the Apostle Paul acknowledged:

425

For we ourselves also were sometimes foolish, disobedient, deceived, serving divers lusts and pleasures, living in malice and envy, hateful, and hating one another. But after that the kindness and love of God our Savior toward man appeared, *Not by works of righteousness which we have done, but according to His mercy He saved us,* by the washing of regeneration, and renewing of the Holy Ghost; Which He shed on us abundantly through Jesus Christ our Savior; That being justified by His grace [unearned gift], we should be made heirs according to the hope of eternal life (Titus 3:3-7, bracketed clarification mine, emphasis added).

(98:8) Their reward is with their Lord: Gardens of Eden underneath which rivers flow, wherein they dwell for ever. Allah has pleasure in them and they have pleasure in Him. This is (in store) for him who fears his Lord.

This passage suggests a return to the extinct Garden of Eden (Genesis 3:23), as opposed to Heaven or the renewed earth after the tribulation period (Isaiah 65:17; 2 Peter 3:13; 66:22; Revelation 21:1). To be impartial, we know that the God of the Bible is able to do all things, and if he wants to recreate something (Revelation 21:1), He is able to do it—and that includes the Garden of Eden!

NOTES:
1. Geisler, *Baker Encyclopedia of Christian Apologetics*, 533. In 1947, in a place called "Qumran" near the Dead Sea, manuscripts were discovered. They included copies of various fragments from virtually every book in the Old Testament except Esther.
2. Ibid. The writings from the Gospel of Mark were found in Cave 7 and dated from around 50 A.D., twenty years before the destruction of Herod's Temple, just as Jesus predicted would happen (Mark 13:2.) They were written on Papyrus, a very strong type of paper created from the papyrus plant, which had become very brittle after 2,000 years.

☪

SÛRAH 99

THE EARTHQUAKE (Az-Zilzâl)
(Revealed at Mecca)

In the name of Allah, the Beneficient, the Merciful.

(99:1) When Earth is shaken with her (final) earthquake,

Ali translates (final) earthquake as *utmost convolution,* Arberry translates *"(final) earthquake"* as a *"mighty shaking,"* and Shakir translates it as a *"violent shaking."* At the End of the Age, Allah will cause a great earthquake; the result will be the end of the world. As we continue to compare the Koran with the Bible, we agree that this seems to be referring to the signs given by Jesus *(Isa)* when He tells His disciples about what to expect regarding the End of the Age (Matthew 24:3; Mark 13:4; Revelation 16:20).

> So they asked Him [Jesus, about the End of the Age], saying, "Teacher, but when will these things be? And what sign *will there be* when these things are about to take place?"

And He said: "Take heed that you not be deceived. For many will come in My name, saying, 'I am *He,*' and, 'The time has drawn near.' Therefore do not go after them. But when you hear of wars and commotions, do not be terrified; for these things must come to pass first, but the end *will* not *come* immediately."
Then He said to them, "Nation will rise against nation, and kingdom against kingdom. And there will be great earthquakes in various places, and famines and pestilences; and there will be fearful sights and great signs from heaven" (Luke 21:7-11, NKJV, bracketed clarifications mine, emphasis added).

The Old Testament also prophesies the events of the End of the Age when Jesus returns accompanied by a great earthquake:

Behold, the day of the LORD come, and your spoil shall be divided in the midst of you.

For I will gather all nations against Jerusalem to battle; and the city shall be taken, and the houses rifled, and the women ravished; and half of the city shall go forth into captivity, and the residue of the people shall not be cut off from the city.

Then shall the LORD go forth, and fight against those nations, as when he fought in the day of battle.

And His feet shall stand in that day upon the Mount of Olives, which is before Jerusalem on the east, *and the mount of Olives shall cleave [split] in the midst thereof toward the east and toward the west, and there shall be a very great valley; and half of the mountain shall remove toward the north, and half of it toward the south* (Zechariah 14:1-4, bracketed clarification mine, emphasis added).

(99:2) And Earth yields up her burdens,

This is probably referring to the earth having various and diverse volcanic eruptions—which are preceded by earthquakes and continue afterward with aftershocks—causing graves to give up their dead. The Bible also talks about the earth giving up her burden in the form of graves giving up their dead:

For the Lord Himself shall descend from Heaven with a shout, with the voice of the archangel, and with the trump of God: and the *dead in Christ shall rise first* (1 Thessalonians 4:16, emphasis added).

In a moment, in the twinkling of an eye, at the last trump: for the trumpet shall sound, and *the dead shall*

428

be raised incorruptible, and we shall be changed (1 Corinthians 15:52, emphasis added).

(99:3) And man say: "What ails her? "

This sûrah seems to be using a lot of exaggeration to make a point. The word "man" represents mankind. People are concerned about what is going on around them and are starting to panic.

(99:4) That day she will relate her chronicles,

> *That day will be the end of the world, and the earth will recall her history throughout all of time (paraphrase mine).*

(99:5) Because your Lord inspires her [the earth] (bracketed clarification mine).

According to this verse, the event referred to in verse 4 will happen because Allah stimulates the earth.

(99:6) That day mankind will issue forth in scattered groups to be shown their deeds.

The Koran is talking about the end of the world when people will be gathered up and separated into various groups, and all they have done—both good and bad—will be revealed; yet before that day comes, we are told that the eternal war against the Jews (as we see continuing in the Middle East today) must come to a conclusion because:

> *The last hour would not come unless the Muslims will fight against the Jews and the Muslims would kill them until the Jews would hide themselves behind a stone or a tree and a stone or a tree would say: "Muslim, or the servant of Allah, there is a Jew behind me; come and kill him;" but the Gharqad [Boxthorn] tree would not say, "for it is the tree of the Jews" (Hadith, Sahih Muslim Book 41, No. 6985, bracketed clarification mine).*

(99:7) And whoso does good an atom's weight will see it then

This verse says that nothing will escape Allah, even the smallest good work will be noticed; however, our works will not impress the God of the Bible:

For by grace are you saved through faith; and that not of yourselves: it is the gift of God: Not of works, lest any man should boast (Ephesians 2:8-9).

(99:8) And whoso does ill an atom's weight will see it then.

And those who have even participated in the least small bit of evil will be exposed.

This is an example of the Koran's flirtation with atomic structure. We address the Koran's use of the term "atom" in Volume III of our three-volume series, *Islam Exposed, Islam: Science—Bible—Archaeology and Myths,* where we offer an extensive exposé of the scientific compatibility of the atom and theology.

We have found that science is more aligned with the Bible as well as its concept of the Trinity, as opposed to the Koran, when it states: "*... call on those whom you set up beside [associate with] Allah! They possess not an atom's weight either in the Heavens or in the earth, nor have they any share [partnership] ...*" (Sûrah 34:22, M. Pickthall, bracketed clarifications mine, emphasis added).

Quantum physics explains how the atom might hold the key to how an entity can be in more than one place at the same time, even when separated by light years apart, yet not truly be separated. (A light-year is the distance it takes for light to travel in one year, which is equal to 5.9 trillion miles).

☪

SÛRAH 100

(THE CHARGERS)
THE COURSERS (Al-Ā'âdiyât)
(Revealed at Mecca)

In the name of Allah, the Beneficient, the Merciful.

(100:1) By the snorting [horses] courses [galloping] (bracketed clarification mine)

The title of this sûrah is a bit uncertain until we read the first verse, which uses the image of a cavalry charge (charging warhorses). Yusuf Ali's expansion of this passage affirms that assumption when he writes:

By the (steeds) that run, with panting (breath).

It appears Gabriel is talking about galloping horses, as suggested by their snorting or heavy breathing. Ali agrees here by his insertion of "steeds."

(100:2) Striking sparks of fire

This could possibly refer to horse hooves striking rocks causing sparks to fly.

(100:3) And scouring to the raid at dawn,

This appears to be a war-like raiding party ready to attack its target first thing in the morning.

Historically, Arabs would attack their enemies at early dawn while their intended victims were still asleep, only to be abruptly awakened and confused.

(100:4) Then, therewith, with their trail of dust,

These raiders are moving with tremendous speed, which stirs up clouds of dust.

431

(100:5) Cleaving, as one, the center (of the foe),

They came upon their helpless foe very quickly and cut right through the middle of them. This concludes the adventurous story of the morning raiders on horseback. Pickthall observes in his footnote, "The meaning of the first five verses is by no means clear."

(100:6) Lo! man is an ingrate unto his Lord

In what is not an uncommon event, we now shift directions in this disjointed sûrah. This verse leads us to understand that most people do not appreciate Allah.

(100:7) And look! he is a witness unto that [through his actions] (bracketed clarification mine);

People show who they are, not necessarily by what they say but by what they do.

(100:8) And lo! in the love of wealth he is violent.

A person may covet wealth, so much so that he is willing to rob or even kill to acquire it.

(100:9) Know he not that, when the contents of the graves are poured forth

For whatever reason, this incomplete sentence cannot be understood without reading the next verse.

(100:10) And the secrets of the breasts are made known,

Continuing from the last verse, we are informed that everything everyone has done, including that which is hidden deep inside of them, will become exposed.

(100:11) On that day will their Lord be perfectly informed concerning them.

Sûrah 100 concludes with this warning:

On that day, Allah will know what an evil person this thief was and punish him accordingly (verses 9-11, paraphrase mine).

In actuality, Sûrah 100 was the 14th revelation Muhammad received in Mecca. There is no biblical parallel for this verse.

Allah's dislike for thieves and robbers stands out overall in this sûrah. When Muhammad received this at that time, he was militarily weak and unable to conduct raids, ambush disbelievers, and subdue them as he did later when he grew stronger, as recorded in the Koran and Hadiths.

In the Koran, the fact is that an entire sûrah was dedicated to taking spoils or booty (plunder). That chapter is Sûrah 8, "SPOILS OF WAR," which was the 88th sûrah revealed to Muhammad long after this sûrah (Sûrah 100 the 14th sûrah) was given to him at a time when he was weak. In Sûrah 8, titled "AL-ANFAL" (SPOILS OF WAR), the opening verse reads:

They ask you (O Muhammad) of the spoils of war. Say: "The spoils of war belong to Allah and the messenger," so keep your duty to Allah, and adjust the matter of your difference, and obey Allah and His messenger, if you are (true) believers (Sûrah 8:1).

We also read in Sûrah 8:41 that provisions have been made for the relatives of the jihadists *"(who have need) and orphans and the needy.* While Allah is always granted a portion of the spoils (loot taken by force), he always receives a cut of the loot even if he is not actually a participant in the battle:

And know that whatever you take as spoils of war, look! a fifth thereof is for Allah, and for the messenger [Muhammad] and for the kinsman (who have need) and orphans and the needy and the wayfarer [traveler], if you believe in Allah and that which We revealed unto Our slave on the Day of Discrimination, the day when the two armies met. And Allah is Able to do all things. And know that whatever you take as spoils of war, indeed! a fifth thereof is for Allah, and for the messenger and for the kinsman (who hath need) and orphans and the needy and the wayfarer, if you believe in Allah and that which We revealed unto Our slave

433

[Muhammad] on the Day of Discrimination, the day when the two armies met. And Allah is Able to do all things (Pickthall, Surah 8:41, bracketed clarifications mine).

It is also interesting to note in another sûrah that Muhammad did not have to share the booty with those who were wealthier than others (himself excluded, of course). Allah left the division of spoils up to Muhammad to decide who would receive the plunder:

That which Allah gives as spoil unto His messenger [Muhammad] from the people of the townships, it is for Allah and His messenger and for the near of kin and the orphans and the needy and the wayfarer [traveler], that it become not a commodity between the rich among you. And whatsoever the messenger gives you, take it. And whatsoever he forbids, abstain (from it). And keep your duty to Allah. Behold! Allah is stern in reprisal (Pickthall, Sûrah 59:07, bracketed clarification mine).

We would be neglectful if we did not point out that Muslim scholars and the Muslim faithful refer to the caravan raids against the Quraysh as "military expeditions," but the result is still the same. Muhammad would lie in wait for a civilian merchant caravan coming out of Mecca, attack it and then take a spoil (rob them of their goods); consequently, Muhammad would receive a fifth of whatever was stolen (Sûrah 8:41).

In *Volume, I* of *Islam Exposed: A Simple Crash Course on Islam*, Chapter 3, in the section titled, "The Spreading of Islam through the Sword," we address those koranic revelations regarding highway robbery. Robbing and killing are permissible if it finances the furtherance of Islam. (Sûrah 2:106 says Allah can go back on his word and change his mind if he chooses to do so.)

☪

SÛRAH 101

THE CALAMITY (Al-Qāri'a)
(Revealed at Mecca)

In the name of Allah, the Beneficient, the Merciful.

(101:1) The Calamity!

Arberry translates *"Calamity"* as *"Clatter."* Yusuf Ali uses the word *"Clamour"* while Shakir agrees with Pickthall and translates it *"calamity,"* which is the title of this sûrah.

(101:2) What is the Calamity?

Now the reader is asked what all the noise and clatter is.

(101:3) Ah, what will convey unto you what the Calamity is!

A.J. Arberry's translation:

> *And what shall teach you what is the clatter (catastrophe!)?*

Gabriel is building the suspense. He has already established that there is an imminent catastrophe, and then proceeds to ask the obvious:

> *"What is it?" "Who can explain it?" "What is to be learned from this horror?" (Paraphrased.)*

(101:4) A day wherein mankind will be as thickly-scattered moths
We are now given the answer: *"The Calamity"* (the title of this sûrah) is an allegory of the Last Day when incalculable numbers of people will be resurrected in a panic—like swarms of moths!

(101:5) And the mountains will become as carded wool.

This passage is not clear, even with A.J. Arberry's translation:

And the mountains shall be like plucked wool-tufts.

Corded wool is a process of combing the wool fibers so that the wool lays parallel to each other, and it removes any impurities that may have been attached to the recently sheered wool (see picture of one type of tool used at the right). Perhaps the mountains will no longer be majestic and solid; they will become flimsy and crumble away.

Fig. 6. Wool Cording Tools

In the Bible, the mountains become flat at the *End of the Age*, which this verse addresses. The following passage is the Bible's *End of the Age* scenario:

And there were noises and thunderings and lightnings; and there was a great earthquake, such a mighty and great earthquake as had not occurred since men were on the earth. Now the great city was divided into three parts, and the cities of the nations fell. And great Babylon was remembered before God, to give her the cup of the wine of the fierceness of His wrath. Then every island fled away, *and the mountains were not found* (Revelation 16:18-20, NKJV).

(101:6) Then, as for him whose scales are heavy (with good works),

This is another disjointed verse, but in all fairness, separating the Koran's dialogue into verses, and then numbering them, were added at a later time, long after Muhammad.

(101:7) He will live a pleasant life.

Together with the previous verse, this reads, "*Then, as for him whose scales are heavy (with good works), He will receive a pleasant life.*" In other words, the one whose good deeds outweigh their bad deeds will be eternally blessed. As we discussed, this sûrah is referring to Judgment Day, which will be a catastrophe for many, except in this case, where apparently a person's good works are tipping the scales of justice in their favor.

Nevertheless, this concept of scales weighing each person's deeds is not a biblical concept, apart from the allegorical passage found in Daniel 5:27, which we will address shortly. The Bible teaches everyone will stand before the judgment seat of God on the last day (Romans 14:10) to make an accounting of their lives, but there are no scales involved. The Bible also teaches that only a blood sacrifice can atone for our sins (Leviticus 4:1-4; Hebrews 9:22).

Evidently, the notion of doing good works as a covering (i.e., atoning for) our sins was created by the rabbis after the Temple was destroyed in 70 A.D. The cold and frightening reality from the Hebrew perspective was that there could no longer be any blood sacrifices offered to God in the Holy Temple to cover their sins. Therefore, an alternative consisting of doing good works was created based on a verse found in Hosea, Chapter 6, which reads: "For I desired mercy, not sacrifice; and the knowledge of God more than burnt offerings" (Hosea 6:6).

In this passage, using scales for judging the good and evil deeds in a person's life was probably influenced by the story in the Book of Daniel when God judged the son of King Nebuchadnezzar, whose name was Belshazzar, and gave the Kingdom of Babylon to Darius, the Medo-Persian. The story is found in Daniel, Chapter 5, when King Belshazzar held a large banquet (drunken feast) and called for the sacred utensils to be taken from the Holy Temple in Jerusalem to be used by his guests. By doing so, he defiled his debauchery filled banquet and out of nowhere, a hand began floating in the air and proceeded to write with its finger on the plastered wall the mysterious words, *"MENE, MENE, TEKEL, UPHARSIN;"* so Daniel, a prophet of God, was summoned to explain the meaning. Daniel told the King:

 And this is the writing that was written, *MENE, MENE, TEKEL, UPHARSIN.* This is the interpretation of the thing:*'MENE;* God has numbered [the days of] your kingdom, and finished it. *'TEKEL;* You are weighed in the balances and are found wanting. *'PERES;* Your kingdom is divided, and given to the Medes and Persians' (Daniel 5:25-28, bracketed clarification mine, emphases added).

This is only one of two times where scales are mentioned in Scripture and only one time for judging a person's works while here on earth. It seems the scales of judgment event was more for the benefit of King Belshazzar and his banquet guests; nevertheless, in this case, the scales had nothing to do with the afterlife and everything to do with ripping away the kingdom from Belshazzar and giving it to Darius in this world. The other reference is found in Job, "Let me be weighed in an even balance that God may know mine integrity" (Job 31:6). Like the previous passage, Job is defending his integrity and has nothing to do with the hereafter.

We should point out, however, in the final book of the Bible, we find the Four Horsemen of the Apocalypse with one of them a Rider on a Black Horse, who is holding a set of scales. Muhammad might very well have been thinking about that rider as he revealed this verse: *"as for him whose scales are heavy."*

This is the description the Bible gives of the rider on a black horse holding the scales, which has nothing to do with weighing a person's deeds on earth, but rather as a means of balancing the cost of food (food on one side balanced by its cost on the other):

 When He opened the third seal, I heard the third living creature say, "Come and see." So I looked, and behold, a black horse, and he who sat on it had *a pair of scales* in his hand. And I heard a voice in the midst of the four living creatures saying, "A quart of wheat for a denarius, and three quarts of barley for a denarius; and do not harm the oil and the wine" (Revelation 6:5-6, NKJV, emphasis added).

(101:8) But as for him whose scales are light,

However, it seems for the one whose good deeds do not outweigh the bad ....

(101:9) A bereft [bereaved] and Hungry One will be his mother,

Out of our four translations, A.J. Arberry ties these two verses together best when he writes:

Shall plunge in the womb of the Pit [of Hell] (bracketed clarification mine).

Together, Sûrah 101:8-9 tells the readers the one whose good deeds do not outweigh the bad shall be plunged into the pit of Hell.

(101.10) Ah, what will convey unto you what she is! -

The tension builds as we are asked if we have figured what she is.

(101.11) Raging Fire.

She is the fire of Hell!

☪

SÛRAH 102

(THE RIVALRY)
RIVALRY IN WORLDLY INCREASE (Takathur)
(Revealed at Mecca)

In the name of Allah, the Beneficient, the Merciful.

(102:1) Rivalry in worldly increase distracts you

This verse deals with greedy competition and self-glorification between people, either as individuals or groups.

When compared to the Bible, this is very similar to the biblical concept of focusing too much on the creation of wealth:

> For the love of money is the root of all evil: which while some coveted after, they have erred from the faith, and pierced themselves through with many sorrows (1 Timothy 6:10).

However, the creation of wealth is not in and of itself sinful:

> But you shall remember the LORD your God: for it is He who gives you the power to get wealth, that He may establish His covenant which He swore unto your fathers, as it is this day (Deuteronomy 8:18).

(102:2) Until you come to the graves.

People work their entire lives plotting and scheming to gain wealth, only to lose it all when they die. Jesus *(Isa)* cautions us:

> Do not lay up for yourselves treasures on earth, where moth and rust destroy and where thieves break in and steal; but lay up for yourselves treasures in heaven, where neither moth nor rust destroys and

where thieves do not break in and steal. For where your treasure is, there your heart will be also (Matthew 6:19-21, NKJV).

(102:3) Nay, but you will come to know!

However, the time will come when we will be told that those who compete for wealth will finally realize...

(102:4) Nay, but you will come to know!

This stanza is repeated for the sake of importance and setting us up for the next verse.

(102:5) Nay, would that you knew (now) with a sure knowledge!

Now we are told for the third time, "No, if only you really understood, you would realize ..." (paraphrase mine).

(102:6) For you will behold hell-fire.

Now for the big reveal! All your hard work is for nothing because your ultimate reward is HELL!

(102:7) Aye [yes], you will behold it [Hell] with sure vision (bracketed clarifications mine).

We are told in the affirmative, for all your competitiveness, you will clearly see it.

(102:8) Then, on that day, you will be asked concerning [your past earthly life] pleasure (bracketed clarification mine).

We conclude this Sûrah with A.J. Arberry's translation of verse 102:8.
    ... then you shall be questioned that day concerning true bliss.

Presumably, we are taught here the irony of working hard all of our lives for gain, only to gain Hell in the end. Then we are asked if all that hard work was worth it (i.e., a short life of wealth followed by an eternity in Hell).

☪

SÛRAH 103

THE DECLINING DAY ('Aṣr)
(Revealed at Mecca)

In the name of Allah, the Beneficient, the Merciful.

(103:1) By the declining day,

This brief sûrah seems to be a shortened representation of man's life and what he needs to do to assure paradise for himself when he reaches the last days of his life.

(103:2) Surely! man is in a state of loss,

Not only are we able to lose our lives in this world, but also in the next. The body will die, but the spirit is immortal and will live forever—the only question is where? The Bible teaches, "... it is appointed unto men once to die but after this the judgment ..." (Hebrews 9:27).

(103:3) Save [except] those who believe and do good works, and exhort one another to truth and exhort one another to endurance (bracketed clarification mine).

The last verse in this sûrah is a continuation of the previous verse, which comprises this sûrah. The thought concludes by affirming salvation can be achieved through good works and sharing Islam with one another.

The Bible tells us just the opposite: works do not save us: For *by grace are you saved* through faith; and that not of yourselves: it is the gift of God: *Not of works,* lest any man should boast (Ephesians 2:8-9, emphasis added).

continued

NOTE: This is the second shortest sûrah in the Koran after Sûrah 108, titled Al-Kauther (Abundance, Plenty).

☪

SÛRAH 104

(THE GOSSIPMONGER MONGER)
THE TRADUCER[1] (Humaza)
(Revealed at Mecca)

In the name of Allah, the Beneficent, the Merciful.

(104:1) Woe unto every slandering traducer,

This sûrah begins by wishing grief on those who are backbiters. Backbiters and gossipers are a problem that transcends every culture. The Bible addresses this, including one of the Ten Commandments, which warns us about lying and telling false stories about others:

You shall *not bear false witness* against your neighbor (Exodus 20:16, emphasis added).

And even as they did not like to retain God in their knowledge, God gave them over to a reprobate mind, to do those things which are not convenient;

Being filled with all unrighteousness, fornication, wickedness, covetousness, *maliciousness;* full of envy, murder, debate, deceit, malignity; whisperers, *Backbiters*, haters of God, despiteful, proud, boasters, inventors of evil things, disobedient to parents (Romans 1:28-30, emphasis added).

(104:2) Who has gathered wealth (of this world) and arranged it.

Muhammad Habib Shakir translates this passage better:

Who amasses wealth and considers it a provision (against mishap).
Allah discourages saving too much money for a rainy day. This thought is continued in the next few verses.

(104:3) He thinks that his wealth will render him immortal.

Realistically, what might be presented here is that a stingy person tends to depend more on his savings than Allah for protection against future emergencies.

(104:4) Nay [No], but verily [truly] he will be flung to the Consuming One (Bracketed clarification mine).

This is a "tease" verse since we are not told here who the *consuming one* is. Muhammad Habib Shakir renders this passage:

Nay! He shall most certainly be hurled into the crushing disaster.

So whether he is consumed or crushed, this person will still suffer a disaster. Despite all of his scheming and saving, his treasure will not save him.

(104:5) Nay [No], but verily [truly] he will be flung to the Consuming One (bracketed clarification mine).

Gabriel is once again using a literary device to build suspense.

(104:6) (It is) the fire of Allah, kindled,

This and verse 5 are self-explanatory. The "Consuming One" is the fire of Hell created by Allah

(104:7) Which leaps up over the hearts (of men).

We are told that this fire consumes what their hearts hold dear—their wealth!

(104:8) Look! it is closed in on them
They are confined and encircled by Hell's fire.

(104:9) In outstretched columns.

This verse is an amplification of verse 7, explaining that the encircling fire towers over them like tall columns (of fire)!

OBSERVATION: As you read these short sûrahs at the end of Volume II of the Koran, keep in mind they were actually the first revelations given to Muhammad by the angel Gabriel. In these first revelations, we see no outreach of love from Allah, only the threat of Hell-fire. There is no doubt that we would be hard-put to find an Allah of love anywhere in the Koran.

The God of the Bible constantly reinforces His love for us. One example is found in 1 John 4:7-21 where we find the love of God mentioned 27 times. Someone could not be faulted if they were to doubt if the God of the Bible wrote the Koran, and if He did, why is the love of God is missing in the Koran? This is only one of many biblical passages we have contrasted with the Koran.

NOTES:
1.	False accuser, slander

☪

SÛRAH 105

THE ELEPHANT (Fil)
(Revealed at Mecca)

In the name of Allah, the Beneficient, the Merciful.

(105:1) Have you not seen how your Lord dealt with the owners of the Elephant?

It is believed that this incredible story, and the miraculous defeat of the mighty elephant army, ushered in the birth of Muhammad. Could this event have been an omen of the future Prophet of Islam? Is this why Gabriel had Muhammad placed it in Koran? It does make for a great story and as a tie-in to Muhammad's birth; it is also included in the Hadith:

Narrated Al-Muttalib bin 'Abdullah bin Qais bin Makhramah:

...from his father, from his grandfather, that he said: *I and the Messenger of Allah*, were born in the *Year of the Elephant* (emphasis added) [1]

This is a fascinating story—which was possibly intended to tie a miraculous event (such as the birth of Jesus) to the birth of Muhammad—while also providing the Koran with at least one miracle. Even so, recent historians have debunked Muhammad's birth in the *Year of the Elephant*—as simply a myth. [2]

This sûrah is regarding an Arabian myth about either a Yemen Jewish or a Yemen Christian leader who attacked Mecca with an army using war elephants. This story is intriguing because—the logistics alone—to move a herd of elephants across the Arabian Desert would have to be an incredible endeavor if, in fact, it could be accomplished at all!

449

(105:2) Did He not bring their stratagem [of war] to naught [nothing]. [?] (Bracketed clarifications mine.)

Muhammad Habib Shakir translation clarifies this passage:

Did He not cause their war to end in confusion?

We know from the previous verse that these elephants and their handlers are an army, although how they managed to deploy them in the Arabian Peninsula is unclear.

(105:3) And send against them swarms of flying creatures,

Yusuf Ali translates it this way:

And He sent against them Flights of Birds,

Allah chooses to deal with this mighty army of elephants by sending a flock of birds against them.

(105:4) Which pelted them [the elephants] with stones of baked clay (bracketed clarification mine),

Apparently, the birds are armed with ammunition, which they *"pelted"* down on the men and their elephants. The elephants were probably not too troubled by the bird's attempt to harm them, but it could have been very troubling for the soldiers to hold up very long under a constant barrage of being pelted! One curious observation is, who baked the small clay stones, and why?

(105:5) And made them like green crops devoured (by cattle)?

Pickthall and Shakir use a question mark in this verse, while Arberry and Ali do not.

A.J. Arberry relates *"green crops"* to *"grass."*

450

And He [Allah] made them [the men and their elephants] like green blades [of grass] devoured (bracketed clarification mine).

Either way, the picture of what was left of the men and their elephants seems to have been total destruction.

As an interesting side note, Muhammad Khan explains that elephants could not have been introduced to the Arabian Peninsula because of its arid environment and lack of water. Elephants require 330 to 375 pounds of food and consume about 18-26 gallons of water each day. They spend almost 80% of the day eating; therefore, deserts could not sustain elephants, even for a short raid. That being the case, elephants would not be able to travel a hundred miles through the Arabian Desert to Mecca since the Red Sea is the only large body of water, and because of its salt content, it is undrinkable. (Camels, like elephants, drink up to 40 gallons of water a day.[3] The difference is, unlike an elephant that must drink water daily, a camel can go days, some zoologists say even months, in cooler weather without water.)

Khan also reveals that there is a pre-Islamic myth regarding what many Arabs considered fact. The myth is a story about a man named Abraha, a monotheist, and his marauding army of soldiers with elephants, who were intent on destroying Allah's house, the Ka'aba in Mecca.

Even more important than the destruction of the Ka'aba, General Abraha was intent on ending Pagan polytheism; however, the elephant army was defeated by Allah's use of many species of birds armed with ammunition.

This seemingly feeble adversary bombarded General Abraha and his elephant army with wave after wave of rocks and pebbles, forcing him and his elephant army to retreat, leaving the Arabian tribes free to worship their 360 Pagan gods, of which Allah was one. The paradox surrounding this story is that Allah defeated an army of monotheists in order to preserve polytheism.

The reason why Allah would want to include a myth, especially this myth, in the Koran remains a mystery[4] unless, of course, as we

451

mentioned at the outset of this sûrah, there seems to be an alleged relationship to the birth of Muhammad. This "miraculous" tie-in is echoed by several Muslims (see vs. 1) like Ibrahim AbuNab, who would also have us believe that the year Mecca was spared of the elephant onslaught was also the same year in which Muhammad was born (570 A.D.).[5]

NOTES:

1. Jami' at-Tirmidhi, *Chapters on Virtues*—Grade: Sahih (Darussalam). English reference: Vol. 1, Book 46, Hadith 3619 Arabic reference: Book 49, Hadith 3979.
2. John L. Esposito, *The Oxford Dictionary of Islam* (New York: Oxford), 2003. "Historians today believe that this event occurred at least a decade prior to the birth of Muhammad."
3. "Elephants and Water," *Canisius Ambassadors for Conservation*. CAC Is a Program of the Institute for the Study of Human-Animal Relations at Canisius College in Buffalo, New York. N.p., n.d. WEB. 24 Aug. 2013.
4. Muhammad A. Khan, "The Chapter Sura Fil (Elephant) of the Qur'an Written Long Before the Advent of Islam." Web. 31 December 2013.
5. Ibrahim AbuNab, "Sûrahs 105 Al-Feel." Sûrahs 105 Al-Feel. N.p., n.d. Web. 18 October 2014.

☪

SÛRAH 106

"WINTER" OR "QURAYSH" (Quraysh)
(Revealed at Mecca)

In the name of Allah, the Beneficient, the Merciful.

(106:1) For the taming [civilizing] of Quraysh.

Arberry uses the word "*composing,* while Muhammad Habib Shakir uses "*taming.*" Yusuf Ali uses the word "*covenants*" but clarifies the meaning of all the words used in his parenthetical clarification:

> For the covenants (Of security and safeguard enjoyed) by the Quraysh,

The Quraysh were the powerful merchant tribe who controlled Mecca during the time of Muhammad. In his commentary, Yusuf Ali says the Quraysh controlled both Mecca and the Ka'aba. The Ka'aba is located near the center of the Great Mosque in Mecca, which is central to the Arabian Peninsula. It housed all 360 Pagan gods of the Arabian tribes, which allowed the Quraysh to be in the enviable position of prestige and power to broker deals and make covenants between the tribes. (See the next verse.)

(As a point of interest, Muhammad was related to members of the Quraysh tribe. Other spellings, in addition to Quarysh, are Qureish, Quraish, Quresh, Qurish, Kuraish, and Coreish).

(106:2) For their taming (We cause) the caravans to set forth in winter and summer.

Because of Mecca's location, they were able to go on their trade journeys to Yemen in the winter, as well as the cooler regions of Syria

and the north in the summer. Because of their travels, the Quraysh "...
became practiced travelers and merchants, [and] acquired much
knowledge of the world and many arts .... "[1]

(106:3) So let them worship the Lord of this House,

This is referring to the Ka'aba after Muhammad conquered Mecca and
purged it of all the other Pagan gods, leaving only Allah to be the *"Lord
of this House."*

(106:4) Who has fed them against hunger

Unlike the other three translators, for whatever reason, Pickthall
divides the last verse into two separate verses; therefore, we will hold
our commentary until the end of the next and final verse in this sûrah.

(106:5) And has made them safe from fear.

Beginning with verse 4, where we read, *"Who has fed them against
hunger,"* tells us that the caravans of the Quraysh not only enriched
them but also drew people from all over to visit and worship in Mecca.
This concluding verse assures the Quraysh tribe, " *And has made them
safe from fear"* because the Ka'aba housed Allah and, therefore, placed
Mecca in a safer position due to its religious importance and centrality
to all the other tribes; this allowed it to be more neutral and avoid the
constant tribal warfare.

The Bible has several similar passages regarding God's protection. We
have listed two:

Yea, though I walk through the valley of the shadow
of death, I will fear no evil: for You are with me; your
rod and your staff they comfort me (Psalm 23:4).

What shall we then say to these things? If God be for
us, who can be against us? (Romans 8:31.)

CONSIDER: Even though Muhammad was related to the Quraysh tribe, he later went to war against them which allowed for this sûrah. The Quraysh tribe revered the moon god, Hubal, also known as Allah, as their tribal deity.[2] Muhammad later converted their god into the god of the Koran and the alleged god of the Bible. Julius Wellhausen (1844-1918) was a Bible scholar and orientalist who teaches Hubal, another name for Allah.[3] Authors David Leeming[4] and Mircea Eliade[5] say Hubal was a god of war and rain deity.

NOTES:

1. Abdullah Yusuf Ali, footnote 6277 for Sûrah 106:5.
2. Hafiz Ghulam Sarwar. *Muhammad: the Holy Prophet* (Lahore Pakistan: Muhammad Ashraf Publ., 1974), 18-19. (This is a Muslim source. *Muhammad Ashraf* is a publishing house that is over 100 years old.
3. "II. The Religion of the Pre-Islamic Arabs"
   "The life of the pre-Islamic Arabs, especially in the Hijaz, depended on trade and they made a trade of their religion as well. About four hundred years before the birth of Muhammad, one Amr bin Lahyo bin, Harath bin Amr ul-Qais bin Thalaba bin Azd bin Khalan bin Babalyun bin Saba, a descendant of Qahtan and king of Hijaz, had put an idol called "Hubal" on the roof of the Kaba…. Besides Hubal, there was another idol called "Shams" placed on the roof of the Kaba…. The blood of the sacrificial animals brought by the pilgrims was offered to the deities in the Kaba, and sometimes even human beings were sacrificed and offered to the god…. Besides idol-worship, they also worshipped the stars, the sun, and the moon." Gerald R. Hawting, *The Idea of Idolatry and the Emergence of Islam: From Polemic to History* (Cambridge: Cambridge University Press, 1999), 112.

4. David Adams Leeming, *Jealous Gods and Chosen People: The Myology of the Middle East* (New York: Oxford Press, 2004), 121.
5. Eliade Adams, *The Encyclopedia of Religion,* Vol. I (New York: Macmillan, 1987), 121.

☪

SÛRAH 107

SMALL KINDNESSES (Mā'ūn)
(Revealed at Mecca)

In the name of Allah, the Beneficent, the Merciful.

(107:1) Have you observed him who belieth [forgoes] religion? (Bracketed clarification mine.)

A.J. Arberry and Muhammad Habib Shakir better translate the meaning of this passage, as noted below:

See you one who denies the Judgment (to come)? (Arberry)

Have you considered him who calls the judgment a lie? (Shakir)

This verse is referring to those who deny the End of the Age and the judgment to come.

(107:2) That is he who repels the orphan,

This verse describes an individual male who shows no charity toward those less fortunate, such as the poor orphans.

(107:3) And urges not the feeding of the needy.

This is also fairly self-explanatory. The man who calls into question Islam (verse 1) tells others not to concern themselves with the less fortunate.

(107:4) Ah, woe unto worshippers

Gabriel is pronouncing grief on people who worship, which is confusing on the surface, but we need to read on to understand his point.

(107:5) Who are heedless of their prayer;

Now we see to whom the woe or grief is directed; it is for those who neglect their prayers.

(107:6) Who would be seen (at worship)

Arberry translates this to say:

> *To those who make display [of their worshiping] (bracketed clarification mine.)*

The continuation of this sentence is suggesting that the objects (people) of this sûrah are hypocrites who only want to be seen worshipping, so others will be impressed by their devotion.

(107:7) Yet refuse small kindnesses!

This sûrah ends with this verse. It explains—while they appear to be godly—these people are neither truthful nor charitable.

NOTE: Although this sûrah has seven verses, it is comprised from only three sentences.

☪

SÛRAH 108

ABUNDANCE (Kâu<u>th</u>ar)
(Revealed at Mecca)

In the name of Allah, the Beneficient, the Merciful.

(108:1) Look! We have given you Abundance;

Gabriel is telling Muhammad that Allah has given him great wealth.

(108:2) So pray unto your Lord, and sacrifice.

Gabriel continues:

> *Because of your blessings, you should show Allah your appreciation through prayer and sacrifice (paraphrase mine).*

(108:3) See! it is your insulter (and not you) who is without posterity.

Gabriel is encouraging Muhammad to watch those who do not accept what he is preaching because they will be the ones who are cursed. Muhammad's enemies will not be allowed the hope of passing on what they have through their children.

It is not clear what this verse has to do with divine revelation to the world; it seems to be directed more toward bolstering Muhammad's self-esteem than a revelation for others. Some Islamic scholars suggest that this was given to Muhammad during the time when he was facing a lot of painful taunts and incidents from his enemies.

While Sûrah 108 is one of the last sûrahs given toward the end of the second volume of the Koran, it was the 15th revelation given to

Muhammad near the beginning of his "ministry," a time when he was militarily weak.

NOTE: This is the shortest sûrah in the Koran.

SÛRAH 109

THE DISBELIEVERS (Kāfirūn)
(Revealed at Mecca)

In the name of Allah, the Beneficient, the Merciful.

(109:1) Say [Muhammad]: "O disbelievers!" (Bracketed clarification mine.).

Once again, in this early sûrah, Muhammad is addressing those who will not accept Islam.

(109:2) I worship not that which you worship;

Muhammad is confronting those who will not accept him and his message from Allah. He acknowledges that he does not worship the Pagan gods.

(109:3) Nor worship you that which I worship.

Muhammad is addressing the obvious—those to whom he is speaking had not recognized his newly reinvented monotheistic, formerly Pagan, tribal moon god, Allah. In context, this seems less like a revelation from a deity and more of a conciliatory speech from a man finding himself in a weak position and not wanting to be considered offensive. This is one of the earlier revelations given in Mecca when Muhammad was relatively weak and did not have many followers. (This was the 18th revelation given to Muhammad.)

(109:4) And I shall not worship that which you worship.

There is no compromising for the sake of dialogue with these infidels! However, Muhammad now has their undivided attention.

(109:5) Nor will you worship that which I worship.

This is redundant; it is just worded differently.

(109:6) Unto you your religion, and unto me my religion.

We are now able to see that this sûrah is one of the first revelations given to Muhammad (the 18th) when he only had a handful of followers. Here Muhammad is speaking passively, accommodating, and is open-minded. He is not forceful or intolerant and is without compromise as he became later on as his ranks grew. It is difficult to imagine that Gabriel is giving Muhammad these conciliatory, moderate and restrained words, considering the fiery rhetoric Gabriel later espouses. To be sure, there is no parallel passage we can find in the Bible—anywhere—displaying such timidity offered by a prophet of God with the possible exception of Jonah, who feared to confront the ruthless Ninevites.

To be sure, this is one of the favorite Koran verses that Muslims love to recite to prove Islam is a "religion of peace," and they would never force anyone to accept Islam. It is also known as *kitman*, which incorporates truth in order to deceive a nonbeliever. While this is an actual verse (truth), it has been abrogated (replaced) by many later, hostile verses.

CONSIDER: This sûrah is the 18th revelation that was among the first revelations Allah gave to Muhammad through the angel Gabriel.[1] It came at a time when the polytheists of Mecca were giving Muhammad some trouble,[2] thereby necessitating the need of a conciliatory revelation of tolerance from Allah. This is quite a contrast to later sûrahs, such as Sûrah 9:5 where Allah tells Muhammad to lie in wait and force Islam on the ambushed, weary unbeliever through the sword. This is also one of the "proof-texts" Muslims like to point to in an attempt to convince the naive western culture that Islam is a "religion of peace."

NOTES:

1. Abdulmageed Falah, "Grammatical Opinions of Abu Hayyan Andalusi between Theory and Practice." Arab Journal for the Humanities. Academic Publication Council, Kuwait University: 29, No. 116 (2011), n.p.
2. The Meccans were tolerant of Muhammad's new religion since there were hundreds of other Arabian gods—that is until he started attacking their beliefs and gods: *[The Meccans] said they had never known anything like the trouble they had endured from this fellow. He had declared their mode of life foolish, insulted their forefathers, reviled their religion, divided the community and cursed their gods* (Ibn Ishaq/Hisham 183).

    "We [the Meccans] have never seen the like of what we have endured from this man [Muhammad]. He has derided our traditional values, abused our forefathers, reviled our religion, caused division among us, and insulted our gods. We have endured a great deal from him" (al-Tabari, Vol.VI, p.101).

☪

SÛRAH 110

(THE PURITY OF THE FAITH)
SUCCOUR (An-Naṣr)
(Revealed at Al-Medina)

In the name of Allah, the Beneficent, the Merciful.

(110:1) When Allah's succour [help] and the triumph cometh (bracketed clarification mine),

Now we are addressing a forceful statement, which is that Allah brings the help needed to triumph over difficult times that give victory. The encouragement is aimed at many minority groups of Muslims who feel persecuted.

This is a biblical concept we can read in many books of the Bible:

For the LORD your God is He who goes with you, to fight for you against your enemies, to save you (Deuteronomy 20:4, NKJV).

The *righteous* cry out, and the Lord hears, And delivers them from out of all their troubles (Psalm 34:17, NKJV).

Cast your burden on the Lord, And He shall sustain you; He shall never permit the righteous to be moved (Psalm 55:22, NKJV).

He shall call upon Me, and I will answer him; I will be with him in trouble; I will deliver and honor him. With long life will I satisfy him, And show him My salvation (Psalm 91:15-16, NKJV).

465

Fear not, for I am with you; Be not be dismayed, for I *am* your God. I will strengthen you yes I will help you; I will uphold you with my righteous right hand (Isaiah 41:10, NKJV).

(110:2) *And you see mankind entering the religion of Allah in troops,*

Shakir renders this verse:

And you see men entering the religion of Allah in companies,

Gabriel is upbeat in this verse, promoting the idea there are many converts beginning to accept the religion of Islam. Those who feel despair need not worry because their small numbers will soon be in a majority status as more converts are helping to grow the faith!

It seems that the promise of triumphing over one's adversaries and problems is a powerful motivator to bring in droves of people to the ideology of Islam.

(110:3) *Then hymn the praises of your Lord, and seek forgiveness of Him. Behold! He is ever ready to show mercy.*

This passage is based on a biblical concept:

Oh, give thanks to the LORD! Call upon His name; Make known His deeds among the peoples! Sing to Him, sing psalms to Him;

Talk of all His wondrous works! Glory in His holy name; Let the hearts of those rejoice who seek the LORD! (Psalm 105:1-4, NKJV).

The previous sûrah ended on a gloomy note regarding the lack of interest people were showing in Islam; yet we see with this sûrah's upbeat theme, Gabriel encourages converts to sing the praises of Allah and repent for having ever doubted Muhammad because Allah is ready to accept and forgive them for having ever questioned his message.

Consider: We are told there is no particular order of the sûrahs because all revelations should be put in the Koran, leaving nothing out.[1] It seems very advantageous, if not a little misleading, that this triumphant sûrah is included at this particular place in the Koran. Historically, this sûrah was the last (114th) one Muhammad received when he was near his peak in both religious adherents as well as military strength; yet it is placed right after Sûrah 109, which was given when Muhammad was just starting out and relatively militarily weak (see Table 1 in our Introduction).

NOTES:

1. An exception to include everything Muhammad claimed to have received in the Koran could be the so-called satanic verses with which Satan supposedly tricked Muhammad. Those verses allowed for intercessory prayers through the three Pagan goddesses to be placed in the Koran but were later removed. (See *Volume III* of our *three-volume series, Islam Exposed, Islam: Science—Bible—Archaeology and Myths*).

   a. Christians and Jews were not the only ones who were confused by the teachings of Muhammad. The Arabs of Muhammad's day might have also felt conflicted because they were told that the Allah of the Koran had no Son, but the Allah of the Arabian pantheon had three daughters by the same names as those goddesses mentioned in the Koran's so-called *satanic verses*. One of the translators of the Koran we referred to for this book, Abdullah Yusuf Ali, explains in his footnote number 5096, on page 1445 of his book, *The Holy Qur'an, Text, Translation, and Commentary*, "Lat, Uzza, and Manat were known as "the daughters of God (Allah).""

☪

SÛRAH 111

(THE TWISTED ROPE)
PALM FIBER (Al-Masad)
(Revealed at Mecca)

In the name of Allah, the Beneficent, the Merciful.

(111:1) The power of Abû Lahab will perish, and he will perish.

Pickthall fails to identify *Abû Lahab,* yet what he does reveal is quite interesting: *"The power of Abû Lahab will perish, and he will perish."*

Yusuf Ali translates this verse as "Perish the hands of the Father of Flame! Perish he!" The "Father of Flame" spoken of by Yusuf Ali is the nickname of Muhammad's uncle *Abû Lahab.*[1]

Muhammad Habib Shakir, A.J. Arberry, and Abdullah Yusuf Ali, all include Abû Lahab's hands in this verse. Muhammad Habib Shakir explains:

> *Perdition [Hell] overtake both hands of Abu Lahab, and he will perish (bracketed clarification mine).*

A.J. Arberry titles this sûrah "Perish." This is an interesting sûrah because Abû Lahab (originally called "Abd al-'Uzzā) was the paternal half-uncle of Muhammad.[2]

Abû Lahab was also a very important leader of the Quraysh tribe, and apparently, bad blood developed between him and Muhammad because he would not accept Islam, nor would his wife, Umm Jamil bint Harb. Muhammad's aunt was known to express hateful words and actions toward him. It is said she would intermingle palm leaves with thorns, put them into bundles, and then place them on paths where

469

she knew Muhammad would be walking when the night sky was dark. She obviously wanted to cause bodily harm to her nephew.

On one occasion, Muhammad called together members of the Quraysh tribe to say that if they did not accept his new religion of Islam, Allah would punish them. His Uncle Abu called out from the crowd, "May your hands perish all this day. Is it for this purpose you have gathered us?" He then threw stones in the face of Muhammad. It is for that reason Allah gave this sûrah against Muhammad's uncle.

> NOTE: This story happened after the Bible was canonized (completed); therefore, it has no biblical relevancy.

(111:2) His wealth and gains will not exempt him.

Gabriel is reassuring Muhammad that even though his uncle is powerful, he will not profit from all of his wealth and earthly possessions.

(111:3) He will be plunged in flaming Fire,

Muhammad is further comforted to know that Allah will send his hateful uncle, who refuses to accept Islam, to Hell.

(111:4) And his wife, the wood-carrier,

We are also informed about the fate awaiting Muhammad's aunt, who hatefully used bundles of palm leaves and thorns as snares in Muhammad's path, would also carry that same wood to fuel Hell's fire!

(111:5) Will have upon her neck a halter of palm-fibre.

Apparently, the weapon of punishment for Muhammad's aunt would be the same one she used against him.

OBSERVATION: The Koran was supposed to have been created at the beginning of time, yet this petty little family schwalbe manages to be inserted in the message for mankind. Think about it. While interesting, these three sentences, which are converted into five verses, are of no relevance, benefit or concern to anyone other than Muhammad, his uncle and his aunt; nevertheless, Allah considered it so important that he made it the 6th revelation given to Muhammad so that this unforgiving condemnation towards his aunt and uncle could be forever enshrined in the Koran.

NOTES:

1. Muhammad Yusuf Ali. *The Holy Quran,* Sûrah 111:1, footnote 6294.
2. Abu Lahab (originally called "Abd al-'Uzzā") was the half-uncle of Muhammad through his paternal grandmother, Fāṭimah bint 'Amr of the Banu Makhzūm clan.

☾

SÛRAH 112

(THE PURITY OF FAITH)
THE UNITY (Ikhlāṣ)
(Revealed at Mecca)

In the name of Allah, the Beneficent, the Merciful.

(112:1) Say: "He is Allah, the One!"

This is a biblical concept found in the Hebrew Shema (Deuteronomy 6:4-9):

> Hear, O Israel: The LORD our God is one LORD (Deuteronomy 6:4).

(112.2) Allah, the eternally Besought of all!

> *... that Allah is eternal, and everyone needs to find him (paraphrase mine).*

The Bible would agree that God is eternal:

> The eternal God is your refuge (Deuteronomy 33:27a).

(112:3) He begets [conceived] not [Jesus], nor was begot (bracketed clarifications mine).

NOTE: As stated before, these last sûrahs are actually among the first revelations given to Muhammad and the beginning of the attacks on the Divinity of Christ.

We can see in the first half of this verse—presented near the outset of the Koran's revelations to Muhammad (this was the 22nd revelation given to him)—how it begins its repetitious mantra that Allah is not the father of anyone.

The last part of this verse, *".... nor was begot ..."* is more biblically accurate, although the irony being that's not the way the Koran actually meant it because Jesus always existed as one with the Father (John 1:1).[1] The Koran claims Allah is the God of the Bible, and we know the God of the Bible was not created, but that is as far as it goes. Previously, we pointed out that the Koran's overarching theme is the denial of the Divinity of Christ Jesus, who the Bible teaches is the Son of God (Proverbs 30:4; Isaiah 9:6; Matthew 26:63-64a, etc.).

> CONSIDER: The unique point regarding Jesus is that most religions feel forced to incorporate Jesus in some manner. Buddhists claim Jesus as an ascended Master and Hindus accept Jesus as another god. In Islam, He is relegated to being a third-rate Muslim prophet, behind Muhammad and the Mahdi. Jesus is also acknowledged as a prophet or Ascended Master by the Bahá'i' faith, Druze, Unitarians, etc. but not as the Savior of

As we just read, the second half of this verse contradicts the Divinity of Christ and denies He is the Son of God, but what does the Bible have to say regarding God having a Son?

Yet have I set my king upon My holy hill of Zion. I will declare the decree: the LORD has said unto Me, You are My Son; this day have I begotten [presented] You (Psalm 2:7, bracketed clarification mine).

Again, there is some confusion over the word "begotten," which we have been forced to address in this and other koranic passages. To review, "begotten" refers to Christ's relationship to the Father, because this passage is thought to mean that Jesus was conceived and thereby a created being, which has resulted in the formation of many cults (e.g., Jehovah's Witnesses, Mormons, etc.).

474

To review the concept of "begotten" (or "to be gotten") leaves one to think about the natural act of procreation; however, because the Koran belabors this point, we must likewise continue to point out that the Greek word used here for "begotten" is *Monos* (Gk., μόνος meaning "solitary/only" or "unique"), *genes* (Gk., γενής" kind/family"). Monogenés, translated as "begotten, is not describing a sexual encounter and is a rather difficult concept to translate into English. It can also mean "brought forth" or "presented"—as in this case—a unique pre-existing entity (God)[2] inhabiting or presented in the body of a man.

When reading the Koran, it soon becomes apparent how conflicted it is over the fact that the Bible not only acknowledged and prophesied the coming of the Son of God (Proverbs 30:4; Isaiah 9:6), who would be born of a virgin (Isaiah 7:14), and would die for our sins (Genesis 3:15; Isaiah 53:3-5), but was also Trinitarian in nature (Isaiah 48:16). Those prophecies—and more—were fulfilled with the birth of Yeshua (i.e., Jesus). Since this is a concept the Koran will not—and cannot— recognize, it is forced to present an *alternative,* monotheistic religion. As long as the Christ of the Bible has atoned for the sins of mankind by living a sinless life, was crucified dead and buried, only to be resurrected on the third day and ascend into Heaven to be with the Father,[3] He is a threat to Islam because the Jesus of the Bible negates the need for another prophet and method of salvation.

> *The Originator of the Heavens and the earth! How can He have a child, when there is for Him no consort, when He created all things and is Aware of all things? (Pickthall, sûrah 6:102).*

The problem with this koranic passage (and the others like it) is its premise. As we have shown, based on the Koran, Muslims erroneously assume that in order for God to have had a Son (Jesus), Christians believe God had to have sex (like the Olympian gods and goddesses) with a "consort" ("wife" or "concubine," Sûrah 6:101; Sûrah 72:2-3). However, that is not what Christians believe based on the Bible's teaching, which is God and His angels are not equipped with reproductive organs. They are immortal beings and, therefore, have no need to reproduce themselves (Matthew 22:30).

475

The Bible also states that Jesus always existed and, therefore, nothing could have existed before Him. The Bible is clear when referring to Jesus: "All things were made by Him, and without Him was not anything made that was made" (John 1:2); so one may ask, "What part of nothing that was made was made by Him does the Gabriel of the Koran not understand?" Jesus could not have been created since He created everything, and nothing that was created was created without Him; therefore, Jesus had to have always existed. Jesus was the reasoning of God, and if the Father could not reason (Gk., *logos*), then He would have not only been incapable, but unable to function at all! This gives us cause for concern since Allah claims he wrote the Bible, and most certainly, he would remember there was no "spousal involvement" required in the formation of the physical body that was needed for the divine Spirit of Jesus to inhabit.

Jesus was not the only person to inhabit a human body without copulation. The Bible informs us of three separate beings who were divinely begotten, or more accurately, brought forth without sexual involvement. The first human, Adam, was begotten (brought forth) by God from the dust of the earth (Genesis 2:7). The second human was Eve, who was begotten by God from out of the body of Adam—not through sperm or an egg—but brought forth out of his side (ribs) (Genesis 2:22). The third was a body created for the pre-existing Jesus to inhabit.

We never think of God as having created Adam and Eve through the act of sex; likewise, we should not think of sex being involved when the earthly habitat of the third human being's body was uniquely created without sex, just like those of Adam and Eve (Philippians 2:6-7).

In the case of Mary, her egg was still just an egg until it was infused with the spirit of life. The Bible tells us how this was accomplished when Christ Jesus:

> Who, being in the form of God [God the Son], thought it not robbery to be equal with God [give up His divine equality]: But made Himself of no reputation, and took upon Him the form of a

servant, and was made in the likeness of men (Philippians 2:6-7, bracketed clarifications mine).

The Koran has no problem with Adam and Eve having been divinely created with fully formed and developed bodies, which consisted of 46 chromosomes each (the sperm and egg only have 23 chromosomes each)—created *without* a sexual encounter or the combining of an egg with a sperm nor a human parent. Yet by admitting the virgin birth, the Koran demonstrates that Mary's child was Divine because Jesus was the only human being in recorded history, to be born of a virgin—a sign prophesied in the Old Testament (Isaiah 7:14) and fulfilled in the New Testament (Luke 1:26-32). Unquestionably, this could only be a divine occurrence. Ignoring this fact, the Koran vehemently insists that the only purpose of this historically unique, miraculous birth was simply to make another third-rate prophet who would take His place behind Muhammad and the Mahdi, whose own births—with all intended respect—were, at the very least, uneventful.

Scientifically, we know that God has also enabled, on rare occasions, some heterosexual creatures to give virgin birth without engaging in a sexual act and without having any sperm involved. While rare, this anomaly is referred to as *parthenogenesis;* therefore, why should it be a problem for God, who can create animals and some plants to abnormally reproduce by this means, not be able to do the same in Mary's body?

The Bible tells us animals have both a soul and a spirit, which a dichotomist would argue are the same (man + spirit/soul = 2); nevertheless, the Bible does say animals were created as living souls (Genesis 1:20, 24, 30). If someone is trichotomous (body + soul + spirit = 3), they believe the spirit and soul are separate. Regardless, the Bible teaches that man and animals hold all things in common (Ecclesiastes 3:18-19) and that animals also have a spirit (Ecclesiastes 3:21).

The passage in Ecclesiastes 3 asks the rhetorical question, "Who knows where the spirit of the beast goes?" It then provides the answer to that rhetorical question in Ecclesiastes 12:7: "... and the spirit returns to God who gave it." It is obvious that the animals (see the following text box), who are created through the process of *parthenogenesis* and possess both a soul (Job 12:10) and a spirit (Ecclesiastes 3:21), do so without a sexual encounter. Therefore, it stands to reason that the same principle was applied to Jesus when He inhabited the ovum in Mary's body.

CONSIDER: While skeptics might dismiss the virgin birth as being impossible, consider the phenomenon of parthenogenesis (not to be confused with *monogenēs* (i.e., unique, one of a kind), *which* we discussed in the commentary for verse 3. The word "parthenogenesis" is from the Greek word *parthenos* (παρϑένος) "virgin" + "genesis" (γένεσις) + "creation." It has been observed by scientists that some heterosexual animals, such as sharks, lizards and snakes, while rare, have the ability to reproduce without the involvement of a male. More than 2,000 species of plants and animals are thought to reproduce "parthenogenetically." Because we are dealing with the Divine, it should come as no surprise that a Divine being is capable of doing as He wishes without a sexual encounter[4]

Because Adam was the head of his family as a husband and father, as well as the priest (e.g., spiritual head), he was responsible for enforcing God's rules. Unfortunately, Adam—the first man—disobeyed God by eating from the fruit "of the tree of the knowledge of good and evil," which God expressly forbade Eve and him to eat (Genesis 2:17); therefore, because Adam was the head of his family, as well as the family of mankind, many theologians believed that our "original sin/sin nature" is inherited and passed on through the fathers (Exodus 20:5, 34:6-7; Deuteronomy 5:9).

> For as in Adam all die, so in Christ all will be made alive (1 Corinthians 15:22).

Many might say, "Okay, we accept that Jesus' spirit was infused into Mary's ovum without any sexual encounter, either physically or spiritually—so what?" That would be a great question—one the Koran totally ignores because it has no answer.

To begin with, it is essential to provide some biblical background. As previously stated, in order for God to walk among the people, and enable them to relate to Him personally—and also provide for them the ultimate blood sacrifice for mankind's sins—He would need a body for the second member of the Godhead to inhabit—thus, allowing the second member of the Godhead not only to be known as the Son of God, but the Son of man as well.

To accomplish that, God repeated the same type of creation that He used when He took a rib from Adam and made Eve. When a body was needed for Jesus to inhabit, God flipped the process by taking a daughter of Eve and creating a male body (Jesus) from her body. Thus, God repeated what He had done when He created both Adam and Eve without the use of sex.

When the Holy Spirit overshadowed Mary—a daughter of Eve—He used a female egg instead of a male rib to create a host body into which the pre-existing divine Spirit of Jesus *(Isa)* was poured—and did so without any involvement from a son of Adam.

We must also pay attention to the biblical description of how God did this by overshadowing Mary's body and not approaching her ovum via the birth canal as would be required by a male human. This allowed her to remain a virgin in every sense of the term while allowing for a member of the Godhead, Jesus, to become fully human while also remaining fully God and His mother to remain fully virgin at the same tune.

This was prophesied hundreds of years before the miraculous event. In the book of Isaiah, it was told, "... the Lord Himself will give you a sign: The virgin will conceive and give birth to a son, and will call Him God with us (Immanuel)" (Isaiah 7:14).

Following are two examples of several biblical Scriptures where Jesus *(Isa)* is proclaimed God's Son. God gives the first example where we read in the Bible:

And Jesus, when He was baptized, went up straightway out of the water: and, behold, the heavens were opened unto Him, and He saw the Spirit of God descending like a dove, and lighting upon Him: And lo, a voice from Heaven, saying, "This is my beloved Son, in whom I am well pleased" (Matthew 3:16-17, bracketed clarification mine).

In another instance, even the demons (known as "jinn" in the Koran) recognized Jesus *(Isa)* as the Son of God:

And when He had come out of the boat, immediately there met Him out of the tombs a man with an unclean spirit, who had *his* dwelling among the tombs; and no one could bind him, not even with chains, because he had often been bound with shackles and chains. And the chains had been pulled apart by him, and the shackles broken in pieces; neither could anyone tame him. And always, night and day, he was in the mountains and in the tombs, crying out and cutting himself with stones.

When he saw Jesus from afar, he ran and worshiped Him. And he cried out with a loud voice and said, "What have I to do with You, Jesus, Son of the Most High God? I implore You by God that You do not torment me." For He said to him, "Come out of the man, unclean spirit!" Then He asked him, "What *is* your name?" And he answered, saying, "My name *is* Legion; for we are many" (Mark 5:2-9, NKJV, emphasis added).

We are reminded that we have been told to validate the accuracy of the Koran by comparing it with biblical scripture (Sûrah 4:82), so once again, we must accept the challenge to prove God has a Son. As we have shown throughout this book, He did indeed have a Son, but not in the usual way of procreation:

Who is a liar but he that denies that Jesus is the Christ? He is antichrist who denies the Father and the Son (1 John 2:22, NKJV).

(112:4 And there is none comparable unto Him.

Biblically, it would seem this is an understatement, especially when compared to Allah's instructions regarding Sûrah 4:82 and Sûrah 5:46-47, which challenge us to compare the Bible with the Koran to see if there are any discrepancies. What we do find (not including the inaccurate biblical stories contained in the Koran) is that Allah could not possibly be the Triune God of the Bible (Isaiah 48:16; Proverbs 30:4; Matthew 3:17; 17:5; Mark 1:11; Hebrews 1:2; 2 Peter 1:17).

> CONSIDER: Even in the shortest and seemingly innocent small sûrahs—which are only composed of a handful of verses—we can still find a tremendous amount of controversy!

NOTES:

1. English Bibles translate this passage differently than the original Greek. Here is the English translation:
   "In the beginning was the Word, and the Word was with God, and the Word was God" (John 1:1).
   In the Original Greek, the word order is like this:
   "In the beginning was the Word, and the Word was with God, and God was the Word" (John 1:1, GK).

2. *Greek-English Lexicon of the New Testament and Other Early Christian Literature* (BAGD, 3rd Edition). Monogenés, Strong's word #3439. Monogenés has two primary definitions "pertaining to being the only one of its kind within a specific relationship" and "pertaining to being the only one of its kind or class, unique in kind."

3. The Bible confirms Jesus' eternal existence with God the Father: "Jesus spoke these words, lifted up His eyes to Heaven. And said: 'Father, the hour has come. Glorify your Son, that Your Son also may glorify You, as you have given Him authority over all flesh, that He should give eternal life to as many as You have given Him. And this is eternal life, that they may know You, the

only true God, and Jesus Christ whom You have sent. I have glorified You on the earth. I have finished the work You gave me to do. And now, O Father, glorify Me with Yourself, with the glory which I had with you before the world was' " (John 17:1-5, NKJV).

4. The Editors of Encyclopædia Britannica. "Partheno-genesis." *Encyclopædia Britannica*. Encyclopædia Britannica, Inc., n.d. Web. 10 June 2017. "The word parthenogenesis is taken from the Greek words *parthos*, meaning "virgin" and *genesis*, meaning "origin."

☪

SÛRAH 113

THE DAYBREAK (Falaq)
(Revealed at Mecca)

In the name of Allah, the Beneficent, the Merciful.

(113:1) Say:" I seek refuge in the Lord of the Daybreak"

When Muhammad first started recruiting converts to Islam from his family and friends, he faced a lot of rejection. This must have been very discouraging for Muhammad; therefore, it is reasonable Gabriel would seek to encourage Muhammad with this sûrah. In this verse, Gabriel is telling Muhammad—when he suffers from depression—to tell those who will not listen to him that he is not dismayed because he takes shelter from their attacks in Allah, who is the creator of the dawn.

(113:2) From the evil of that which He created;

This verse is troubling from a biblical point of view because when God created the world and all that is in it, He said it was good (Genesis 1:4, 12, 21, 25). In fact, God said all He made was "very good" (Genesis 1:31). It appears that the Allah of Islam is the originator of evil, unlike the God of the Bible, who cannot tolerate evil (Habakkuk 1:13). God created angels and people to have free will, thus allowing for the possibility they may choose to become evil as opposed to creating them evil. Without question, God could have created living computers programmed to automatically love Him. On the other hand, without the possibility of rejection, could that really be love? Could God realize the true satisfaction of being loved by those who are just robots? Could God return true love toward those who have no choice but to love Him? Of course not. God desired real love and devotion from creatures who worship Him out of their own free will, but with that kind of love, there is a price. Free will allows for rebellion and sin, which is evil—not created by God—but created by the subjects of His affection!

We are also informed in Sûrah 3:54 that Allah is a schemer (deceiver), whereas we know the God of the Bible does not lie or change His mind (Numbers 23:19). The Bible tells us it is Satan who is the father of lies and a murderer from the beginning, not God (John 8:44).

Sin is basically the rejection of God and the rules of conduct He gave us in order for us to have a blessed life. One might ask why God created such a creature with the ability to reject Him. The answer is because God desires His angels and humans to be able to choose, as opposed to being forced to love Him. If God only wanted creatures who could never reject Him and only love Him continually, He could have created programmed automatons or cyborgs.

(113:3) From the evil of the darkness when it is intense,

Gabriel is continuing with the last thought of this sentence, which is to seek protection in Allah from evil, especially when it is encased in darkness and becomes intense.

(113:4) And from the evil of malignant witchcraft,

A.J. Arberry is closer to the original Arabic revelation, which translates:

> ... from the evil of women who blow on knots.

Pickthall, in his comments, agrees with Arberry, who explains this unusual saying of *"blowing on knots"* as "... a common form of witchcraft in Arabia for women to tie knots in a cord and blow upon them with an imprecation [curse]" (bracketed clarification mine).[1]

(113:5) And from the mischief of the envious one as he practices envy.

Basically, Gabriel is telling Muhammad not to be troubled when jealous people attack him out of envy.

NOTES:
1. Pickthall, the *Koran*, 677, Sûrah 113:4, fn 1.

☪

SÛRAH 114

MANKIND (Nās)
(Revealed at Mecca)

In the name of Allah, the Beneficient, the Merciful.

(114:1) Say:" I seek refuge in the Lord of mankind,"

Gabriel is telling Muhammad to say he takes *"refuge in"* [Allah], *"the Lord [over all] of mankind"* (bracketed clarifications mine).

(114:2) The King of Mankind,

For emphasis sake, Gabriel builds on this theme, claiming that Allah is also *"the King of mankind."*

(114:3) The God of mankind,

Gabriel concludes that the glorification of Allah—with the observation *"The God of Mankind."*

A.J. Arberry translates it, *"The King of men, The God of men."* While Abdullah Yusuf Ali uses the clarification in parenthesis—*"The God "(or judge) of men."*

(114:4) From the evil of the sneaking whisperer,

Now Gabriel explains why refuge is sought; it is from the evil one who whispers evil things in your ears and changes your heart's desires.

Muhammad Habib Shakir translates it:

From the evil of the whisperings of the slinking (Shaitan).

Note: *Shaitan* is "Satan" in English

(114:5) Who [also] whispers in the hearts of mankind (bracketed clarification mine),

It is Satan who whispers evil thoughts into the ears and minds of unsuspecting people.

(114:6) Of the jinn and of mankind.

The jinn (or genies) are mischievous creatures similar to the Irish leprechauns who can sometimes be very troublesome. Here we see Satan (also a jinn in Islam[1]) is the cause of evil mischief with both these creatures.

Perhaps this short sûrah is Muhammad's way of dealing with doubt. This last sûrah was actually Muhammad's 21st revelation and came at a time of great rejection by those whom he sought to convert. Possibly, the whispers of Satan (verse 5) were simply Muhammad's way of explaining his failure. We do know, as Muhammad was eventually able to convince more people of his message of Islam, he was able to overcome doubt; however, as he gathered more and more followers, his timidity turned more and more violent and aggressiveness.

NOTES:

1. Gauvain, Richard. *Salafi Ritual Purity: In the Presence of God*. (New York: Routledge, 2013), 73. Islamic scholars agree that Satan was an angel, but contemporary scholars also regard him as a jinn too.

☪

SOURCES CONSULTED

Abdul-Fattah, Muhammad M., Reima Youssif Shakeir, trans. *A Selection of Authentic Qudsi (Sacred) Hadiths.* ed. vol. 2. Dar Al-Manarah for Translation, Publishing & Distribution n.d.

Adams, Eliade. *The Encyclopedia of Religion,* Vol. I (New York: Macmillian, 1987).

"Alexander the Great." - *Oxford Islamic Studies Online.* Oxford University, n.d. Web. 13 September 2016.

"AL-LAHAB." *Center for Muslim-Jewish Engagement.* University of Southern California, n.d. Web. 12 September 2016.

Abu Nab, Ibraham. "Sûrahs 105 Al-Feel." Sûrahs 105 Al-Feel. N.p., n.d. Ibrahim AbuNab (1931-1991). Web. 18 October 2014.

Al-Bukhari Sahih, al-Jaami' al-Sahih al-Musnad al-Mukhtasar min Umur Rasool Allah wa sunanihi wa Ayyamihi. Book 59, Hadith 584, n.d.

_____. Vol.4., Book 19, Number 4294, 'o.'

Al-Mehri, A. B. *The Qur'ān: with Sūrah Introductions and Appendices: Saheeh International Translation.* Birmingham, UK: The Qur'ān Project, 2010.

Al-Tirmidhi, Jami.'-*Chapters on Virtues - Grade: Sahih* (Darussalam) English reference: Vol. 1, Book 46, Hadith 3619 Arabic reference: Book 49, Hadith 3979.

Ali, Abdullah Yusuf, trans. *The Holy Qur'an* (Hertfordshire: Wordsworth Edition Limited, 2000).

Anderson, Andrew Runni. "Alexander's Horns." *Transactions and Proceedings of the American Philological Association*, vol. 58, 1927

Andrae, Tor. *Mohammed: The Man and His Faith*. (Mineola: Dover Publications, 2000).

Arberry, A. J. (Arthur, John). *The Koran Interpreted* (New York: Touchstone, 1955).

Armstrong, Karen. *Islam: A Short History*. New York: The Modern Library, 2000.

Asad, Muhammad. *The Message of the Qur'an* (London: The Book Foundation, 2012).

Aziz, Dr. Zahid. "Shakir Identified." The Lahore Ahmadiyya Islamic Movement, n.d. Web. 25 March 2015.

Ayoub, Mahmoud M. *The Qur'an and Its Interpreters:* v.1: Vol 1 (Albany: State University of New York Press, 1984).

Barker, Kenneth ed., The NIV Study Bible (Grand Rapids: Zondervan, 1985).

Baring-Gould, S. - trans. *Myths of The Seven Sleepers of Ephesus*. Whitefish: Kessinger, LLC, Publ., 2010.

Barnhart, Clarence L. ed. "The Dark Ages." The American College Encyclopedic Dictionary. vol. I and II (Chicago: Spencer Press, Inc., 1959).

Bible Hub. "Bible Timeline." n.d.; Web. 28 June 2013.

Bickerman, Elias J. *Chronology of the Ancient World*. 2nd edition. (Ithaca: Cornell University Press. 1980).

Bietenholz, Peter G. Historia and Fabula: *Myths and Legends in Historical Thought from Antiquity to the Modern Age* (New York: E.J. Brill, 1994).

Campo, Juan Eduardo. *Encyclopedia of Islam*. "Idris" (New York: Infobase Publishing, 2009).

Cartledge, Paul. *Alexander the Great: The Hunt for a New Past* (Michigan: The University of Michigan Press, 2004),

"Chronological Order of the Qur'an." - *WikiIslam*. N.p., n.d. Web. 30 Mar. 2016.

Cowan, J. Milton (ed). *The Hans Wehr Dictionary of Modern Written Arabic.* Ithaca: Spoken Language Services, Inc., 1976.

Caner, Ergun Mehmet, and Emir Fethi Caner. *Unveiling Islam: An Insider's Look at Muslim Life and Beliefs* (Grand Rapids, MI: Kregel Publications, 2002).

"Dates of Abraham's Life." - Conservapedia. N.p., n.d. Web. 2 July 2013.

Dawkins, R. M., and Andrew Runni Anderson. *Alexander's Gate, Gog and Magog, and the Enclosed Nations: By Andrew Runni Anderson* (Cambridge: Medieval Academy of America, 1932).

"Elephants and Water." *Canisius Ambassadors for Conservation*, CAC Is a Program of the Institute for the Study of Human-Animal Relations at Canisius College in Buffalo, New York. N.p., n.d. WEB. 24 Aug. 2013.

Encyclopaedia of Islam, New Edition, Volume V. Ledin: E.J. Brill, 1986.

Esposito, John L. *The Oxford Dictionary of Islam* (New York: Oxford UP, 2003).

Falah, Abdulmajeed. "Grammatical Opinions of Abu Hayyan Andalusi between Theory and Practice." Arab Journal for the Humanities. Academic Publication Council, Kuwait University: 29, no. 116 (2011): np.

Freedman, Saul S. *A History of the Middle East* London: McFarland & Co., 1937.

Freeman, Philip. *Alexander the Great* (New York: Simon & Schuster, 2011).

Gauvain, Richard. *Salafi Ritual Purity: In the Presence of God*. New York: Routledge, 2013.

Geisler, Norman L., and Abdul Saleeb. *Answering Islam: The Crescent in Light of the Cross*. Grand Rapids, MI: Baker, 2002.

_____. Baker *Encyclopedia of Christian Apologetics* (Grand Rapids: Baker Books, 2000).

Gibson Shimon, *The Cave of John the Baptist* (New York: Random House, 2005).

Gill, John. Numbers 10:29 Commentaries: Moses's Father-in-Law. N.p., n.d. Web. 24 September 2013.

"Hajj." *ACADEMIC*, Enacacademic, enacademic.com/dic.nsf/enwiki/46076.

Hanson, Erin. "Oral Traditions." *Indigenousfoundations*, University of British Columbia, 2009, N.p., n.d. Web. 18 June 2013.

Hawting, Gerald R. *The Idea of Idolatry and the Emergence of Islam: From Polemic To History* (Cambridge: Cambridge University Press, 1999).

Ibn al-Hajjaj. *Muslim Sahih Muslim*, trans. Abdul Hamid Siddiqui (Houston: Dar-us-Salam Publications, 2007), [number 1676].

490

Ibn Isḥāq. *The Life of Muḥammad: A Translation of Ibn Isḥāq's Sīrat Rasul Allāh with Introduction & Notes by Alfred Guillaume* (Oxford: Oxford UP, 1955).

Jacobs, Joseph, and Louis H. Gray. "JewishEncyclopedia.com," The Kopelman Foundation *SABEANS*

Jeffery, Arthur. *Islam: Muhammad and His Religion*. (Indianapolis: Bobbs-Merrill Co. Inc., 1958).

Kahn, Muhammad A, "The Chapter Sûrah Fil (Elephant) of the Quran Written Long Before the Advent of Islam." Web. 31 December 2013.

Keohane, Jonathan and Jim Lochner. *National Aeronautics and Space Administration Goddard Space Flight Center*. "Imagine the Universe: How many times the earth would fit inside the sun?" *NASA, 1997,* Web. 16 July 2013.

Leeming, David Adams. *Jealous Gods and Chosen People: the Myology of the Middle East* (New York: Oxford Press, 2004),

Lewis, Bernard. *The Arabs in History* (Oxford: Oxford Univ., 1993).

Liddell, Henry George, Robert Scott, Eric Arthur Barber, Henry Stuart Jones, and Roderick McKenzie. *A Greek-English Lexicon with a Supplement* 1968 (Oxford: Clarendon, 1940).

Lull, Timothy F. and Wm R. Russell, Ed., *MARTIN LUTHER'S BASIC THEOLOGICAL* WRITING, 2nd ed. Minneapolis: Augsburg Fortress Press, 2005

Lyons, Elizabeth, Heather Peters, *Buddhism*: *The History and Diversity of a Great Tradition* (Philadelphia, University of Pennsylvania Museum of Archaeology and Anthropology, 1985), 5.

Mark, Joshua J. "Magic in Ancient Egypt." *Ancient History Encyclopedia*, Ancient History Encyclopedia, 24 Feb. 2017.

"Maya." *Oh Baby! Names*, 22 Oct. 2014, ohbabynames.com/all-baby-names/maya/.

Queen Māyā is also the name of the mother of Buddha. As a Latinate form of "May", Maya may also be considered a nickname for Mary or Margaret, meaning "beloved" and "pearl,"

Maspero, Gaston. *Manual of Egyptian Archaeology and Guide to the Study of Antiquities in Egypt: For the Use of Students and Travellers (1914)*. (Reprinted Ithaca: Cornell U Library, 2009. ed.)

Menner, Robert J. "Nimrod and the Wolf in the Old English 'Solomon and Saturn.' " Journal of English and Germanic Philology, 37, 1938.

Meri, Joseph W. ed. "Jinn." *Medieval Islamic Civilization - An Encyclopedia* vol. 1 ed. (New York: Routledge, 200).

Mohamed, Mamdouh N .*Hajj and Umrah From A to Z*. Self-Published (the USA, 1996).

Muller, Herbert J. *Arabia before Islam Arabia Before Islam*, "Political Conditions in Arabia," n.d. Web 20 July 2013.
"Muslim Mastectomy or The Miracle of Disappearing Breasts Surah An-Naba' (78:33)." *Surah An-Naba' 78:33*, www.answering-islam.org /Quran/Versions/078.033.html. Accessed 15 June. 2013.

New World Dictionary-Concordance to the New American Bible (New York: World, 1970).

Nooeuddin, Allâmah. *Exegesis of the Holy Qur'ân: Commentary and Reflections*. Translated by Amatul Rahmân Omar and Abdul Mammân Omar, Noor Foundation International Inc, 2015.

Ohlig,Karl-Heinz, Gerd-R Puin, Die dunklen Anfänge: neue Forschungen zur Entstehung und frühen Geschichte des Islam (Berlin: H. Schiler, 2006).

Peterson, Daniel C. Foreward by Khaleel Mohammed. *Muhammad, Prophet of God*. Grand Rapids: Wm. B. Eerdmans Publ. Co., 2007.

Pickthall, Marmaduke. *The Meaning of the Glorious Koran*. 7th ed. (New York: Everyman's Library, 1993).

"Purgatory | Roman Catholicism." Encyclopædia Britannica Online. *Encyclopædia* Britannica, n.d. Web. 13 September 2013.

"Quran Verses in Chronological Order." *Qran.org.* اقرا قرآن في طريق آسون, n.d. Web. 30 March 2016.

Rane, Halim. *Reconstructing Jihad Amid Competing International Norms*. New York: Palgrave MacMillan, 2009.

Rippin, Andrew. *The Qur'an : Formative Interpretation*. Aldershot: Ashgate, 1999. Print. Quoting Norman Calder.

St. Clair-Tisdall, M.A., Rev. W^m, *The Source of Islam*. Edinburgh Privately Published, 1901; reprint, Nashville: Center for the Study of Political Islam, 2011.

Schaff, Philip. *History of the Christian Church*. vol. IV (Peabody: Hendrickson Publishers, Inc., 2006).

Schimmel, Annemarie. And Muhammad is His Messenger: The Veneration of the Prophet in Islamic Piety. Chapel Hill: The University of North Carolina Press, 1985.

Scott, Noel and Jafar Jafari. *Tourism in the Muslim World*. (Bingley: Emerald Group Publishing Ltd., 2010).

"Seven Sleepers." *Wikipedia*. Wikimedia Foundation, n.d. Web. 14 September 2016

Shaikh, Fazlur Rehman. *Chronology of Prophetic Events,* (West Norwood: Ta-Ha Publishers Ltd, 2001).

Shakir, Muhammad Habib. trans. *The Qur'an*, 11th ed. (Elmhurst: Tahrike Tarsile Qur'an, Inc.), 1999.

Shorrosh, Dr. Anis A. Islam Revealed: *A Christian Arab's View of Islam*. (Nashville: Thomas Nelson, 1988).

Seven Sleepers. (2017, May 15). *Wikipedia, The Free Encyclopedia*. Retrieved 23:11, August 28, 2019

Spencer, Robert. *The Complete Infidel's Guide to the Koran* (Washington, DC: Regnery Pub., 2009).

"Sûrah Al-Baqara" 2:87-90 - Towards Understanding the Quran - Quran Translation Commentary - Tafheem Ul Quran." *Sûrah Al-Baqara 2:87-90 - Towards Understanding the Quran - Quran Translation Commentary - Tafheem Ul Quran*. Islamic Foundation UK, n.d. Web. 21 Sept. 2016.

Talbert, Richard J.A., *Plutarch on Sparta* (London: Penguin Books, 1988).

Talk: Haman (Islam). Web. 12 May 2013. https://en.wikipedia.org/wiki/Talk:Haman_(Islam)

Taqi-ud-Din, Dr. Muhammad, and Dr. Muhammad Muhsin Khan Trans. *Interpretation of the Meanings of the Nobel Qur'an in the English Language.* (Riyadh: Saudi Arabia, Darussalam Publ. 1999).

The Arabic Gospel of the Infancy of the Saviour. Ante-Nicene Fathers. Ed. Alexander Roberts and James Donaldson. 4th ed. Vol. 8. (Peabody: Hendrickson, 20).

The Bible Study Site, Abraham's Journey Map. Web. 2 July 2013.

The Editors of Encyclopædia Britannica. "Harut and Marut." *Encyclopædia Britannica, Inc.,* 20 July 1998. Web. 17 February 2016.

_____. "Julian Calendar."*Encyclopædia Britannica.* Encyclopædia Britannica, Inc., 28 Apr. 2017.

_____."Partheno-genesis." *Encyclopædia Britannica.* Encyclopædia Britannica, Inc., n.d. Web. 10 June 2017.

"The Glorious Koran." Tran. by Marmaduke Pickthall. New York: EVERYMAN'S LIBRARY, 1992. Print.

The New American Bible. Saint Joseph Edition (New York: Catholic Book Publishing Co., 1970).

"The Qur'an Interpreted." Tran. by A.J. Arberry. New York: TOUCHTONE, 1955. Print.

"The Holy Qur'an." Trans. by A. Yusuf Ali. 2nd ed. n.c.: American Public Trust, 1997. Print.

"The Qur'an Translation." Trans. by M. H. Shakir. 14th ed. New York: Tahrike Tarsile Qur'an, Inc.,.2003. Print.

"The Timeline of the Bible." Joseph in Egypt to Moses and the Exodus. Web. 9 June 2013.

Tisdall, Rev. W. St. Clair. *The Source of Islam*. Reprint. Edinburgh: Privately Published, 1901. Nashville: Center for the Study of Political Islam, 2011.

University of British Columbia (n.d.): Oral Traditions. Web. 18 June 2013

Van Bladel, Kevin. *The Alexander Legend in the Qur'an* (New York: Routledge, 2007).

van der Horst, Pieter Willem, et al. "The Thirteenth International Orion Symposium: Tradition, Transmission, and Transformation: From Second Temple Literature Through Judaism and Christianity in Late Antiquity." Brill, *Tradition, Transmission, and Transformation from Second Temple Literature Through Judaism and Christianity in Late Antiquity: Proceedings of the Thirteenth International Symposium of the Orion Center for the Study of the Dead Sea Scrolls and Associated Literature, Jointly Sponsored by the Hebrew University Center for the Study of Christianity, 22-24 February 2011*, 2015.

Viscount Bryce Intro. *The Book of History; A History Of All Nations From The Earliest To The Present* (Charleston: Nabu Press, 2011).

Watt, W. Montgomery. *Muhammad at Medina* (Oxford: Clarendon Press, 1956).

Watt, William Montgomery. *The Encyclopedia of Islam*. 2nd ed. Vol. IV. (Leiden: Brill, 1997). Print.

Wessels, Anton. *The Torah, the Gospel and the Qur'an: Three Books, Two Cities, One Tale* (Grand Rapids: Wm. Eerdmans Publishing, 2013).

Wikipedia contributors, "Alexander the Great in the Quran," Wikipedia, The Free Encyclopedia. Web. 20 June 2013.

_____. "Hajj." Wikipedia, The Free Encyclopedia. Web. 24 June 2013.

_____."Muhammad Muhsin Khan," Wikipedia, The Free Encyclopedia. Web. 15 March 2015.

Wilson, Christy. "The Qur'an." *In The World's Religions* (Oxford: The New Lion Handbook, 2008).

ABOUT THE AUTHOR

As a student of history and theology, Dr. Sloane has researched not only the diversity of Christianity, but he has also explored the various other religions, sects, and cults in order to understand how they interact, challenge, and influence each other. It was because of his quest for knowledge that he embarked on over 30 years of higher education, graduating from a special program at Purdue University that was sponsored by the Indiana Council of Churches. He also graduated from the Institute of Charismatic Studies at Oral Roberts University, the Moody Bible Institute, and Institute of Jewish-Christian Studies. He earned a B.A., *Summa Cum Laude,* from the Master's College, where he attended their IBEX campus in Israel. While at the Master's College, he earned an M.A. in Biblical Counseling. At Trinity Theological Seminary, he earned a Doctorate of Ministry as well as a Ph.D., *With Distinction*, in Religious Studies.

Throughout the years, Dr. Sloane has appeared on such television programs as the 700 Club, Lester Sumrall Today, Richard Roberts Live, LeSea Broadcasting's Harvest, and Trinity Broadcasting Network's Praise the Lord, to name a few.

Publications Dr. Sloane appears in include, "Who's Who in the World" and "Who's Who in America." He is also featured in the "Dictionary of International Biography" and "2000 Outstanding Intellectuals of the 21st Century" (Cambridge, England).

Continued . . .

Dr. Sloane is seen here working at the "John The Baptist" dig during his

undergraduate work in Israel, under the direction of the Israeli *Antiquities* Authority and the supervision of Dr. Shimon Gibson (adjunct Professor of Archaeology at the University of North Carolina at Charlotte). This site is located in the orchards of Kibbutz Tzuba, near the village of Ein Karem, which is also believed to be the traditional birthplace of John the Baptist (located west of Jerusalem). "From a historical point of view, the uniqueness of this cave is that it contains archaeological evidence that comes to us from the very time of the personalities and events described in the Gospels ... in the cave is the earliest ever Christian art depicting John the Baptist as well as the three crosses of the crucifixion."[1]

NOTE:

1. Shimon Gibson, Ph.D., *The Cave of John the Baptist* (New York: Random House, 2005), back cover.

www.ingramcontent.com/pod-product-compliance
Lightning Source LLC
Chambersburg PA
CBHW031942090426
42739CB00006B/58